COMMUNITY ORGANIZING

COMMUNITY ORGANIZING
THEORY AND PRACTICE

Douglas P. Biklen
Syracuse University

Prentice-Hall, Inc., Englewood Cliffs, New Jersey 07632

Library of Congress Cataloging in Publication Data

Biklen, Douglas.
  Community organizing.

  Includes bibliographical references and index.
  1. Community organization.   2. Social action.
  3. Social problems.   I. Title.
  HN17.5.B53 1983   361.8   82-16599
  ISBN 0-13-153676-1

HN
17.5
.B53
1983

Printed in the United States of America

10 9 8 7 6 5 4 3 2 1

Editorial/production supervision:
  Maureen Connelly
Cover design: Zimmerman/Foyster Design
Manufacturing buyer: John Hall

ISBN 0-13-153676-1

Prentice-Hall International, Inc., *London*
Prentice-Hall of Australia Pty. Limited, *Sydney*
Prentice-Hall Canada Inc., *Toronto*
Prentice-Hall of India Private Limited, *New Delhi*
Prentice-Hall of Japan, Inc., *Tokyo*
Prentice-Hall of Southeast Asia Pte. Ltd., *Singapore*
Whitehall Books Limited, *Wellington, New Zealand*
Editora Prentice-Hall do Brazil, Ltda., *Rio de Janeiro*

To Sari Knopp Biklen

CONTENTS

PREFACE

As a junior high school student, I belonged to a discussion group called Concern. We met regularly every other Friday evening to talk about issues in which we were interested, but which were not discussed at school—issues like nuclear disarmament, the pros and cons of bomb shelters as a defense against nuclear war, the injustice of racism, and the merits of non-violent protest. As I recall, we even spent one session discussing Erich Fromm's *The Art of Loving*.

On a few occasions in conjunction with our discussions of political topics, we took action. We picketed a local NIKE missile site, for example. That action prompted one citizen to write a letter to the editor of the local newspaper. The author called us "still wet behind the ears" as if to say, "you'll know better than to demonstrate against such things when you get a bit older." How wrong he was. From this protest and his subsequent letter, we realized we could act on our beliefs *and* have some effect.

Our next site was a department store. We joined a picket sponsored by the local NAACP and some religious groups outside a Woolworth's store in Norwalk, Connecticut—it was a sympathy boycott to express allegiance with people in southern states who were desegregating Woolworth's lunch counters. Many shoppers tried to ignore us. A few stopped to talk, and voiced their support of our cause. And some argued with us: "Why picket this store when the real problem is prejudice in the South?" they said. Some of our critics charged us with being ill-informed and, therefore, presumptuous. It was just another version of the "still-wet-behind-the-ears" argument. "Who are you to protest against this northern store? Don't you know that it will just hurt the local store owners and won't have any effect on the Woolworth's southern operation?" We did not always have good, crisp answers for these charges. In retrospect, that is understandable. We were still young and had a great deal of learning ahead of us. The questioning spurred us on. A few years later, I came to realize that such complaints had many forms (for example: "How can you be sure you are right? After all, the officials have more information than you"; "I agree with your goals but not with your confrontation approach"; and "You are just going to alienate the very people you want to change").

When we entered high school, most of us who had been active in Concern got involved in our high school newspaper. One day we received a call from the editor of a neighboring school paper, whose paper was embroiled in controversy. She had written an editorial in which she questioned the value of patriotism and advocated international harmony. Somehow, the editors of *Life* magazine were interested enough in her thoughts to write their own editorial entitled "Dear Virginia," in which they criticized her views as "naive". Bertrand Russell heard of the controversy and wrote a letter to Virginia in which he defended her perspective and lambasted *Life*. Virginia's advisors would not allow her to publish the Bertrand Russell letter in her paper. Would we publish it? We jumped at the opportunity, thrilled with the thought that a high school newspaper would get to publish an original statement by a Nobel Prize winner. Clearly it belonged on the front page. But that would not come to pass. Our faculty advisor, fearful of potential controversy, insisted that we publish the Russell letter as a regular "letter to the editor," and not on the front page. Naturally we were disappointed, perhaps even angry, but what I remember most vividly about that event was that we did not know how to handle the situation. Should we have quit the paper? Should we have taken our case to a higher authority? Should we have organized a student protest? Should we have contacted the American Civil Liberties Union? What we did was to acquiesce to our advisor.

While in college, I joined more than a hundred other student government presidents from across the country in signing an antiwar (Vietnam) letter to then-President Johnson, which the *New York Times* gave front page coverage. The *New York Daily News* labelled our sympathy with draft resistance "commie line stuff." We won a more measured response from the U.S. Department of State. The then-State Department Secretary Dean Rusk published a booklet which included our letter and his detailed response. Of course our letter/petition did not change the government's mind. But, that was not really the point. The significance of our letter was that it was one of hundreds of antiwar actions by small ad hoc groups throughout the country which had the effect of helping to change the tide of public opinion on the war. We had joined an informal network of groups who felt they could make a difference and who felt a sense of community through their organizing.

Over the next few years, as so many of my generation who reached adulthood during the 1960s, I continued to be involved in organizing. The Vietnam antiwar movement lasted more than a decade. I spent two years in Africa as a Peace Corps volunteer organizing a farm cooperative at local level. When I returned to the U.S. as a graduate student, I joined the Committee of Returned Volunteers, a local peace and justice group known as the Syracuse Peace Council, and several other activist organizations. I worked on civil rights, antiwar, feminist, and civil liberties organizing.

Then, as if all my previous training had been in preparation for what lay ahead, I chanced to hear Burt Blatt speak on the horrors of America's retardation institutions. From that moment on, the greatest part of my organizing efforts would focus on addressing that problem. It was a problem I had known nothing about, nor had I even thought about prior to hearing the talk and seeing photographs that Burt Blatt and Fred Kaplan had secretly taken in some of America's largest institutions. In the next several years I visited a half dozen such institutions, I got to know hundreds of families of retarded children, I began to write about what I was learning, and I began organizing.

In 1970, a group of us in Syracuse, New York, founded the Center on Human Policy. The Center's mission is to promote equal rights and the maximum possible social integration for people with disabilities. We organize for the right to education, deinstitutionalization, upgrading of quality in a whole range of human services, and an end to handicapism. In many ways, this book represents a summation of what I have learned about organizing in ten years at the Center on Human Policy.

While the Center's focus has been almost exclusively on disability rights, its work transcends single issue organizing. Disability issues are clearly inseparable from issues of poverty, health service delivery, public education, housing, and other social policy questions. More to the point in terms of this book, the Center has systematically studied other community organizing efforts and social movements to find effective approaches to change. Examples of our work appear throughout this book. The Center has used nearly every type of traditional and innovative approach: neighborhood organizing, national organizing, community-wide organizing, whistleblowing (within organizations), and self-help organizing. Our strategies have included action research, litigation, negotiations, social protest, organization building, public forums, press conferences, demands, and more.

With each action, sometimes protest, other times a teach-in, a "letter to the editor," a heated negotiation session with people in power, or an action research report, I learned that it was nearly impossible to predict our exact effect. Nor could I or any other organizer ever expect to control the organizing group's choice of tactics and even goals, or, for that matter, who might get involved on either side of an issue. Organizing embraces the unpredictable. It defies domestication. That fact always left me and everyone else two choices: don't get involved and therefore never be in a position to have to compromise, or get more involved and try to shape the goals and tactics to our liking even if it means having to make compromises. I nearly always chose the latter option. And while it is sometimes difficult to work in groups, that difficulty is part of what makes organizing so exciting: goals, action strategies, and the public's reaction keep changing. In writing this book, I hope to have provided a resource that will help others become more involved in community organizing.

Thus far, this brief biographical account of some of my own organizing has mentioned only one of the many people from whom I have learned about issues and organizing. Let me rectify that situation now. I am indebted to the many people who have been associated with the Center on Human Policy for their friendship and advice, particularly to Burton Blatt, Bob Bogdan, Ellen Barnes, Steve Taylor,

Helen Timmins, Jo Scro, Diane Murphy, Bernice Schultz, Carol Berrigan, Hillery Schneiderman, Milt Baker, Sally Johnston, Liz Altieri, Carole Hayes, Diane Apter, Claudia Stockley, Stan Searl, Jane Conoley, and Gunnar Dybwad.

I have learned about organizing from a number of people outside the Center as well. I feel especially indebted to Honey Knopp, the adult who founded our original Concern group, and to Tony Avirgan, Martha Honey, Mark Morris, Peg Averill, Dik Cool, Maud Easter, David Easter, Sari Knopp Biklen, and Alex Knopp.

I would like to acknowledge the reviewers who commented on this book at its various stages: Morris Cohen, University of North Carolina–Chapel Hill; Alan N. Connor, formerly of University of Michigan–Ann Arbor; John M. Haynes, State University of New York at Stony Brook; Julius Newman, University of Connecticut, Greater Hartford Campus; and Theodore Walden, Rutgers University.

For his assistance in helping with bibliography searches I thank Ye Kai. For their assistance in typing drafts of the manuscript, I thank Loraine Kotary and Helen Anderson.

For their assistance in the areas of negotiations and lobbying respectively, I want to thank Karen Beckwith and Polly Rothstein.

For their love and support I want to thank my parents, Anne and Paul Biklen and my father-in-law, Burton Knopp. For their love and good spirit, I want to thank Molly Knopp Biklen and Noah Knopp Biklen.

Douglas P. Biklen
Syracuse, New York

COMMUNITY ORGANIZING

PART ONE
THEORY

In this book, we examine both the theoretical and practical aspects of community organizing. Certain fields allow their participants to engage in theory alone or practice alone. Sociologists, for example, frequently limit their role to formulating theoretical ways of understanding social structures and social systems. Often, social work is regarded as the practical side of sociology. Social workers get involved in the real world in seeing first hand and having to grapple with social structure, social systems, and their effects on individuals. In truth, though, good sociology cannot afford to be out of touch with the reality of daily life in social structures. Neither can social work ignore theories which explain or give insight into practice. The same is true for community organizing. Community organizing requires theory and practice. Good practice is rooted in theory. Similarly, good theory, by which we mean useful theory, derives from, accounts for, and even helps shape effective practice.

Social scientists have no shortage of theories—for example, Marxism, structural functionalism, symbolic interactionism, conflict theory, and behaviorism—by which to explain daily life and the major social structures which dominate daily life. Some overlap. Some contradict each other. What concerns us here are those theoretical perspectives which community organizers have found particularly useful in their practice. In other words, what theoretical viewpoints can help a community organizer achieve success in understanding issues of the day, in building community, in giving leadership, and in creating change?

In Part I, we examine the principal theoretical roots of organizing. Four theoretical areas constitute our major focus: (1) ideology or values, (2) power, (3) analysis of social conditions, and (4) leadership. Each chapter in this part covers one of these four areas.

First, we look at values. Community organizing is not new to America. It has come to us through a long tradition of concern and activism. It reflects particular values in the culture which its adherents felt worthy of their commitment. In Chapter One, Creating the Future, we examine these values.

Second, the status quo, for example vastly disparate housing conditions or unequal provision of health care, continues unabated unless people have the ability to change it. For this they need power. But since community organizing usually focuses on the interests of the traditionally powerless, that is no simple task. Who currently exercises power? How do they exercise power? How can ordinary citizens become more powerful? These are the central questions covered in Chapter Two.

Third, even if people are able to exercise power, for what shall they organize? As we noted, social scientists have developed many theories by which to explain or understand the human social condition. Which of these many ways should we choose? To put it more directly, what social problems demand community organizer's attention? And, who should decide which to tackle first? In this chapter we examine a variety of the dominant ways social scientists develop their analyses of society and we identify those theoretical perspectives which organizers have found most useful.

Fourth, in the final chapter of Part One, we look at the role of the individual community organizer. Although its roots lie in charity organizing and the ideology of professional service, the organizer role parts company with both. This chapter includes a careful accounting of organizing's early origins, not merely to debunk charity for its often patronizing ways or professionalism for its elitism, but to help clarify the current nature of leadership which community organizing has adopted as its own.

CHAPTER ONE
CREATING THE FUTURE: VALUES AND METHODS

Community organizing spurs social change. The history of community organizing's effect on our society is rich. Neighborhoods have organized to demand building and health code enforcement in housing. Disability rights groups have used organizing to win educational rights for all school age children, regardless of the severity of their disabilities. In the recent past, activist students, unions, churches and other citizens groups organized to pressure the government into ending its involvement in the Vietnam War. Ecology groups organized for the clean air and water acts. Homeowners' groups have organized to expose industrial dumping of toxic wastes in their communities. Civil Rights advocates forced the integration of lunch counters, transit systems, schools, public accommodations, and a variety of other settings. Poor people have used organizing to fight forced relocation brought on by highway projects. Welfare recipients have organized to demand and win increases in welfare benefits. Organized older people have monitored and exposed abhorrent conditions in nursing homes. They have also organized effectively for community based alternative living arrangements for older people. In one city, a women's health collective produced a book entitled *Our Bodies, Ourselves* which became a national bestseller. The book created a new consciousness about women's health care and helped support women's demands nationally for changes in health care practice. In the area of criminal justice, prisoners have staged strikes and prison takeovers to push their demands for reform. Local organizers have formed self help groups, alternative sentencing programs, reform bail bond services, and community based dispute resolution centers.

As society has changed, so too has the nature of community organizing. Several fundamental social changes have affected the way in which community organizing takes place. First, since the early 1950s society has shifted its emphasis away from being nearly exclusively goods producing to being service centered. The human service sector of the economy has increased at a remarkable pace. A second, parallel, phenomenon is the obvious concentration of economic and political power in fewer and fewer major corporations. Corporate power has grown and become more international. The effect of this latter change is that traditional political structures enjoy less control over the society's future. A third important change concerns the effects of industrial production. On the manufacturing, or goods-producing side of the economy, petrochemical and other high technology industries have grown enormously. These industries produce significant amounts of toxic wastes that are now recognized as potentially dangerous health hazards. Fourth, and finally, the shift to a service-oriented society and the emergence of multi-national corporations has been attended by an ever larger government bureaucracy. In other words, both the corporate and government contexts have changed radically in recent years. These developments have strongly influenced both the focus of community organizing (that is, its goals) and the methods or strategies of community organizing.

In this book we will examine the nature of community organizing today. Both theory and methods of practicing community organizing will be discussed. Some of the goals associated with modern-day organizing have changed little from those traditionally espoused by activists while others are new. These present goals reflect how society itself has changed. Organizers still concern themselves with issues of justice and equality. They still pursue the goal of greater self-determination for traditionally powerless people. They still regard organizing as a way of "practicing democracy." However, some of the current concerns, such as how to make human services more responsive to consumers and how to address scientifically complex issues like toxic waste, are new.

Anyone can exploit community organizing strategies and techniques for any cause. Single issue groups can do action research. Sectarian demagogues can hold press conferences with aplomb. Elite power brokers can create slogans and public education campaigns to convince the public of things that are counter to its own interests. But community organizing is more than a grab bag of techniques available for the asking. The techniques themselves complement a way of thinking, an outlook, a set of values. Effective community organizers need to have both technique and vision.

Both old and new values of community organizing reveal a spirit and commitment to fundamental social change. While organizing methods are available to demogogue, ideologue, and egalitarian alike, the concept of community organizing enjoys a progressive tradition in America. It is non-sectarian, yet passionate. It is egalitarian, and practical. It is radical, yet rooted in the real needs and interests of local communities. Community organizing supports a set of values, old and new, that have a broad base of support. First among these values is justice.

Justice

A just society requires three kinds of justice: (1) a system of justice to which all people, rich and poor, powerful and powerless, disabled and non-disabled, old and young, minority and non-minority enjoy access; (2) fair treatment for all within the justice system; and (3) societal conditions which are themselves just. In regard to the first, a legal system is required in which the principles of law (for example, the right to trial by jury and the right to use the courts to protect individual rights against excessive corporate or state power) are available on an equal basis to all. Second, justice must be applied impartially. In this legal system, the accused and accusor, defendant and plaintiff, powerful and powerless are peers. The third kind of justice means that all people, including the most vulnerable, powerless and poor, enjoy basic social goods such as shelter, clothing, food, medical care, education, and freedom of movement. These goods are basic to a just society. They are the signs of a society's moral development. Wherever a society fails to guarantee basic social goods, or where a society forces people to beg and compromise themselves, their pride, and their dignity for such goods, then that society fails to guarantee justice.

Independence and Freedom

No one likes big government. But neither do most people like giant institutions of any kind whether these institutions be superconglomerates having no allegiance to anyone or anything except growth and profit or massive, impersonal "human service" bureaucracies. Rather, people want to feel a sense of self-importance and have a real ability to make decisions that affect their own lives. They need to influence their own futures and to take risks. People do not like playing the role of pawns held in the controlling grip of a few corporate giants. Bigness, impersonal and mechanistic treatment, and unresponsiveness are the enemies of most people, particularly of those who do not enjoy access to the highest decision-making circles of America's institutions. People want to experience life on a human level. People want to experience life in a human way, where they do not lose themselves in jargon and unrelenting procedures. At some inner level of awareness, most people recognize that the really important issues of our lives (for example, how we learn, what values we should pursue, how to make the world safe, how to raise children, and how to practice democracy) are not subject to instantaneous, technocratic solutions. These activities and goals take time, commitment, and creativity. They require independence and the freedom of people to experiment, reflect, and change.

Community Life

Some people, though not many, choose to live in isolation from other people. But aside from rural hermits and urban recluses, most people want the chance to experience a feeling of belonging. People generally want to find their own community or, to put it more accurately, to create their own community, whether it be one of friends, neighbors, workers, or believers. And, no wonder—when people find community, they find they have greater power over their lives. They find ways of resolving problems. They find support and a sense of belonging. They find greater meaning in life. By the same token, when people are forcibly isolated, they frequently become victims of exploitation, authoritarianism, and alienation. They feel powerless, vulnerable, and unimportant. Those of us who believe in community organizing choose the opposite. We choose community as a way of exerting control over our lives.

Individuality

People with disabilities, older people, poor people, minority groups and all others who experience discrimination have not always been recognized or treated as individuals. People with disabilities, for example, have been called "vegetables," incompetent, violent, sexless, oversexed, nauseating, God's gift, and any number of other *things*. They have experienced stereotyping, prejudice, and discrimination writ large. Like all people, those with disabilities want to be regarded as individuals. To have a particular kind of disability, or a particular difficulty related to a disability (for example, coordination problems or communication impediments) is to experience life, or an aspect of life in a certain way. It should not justify treating the person as an object of pity, an object of scorn, an object of fear, an object at all. All kinds of traditionally vulnerable, exploited, and powerless groups have used community organizing to establish group solidarity and group power, but always for the end, at least in part, of reestablishing the individual's worth.

Social Responsibility

As long as one person suffers from unjust social policies and practices we all suffer from them. Even if we did not build large, dehumanizing institutions which segregate those with so-called mental illness, even if we do not personally condone the warehousing of older people in nursing homes, proprietary homes, and single room "apartments," even if we never with our own actions excluded a single child from public schools, even if we never again denied quality health care to poor people—so long as such conditions prevail, and so long as we pay the taxes that finance such practices or remain silent as others act on our behalf (albeit against our conscious will), then we collaborate. Those of us who advocate community organizing ally ourselves with those most vulnerable before the large and powerful institutions of the society. We believe that only when their individual interests are regarded as being on an equal footing with those of the most powerful will the common good prevail. For some groups, such as older people and people with disabilities, equality even means making extra efforts to provide opportunities and to adapt society to people's unique needs. Far from seeing any contradiction between the goals sought by minority interest groups and the public interest, we see the two as inseparable.

Accountability

We hold the government accountable for its actions. No one, ourselves included, condones government waste. Frivolous research, unneeded and unread paperwork, and expensive junkets for officials are the trappings of a system that lacks adequate accountability to the real needs of people. We do not condone government policies which treat the traditionally powerful and prestigious differently than those judged average or ordinary. Government action must be responsive to the interests of ordinary citizens and not to those who can buy government action. Moreover, we believe that good government should work with us to demand accountability from the other major institutions of society, particularly corporations. We want government to help protect the water, air, and earth and thereby protect our health.

Self-Determination

"I don't want to be a charity case." This is a familiar line. The fact is that no one wants to feel completely dependent. No one wants other people to make all their decisions for them. People want the chance to affect their own future, to make choices, even if they are the "wrong" choices. People want the freedom to succeed, even if this implies the possibility of failure. Most people believe they can make some contribution to their own and to society's betterment. If some people never have the chance to try, then we as a society suffer from that lost opportunity. A sense of accomplishment comes from engaging in action, not from being acted upon. Community organizing assumes that all people have some potential to represent their own interests, to speak on their own behalf, to help as well as be helped, and to make change.

Change

Finally, we in community organizing believe in change. In 1972 there were few group homes or supportive apartments available for people with developmental disabilities. School exclusion for these people was acceptable or at least commonplace in most communities and states. At that time the terms handicapism and sexism had not yet been coined. Several decades ago racial segregation in schools was pervasive and legal. Until very recently, industrial pollution went unabated and even unquestioned. Now, only a decade later, community residences, educational rights, the struggle against handicapism, and an advocacy movement able to recall the early contributions of parent activists are a reality. The past activism of Helen Keller, and the present radicalism of the National Federation of the Blind confirm just how far we have come in the field of disability rights. Environmental activists have led the way in establishing national legislation and a national consciousness about environmental concerns. Feminism is here to stay. The struggle against racism has outlawed Jim Crowism, although the struggle to defeat prejudice, stereotyping, and discrimination must continue. We can clearly see the products, however fragile, of community organizing. These products are signs. They signal the fact that change can happen. And, if change has happened in the past, it can happen in the future. Hence our optimism.

Just as the values of organizing are a blend of the old and the new, so too are the methods. On the one hand, many strategies look familiar. Social protest is a good example of a familiar strategy. Organizing groups hold demonstrations and picket in front of organizations with which they have a dispute. They issue demands as well as organize boycotts. Negotiating is another familiar strategy. Groups develop their issues, prioritize them, form negotiating teams, and negotiate on behalf of their own interests. Lobbying, an activity similar to negotiating, also continues to be a popular organizing strategy. At the same time, however, organizing has some dramatically new methods at its disposal. Law, for example, has become a much more universally recognized action strategy. Local and national groups produce legal handbooks to inform service consumers and particular segments of society (for example, women, prisoners, poor people) of their rights. With the advent of government and private support for legal services, more groups have been able to bring their issues to court. Similarly, action research has developed as a major type of strategy. In the style of muckraking, organizing groups do research on such things as bank mortgage policies in poor neighborhoods, schools' exclusion of disabled and poor children, health care costs, and nursing home conditions. As organizers have become more sophisticated in their ability to analyze issues, policies and practices, they have also developed greater effectiveness in using the mass media to project their interests. In response to the growth of corporate and bureaucratic power, a few especially courageous organizers on the inside of mainstream social institutions have perfected a risky organizing strategy known as the art of *"whistleblowing."* In conjunction with the emergence of the "service society" and its attendant professionalism, *self-help* advocacy (for example, rape crisis centers, the Mental Patients Liberation Front, and the Grey Panthers) has proliferated at an unprecedented rate.

In this book we will examine community organizing today and how it incorporates the old and the new. Part I focuses on the theory behind organizing. It includes an analysis of power and its uses, the historical context and role of organizing and its relationship to leadership, and the politics of defining interests, issues, and changes. Part II is concerned with the major action strategies of community organizing. These include legal advocacy, social protest and demands, whistleblowing, negotiations, lobbying, use of the media, and action research. In both sections, the book incorporates examples of organizing in a full range of issue areas.

CHAPTER TWO
POWER

INTRODUCTION

In the early 1960s Stanley Milgram, a professor at Yale University, conducted a study of obedience. It was, in his own words, "a simple experiment":

> A person comes to a psychological laboratory and is told to carry out a series of tasks that come increasingly into conflict with conscience. The main question is how far the participant will comply with the experimenter's instructions before refusing to carry out the action required of him.[1]

The design was indeed simple. And, as is so often the case, simplicity proved compelling.

"WE WILL PAY YOU $4.00 FOR ONE HOUR OF YOUR TIME."[2] So read the headline of an advertisement that Dr. Milgram placed in local newspapers. He offered to pay $4.00 plus 50¢ car fare to people of diverse backgrounds between the ages of 20 and 50 (excluding students) to participate in the experiment. Subjects were invited to Yale University's psychology laboratory where they received their instructions on how to participate in the experiment. Each subject entered the laboratory with another person. The former assumed that the latter was a subject as well. In fact, the other person was a paid actor. The subject and the actor were instructed in the procedures of the experiment by an experimenter. The experimenter designated the subject as a "teacher" in the experiment. The other person (the actor) became the "learner."

The experiment was described to the subject as a study of memory and learning. The subject watched as the experimenter led the learner into a separate room. The learner was then strapped into a chair and an electrode was attached to his or her wrist. The subject was then instructed to sit in the main experimental room before "an impressive shock generator." The generator had a panel of 30 switches, each for a different voltage that varied from 15 to 450 volts. The subject (teacher) was then instructed to give a learning test to the man or woman in the other room. For each incorrect answer, the teacher was to administer a progressively more powerful shock to the learner. The experiment would end when the teacher reached the 450 volt switch.

The real research question was simple. Would Dr. Milgram's subjects be willing to shock the learner? And if the answer was yes, would they be willing to shock the learner with a full 450 volts?

Each subject was given a sample shock of 45 volts. Each time the learner made a mistake, the experimenter told the teacher to announce the voltage level before administering the shock. If the subject balked about giving the shock the experimenter responded "with a sequence of prods" such as "please continue," "please go on," and "you have no choice, you must go on." There were other prods. There were also numerous variations on the experiment. However, the basic experiment was as it has been described.

How did subjects respond to this situation? We might expect that most people would refuse to administer a 450 volt shock. In fact, most subjects gave the full shock. In the first experiment the teacher could not see or hear the learner, although at the level of a 300 volt shock, "the laboratory walls resound as he pounds in protest" (Milgram, 1974, p. 32). Thereafter, the teacher hears no further complaints. Sixty-five percent of the subjects were willing to administer the full 450 volts. Five of the subjects stopped at the 300 mark. In a second experiment, where subjects could hear the voice protests from the learner, 62.5% were willing to administer the full 450 volts. In still a third variation, where the teacher and learner sat in the same room, full compliance dropped to 40%.

The lesson of Milgram's study seems obvious enough. People are affected by their context to a remarkable extent. People who in many cases saw themselves as caring, moral people, obediently followed instructions, even if it meant acting counter to their own values.

Political scientists have defined the term "power" in various ways. The common definition is "the ability to get someone to do something he or she would not ordinarily do." That was Milgram's accomplishment. He created a particular context, a psychological experiment, in which individuals acceded to the demands of authority. In a less global context, he did what slave owners, Nazi "technicians," army officers, political leaders, and directors of bureaucracies have historically done. He won obedience from his subjects.

Yet in one very obvious respect, Milgram's experiment does not and cannot resemble social relations in general. True, Milgram demonstrated in no uncertain terms that individuals respond to their environment. Only in some of their best dreams and fantasies do people dominate their social context in such a way as to become, in any sense, autonomous beings. Real life is no neutral playing field.

Barriers, pitfalls, slippery spots, diverse opponents, and many other known and unknown forces impinge on people's wishes for autonomy. Milgram demonstrated all of that in his experiment. But, unlike the Yale experiments, the social environment is not of such a simple design.

For example, Binstock and Ely's description of people who experience powerlessness in nearly all aspects of their daily lives shows the complexity of the social environment.

> Some people are powerless in virtually every aspect of their lives. On all fronts it seems that active steps to improve their lot are predestined to fail. They have barely enough to eat, and find it difficult to get and hold jobs that would provide them with more than subsistence wages. They live in overcrowded, unsanitary shelters. If their incomes increase sufficiently for them to afford better housing, social restrictions preclude them from doing so. Their children have trouble staying in school and, when they do, they end up with diplomas rather than educations.
>
> Repeated frustrations in the pursuit of specific goals lead to a more general condition of powerlessness—an overwhelming sense of dependence and little opportunity for self-determination. Daily existence becomes threatening and degrading. An application for welfare assistance can subject one's character and intimate personal relations to scrutiny by a government social worker. Standing or sitting on a street-corner can mean sudden confrontation, search, and arrest by the police. Capricious acts of strangers and turns of fate are more important than conscious plans. It seems impossible to have *autonomy* in any area of one's life.[3]

The single most obvious difference between real life situations like these and the laboratory experiment just described is the degree of complexity involved. In Milgram's experiment, the environmental variables may explain how individuals' behaviors can be isolated, manipulated, and analyzed. In real-life situations, we have greater difficulty explaining how the particular situations affect the behavior of individuals. Do children perform poorly in school because they lack the requisite intelligence, because they refuse to accede to their teachers' racist attitudes, because their parents do not value education, because they have come to believe that education cannot improve their life chances, or because certain social and economic forces have destined them to failure?

Political scientists, sociologists, social workers and community organizers, among others, try to understand life situations, particularly those such as Binstock and Ely describe. While explanations of causality may differ markedly, most social analyses address the issue of power in varying fashion. One way to explain educational failure, hanging out on the street-corner, or drunkenness is in psychological terms. In this framework, the problem becomes rooted in or is at least resolvable through the individual psyche. I. Ira Goldenberg, speaking of how a psychiatric counselor might approach a person who is unemployed, believes that the psychological orientation masks other social forces:

> There is a very "simple" reason for the therapist's inability or unwillingness to let the relatively "mundane" question of employment intrude itself in the rehabilitative process: it is the belief that somehow, in some vague, unspecified, and almost mystical

manner, the truly healthy person will naturally and with little difficulty deal with the problem on his own.[4]

As contradictory as this narrow psychological analysis is from the perspective of economic, political and social analyses (for example, economically created unemployment, racism, and political disenfranchisement), it nevertheless addresses the issue of power. With enhanced self-esteem, the individual will become more effective in garnering power.

Those who call for systemic change, for reallocation of resources, for a better economic and social life through structural change, also address the issue of power. But their pursuit is towards something more than self-actualization or personal growth. Some see political organization as the best way of improving the individual's condition. Alinsky espoused this view:

> The only reason people have ever banded together and the only reason they ever will is the fact that organization gives them power to satisfy their desire or to realize their needs. . . . Even when we talk of a community lifting itself by its bootstraps, we are talking of power. It takes a great deal of power to lift oneself by one's own bootstraps.[5]

Piven and Cloward have proposed still another path to social change.[6] They prescribe protest, not organization building. When organizers concentrate on organization building, they miss the opportunity to capitalize on popular unrest and leave themselves open to being co-opted by the elite opposition.

Each of these analyses—and there are many more available—attempts to explain and propose remedies for offensive social conditions. While each one calls for different actions, presumably because each understands social conditions and their causes somewhat differently, each in some measure, comes back to questions of power. How is it that some people are more powerful or less powerful than others? What factors enhance power? How does power work in complex social contexts? How can individuals transform power relations? These are central questions for organizers.

DEFINITION OF POWER

Virtually every commentator on power shares a belief in its importance. Yet social theorists disagree profoundly about how power manifests itself. Some view power as something which individuals seek essentially for themselves. According to this view, power primarily serves the individual's interests. That is generally labeled a Machiavellian vision of power. Another school of thought holds that power ultimately serves the common good. Groups of people exchange power endlessly in quest of consensus. This is called a consensus-building, pluralist, and/or functionalist perspective. Another vision of power is an essentially psychological one. It defines power as an expression of the social self. Still another view, a Marxist one, suggests that power belongs to those who own the means of production, which constitute the economic structure of society.

Michael Korda (1975), in his book *Power!* epitomizes the modern day Machiavellian view.[7] Power becomes an end in itself, something that enhances individual experience.

> All life is a game of power. The object of the game is simple enough: to know what you want and get it. The moves of the game, by contrast, are infinite and complex, although they usually involve the manipulation of people and situations to your advantage. As for the rules, these are only discovered by playing the game to the end.
>   Some people play the power game for money, some for security or fame, others for sex, most for some combination of these objectives. The master players (some of whose games we shall study) seek power itself, knowing that power can be used to obtain money, sex, security or fame. None of these alone constitutes power; but power can produce them all.[8]

Korda's context for power involves sexual relationships (including marriage) and the American corporation. The fact that racism, class divisions, forced unemployment, and other conditions related to social structure and ideology remain outside his discussion probably reflects his own position among the "successful." The goal for Korda is not social change in the sense of redistributing power but, rather, individual success and access to the top. He advises people on such things as how and where to sit in an office, what to say, when to cry (for best effect, to get one's way), when to speak out, and how to dress.

Another popular view of power is the "consensus" or functionalist model. Parsons, the leading proponent of functionalism, holds that various factions and interest groups compete in the marketplace until consensus emerges. According to this theoretical perspective, the public good is served by the "open" competition of interests. Martin has characterized the Parsonian view this way:

> The assumption of conflict and antagonism is built into the definition: A overcomes the resistance of B, implying that the interests of B are being sacrificed to the interests of A. But this ignores the possibility that power relations may be relations of mutual convenience: power may be a resource facilitating the achievement of the goals of both A and B—in the same way as money may facilitate the achievement of the goals of both borrower and lender in a credit relation. Transposed onto a societal level, power may be seen as a generalized means for the achievement of collective goals, instead of a specific means for the satisfaction of limited, sectional interests.[9]

Blau's exchange theory is not much different than the Parsonian analysis. He envisions, and has described, power relationships as ongoing exchanges between individuals, groups and social structures. Briefly his thesis is as follows:

> Exchange processes . . . give rise to differentiation of power. A person who commands services others need, and who is independent of any at their command, wins power over others by making the satisfaction of their need contingent on their compliance. . . .
>   Differentiation of power in a collective situation evokes contrasting dynamic forces. . . .
>   Under the influence of these forces, the scope of legitimate organization expands to include ever larger collectivities, but opposition and conflict recurrently redivide these collectivities and stimulate reorganization along different lines.[10]

According to Blau, opposition movements came into existence to promote "adjustments" to the system and its prevailing institutions. Yet, it is inevitable, he argues, that even opposition movements will eventually become institutionalized, and therefore, rigid, thus laying the groundwork for new opposition. If all this sounds rather like the Marxian notion of a dialectical process, it is. The main difference is that Blau, Parsons, Lindblom, and other consensus-building or pluralist theorists do not perceive current patterns of power distribution as being highly concentrated in the hands of business elites, nor do they adhere to a Marxian economic world view.

There are several problems with Parsonian theory. While it has the advantage, as far as the community organizer is concerned, of moving beyond Korda's "looking out for number one," it adheres to a naive notion of social interaction. It ignores the real and observable fact that certain segments of society, particularly those groups that are powerless and oppressed, have neither the resources nor the avenues with which to catapult their interests into the fray. Thus societal interests or the public good become synonymous with the good of those who can engage regularly and effectively in power relations.

Parsons epitomizes the current views of proponents of consensus, pluralist politics. He assumes an ever emerging commonality of values, a nascent public good:

> I conceive of power to be a generalized symbolic medium which circulates much like money, the possession and use of which enables the responsibilities of an office with authority in a collectivity to be more effectively discharged.
>   Power I conceive . . . to be a primary instrumentality of effective performance in that position. To be effective, a unit must have an income of power, must be willing to spend it, and yet must be prudently rational in doing so.[11]

But what is the public good? Is it not defined de facto as protection of particular interests? Parenti describes Parson's theory as a defense of collusion: "The ideal purpose of collusion is to build such a preponderance of support for a particular interest as to forestall the emergence of competing interests, thereby sustaining the appearance of an unopposed collective interest."[12] In other words, public good or consensus politics may well mean consensus for dominant groups and exclusion, disenfranchisement, or oppression for marginal groups.

This is essentially the view taken by Gouldner. While he has no quarrel with the notion that power could be manipulated like money, he questions Parson's conclusion that it will be used for effectiveness, rationality, and collective goals. Where Parsons asserts noble interests, Gouldner displays skepticism:

> The current conception of power as a resource for fulfilling collective or public goals, rather than the selfish ambitions of office-holders reflects the sociologist's access to and ease with established power centers.[13]

In Gouldner's view, "Power is . . . just this ability to enforce one's moral claims."[14] With the recent emergence of single issue special interest politics (for example, disability rights, ecology, and antinuclear groups) critics sometimes ask,

"Can society afford to jeopardize the common good by meeting the demands of special interests?" In effect, this rhetorical question suggests that the common good excludes certain minority interests. Of course minority groups would argue that the common good will only be achieved when marginal groups have equal access to decision-making processes and have their concerns incorporated into mainstream social policy.

Some scholars of power attempt to understand its social characteristics in personal, psychological terms. Since individuals create and use power, the way to study power, so the argument goes, is to study what it means psychologically for individuals. The goal here is presumably to show individuals how to develop power in ways that are both personally valuable and socially beneficial.

Psychologist Rollo May explains power in such terms. Power is, he says, the ability to act, to create change, and to influence others. Through power, people affirm their existence and their being.[15] According to May, power takes five forms: (1) exploitative, as in the instance of slavery; (2) manipulative, power over another person; (3) competitive, power against another; (4) nutrient, power for the other, or in caring for one's children, or loved ones; and (5) integrative, or power with the other person. Interestingly, May does not assume a "consensus" view of power. He does not, for example, presume that "nutrient" and "integrative" power are essential. He says that competitive power is perfectly acceptable because at least you are not considered inferior to others when you compete with them. Yet for all its value in helping explain the individual's psychological relation to power, May's typology does little to explain how power is distributed in society and how it may be used. For that reason, psychological theories have raised little interest among community organizers.

Before we outline the notion of power that community organizers have found most compelling and useful, it is important to discuss the remaining major conception of power, one that has contributed largely to community organization practice. Marxists define power as control of the means of production in society. Malcolm X espoused this view:

> The black man in North America was economically sick and that was evident in one simple fact: as a consumer, he got less than his share, and as a producer gave least. The black American today shows us the perfect parasite image—the black tick under the delusion that he is progressing because he rides on the udder of the fat, the three-stomached cow that is white America. For instance, annually, the black man spends over $3 billion for automobiles, but America contains hardly any franchised black automobile dealers. For instance, forty per cent of the expensive imported Scotch whiskey consumed in America goes down the throats of the status-sick black man; but the only black-owned distilleries are in the bathtubs, or in the woods somewhere. Or for instance—a scandalous shame—in New York City, with over a million Negroes, there aren't twenty black-owned businesses employing over ten people. It's because black men don't own and control their own community's retail establishments that they can't stabilize their own community.[16]

The existence of ruling elites in America has been chronicled again and again, sometimes along racial lines, as in the case of Malcolm X's analysis, and more often strictly in economic and social terms. Floyd Hunter described an elite in Atlanta in his famous study of community power structure:

> Businessmen are the community leaders in Regional City as they are in other cities. Wealth, social prestige, and political machinery are functional to the wielding of power by the business leaders in the community . . .
>
> In the general social structure of community life, social scientists are prone to look upon the institutions and formal associations as powerful forces, and it is easy to be in basic agreement with this view. Most institutions and associations are subordinate, however, to the interests of the policymakers who operate in the economic sphere of community life in Regional City. The institutions of the family, church, state, education, and the like draw sustenance from economic institutional sources and are thereby subordinate to this particular institution more than any other. The associations stand in the same relationship to the economic interests as do the institutions. We see both the institutions and the formal associations playing a vital role in the execution of determined policy, but the formulation of policy often takes place outside these formalized groupings. Within the policy-forming groups, the economic interests are dominant.[17]

In *Middletown, USA* (Muncie, Indiana), Robert and Helen Lynd identified the elite as one dominant manufacturing family:

> If I'm out of work I go to the X plant; if I need money I go to the X bank, and if they don't like me I don't get it; my children go to the X college; when I get sick I go to the X hospital; I buy a building lot or house in an X subdivision; my wife goes downtown to buy clothes at the X department store; if my dog stays away he is put in the X pound; I buy X milk; I drink X beer, vote for X political parties, and get help from X charities; my boy goes to the X Y.M.C.A. and my girl to their Y.W.C.A.; I listen to the word of God in X-subsidized churches; if I'm a Mason I go the X Masonic Temple; I read the news from the X morning newspaper; and, if I am rich enough, I travel via the X airport (Comment by a Middletown man, 1935).[18]

Certainly one of the most famous critiques of ruling elites is contained in C. Wright Mills' *The Power Elite*. Mills described the unequal nearly monolithic distribution of power he found on a national and international level. It was no different than that which Hunter found in Atlanta, that the Lynds found in Middletown (Muncie), and that Malcolm X found between Blacks and Whites:

> Within each of the most powerful institutional orders of modern society there is a gradation of power. The owner of a roadside fruit stand does not have as much power in any area of social or economic or political decision as the head of a multi-million-dollar fruit corporation; no lieutenant on the line is as powerful as the Chief of Staff in the Pentagon; no deputy sheriff carries as much authority as the President of the United States. Accordingly, the problem of defining the power elite concerns the level at which we wish to draw the line. By lowering the line, we could define the elite out of existence; by raising it, we could make the elite a very small circle indeed. In a preliminary and minimum way, we draw the line crudely, in charcoal as it were: By the power elite, we refer to those political, economic, and military circles which as an intricate set of overlapping cliques share decisions having at least national consequences. In so far as national events are decided, the power elite are those who decide them.[19]

The distinguishing feature of elite power is its seeming monolithic quality. As Mills demonstrated, power elites set the limits within which others less powerful than themselves make choices or decisions. Because elites circumscribe the range of choices, the individual's range of freedom is predetermined. If Mills' analysis is correct, the work of community organizers is at best monumental:

> On the bottom level there has come into being a mass-like society which has little resemblence to the image of a society in which voluntary associations and classic publics hold the keys to power. The top of the American system of power is much more unified and much more powerful, the bottom is much more fragmented, and in truth, impotent, than is generally supposed by those who are distracted by the middling units of power which neither express such will as exists at the bottom nor determine the decisions at the top.[20]

THE COMMUNITY ORGANIZER'S VIEW OF POWER

Max Weber defined power as "the probability that one actor within a social relationship will be in a position to carry out his own will despite resistance, regardless of the basis on which his probability rests."[21] That definition of power dominates all others in the field of political science. Scholars have restated it again and again. David Easton calls power "a relationship in which one person or group is able to determine the action of another in the direction of the former's own ends."[22] Lewin defines it much as a professor of physics might. The message is still the same, and that is to get others to do what you want them to do:

> We might define power of b over a (pow b/a) as the quotient of the maximum force which b can induce on a ($i^b f_{a,x}^{max}$), and the maximum resistance ($f_{a,x}^{max}$) which a can offer. (x indicates the region into which a should locomote according to the will of b; $f_{\overline{a,x}}$ indicates a force in the direction opposite to $f_{a,x}$).[23]

Dahl's definition reiterates this kind of theme: "My intuitive idea of power, then is something like this: A has power over B to the extent that he can get B to do something that B would not otherwise do."[24] Community organizers tend to subsume these bare bones definitions in a larger view of power.

Taken as a group, organizers tend not to be doctrinaire in their vision of power. While it is certainly true that some have espoused particular, well defined ideological perspectives—"New Left" organizers, for example, tended to adhere to a neo-Marxist politics—most have not. Alinsky epitomized the eclectic approach that community organization took in regard to the concept of power. He saw power concentrated in the hands of elites and their organizations. However, his writings express the belief that organized communities can challenge elites and their institutions without radically restructuring the economic nature of society. He describes organization building and neighborhood strategizing in the context of a democratic process where competing forces meet, yet he never invokes the Parsonian spectre of an ever-emerging collective good. He describes power as the ability to get others to do what one wants, but he also describes power in more cooperative terms as well, such as the ability of a group to build a power base.

Community organizers tend to endorse what might be called an interactional view of power. *Power exists whenever people cooperate and/or obey.* In the words of a leading student of interactional power, "power is inherent in practically all social and political relationships.[25] Sharp believes that the manner in which people define their own relationship to government and other social institutions such as corporations, schools, and medical care centers, determines whether they can consider social change, how they approach social change, and the outcome of their social change activities:

> Basically, there appear to be two views of the nature of power. One can see people as dependent upon the good will, the decisions and the support of their government or of any other hierarchical system to which they belong. Or conversely, one can see that government or system dependent on the people's good will, decision and support. One can see the power of government as emitted from the few who stand at the pinnacle of command. Or one can see that power, in all governments, as continually rising from many parts of the society.[26]

Sharp concludes that nonviolent action and (one might add) community organization, are founded on the latter views. In other words, governments and other social institutions depend on people.

This notion of power has several corollaries which, in addition to clarifying the dynamics of power, are of obvious importance to community organization. First, since power requires support, in the form of cooperation and obedience, power is not necessarily durable, monolithic or immutable. Indeed, it is dynamic and even fragile. A school superintendent's power, for example, derives from a cooperating school board, from citizens who pay taxes, from cooperative or obedient teachers or a teachers union, and from parents who go along with the superintendent's policies. A public speaker enjoys the power to be heard and the potential power to persuade or influence others only so long as people will listen. A political leader needs popular support in the form of votes. At a societal level, those who would wield power have a never-ending thirst for support. Power is "always dependent for its strength and existence upon a replenishment of its success by the cooperation of a multitude of institutions and people—a cooperation which may or may not continue."[27] Similarly, Karl Deutsch wrote in his article, "Cracks in the Monolith," that enforcement of orders requires a society's compliance.[28]

The second corollary is that since the source of power rests with people and that it can and does change, power itself belongs to no one person. Groups of people can create power by joining together in mutual action, either to influence others by giving or withholding cooperation and obedience or to create their own social institutions (for example, a food cooperative, a self-help clinic, a neighborhood center). In the words of Hannah Arendt, "Power is always as we would say, a power potential and not an unchangeable, measurable, and reliable entity like force or strength."[29]

Third, power depends not on quantifiable physical resources such as money or property, but on the significance that people give to such things. Rich people frequently wield power because others want their money and are willing to offer services or follow commands in order to get it. Consumers can wield power by refusing to purchase particular products (for example, gas-guzzling automobiles). Thus, money and other forms of property may be tools which people can use to achieve influence or control power. They may do so only as long as people defer to money and property.

Fourth, the same can be said of authority that has been stated about money. Even legitimized power (that is, authority) depends on the support of people to execute its functions. Contrary to conventional wisdom,

> the decision as to whether an order has authority or not lies with the person to whom it is addressed, and does not reside in persons of authority or those who issue orders.[30]

That this characteristic of authority has been lost on many people helps explain what Sharp called the other view of power, that power *belongs* to the elite few who exercise it. The origins of authority have simply become obscured. Bertrand De-Jouvenal, in his classic book, *On Power,* explains just how obscured the origins of authority have become:

> When he gets a warning from the tax collector or a summons to barracks from the policeman, the recipient is far from seeing in the warning or in the travel voucher an exercise of his own will, however much extolled and transfigured for him that will may be. Rather they are for him the dictates of a foreign power, of an impersonal master now popularly called ''they'' but in other days known as the evil spirits.[31]

Bertrand Russell wrote nearly identical words to those of DeJouvenal in the same year, 1949:

> The ordinary voter, so far from finding himself the source of all power, or army, navy, police, and civil service, feels himself their humble subject, whose duty is as the Chinese used to say, to ''tremble and obey.''[32]

Not even authority backed by death-inflicting force can guarantee power's reign. The Nazi concentration camps provide a case in point. One might logically expect that prison authorities and guards would be able to exert complete power over prisoners in this situation. This is almost never the case. As Steiner reported in his account of the Nazi camps, the Germans depended upon cooperation and obedience from prisoners and potential prisoners alike.[33] German ''technicians'' divided Jewish ghetto populations into those with cards and those without, thus causing the Jews to believe that their future rested in the hands of fate (luck) rather than on something they themselves could influence.

> The Germans issued work certificates, saying that the bearers would have to present them only during raids. The ghetto was divided into two camps: those who had

certificates and who were lulled by the sense of security they derived from them, and those who did not have them and who felt vulnerable, isolated, abandoned. The raids resumed, striking those "without certificates." For the privileged, it was the beginning of compromise. By brandishing their certificates during a raid, they dissociated themselves from their own people, they lost the sense of the oneness of the destiny of their people.

But soon the privileged themselves were divided, the certificates became of two kinds: with and without photograph. They wondered which kind offered the best protection. "With photograph," concluded the majority, for the photograph made the document seem more official. The Technicians distributed a large number of these and carried out a small raid on those without photographs. Our point, thought those with photographs. Then the certificates with photographs were abolished and replaced by blank certificates bearing the seal of the labor bureau of Ponar. The word caused alarm and the "blanks" did not have much success, until a second raid descended upon those without photographs and those without certificates, sparing only those with blanks. Then the "blanks" were in turn divided into two categories—those with and those without the qualification "skilled worker."[34]

And so it went: division, dissension, desperation, demise. Yet even under such diabolical conditions a resistance movement grew.

For instance, at Treblinka there would be a prison camp revolt. What Steiner confirms in his book *Treblinka,* is that resistance begins with an affirmation of self, even in the face of death. Indeed the ability to resist may, in the most extreme situations, come only when people decide they can challenge death. In the words of Frederick Douglass:

It was a resurrection from the dark and pestiferous tomb of slavery, to the heaven of comparative freedom. I was no longer a servile coward, trembling under the frown of a brother worm of the dust, but my long cowed spirit was roused to an attitude of independence. I had reached the point at which I was not afraid to die. This spirit made me a free man in fact, though I remained a slave in form.[35]

Douglass recognized that even in a master-slave relationship, with all the violence that it implies, power in authority is a two-way affair. Gandhi came to precisely the same conclusion:

The moment the slave resolves that he will no longer be a slave, his fetters fall. He frees himself and shows the ways to others. Freedom and slavery are mental states. Therefore, the first thing is to say to yourself: "I shall no longer accept the role of a slave. I shall not obey orders as such but shall disobey them when they are in conflict with my conscience."[36]

The fifth and final major principle or corollary implied by the interactional definition of power has to do with the reasons for people's cooperation and obedience. Sharp suggested that, in part, people fail to act in their own interests or for progressive interests because they perceive themselves as passive objects "dependent upon the goodwill, the decisions, and the support of their government or of any other hierarchical system to which they belong.''[37] The alternative vision, that people through their ability to give or withhold support control the exercise of power, leads to one major question. It is a question that may well shape an organizer's activities: "If people find policies and practices which they do not like, then why do they not act to change them; why do they not become more active in consciously changing how they give and withhold their cooperation and obedience?" Put more simply, "why do people cooperate and obey?" In the words of Gerth and Mills, "an adequate understanding of power relations . . . involve a knowledge of the grounds on which a power holder claims obedience, and the terms to which the obedient feels an obligation to obey."[38]

REASONS FOR INACTION

The interactional definition appeals to organizers because it admits to the fragile, diffuse, and fluid nature of power. It invites change. It suggests that everyone can participate in its use. It places people above things. It encourages skepticism toward authority. And it asks the important question of why people sometimes fail to act on their beliefs and interests. This last question is of central importance to organizers.

The answer to why people cooperate and obey must necessarily reflect the particular institutional or social context in which it is asked. We would, for example, expect that in a capitalist society, particularly in those sections of society where pursuit of wealth is greatest, that cooperation and obedience may well be linked to the desire to be rich. By contrast, in a non-capitalist context (e.g., a hunter-gatherer culture), a million dollars could be expected to win neither cooperation nor obedience. Similarly, we might expect that the reasons for people's cooperation and obedience would vary from one type of institution to another (e.g., the army, a hospital, a school, a corporation). Yet, the *general* type of reasons for cooperation and obedience are universal. It is their application to particular social and institutional contexts which vary. The organizer's task is to examine the reasons for cooperation and obedience in particular contexts.

Ideology, Beliefs, World View

Part of the reason why people cooperate and obey can be understood only upon examination of their ideological perspectives. People who believe in the Darwinian view of human existence (survival of the fittest) may use that belief to justify all kinds of economic, political, and social inequality. Instead of resisting policies which foster or preserve inequality, people who hold such beliefs may openly embrace them. In contrast are those people who favor democratic socialism. The latter group will, more likely than not, favor state intervention in order to promote not only equal opportunities, but also equal benefits. These are just two examples of ideological orientation chosen from the many that are possible. They demonstrate the importance of ideology in action taken by an individual.

On a less grand or at least more narrow scale, ideological belief structures still influence individual and group action. We can expect, for example, that in a society which devalues the condition of being old, large numbers of people in the society will see nothing wrong with supporting policies and practices which consign older persons to a subsistence existence. Policies will be supported which cut off older persons from the social mainstream, and which place the needs of older persons after the needs of more valued groups such as the young and the middle-aged.

Certain ideological perspectives, including the two mentioned above, militate against social action. The belief, for example, that most, if not all, social problems can be solved by careful application of scientific expertise, removes the ordinary person from the change process. It puts the future in the hands of experts. Another dominant ideological theme is the one described by William Ryan. It consists of "blaming the victim," and holds that the source of most social problems such as poverty, ignorance, and lack of adequate housing inheres in poor persons' bad work attitudes, lack of interest in education, and low respect for property and for social advancement.[39] This thesis completely ignores the relationship between national economic policies and poverty, between racism and poor schooling, between powerlessness and hopelessness. Still another ideological view is that "more is better." This view holds that increased social programs translate into social progress. While it is true that additional social programs usually attract users, the thesis that more is better obscures the reality that more social programs may do nothing to counter the structural causes of inequality.

Some ideological perspectives, like the technicist one cited above, militate against social change (structural change), even though they are not in any gross or intentional way racist, classist, or otherwise discriminatory. Take for example Parsons' outlook. Parsons envisions the world as a large arena in which interests are played out and consensus is achieved. But, as we noted earlier, because of how society is already established—economically, politically, and socially—certain interests do not have an equal chance once they enter the conflict. Some never get into the fray at all. In contrast, Mills' notion of a power elite dramatically portrays the reality of the unequal social context. Mills' view, like Alinsky's, Fox and Piven's, and Hunter's does not mask political reality. If anything, his view magnifies it. Mills reminds us that to be effective, action must in some tangible way call into question existing distributions of power.

Practically speaking, organizers may adopt any one or a combination of stances with respect to ideology. Also, they may organize others to accept their ideological viewpoint. Alternatively, they may organize consciousness-raising groups with the expressed interest of encouraging groups of people to examine the relationship of particular policies and practices to ideologies, thus laying the groundwork for formulation of an ideological view that the group feels is best suited to its interests. They may choose, as Alinsky did, to adopt an ideological viewpoint that will have strong appeal within particular constituencies, be non-doctrinaire, be low profile and be hard to refute, even in the enemy camp.[40] Alinsky espoused a democratic ideology and also believed in the rights of poor and disenfranchised persons to challenge traditional, elite power blocs.

Habit, Custom, Standard
Operating Procedure

Sometimes people point to tradition or habit to rationalize or justify conforming to policies and practices, even those they dislike. In a nutshell, "that's the way it's always been done." However, the fact that something has been regarded as "standard operating procedure" does not make it best or even desirable. To the extent that particular policies and practices survive as a matter of inertia or because they are rooted in tradition, the organizer's role is clear: (1) to examine and question tradition; (2) to show that times have changed, thus opening the way for new policies and practices; and (3) to present alternatives.

It is no accident that community organization efforts challenge tradition, particularly if they involve such strategies as action-research, lobbying, litigation, demands (including the development of recommendations), alternative models, and blueprints. One of the simplest retorts to the claim that "we've always done it this way" and "it's the only way we know," is to present evidence that practical, workable alternatives already exist. The second best defense is to unveil an alternative blueprint. That has been a frequent strategy of Common Cause, Public Interest Research Groups, and numerous other social change organizations. Nearly all action-research reports (as defined and described in the Action-Research Chapter) include extensive proposals to remedy the conditions they expose.

In 1971 the National Urban Coalition, an organization created in the wake of urban riots of 1967, published *Counterbudget: A Blueprint for Changing National Priorities, 1971–76.*[41] In the words of Sol Linowitz, former National Coalition Chairperson, the counterbudget marked "the first effort by a major non-government group to set forth a complete and comprehensive plan for revising national priorities." The coalition put forth a five year counterbudget that called for national health insurance, massive transfer of expenditures from defense to health and human needs, support for housing, increased public jobs, and expanding early education programs. One of the proposals of the coalition was to abolish welfare. The Coalition report recommended that the welfare system be replaced by a cash assistance grant based on family size that would be reduced by a preset rate (say 50¢ on the dollar) as family members earned income through work. The point of all these recommendations was *not* to supplant the official budget (the President's budget) with the counterbudget, but to force serious discussion and possible implementation of some of the alternatives. The counterbudget challenged the knee-jerk budget process that, with but a few exceptions, makes across-the-board increases on the previous year's budget items. It challenged habit, custom, and standard operating procedure.

Rewards and Sanctions

People often act out of fear of sanctions and also for the hope for rewards. Max Weber considered fear and hope central to the unfolding of power:

Obedience is determined by highly robust motives of fear and hope—fear of vengeance of magical powers or of the power holder, hope for reward in this world or in the beyond.[42]

On the question of hope for one type of reward, that of prestige, Weber wrote, "Striving for prestige pertains to all political structures."[43]

Hope for reward takes numerous and diverse forms, including the desire for prestige, wealth, and a sense of self-worth. Gaetano Mosca has argued that the number of social inducements that give rise to hope is on the rise: "As civilization grows, the number of the moral and material influences which are capable of becoming social forces increases."[44]

For some people, cooperation and obedience become necessary for survival. That is, the reward for which many people strive is often life itself. Tolstoy put it this way:

> A worker only agrees to live all his life underground, or to make the one hundredth part of one article all his life, or to move his hands up and down amid the roar of machinery all his life, because he will otherwise not have means to live.[45]

For others, cooperation and obedience may mean keeping a job, getting promoted, or "holding on to what you have." A quick survey of whistleblowers, for example, reveals that those who speak out against injustice and malfeasance in their own workplace often lose their jobs. Particular strategies which whistleblowers and other organizers can use to protect themselves against unwanted sanctions are discussed further in Chapter Seven.

Authority and Sense of Self

People's readiness to obey or cooperate with others depends heavily on their sense of self. A person who has little confidence in his or her personal judgment would be expected to follow others rather than him or herself. Conversely, strong-willed people might display less willingness to submit to the demands of others and more propensity to consciously choose precisely when to give or withdraw support of power. In other words, individual personality characteristics may influence our readiness to sanction the authority of others.[46] Bertrand Russell, a deeply committed individualist, once lamented the fact that

> Wherever there is inequality of power, it (self respect) is not likely to be found among those who are subject to the rule of others: One of the most revolting features of tyrannies is the way in which they lead the victims of injustice to offer adulation to those who ill-treat them.[47]

Who can doubt the importance of a person's sense of self, values, moral outlook, and feelings in determining readiness to cooperate or obey? Even our disposition is crucial. Chester Barnard, for example, cites apathy or "zones of indifference" as a major determinant of obedient behavior.[48] On the other hand, many people decide to follow or "go along" on the basis of perceived charisma in leadership.

Milgram's work suggests that people may be particularly responsive to the commands of scientists or what they perceive to be "the interests of science." Similarly, people sometimes bow to patriotism or duty. Presidents have been known to request obedience and cooperation by invoking the vague proscriptions of ''national security interests.''

While few people will admit to being easily cowed by apparent authority—upon hearing of the Milgram experiment many people say, ''I would never have given those shocks''—none of us can claim freedom from influence. Our hearts flutter and our adrenalin surges when we come face to face with authority.

We are particularly apt to question ourselves, our abilities, and even our rightness when we feel isolated. Because of this tendency, it is not at all uncommon for officials to prefer dealing with people individually. This is done in the name of protecting individual privacy, but it has the effect, whether intentional or not, of isolating the individual and rendering him or her less powerful. Because organizers must regularly confront authority they, perhaps more than others, can ill afford to ignore this fact.

It takes confidence and an almost unending supply of optimism to keep fighting injustice. It takes confidence to question particular authorities, whether they are health planners, mayors, housing authority directors, or school superintendents. It takes confidence to hold a press conference. It takes confidence to make public demands on officials. To meet this need for confidence, organizers have turned to such strategies as assertiveness training, role playing, and training in the arts of negotiation and group building.

Expertise

Modern science, technical expertise, and professionalism may not always be the organizer's best friends. Michael Parenti has noted that technical, scientific expertise can be used to exclude affected groups (for example, poor people, racial minorities, older people, people with disabilities) from participating in social change.[49] ''The modern scientific view that almost all problems are subject to solution by rational investigation and manipulation seemingly allows all the room in the world'' for rational change.[50] He continued, however, by saying that the modern scientific view avoids political reality; it fails ''to draw any link between the social problems of the have-nots and their powerlessness, or more generally, between social problems and power distribution.''[51] In the scientific view, the politico-economic social order is taken as a given. People's problems are viewed as technical problems and not as political (power) problems. Hence, the organizer and affected groups are relegated to an observer status. They must stand aside while the experts, who ''know best'' by virtue of their training, accomplish social engineering.

Society's increasing professionalization (for example, more fields require professional licensing, more fields are dividing into increasingly narrow specialties) poses a serious threat to organizers. Once a field becomes professionalized, the consumer or lay person is relegated to the role of outsider. Yet, to combat the reign of experts by declaring that prevailing social problems are not essentially technical smacks of advocating a retreat from the technological revolution. In point of fact, organizers recognize their dilemma. Thus, it is not unusual to find them becoming expert in a professional area (for example, health care, disabilities, education, special education, physical planning, transportation, welfare, criminal justice, rights of mental patients) while at the same time they seek political solutions to problems. Expert skills thus become an additional, though not completely sufficient, tool of community organization. Technique must be linked to power.

Skills

Good intentions, noble goals, and even popular support do not guarantee successful social change. Organizers require a broad repertoire of skills in order to practice their trade. They must know how to research a law. They must know how and when to hold a press conference. They must know the basic principles of effective negotiating, of public speaking, of letter writing, of lobbying and demonstrating. They must have a sense of strategy. They must know when they are being co-opted and how to guard against co-optation. Each of these abilities is a learned skill. Each is perfected through practice. The very use of power is a skill. As Si Kahn puts it, "The organizer . . . must serve as a tactician skilled in the use of power tactics if he (she) is to be effective . . ."[52]

When student aptitude test scores and literacy abilities began to drop several years ago, there was a tendency for commentators to say things like, "they are watching too much television," "they live in an electronic culture," and "reading is becoming a lost art." Some teachers welcomed these explanations, for they placed blame outside the classroom. Similarly, an organizer might wish to explain away the news conference that news reporters do not attend as just one more example of "how the system keeps our views from the public eye." Indeed, there may be some truth in such charges. But blaming a whole culture for declining reading scores or "the system" for an unattended news conference does little to promote change. Even if the "conspiratorial system" analysis is correct, the organizer's task is, in the case of a news conference, to attract the news media. To accomplish that, the organizer must know *when* to call a news conference, *how* to make an effective news presentation, *how* to compose a news release, and *who* to invite. The good organizer, like the good teacher, must ask, "how can I do things differently in order to achieve different results?"

We also need resources. Community organizing costs money. Newsletters, training materials, and research reports also cost money to produce. Litigation requires expensive legal talent and incurs potentially burdensome court costs. Phone bills, postage, office supplies, office equipment, and office space costs mount up quickly. Hence, fundraising, while seemingly unrelated to community organizing, becomes a regular and necessary aspect of the work. Typical strategies for fundraising include membership dues, establishment of a "defense fund," door-to-door soliciting, direct mail, grant writing, fee-for-service, and sale of publications.

Language

It has been suggested that the "most universal form of human cooperation and the most complex, is speech."[53] We create words in the process of creating society as a means of institutionalizing human actions, to both expand and constrict our experiences. Hannah Arendt put it this way: "Power is what keeps the public realm, the potential space of appearance between acting and speaking men, in existence."[54] Words mean nothing until a listener hears them or cooperates with them. Language plays a central role in power because people must share words and symbols in order to communicate, experience cooperation, and obey or disobey those who exercise power.

People sometimes use words to dehumanize others. The effect of this kind of usage frequently renders people less powerful. Just as people may experience an opening up of their lives through art, communication and through shared experiences, so too they may find themselves objectified by words. Pejorative labels like "nigger," "chick," "retard," "idiot," and "gook" are examples of such objectification. These labeling terms deny people their humanness. Other classifications such as medical diagnoses, differentiation by educational experience, and racial designation, while not always pejorative, frequently influence how people are perceived and treated. Such classifications influence people's life experiences and therefore affect power relations as well. Can there be any question that labels such as "disturbed," "retarded," "Black," "genius," or "gay" influence people's lives? Each institution, school, or human service has its own typification symbols or words. That these words relate closely to expressions of power can be easily demonstrated. Gerth and Mills wrote:

> Certain emblems and modes of language not only recur in given social contexts but seem to be more important to the maintenance of certain institutions, to their chains of authority and to the authoritative distribution of their roles.[55]

In school, children are often referred to by the grades they occupy (for example, "that fifth grader"). In large state mental hospitals and prisons, people are sometimes referred to by numbers, hardly ever by their full name, or by Mr. or Ms. In health care settings, familiarity with technical medical language is highly associated with access to decision-making circles. The consumer's place is defined by the all-purpose, leveling label of "patient."

Edelman has suggested that people in authority positions employ vague cue words to evoke vivid and sometimes prejudicial images. He holds that language relates closely to power. It not only serves to describe events but is "part of events, strongly shaping their meaning and political roles . . ."[56] For example, Edelman regards "welfare" as a social cue word:

> The "welfare" label connotes to a great many people that the problem lies in public dole, which encourages laziness. This widespread belief about the cause of poverty is further reinforced by other political terms, such as the "work test" provisions widely

publicized in the 1967 and 1971 Social Security Act Amendments. Our language creates a picture of hundreds of thousands of welfare recipients refusing a plentiful supply of productive work, but the pertinent research shows (1) that only a very small percentage of the recipients are physically able to work and even these typically cannot find jobs, with unemployment levels running between 5 and 6 percent of the labor force and usually far higher in localities where recipients are concentrated; and (2) that welfare benefits do not detract from work incentive.[57]

Organizers have long understood the importance of language. Terms like "Blacks," "racism," "feminism," "woman" (as opposed to lady or girl), "gray panthers," "handicapism," "ageism," and "Chicano," declare the spirit of self determination. The words themselves demand new relationships based on equality.

Corporate and government leaders are also quite aware of the importance of language. Few situations better illustrate this fact than crises which "the authorities" attempt to mediate for the public by carefully choosing their words. At times the particular choice of words is, or borders on, the misleading. A prime example of this is the words selected by corporate officials to describe the Three Mile Island nuclear accident in Harrisburg, Pennsylvania. At 10:00 P.M. on March 28, 1979, a Nuclear Regulatory Official stated, "At this point we have found no mechanical damage at all. The reactor is stable. There is no problem with the containment."[58] Note the insertion of the word mechanical. Earlier that afternoon this official and others knew there had been core damage. The official knew the core had been uncovered. A special task force report on the accident found that the same official, only a few minutes later "resorted to what is called a 'classic example of fudging' when he was asked whether the core was damaged. 'No,' the official replied, 'there appears to be no *significant* core damage.' The report said that by inserting the word 'significant' the official left the impression that there had been no damage to the core, even though he had told Lieutenant Governor William W. Scranton, Jr. earlier that the reactor *was* damaged."[59] The official was apparently trying to control how the event was reported, presumably because he wanted to control how people responded to the Three Mile Island accident. Presumably, he hoped to limit the public's negative reaction to nuclear power in general.

CONCLUSION

Power has a bad name. Certain worn phrases like, "Power corrupts; absolute power corrupts absolutely" stick in people's minds and prejudice them against it. The concept smacks of control by one group over another. For some it is a synonym for oppression. For others it seems a hopeless dream. One may just as well hope to win at the lottery as become powerful.

This chapter offers no panaceas by which the "powerless" can become "powerful." Nor is there intent here to imply that power-shifts come easily or without pain. To say that power belongs to everyone, that we all collaborate in it as its source, that it is fragile and malleable, is not to say that it can be coralled with ease.

Power takes shape in particular ways through interaction of complex forces. One component of these forces is individual action (for example, a person has an important and revolutionizing idea). Other components can only be understood as societal or even transnational (for example, capitalism, socialism, multinational corporate economics). At the risk of sounding polly-annaish or overly optimistic, it seems fair to say that by revealing a basic framework for examining power which includes the complex forces shaping it, we can begin to create strategies by which to transform the prevailing patterns of power to serve new ends, new interests, and different alignments of people. In the context of community organization, we use this interactional definition of power to provide a practical tool for social analysis. If used, the power analysis (analysis of why people cooperate and obey in particular institutional and social contexts) can provide an outline for community organization strategies.

NOTES

[1]Stanley Milgram, *Obedience to Authority* (New York: Harper & Row, 1974), p. 3.

[2]Milgram, *Obedience*, p. 14.

[3]Robert H. Binstock and Katherine Ely, *The Politics of the Powerless* (Cambridge, MA: Winthrop, 1971), p. 1.

[4]I. Ira Goldenberg, *Oppression and Social Intervention* (Chicago: Nelson-Hall, 1978), pp. 14–15.

[5]Saul Alinsky quoted in Binstock and Ely, *Powerless*, p. 238.

[6]Frances Fox Piven and Richard A. Cloward, *Poor People's Movements: Why They Succeed, How They Fail* (New York: Pantheon, 1977).

[7]Michael Korda, *Power!* (New York: Ballantine, 1975).

[8]Korda, *Power!*, p. 4.

[9]Roderick Martin, *The Sociology of Power* (London: Routledge and Kegan Paul, 1977), p. 37.

[10]Peter M. Blau, *Exchange and Power in Social Life* (New York: John Wiley, 1964), p. 22.

[11]Talcott Parsons, "The Political Aspect of Social Structure and Social Process," in *Varieties of Political Theory*, ed. David Easton (Englewood Cliffs, NJ: Prentice-Hall, 1966), p. 79.

[12]Michael Parenti, *Power and the Powerless* (New York: St. Martin's Press, 1978), p. 22.

[13]Alvin Gouldner, *The Coming Crisis in Western Sociology* (New York: Basic Books, 1970), p. 299.

[14]Gouldner, *Crisis*, p. 299.

[15]Rollo May, *Power and Innocence* (New York: W. W. Norton & Co., Inc., 1972).

[16]Malcolm X in Binstock and Ely, *Powerless*, pp. 6–7.

[17]Floyd Hunter, "Community Power Structure," in *The Search for Community*, eds. Willis D. Hawley and Frederick W. Wirt (Englewood Cliffs, NJ: Prentice-Hall, 1968), p. 56.

[18]Robert S. Lynd and Helen M. Lynd, "Middletown's X Family: A Pattern of Business-Class Control," in *The Search for Community*, eds. Willis D. Hawley and Frederick W. Wirt (Englewood Cliffs, NJ: Prentice-Hall, 1968), pp. 41–42.

[19]C. Wright Mills, *The Power Elite* (New York: Oxford University Press, 1956), p. 18.

[20]Mills, *Power Elite*, pp. 28–29.

[21]Martin, *Power*, p. 36.

[22]Parenti, *Powerless*, p. 6.

[23]Dorwin Cartwright, ed., *Studies in Social Power* (Ann Arbor, MI: Research Center for Group Dynamics, Institute for Social Research, The University of Michigan, 1959), p. 188.

[24]Dahl in Martin, *Power*, p. 36.

[25]Gene Sharp, *The Politics of Nonviolent Action* (Boston: Porter Sargent, 1973), p. 7.

[26]Sharp, *Nonviolent Action*, p. 8.

[27]Sharp, *Nonviolent Action*, p. 12.

[28]Karl W. Deutsch, "Cracks in the Monolith," in *Totalitarianism*, ed. Carl J. Friedrick (Cambridge, MA: Harvard University Press, 1954).

[29]Hannah Arendt, *The Human Condition* (Garden City, NY: Doubleday, 1959), p. 179.

[30]Chester I. Barnard, *Functions of the Executive* (Cambridge, MA: Harvard University Press, 1948), p. 163.

[31]Bertrand DeJouvenal, *On Power, Its Nature and the History of Its Growth*, trans. J. F. Huntington (New York: Viking, 1949), p. 8.

[32]Bertrand Russell, *Authority and the Individual* (New York: Simon & Schuster, 1949), p. 46.

[33]Jean Francois Steiner, *Treblinka*, trans. Helen Weaver (New York: New American Library, 1966).

[34]Steiner, *Treblinka*, p. 31.

[35]Frederick Douglass, *Life and Times of Frederick Douglass* (New York: Collier Books, 1962), p. 143.

[36]Mahatma Gandhi in Sharp, *Nonviolent Action*, p. 59.

[37]Sharp, *Nonviolent Action*, p. 8.

[38]Hans Gerth and C. Wright Mills, *Character and Social Structure* (New York: Harcourt Brace Jovanovich, 1953), p. 194.

[39]William Ryan, *Blaming the Victim* (New York: Vintage Books, 1971).

[40]Saul D. Alinsky, *Rules for Radicals* (New York: Vintage Books, 1972), p. 40.

[41]Robert S. Benson and Harold Wolman, eds., *Counterbudget: A Blueprint for Changing National Priorities, 1971–76* (New York: Holt, Rinehart and Winston, 1971).

[42]Hans Gerth and C. Wright Mills, *From Max Weber* (New York: Oxford University Press, 1946), p. 160.

[43]Gerth and Mills, *Weber*, p. 160.

[44]Gaetano Mosca, "The Ruling Class," in *Power in Societies*, ed. Marvin Olson (New York: Macmillan, 1970), p. 135.

[45]Leo Tolstoy, "The Slavery of Our Times," in *Patterns of Anarchy*, ed. Leonard Krimmerman and Lewis Perry (Garden City, NY: Doubleday, 1966), p. 77.

[46]Cartwright, *Social Power*.

[47]Russell, *Authority*, p. 48.

[48]Barnard, *Executive*.

[49]Parenti, *Powerless*.

[50]Parenti, *Powerless*, p. 25.

[51]Parenti, *Powerless*, p. 25.

[52]Si Kahn, *How People Get Power* (New York: McGraw-Hill, 1970), p. 74.

[53]Barnard, *Executive*, p. 46.

[54]Arendt, *Human Condition*, p. 179.

[55]Gerth and Mills, *Character*, pp. 275–76.

[56]Murray Edelman, "Language, Myths, and Rhetoric," *Society*, July/August, 1975, p. 14.

[57]Edelman, "Myths," p. 18.

[58]David Burnham, "Panel Says Atomic Officials Played Down Reactor Peril," *The New York Times*, November 5, 1979, p. A16.

[59]Burnham, "Panel Says," p. A16.

CHAPTER THREE
THE MAKING
OF SOCIAL PROBLEMS

THE EYE OF THE BEHOLDER

A precondition for community organization is a social problem. This kind of problem is the organizers' life blood. Without it there is no cause for action and no condition to change. A social problem is to a community organizer roughly what an aggrieved party is to a lawyer. Unless a person has been harmed (for example, psychologically, economically, physically), he or she has no legal claim against another. Similarly, without a social problem the organizer has no reason to organize.

This fact, that organizers need problems, may at first glance seem trivial. After all, social problems abound. To some people, they seem almost cancerous, spreading uncontrollably through society, attacking individuals and groups of people alike. So, to say that organizers need problems is a bit like saying people need air and there is an abundance of both. While most of us agree that society has many social problems, each of us does not necessarily define like conditions as problematic. In the words of Fuller and Myers, "social problems are what people think they are and if conditions are not defined as social problems by the people involved in them, they are not problems to those people, although they may be problems to outsiders or to scientists . . ."[1] Thus the poverty stricken condition of illegal aliens may constitute a social problem to the aliens themselves or to community organizers, but not to the sweatshop operators who exploit them. By the same token, off-shore oil exploration and drilling may be problematic to the fishing industry, tourist trade, and environmentalists, but not to oil companies. The high school dropout rate in major urban areas may be a problem to educators, parents of the youths, and to the youths themselves, but perhaps not to affluent suburban college bound students and their families. Jessica Mitford notes the politics of defining problems when she examines the issue of crime:

> When is conduct a crime, and when is a crime not a crime? When somebody up There—a monarch, a dictator, a pope, a legislature—so decrees. If one were to extend [the] . . . map of high crime areas (as defined by official statistics), one might find manufacturers of unsafe cars which in the next year will have caused thousands to perish in flaming highway crashes, absentee landlords who charge extortionist rents for rat-infested slum apartments, Madison Avenue copywriters whose job it is to manipulate the gullible into buying shoddy merchandise, doctors getting rich off Medicare who process their elderly patients like so many cattle being driven to the slaughterhouse, manufacturers of napalm and other genocidal weapons—all operating on the safe side of the law, since none of these activities is in violation of any criminal statute. Criminal law is essentially a reflection of the value, and a codification of the self interest, and a method of control, of the dominant class in any given society.[2]

To make matters even less certain, people do not always agree on what constitutes "the facts" or "objective conditions." That is to say facts, like problems, are social constructs and not scientific, natural, indisputable entities. For example, what does it mean to refer to a segment of the population as being "hard core unemployed?" Are the people so defined those who do not want to work, those who cannot find work, or those untrained for particular types of work? Who should we include in such a category? Similarly, who is poor? As we all know, the definition of where to draw the poverty line is an administrative decision, usually made be economists and politicians who use the poverty determination to judge who shall become eligible for various social programs. But typically, politicians manipulate the definition of poverty from time to time, thus altering the patterns of social welfare. When Ronald Reagan became President in 1981, for example, he and his economic advisors argued that social programs had cast too wide a net and that those programs would have to shrink substantially. Naturally, this meant redefining who might be eligible. They then began to say that only the "truly needy" would be eligible for food stamps, aid to dependent children, social security supplemental income and other social welfare programs. The economic position of people had not changed, but the definition of who was "truly" poor had changed, and with this came a new definition of a problem. Incredibly, even in fields presumably dominated by scientists, the definition of facts eludes scientific expertise. Defining disabilities is a case in point. It should be possible to tell, scientifically, whether or not a person has a disability. Or should it? In fact, so-called scientific definitions of disabilities change from time to time depending on prevailing social norms, the activism of people so labelled, the ideological perspective of those who would apply labels, and other *social* conditions. In recent years, for example, the American Psychiatric Association declassified homosexuality as a mental illness. Obviously, this change reflected changing social attitudes and the influence of the gay social movement rather than any change in the "objective condition" of homosexuality. It is equally surprising to learn that some apparently quite healthy people are able to

"qualify" as being disabled for purposes of receiving disability compensa...
Even so seemingly static a condition as mental retardation, long regarded by many
as a social problem and by nearly everyone as an objective condition, has not been
immune to definitional controversies. Definitions of who is retarded and who is not
retarded vary from state to state, depending on how the definitions are formulated,
who applies them, and in what context they are applied. More people, for instance,
are defined as retarded during school years than at any other time in the life span,
largely because schools administer certain tests and in fact place people into various
categories. Thus many people classified by schools as mildly retarded are never
defined as retarded again after they leave school. Interestingly, there is even controversy over who is severely retarded. In 1952, the American Psychiatric Association
defined severe retardation as the condition of people in need of custodial care. At
that time, psychiatrists generally believed that severely retarded people could not
benefit from an education. Now all that has changed, including the definition of
severe retardation. Today, psychiatrists tell us that everyone can learn, develop, and
benefit from active programming. People with severe and profound retardation now
participate in a full range of community living experiences, including schooling,
work, and self-help skills learning. Also, a majority of people defined as severely
retarded in 1952 are now considered only moderately retarded. These examples
show that even the "facts" used for defining social problems and mounting social
plans and programs are, to a large extent, socially created.

As Howard Becker has noted, "no amount of factual research can resolve . . . differences [over facts], for they do not arise from a disagreement about
facts but from disagreement about how facts are defined and interpreted."[3] Thus
two observers would probably not disagree on the matter of how much money a
family earned, yet they could easily disagree on whether the family is poor or
wealthy. Similarly, any two people could probably agree that a given person could
or could not read, yet they might argue vehemently over whether the person was
retarded and, if retarded, how retarded. It is therefore clear that both the definition
of facts and the translation of facts into social problems is not an objective, scientific process. Rather, it is a subjective, social process. We might even refer to
problem definition as the politics of defining social problems, for the way in which
people characterize certain facts or conditions as problems reflects their values and
interests:

> A problem is not the same to all interested parties; indeed, there will be as many
> definitions of the problem as there are interested parties. When we speak of adoles-
> cence or race relations, the terms do not define a problem. They only point to phe-
> nomena someone defines as a problem; the definitions will not all be alike.[4]

According to both Becker and Mills, people tend to define as problems those
conditions which infringe on their interests or, to use Becker's words, "interfere
with the satisfactions or make the dissatisfactions more likely to occur."[5] However,
discomfort does not make change automatic or even obvious. One reason for this is
that people often have conflicting values and these can inhibit social change. Becker

notes, for example, that professionals may abstain from involvement in a particular social issue for fear of losing income, prestige, or position. For instance, as much as a doctor might regard teenage pregnancy as highly problematic and abortion as a reasonable social response to pregnancy, he or she might fear the potential effects of becoming involved in the abortion controversy. Similarly, a college administrator may regard certain faculty hiring procedures as racist or sexist, but fear personal loss of position if he or she advocates fundamental policy changes. Indeed it is frequently the case, particularly for people in occupations that carry prestige, position, and high income, that one set of values conflicts with another.

For some people, the problem of making social change lies not so much in recognizing that one has a problem, but in identifying its existence in a way that might make it resolvable. As Mills suggests, American culture has developed a peculiar tendency to adjust to symptoms of particular, troublesome conditions rather than to explore the full range of conditions and their causes. In other words, we do not adequately define facts and problems so that they become resolvable. Facts and issues remain vague and confused and thus are cause for uneasiness and indifference, but not action. As a consequence, Mills argues, we seem more willing to pursue psychological adjustment than social or structural change. In his words, "Many great public issues as well as many private troubles are described in terms of 'the psychiatric'—often, it seems, in a pathetic attempt to avoid the large issues and problems of modern society."[6] We have failed, Mills says, to keep an eye on the economic issues and on the major institutions of our society. We deal with symptoms like spouse and child abuse as solely psychological problems rather than as social phenomena that may have their roots in the relationship of the family to other major institutions. We confront hunger as a problem of individuals and groups to be solved by providing case by case services (for example, food stamps, meals on wheels programs, and school lunches) without ever addressing the large social forces which cause some people to have an inadequate supply of nutritious food.

Since social problems exist only when defined as such, it also follows that we develop preferred ways of defining problems. Fuller and Myers prefer a consensus model for problem identification. That is, whatever people (meaning most people or all people) call a problem is a problem. The idea is that through the democratic process, people will achieve consensus on what constitutes a problem. This is essentially the model of problem identification that Manis labels the "public opinion paradigm." But what of conditions which may be harmful but which go undetected by most people? Should we not define them as social problems too? Manis suggests a professional model of problem identification for these kinds of situations. He says, "I define social problems as those social conditions identified by scientific knowledge and values as detrimental to human well-being."[7] If we accept Manis' thesis, problem identification belongs to professionals, to the experts. In this framework, organizers and the general populace might just as well sit on the sidelines and wait for others to define the issues. Actually, while Manis seems to prefer the professional model, he recognizes a typology of kinds of social problems. Yet at no point does he forsake his own position which is that problems are best identified scientifically by consideration of knowledge and values. Essentially, he seems to argue that we should seek to find the best definition of social problems or, as he puts it, the "real problems." Manis' typology includes the following:

> Perceived social problems are those social conditions that are identified by groups or individuals as contrary to their group or personal values. . . .
> Using popular values as criteria is not neutral nor appropriate for the knowledge-values of science. . . .
> Adjudicated problems are those conditions in society deemed harmful by knowledgeable people. . . .
> Unrecognized social problems are those conditions deemed harmful by knowledgeable persons that are not so identified by other members of society. . . .
> Demonstrable social problems are social conditions identified as detrimental to human well-being on the basis of reasonable evidence. . . .
> Hypothetical social problems are social conditions assumed to be harmful on the basis of reasonable interpretations or theories. . . .
> Spurious social problems are those perceived social problems that are not contrary to personal or group values or are not detrimental to human well-being [Manis gives examples such as long hair, witches, fluoridation, and homosexuality].[8]

Despite the neat appearance of Manis' typology, his argument that problem identification is increasingly and justifiably scientific does not hold up under scrutiny. Because the very definition of social problems is subjective, involvement of scientists or experts in the definitional process cannot render the final product, the problem, a scientific truth. If science lends credibility to particular problem definitions, it does so by providing an *air* of legitimacy and authority, not because it *proves* the reality of a problem. No matter how people define problems, the ultimate act of definition is still subjective, still shaped by values, interests, and ideologies.

COMPETING WAYS TO DEFINE PROBLEMS

Social problems are by definition phenomena of a society and do not pertain solely to individuals. A single person may experience a social problem first hand, but it would be impossible to say that a *social* problem exists where only one individual experiences it, or where the individual's experience can be attributed to strictly personal troubles. C. Wright Mills has identified this division between what he calls "private troubles" and "public issues" as the central factor to be considered when one defines a condition or conditions as problematic. "Troubles," he says, "occur within the character of the individual and within the range of his immediate relations with others."[9] In other words, private troubles emerge from our own immediate social relations and not from social condition or social structure at large. Issues, on the other hand, "have to do with matters that transcend these local environments of the individual and the range of his inner life."[10] Issues grow out of our experiences with social institutions, social attitudes, and social and economic structure. Mills he example of unemployment to explain the difference between a private trouble and a public issue:

> When in a city of 100,000, only one man is unemployed, that is his personal trouble, and for its relief we properly look to the character of the man, his skills, and his immediate opportunities. But when in a nation of 50 million employees, 15 million . . . are unemployed, that is an issue, and we may not hope to find its solution within the range of opportunities open to any one individual. The very structure of opportunities has collapsed.[11]

In this framework, even seemingly personal aspects of life may not be explainable in purely personal terms. The problematic experience that many men and women have with marriage or child rearing, for example, may well reflect society's social and structural conditions more than the accumulation of a large number of merely personal problems.

The role of the social analyst and, therefore, of the community organizer, is to understand the place of the individual in social and historical contexts. Like everyone, organizers come to the problem identification or problem creation enterprise with particular outlooks, with particular ways of looking at the world. In addition, much of their work involves trying to understand how others look at the world. It also involves helping others "develop an analysis," a consistent way of defining issues and solutions.

Organizers must ask two important questions: (1) What are the dominant ideologies through which people define problems? and (2) Once problems are defined along certain ideological lines, what does this suggest for community organization?

The dominant perspectives or ideologies through which people define social problems today are (1) the culture of poverty model; (2) the technicism model; (3) social and economic democracy models; (4) the competing social pathology and civil liberties models; and (5) the sociobiology model. Virtually every articulated social problem owes its existence to one or several of these ideological perspectives. Sometimes perspectives overlap and frequently people use more than one perspective at the same time to address a single set of conditions.

Culture of Poverty

During the 1960s it became commonplace to explain various social phenomena and conditions as products of the culture of poverty. That culture was presumed to include such characteristics as fatherless black families, unemployment, low educational background of parents, lack of occupational skills, poor nutrition for children, social disorganization linked to the 200 year legacy of slavery in America, and inadequate health care, among other things. Such deplorable conditions were said to yield poor attitudes and scant preparation for work, education, and family life. While this ideology masqueraded as a sympathetic, caring perspective on the devastating conditions under which poor people lived, it placed the ultimate responsibility for being poor on poor people themselves. It suggested that poor people, cast into bad circumstances, learned a culture of poverty, replete with laziness, defeatism, irresponsible family behavior, sexual promiscuity, ignorance, and violence. And, equally importantly, it ignored altogether the possibility that people were out of work because there were no jobs or that poor children did not succeed in school because they faced racism and other forms of discrimination on a daily basis. Indeed the "culture of poverty" served as both the dominant social problem and the chief means of justifying the status quo. People suffered in the "culture of poverty." Those same people would find it difficult to flee the culture of poverty unless they could learn new attitudes and skills, that is, rid themselves of socialization to the culture of poverty. According to this viewpoint the way to solve social problems was by creating special remedial programs to change the individuals who had been or likely would be socialized to the culture of poverty. Social programs took such forms as job training and retraining, compensatory education, Headstart, community mental health services, and public housing. The reform-minded but essentially change-absent social programs approach to individual adjustment and status quo preservation was so apparent to one social commentator that he jokingly wrote a speech on the urban condition entitled, "How Community Mental Health Helped Stamp Out the Riots."[12] His point was that urban programs which attempt to mollify individuals could pacify those who might be expected to fight for structural social change. However, these same programs would not in any significant way challenge dominant social forces such as racism and unemployment, which cause the so-called culture of poverty conditions in the first place.

This perspective on the social condition has been characterized by William Ryan as "blaming the victim." In his book by the same name he argues that victim blaming avoids the simplistic and rebuttable arguments of social darwinism, namely that people reflect their genetic or hereditary background and behave accordingly. Rather, exponents of victim blaming ideology are able to use it to say that social problems are caused by poverty, exploitation, and discrimination. Yet it also allows its adherents to label poor, exploited, and discriminated-against-people as damaged by their condition (that is, the culture of poverty). Thus the problem definition switches its focus from cause to victim. The problem, in this view, is damaged people. Ryan explains it this way:

> Blaming the Victim is, of course, quite different from old-fashioned conservative ideologies. The latter simply dismissed victims as inferior, genetically defective, or morally unfit; the emphasis is on the intrinsic, even hereditary, defect. The former shifts its emphasis to the environmental causation. The old-fashioned conservative could hold firmly to the belief that the oppressed and the victimized were both that way—"that way" being defective or inadequate in character or ability. The new ideology attributes defect and inadequacy to the malignant nature of poverty, injustice, slum life, and racial difficulties. The stigma that marks the victim and accounts for his victimization is an acquired stigma, a stigma of social, rather than genetic, origin. But the stigma, the defect, the fatal difference—though derived in the past from environmental forces—is still located *within* the victim, inside his skin.[13]

In order to define social conditions in a "blaming the victim" or "culture of poverty" fashion, we must utilize a process of what might be called problem location. As Ryan notes, the culture of poverty thesis, unlike social darwinism, is a bit sophisticated and, therefore, is not easy to disown. In the final analysis, though, Ryan finds the process and its outcome—poor people are defined as their own worst enemies—a simple case of self-interest in which middle class people exonerate themselves from any responsibility for the condition of poor people:

> Blaming the Victim depends on a process of identification (carried out, to be sure, in the most kindly, philanthropic, and intellectual manner) whereby the victim of social problems is identified as strange, different—in other words, as a barbarian, a savage. Discovering savages, then, is an essential component of, and prerequisite to, Blaming the Victim, and the art of Savage Discovery is a core skill that must be acquired by all aspiring Victim Blamers. They must learn how to demonstrate that the poor, the black, the ill, the jobless, the slum tenants, are different and strange. They must learn to conduct or interpret the research that shows how "these people" think in different forms, act in different patterns, cling to different values, seek different goals, and learn different truths. Which is to say that they are strangers, barbarians, savages. This is how the distressed and disinherited are redefined in order to make it possible for us to look at society's problems and to attribute their causation to the individuals affected.[14]

Ironically, even some of the most sensitive forms of social service promote the victim blaming ideology. Advertisements which warn children not to eat lead paint, but which fail to inform us that slum landlords use lead paint and fail to cover it over when it begins to peel also contribute to a victim blaming mentality. The advertisement leaves us with the distinct impression that if children do eat lead paint, it will be the fault of unwatchful parents. Using this same outlook, we learn that poor people do not like to work, when in fact enforced unemployment among black teenagers regularly runs between 35 and 50 percent. In Baltimore, when the General Service Administration announced the availability of a handful of middle-income jobs (that is, more than $10,000 each), 10,000 people applied. Thus Ryan asks, as well we might:

> Are the poor really all that different from the middle class? Take a common type of study, showing that ninety-one per cent of the upper class, compared to only sixty-eight per cent of the poor, prefer college education for their children. What does that tell us about the difference in values between classes?
>
> First, if almost seventy per cent of the poor want their children to go to college, it doesn't make much sense to say that the poor, as a group, do not value education. Only a minority of them—somewhat less than one-third—fail to express a *wish* that their children attend college. A smaller minority—one in ten—of the middle class give similar responses. One might well wonder why this small group of the better-off citizens of our achieving society reject higher education. They have the money; many of them have the direct experience of education; and most of them are aware of the monetary value of a college degree. I would suggest that the thirty percent of the poor who are unwilling to express a wish that their children go to college are easier to understand. They know the barriers—financial, social, and for black parents, racial—that make it very difficult for the children of the poor to get a college education. That seven out of ten of them nevertheless persist in a desire to see their children

in a cap and gown is, in a very real sense, remarkable. Most important, if we are concerned with cultural or subcultural differences, it seems highly illogical to emphasize the values of a small minority of one group and then to attribute these values to the whole group. I simply cannot accept the evidence. If seventy percent of a group values education, then it is completely illogical to say that the group as a whole does *not* value education.[15]

The problem with the culture of poverty outlook is that it serves the interests of those who use it and not those who are subjected to it. Victim blaming obscures the simple truth that most people, not just the middle class, would like to earn money if they had the chance. Most people would probably like to get a good education, achieve a modicum of status, enjoy leisure, and provide for their children if they had the chance. But, not surprisingly, when faced with one obstacle after another, most people will begin to question whether it is advisable, indeed even possible, to pursue that which they value. It may serve the interest of the middle class to define the condition of poor people as self-induced, but that does not make it true. Again, to cite Ryan:

> The simplest—and at the same time, the most significant—proposition in understanding poverty is that it is caused by lack of money. The overwhelming majority of the poor are poor because they have, first: insufficient income; and second: no access to methods of increasing that income—that is, no power. They are too young, too old, too sick; they are bound to the task of caring for small children, or they are simply discriminated against. The facts are clear, and the solution seems rather obvious— raise their income and let their "culture," whatever it might be, take care of itself.[16]

Probably no issue has been a more frequent target of victim blaming than welfare. Ask any citizen what comes to mind when you mention "the welfare problem" and you will grasp how far the reach of victim blaming mythology has extended. In fact, the term "welfare" seems to be associated with freeloading. When people were asked in a CBS/New York Times poll whether they believed most people on welfare could get along without it, more than half said they felt most could. When asked if they supported government sponsored welfare programs, 58 percent of the 1447 people interviewed said, "No." However, when the word "welfare" is taken away and people consider specific needs and programs, they embrace welfare. Sixty percent of the people interviewed support a national health care program. Eighty-one percent support food stamps for poor people. Eighty-one percent support aid to poor families with dependent children. And 82 percent endorse government-funded health care for poor people.[17]

The problem of victim blaming so plagued people in need of welfare that the National Welfare Rights Organization (NWRO) decided to counter the biggest welfare myths by drawing on federal and private research statistics. Rebutting the myth that hard work is the answer to the welfare problem, NWRO noted that less than one percent of the country's able-bodied men are on welfare and all of them must be registered with employment agencies. Many poor people on welfare do work, but working does not provide an adequate income. Three quarters of all welfare recipients are mothers and their children. Many of these mothers could work if day care were provided, but more often than not it is not provided. In answer to the myth that most welfare recipients are cheaters, NWRO cites a study which found that only four tenths of one percent obtain welfare fraudulently. Debunking the myth that welfare is a good life, NWRO noted that the family of four on welfare has annual income 43 percent below the poverty-level index. And as for the myth that welfare uses up most of the tax dollars, NWRO demonstrated that a far greater percentage of tax receipts go to such things as military programs and interest on the national debt.[18]

Technocracy

A less pernicious though still troublesome ideology is what might be called a technocratic perspective. According to this paradigm, social problems can be defined in terms of such things as "malfunction," and technological obsolescence. Problems surface, so the argument goes, when people cannot keep up with or adjust to technological demands or when technological systems themselves fail to keep pace with societal demands or when technology itself breaks down. The technocratic view assumes that the ideal society is entirely planned and founded upon social planning theory and scientific know-how. It entertains such goals as comprehensive service systems or service integration. Technicists believe that such goals can be achieved through rational, bureaucratic planning. Their planning and problem definition activities incorporate a range of computer associated and technocratic words like feedback, interface, variables, component, capacity building, output, input, indicators, impact (as a verb), yields, and tolerance factors.

Technocracy amounts to a new scientism in which seemingly technical, precise language projects an air of scientific correctness to political policies and practices. Perhaps most important, it smacks of neutrality. It sounds value free. Words like racism, sexism, discrimination, oppression, exploitation, and class bias have no place in this technocratic model.

When technicists define social problems, they generally isolate social conditions and define problems in terms of those specific conditions and put forth narrow, technical solutions. Their approach deems narrow technical solutions as "practical" and views a broader social analysis which recognizes the interrelationship of wide ranging conditions and problems as "impractical" or "romantic."

The technocratic ideology causes us to view social problems as technical ones capable of only technical solutions. In this framework, we should turn to science for a cure to social ills. Ignorance becomes a problem of a technically weak curriculum; unemployment becomes a function of our people and industries in need of some technical retuning; poor housing results from such things as miscalculated housing needs and fluctuating fiscal variables—and so it goes. Failure to make human services universally available is seen not as a result of prejudice or insensitivity but as a result of "gaps" or cracks in the system. As noted above, complex and related social events are usually conceptualized as separate, unrelated phenomena, each capable of being technically adjusted. In this scheme, large issues of morality and ethics are absent altogether. Indeed, using this way of thinking, morality, political beliefs, and passion are the failings of those who are nonscientific and biased. Technocrats consider such human intangibles as, at worst, contaminants and, at best, irrelevancies. After all, ethics and political ideology cannot easily or reliably be reduced to numerical form.

One critic of the technocratic ideology warns that American education has given itself over to propagating the technocratic viewpoint. This is particularly apparent in so-called "engineered classrooms" for behavior problem children. However, as Bowers notes, it is also true for typical children, youth, and even their teachers, all of whom learn that the goal of education is not so much to gain broad knowledge as "specific competencies." Bowers states: "The traditional view of education . . . recognized that the beliefs and practices of one's society must always be subjected to rational scrutiny."[19] Competency-based instruction, on the other hand, "reflects a revolutionary shift" to a "technocratic consciousness." In effect, the individual who learns this system of knowledge becomes a "component" in or a "product" of the system. "Concern with orderliness and efficiency are also paramount to the technocratic mind set of competency-based educators."[20] Thus Bowers argues that the technocratic individual achieves inconsequential, taken-for-granted status in the economic, technological social order.

Like the victim blaming ideology of problem identification, the technocratic model attributes causation for social problems to environmental conditions (that is, poorly engineered social environment). What is unique about this model is its seemingly antiseptic quality. It conjures up images of malfunctioning technological systems rather than the profiteering of one group of people from another or the insensitivity of one group to another. It seemingly neutralizes the human element altogether. Through this model, we lose sight of people, whether they are victims or victimizers.

Social and Economic Democracy

An alternative perspective on social problems, one embraced by many organizers, is that corporate power, upper class power, uneven distribution of wealth, and prejudice cause social problems. At the risk of oversimplifying, the problem is not one of poverty, but of enormous wealth. The problem is not one of gaps or cracks in an otherwise fine system but of a system which perpetuates prejudicial views concerning race, sex, age, and disability. The problem is not one of incompetence but of barriers to education, jobs, and power. Accordingly, as long as there is a deep gulf between social classes, both in terms of wealth, power, and outlook, traditional social programs will act merely as palliatives to oppression and not as a way of ending large scale human misery. This perspective is, above all, eclectic. It embraces Marx's criticism of social class inequality but is not *only* a social class analysis. It is anti-racist, but it is not *only* a theory of race equality. It favors democratic distribution of power but is also an economic theory. It can be called a social and economic democracy perspective.

According to this thesis, a relatively few number of people in the United States earn extraordinarily large amounts of money—hundreds of thousands of dollars per day and pay little or no taxes on these gains. Such practices have been called welfare for the rich. Philip Stern gives the example of Jean Paul Getty who in a given year earned 70 million dollars and paid the same amount of taxes—a few thousand dollars—as a middle-income engineer or professor might pay.[21] Under this system of tax welfare, a person's property can accumulate in value year after year without every being taxed. Moreover, profits from sale of property are taxed at a lower rate than regular earned income. But, more to the point, people with wealth can invest in so-called tax shelters, such as oil drilling operations, and thereby reduce their taxes dramatically. Similarly, people who can afford to invest large blocks of money can buy municipal and other government capital construction bonds which yield tax free interest. These are some of the most common tax avoidance and tax reduction methods but, in fact, such options for the wealthy number in the hundreds. To demonstrate the incredible gulf between the wealthy and the poor, Stern cites one Brookings Institute study which found that of "77.3 billion in tax 'handouts,' just over $92 million goes to the six million poorest families in the nation, while 24 times that amount . . . goes to just 3,000 (wealthy) families."[22] In one year, the government paid out 14.7 million dollars for the food stamp program while providing five times that amount in "tax welfare" to families that make more than $100,000 per year.[23] In other words, the wealthy do well. The number of millionaires in America increased from 13,000 in 1944 to 148,000 in 1969.[24] As Goode notes, "even with allowance for the fall in the purchasing power of the dollar and the growth of population, this increase is remarkable." To put it simply, America's "progressive" income tax and other taxes have not had a very important leveling effect. In referring to the income tax, Goode finds "the impact on income distribution is not impressive."[25]

Federal tax policies on mortgage interest and housing investment typify how tax structures which purport to help the poor and middle-class person actually benefit the affluent most. Rolf Goetz explains how it works:

> Federal tax provisions (tax breaks in the form of interest and investment write-offs) encourage those in upper tax brackets to over-invest in scarce housing as an inflation hedge. This drives up prices and leaves too little housing for others. These tax deductions now threaten to divide those who already have their homes (or can find the resources to invest) from the have-nots who must count on more government aid—more than can ever be provided.[26]

Tax policies allow the wealthy to bid up housing prices thus forcing poor people out of the market. Such policies may revitalize urban areas, but only for the affluent, not for poor and middle-class people.

Writers and organizers who define social problems in terms of social and economic democracy see problems not as the experiences of poor people, but as the relationship of poverty to wealth and exploitation. The example of migrant chicano farm workers in Texas is one illustration of this relationship. In the words of one

United Farm Worker organizer, Gilberto Padillo, "One problem we have is that the Rio Grande Valley is still in the middle ages. South Texas is a place of lords and serfs. Or maybe slaves."[27] A local teacher calls it the poorest part of America and a local planner says 35,000 new homes are needed now.[28] Forty-six percent of the existing "homes" have no plumbing. People live in mud and straw houses. Some have outhouses. Others do not. "There are no stoves. In the winter the people burn wood in washtubs and carry the ashes and coals into the huts for warmth when the temperature drops below freezing, as it often does."[29] One random survey of workers in twelve barrios found them making from $.45 to $1.00 a day. Another survey found that 75 percent of residents in one county earned less than the poverty level income.[30] Father Hesburgh, chairperson of a United States Commission surveying conditions of workers in the Rio Grande, declared that "many of the migrant farm workers in the lower Rio Grande Valley were living under conditions close to peonage or slavery."[31] As Steiner notes, there are hundreds of such communities in the Southwest. "Unseen and uncounted, the families that live in these colonies are not even statistics."[32] In stark contrast to their condition is that of the wealthy:

> Under the palm trees the tourists bask in the sun. Come to vacation amid the "palm-lined citrus groves and fresh vegetables in superabundance as far as the eye can see," says a brochure of the lower Rio Grande Valley Chamber of Commerce. "This is the Fun Coast of Texas." Civic pride has named it "The Magic Valley." "Ever pick a sweet, juicy, ruby red grapefruit or an orange right off a tree?" asks a tourist come-on.[33]

Thus the fruit growers and the Chamber of Commerce project a false public image of paradise in the Rio Grande Valley while they exploit the migrant farm workers.

Similar, if less drastic exploitation and insensitivity occurs throughout society in nearly every aspect of social policy. In health care for example, while most people favor national health care, the medical profession successfully resists health insurance plans which would limit their earning power (for example, require doctors to work for salaries rather than on an ever inflatable fee-for-service basis). Moreover, preventive health service receives little attention because, in a profit maximizing medical system, prevention generates little profit. In his classic study of the American system of blood banks, Richard Titmus found that the operation of commercial blood banks and the lack of a national blood system has led to a virtual scourge of hepatitis among blood recipients in many big urban centers.[34] Titmus' conclusion is that such a system regards the human condition as less important than the economic profit of a few individuals and corporations.

The theme of profit superseding individual well-being flows through this antimonopoly view of social problems. On the one hand, poor and middle income people find their lives deformed by their meager or nonexistent ability to pay for goods and services. Wealthy people, on the other hand, find that their relative position, in terms of wealth and power, grows with their ability to maintain the gulf between social classes. Thus monopolies or concentrated wealth plays a large part in creating social problems. Indeed, one might say, monopolies and policies which promote the former or concentrations of wealth are the problem. The food industry provides a good example of this. The Federal Trade Commission estimates that in most of the country's 200 largest metropolitan areas, a few large food chains control grocery prices.[35] And the food oligopolies are not anxious to give up their control:

> When I began research for this article, I wanted to find statistics which could explain precisely how many cents in last week's grocery bill we could blame on these food oligopolies. The FTC estimates $2.1 billion in overcharges in just thirteen food lines; Ralph Nader maintains that a secret FTC staff report shows that if the oligopolies were broken up, food prices would drop by 25 per cent. But no one seems to have more specific data. "The brutal reality is we don't know how corporations are manipulating prices and profits in individual food lines," an FTC official told me. The Congressional Joint Economic Committee recently subpoenaed supermarket records, and the FTC has been trying to pry some figures out of major food manufacturers' books. "We've been getting one hell of a lot of resistance from all quarters, except consumers," the FTC official complains.[36]

Furthermore, other oligopolies own the separate food sectors represented on the supermarket shelves. As one critic of the food industries put it when he described the beer industry, even in a time of expanding markets, prices, and profits, the market power of the beer oligopoly is enough to force competitors out of markets. "The power of the giants is the power to come into practically any market and dominate it. Local brews exist at the discretion of the major brews."[37] In 1980, it was estimated by the U.S. Department of Agriculture that consumers paid $16 billion in excess food charges because of food industry oligopolies.[38] Clearly, once a corporation like American Telephone and Telegraph (phones), United Fruit (bananas), or ABC, NBC, and CBS (television) gains control of more than half the sales in its product area, it can literally control prices. Faced with a take-it-or-leave-it situation, the consumer has little choice but to go along.

Not surprisingly, corporations have generated a stream of rhetoric against government involvement in and regulation of business. At the same time, the large corporations have welcomed favored treatment status, in the form of government subsidies (for example, guaranteed loans, tax waivers, economic development grants, price supports, massive governmental countracts). Ironically, corporate interests have argued that government is growing too large because unleashed bureaucracies tend to multiply themselves. However, those who define social problems as essentially the result of an unfair and unequitable distribution of wealth and power see the concentration of corporate wealth as largely responsible for government growth:

> The dramatic growth of the state is not, as some conservatives would have it, solely a result of the aggrandizing propensities of bureaucrats, but primarily a response to the growing needs of advanced capitalism. As the multinational conglomerates expand, as they face deepening economic crises, so must government expand, now trying to ease the ensuing social unrest with welfare palliatives, now intensifying the use of surveillance, force, and violence against rebellious elements at home and abroad, and all the while carrying at public expense many of the immense costs of private business,

including direct grants, subsidies, loans, leases, rebates, research and development, tax shelters, risk guarantees, loss compensations, tariff protections, and safeguards for overseas investments.[39]

Parenti argues that these developments in government do not constitute a slow adoption of socialism in America. Rather, he argues, big government is now in the business of managing the social costs (that is, social problems like pollution, seasonal unemployment, work-related injuries, family disruption) which the big corporations themselves spawn.

Social activist Tom Hayden catalogues what he regards as the major social costs associated with relatively unchecked corporate power: *centralization of power,* production and wealth in the hands of a few corporate giants, mainly multinational corporations—the Fortune 500 employ 72 percent of all workers; corporate America magnifies the *unequal distribution of wealth*—the wealthiest one percent earn 51 times the per capita income of the poorest 20 percent; multinationals *export jobs* to foreign countries where they enjoy cheaper labor and higher profits; *monopolistic practices* reduce price and quality competition and increase inflation; corporate attention to *nonproductive military production* and corporate pursuit of government subsidies has stymied innovations and productivity; corporations have persisted in *discriminating against minority groups*—"Black males earn 60 percent of the wages of white males, while female workers earn less than 60 percent of the wage of their male counterparts"; corporations tend to *pursue profit before social responsibility*—the Environmental Protection Agency estimates 23 billion in health and property damage in 1977 alone and the World Health Organization and National Cancer Institute estimate that between 80 and 90 percent of human cancer is environmentally caused; the *profit imperative yields too many unsafe products*— "product-related accidents kill as many as 30,000, permanently injure 110,000, hospitalize 500,000 and force 20 million to seek medical treatment"; a number of major corporations have engaged in *white collar crimes* including cover-ups of toxic chemical dumping; corporate *advertisers manipulate* rather than inform viewers and readers; and big business, particularly conglomerates, unlike small business, take less interest in and *contribute less to civic welfare* (for example, community projects, schools, libraries, cultural institutions).[40]

Certainly one type of social cost outstrips all others in terms of the sheer suffering it imposes. Chemicals and radioactivity cause more human misery than any other kind of industrial waste. Therefore, it is only natural that these substances have come to symbolize corporate power and social irresponsibility. Again, in the words of organizer Tom Hayden:

The final legacy of the petrochemical age may be a humanity and an earth in terminal states of illness. . . .
    The false assumption that the frontier environment was both a source of unlimited resources and a sink for unlimited disposal of toxic waste has given us a landscape pockmarked with poison. In addition to nine million cubic feet of high-level radioactive waste stored since World War II, the nuclear industry produces on the

average 30 tons of radioactive waste per reactor every year—with the long-promised technology for safe disposal still not in sight. Chemical waste is nearly as harrowing a problem for future generations: 70 billion pounds of hazardous waste is deposited annually in 30,000 dumps, many of which are already overflowing, leaching, flammable time bombs. . . .

The petrochemical industry seeking to avoid any social controls on its ecologically destructive behavior works to convince us that disease is but a necessary by-product of progress.[41]

Social analysts who subscribe to social and economic democracy argue that class divisions and therefore, human suffering, are fostered not only by economic forces, but by social institutions which respect economic factors. In health care, for example, the wealthy learn to expect and value individualized treatment. The poor learn to accept medical treatment in large, nonprivate emergency rooms and clinics, if they receive it at all. Likewise in transportation, poor people depend on unreliable public transportation, while people with money can buy transportation options (for example, air travel, commuter trains, private automobiles). In each of these spheres of social experience there is clearly a symbiotic relationship between wealth, quality, and choice of service. However, it is also clear that even when poor and wealthy people use the same service, (for example, a physician's services) upper class people receive more personalized attention. That is to say, as a rule professionals pay more attention and show more deference to those whom *they* perceive as peers or as of greater status than themselves.

No area of social service more clearly demonstrates America's class attitude and racial bias than does the public school system. Policy makers have traditionally looked to the school as a major melting pot institution, as a place where equal opportunity can be realized, where children and youth can practice democracy. Unfortunately, there is substantial evidence that a child's school experience correlates closely with his or her social class and race. Ray Rist tells the story of a not unusual classroom in which a teacher assigned children to one of three tables. She had no overt criteria for placement. However, as it turned out, she assigned the children she regarded as high status to Table 1, which she came to consider the fast learner table. None of the children at this table were from families on welfare. The children at the remaining two tables were considered to be of lower status and were also seen as slow learners. The teacher expected the latter students not to do well in their school work. The students at Table 1 were more verbal than the others, spoke more Standard American English than the others (some of whom used Black English), and came from two parent households. Their parents had attained higher levels of formal education than the others' parents and had a greater income as well. Rist found that the teacher *taught* the children at Table 1 and *controlled* the children at Tables 2 and 3. At the end of the year, the teacher described the children at Table 1 as more interesting and interested than the children at Tables 2 and 3, who were described as problematic:

TABLE 1
I guess the best way to describe it is that very few children in my class are exceptional.
I guess you could notice this just from the way the children were seated this year.

Those at Table 1 gave consistently the most responses throughout the year and seemed more interested and aware of what was going on in the classroom.
TABLES 2 and 3
It seems to me that some of the children at Table 2 and most all the children at Table 3 at times seem to have no idea of what is going on in the classroom and were off in another world all by themselves. It just appears that some can do it and some cannot. I don't think that it is the teaching that affects those that cannot do it, but some are just basically low achievers.[42]

Not surprisingly, children learn messages taught to them. Children of middle- and upper-class backgrounds learn that they have options in life. Poor children, or at least many poor children, learn that they do not. Richard deLone examines this question in his controversial, Carnegie-funded study of inequality in education. In his book, *Small Futures,* he reproduces two interviews with children concerning their attitudes toward work and career:

Interview 1:   Sally

Int:	Do you know what your father does?
Sally:	Sort of. He bosses other people around. Not really bosses, but he tells them how to run the schools.
Int:	Would you like to have that job when you grow up?
Sally:	No.
Int:	Why?
Sally:	You have to do too much work at home.
Int:	What other jobs are there?
Sally:	Well . . . doctors, lawyers, nurses. People who make new things.
Int:	People who make new things?
Sally:	Yeah, like inventors.
Int:	Would you like to do any of those things?
Sally:	Yeah, I guess so. I don't really know.
Int:	What job would you like best?
Sally:	Maybe . . . maybe a nurse or a doctor. I don't really know.
Int:	Can you think of any other jobs?
Sally:	Hmmm. People in the supermarket when you pay. But I don't think I could do that. My fingers aren't fast enough.

Interview 2:   Joseph

Int:	Do you like school?
Joseph:	It's OK.
Int:	Do you like the teacher?
(Joseph shrugs and smiles noncommittally)	
Int:	Do they give tests at your school?
Joseph:	Yeah.
Int:	Are they hard?
Joseph:	Yeah.
Int:	Do you try to do well on the tests?
Joseph:	Yeah.
Int:	Why?
Joseph:	'Cause if you don't, you don't move on up.
Int:	Why is it important to move on up?
(Joseph squirms in his seat, folds his hands, doesn't answer.)	

Int: Why do you think it's important?
Joseph: So you can get out of school.
Int: And what happens when you get out of school?
Joseph: Then you go to work.
Int: What kind of work do people do?
Joseph: They do different kinds.
Int: Can you tell me some kinds?
Joseph: Some people work in gas stations.
Int: Anything else?
Joseph: Some people sell candy in the candy store.
Int: What kind of work would you like to do?
Joseph: I might be working in the candy store. Or maybe go in the army.
Int: Can you think of any other kind of work you might do?
Joseph: (thinks for a moment): What work do you do?[43]

DeLone concludes that these children can at once be aware of the diversity of occupations available yet find themselves limited to thinking about going into jobs which reflect their own class backgrounds.

The lesson for organizers in all of this is that if we define social and economic differences (that is, concentrated wealth and power vs. poverty and disenfranchisement, and prejudice vs. acceptance) as the primary social problems, we need a vision of public policy which will accomplish a redistribution of wealth, power, and human worth. Further, organizers also need a strategy for combatting prejudicial social class and race attitudes such as those which manifest themselves in schools, hospitals and virtually every other social institution.

Social Pathology and Civil Liberties

Sociologists often speak of deviance as a type of social problem or as a way of defining social problems. Here, the social problem is rule breaking. Those people who behave in ways that fail to conform to certain social norms are viewed as problematic. Explanations put forth by psychiatrists, sociologists, social workers, politicians, educators, and others regarding the cause of deviant behavior are myriad. Some say a bad home environment is to blame. For others it is an organic, physiological problem of the individual. Still others point to high unemployment and squalid living conditions, as unsavory aspects of the environment that lead to deviance. Some believe that rule breaking stems from unmet expectations. Others claim rule breaking occurs more frequently among the less intelligent. Whatever the explanation, the resultant problem tends to be defined as deviance.

Organizers have never been much attracted to the deviance model of defining social problems. They have found it an unhelpful way of looking at the world. However much it accounts for the possible causes of deviance, it tends to blame certain groups of people for failing to live up to dominant, usually middle-class, standards. Also, by its nature the deviance model calls into question the very people with whom organizers so frequently ally themselves. Most importantly, the deviance model of problem definition says, in effect, that deviants should "clean up their act'' and adjust to the ''realities of life,'' namely middle-class behavior. Put another way, the deviance perspective cries out for social programs as treatment for what are considered bizarre behaviors. However, at the same time these ''programs'' would be ignoring the larger social context. To use Mills' terminology, in concentrating on social pathology we miss social structure altogether or regard it as impractical to change. In these ways the deviance model has much the same limitations as the victim blaming model.

The experience of older people in America reveals a great deal about the deviance outlook and deviance-based social planning. By almost any sociological, political or economic standard, older people as a group occupy a ''marginal,'' ''surplus,'' ''deviant,'' or ''devalued'' position. Jokes about old age, beliefs that old age breeds incompetence, and other stereotypes (for example, you can't teach an old dog new tricks; they like to be by themselves; they cannot contribute to society) pervade society. The only people in this group who are not ''marginal'' are selected older people, (for example, corporation chairpersons and political leaders) who enjoy tremendous power, wealth, and status. However, the experiences of these few do not erase or ameliorate the situation for most older people. Society victimizes older people as well as poor people, Blacks, and Hispanics.

The social pathology model of deviance only exacerbates older persons' difficulties. Once catalogued as deviant, older people become proper targets for social reformers' programs. That perspective can translate into special programs to rehabilitate old people to make them less deviant. It already has helped to create a special field devoted exclusively to the study of older people that is called gerontology. Special housing projects, recreation centers, special medical programs, volunteer programs, and modest financial supports have also resulted. In other words, the deviance model, like the victim blaming model, paves the way for exceptionalistic programs. While no one would argue that the special programs do not at least partially meet individual needs, few people would boldly say they guarantee older people sociopolitical equality. Ironically, these programs actually guarantee that older people will continue to live marginal and, to some extent, deviant lives. Special programs keep older people dependent in a way that separates them from other people (for example, through special drop-in centers, special food programs, special clinics, and separate housing projects). These programs are available often only after an older person has been stripped of his or her wealth, power, status, and even credibility.

The example of older persons' programs typifies the dominant social policy response of the deviance or social pathology school. It is one of rehabilitation as opposed to social, political and economic structural change. That is, society treats the symptoms as the problem and nearly ignores or merely pays lip service to the conditions, policies, and practices which may create the symptoms. Unfortunately, this kind of treatment frequently reaffirms the differentness or deviance of the client group. Interestingly, for truly difficult sorts of nonconformity such as delinquency and other behavior which social authorities find problematic, social services usually take the form of forced or involuntary treatment.

To some extent, organizers have found specialized services of all kinds, whether voluntary or involuntary, to be objectionable unless controlled by consumers themselves (that is, self-help groups). Thus they are fair targets for organizing. Such organizing strategies take the form of campaigns for racial integration in services, equal protection (see law chapter) in services, accessibility for the disabled, antisex discrimination, tax reform movements, and so forth. Ideologically, organizers point to civil liberties, self-determination, and the politics of nonintervention as their philosophical justification for opposing the proliferation of separate or what Ryan calls "exceptionalistic" programs. The extent of this kind of organizing is discussed at length in the chapter on self-help movements (Chapter 8). Here, one example of a major controversy over involuntary treatment will suffice. The example offers evidence of why organizers find so little solace in the deviant outlook.

Society is usually willing to tolerate a certain amount of deviant behavior. It may even co-opt it, that is, take the deviant behavior as its own and thereby make it normal. Long hair, short skirts, opposition to the Vietnam War, and feminism were at one time controversial, indeed even considered deviant. People who advocated opposition to the Vietnam War were given labels such as communists, anti-American, or yellow. People who spoke for women's rights were characterized as "bra-burners" and "women's libbers." In time, however, society came to accept much if not all of the very same beliefs it once regarded as deviant.

Obviously, society does not always change. Rather, it remains more or less intransigent in its unwillingness to accept or tolerate certain behavior. A prime example of this is society's treatment of people it perceives as bizarre, people it labels "mentally ill." Thomas Szasz, along with hundreds of mental patient activists, and other socio-political analysts, believes that mental illness is a metaphor.[44] That is, society finds certain social behavior obnoxious and in need of control. Society then labels such behavior the manifestation of a sickness, in this case sickness of the mind. Once this behavior is called sick, institutional psychiatry, with the blessing of the state, can lock up and treat the "sick" with therapy, tranquilizing drugs, simple incarceration, electric shock, or, in some extreme cases, with brain surgery (to remove part of the brain). According to Szasz, institutional psychiatry (as distinct from individual, voluntary behavior therapy for what Szasz calls problems of living, not "sickness") claims to help the patient, but in fact its purpose is to exorcise society by protecting it from unwanted people and their behavior. From this view, mental illness is, as he argues, very much like witchcraft. So too is society's response to it:

> The concept of mental illness is analogous to that of witchcraft. In the fifteenth century, men believed that some persons were witches, and that some acts were due to witchcraft. In the twentieth century, men believe that some people are insane, and that some acts are due to mental illness. . . . The concept of mental illness has the same logical and empirical status as the concept of witchcraft; in short, that witchcraft and mental illness are imprecise and all-encompassing concepts, freely adaptable to whatever uses the priest or physician (or lay "diagnostician") wishes to put them. . . . The concept of mental illness serves the same social function in the modern world as did

the concept of witchcraft in the late Middle Ages; in short, . . . the belief in mental illness and the social actions to which it leads have the same moral implications and political consequences as had the belief in witchcraft and the social actions to which it led. . . .

Like the typical European witch in the fifteenth century, the typical mental patient today is usually a poor person in trouble or accused of making trouble, who is declared mentally ill against his will.[45]

What are the social consequences that Szasz warns against? One certainly is incarceration. A second and equally unfair consequence is the stripping of a person's legitimacy. In Szasz's own words, "instead of recognizing the deviant as an individual, different from those who judge him, but nevertheless worthy of their respect, he is first discredited (by being called sick) as a self-responsible human being, and then subjected to humiliating punishment defined and disguised as treatment."[46] Thus the case of involuntary mental health services provides perhaps the starkest example of how special treatment which is supposed to rehabilitate may in fact confirm and even manufacture further deviance or perceptions of deviance. Other social analysts have discussed similar effects of special programming on poor people, those with disabilities, women, and juvenile delinquents, to name just a few. In each instance, specialized programs tend to magnify perceived differences between labelled (deviant) and nonlabelled (normal) people.

Critics of the social pathology approach propose civil liberties (protection from unwanted treatment), self help (that is, treatment designed and provided by marginal groups themselves), and radical nonintervention (conscious decision not to treat) as remedies. Basically, the critics and their models share a common perspective. They all agree that most variance from prescribed social norms does not justify social controls even if garbed in the language and technique of treatment. Rather, the critics favor greater social acceptance of differences. Applied to one kind of "deviance," juvenile delinquency, this noninterventionist approach

implies policies that accommodate society to the widest possible diversity of behaviors and attitudes, rather than forcing as many individuals as possible to "adjust" to supposedly common societal standards. This does not mean that anything goes, that all behavior is socially acceptable. But traditional delinquency policy has proscribed youthful behavior well beyond what is required to maintain a smooth-running society or to protect others from youthful depredation. Thus, the basic injunction for public policy becomes: leave kids alone wherever possible, and the basic injunction for problem definers becomes: wherever possible find solutions to delinquency by changing social structure and values, not by singling out specific individuals as culprits.[47]

Sociobiology and Other Forms of Neosocial Darwinism

In the late nineteenth and early twentieth century, it was not uncommon for social analysts in general and progressive social analysts in particular, such as Havelock Ellis and Margaret Sanger, to recommend selective breeding (what might today be called human genetic control) as a means of solving urban crime, unemployment, family disintegration, and a host of other social problems. Simply put, leading scientists and social reformers believed that "inefficient" and "immoral" or "morally degenerate" "human stock" was at the root of much of what troubled industrial society. That view began to lose credibility as it became clear that: (1) mentally retarded people could be born to people of all intellectual levels and (2) that the intelligence of offspring tend toward the mean or average intellect of the society. Whether or not the goal of human genetic management (eugenics) was desirable, scientists and social reformers were certainly incapable of achieving it. Progressives actually rejected eugenics only after Hitler espoused it as his strategy for creating a master race. To post World War II reformers, eugenics seemed an affront to cherished social values, namely those of equality and democracy. It had been irrevocably tainted by Hitler's antisemitism and blatant racism.

However, while society may have scrapped eugenics, it did not altogether reject social darwinism. Social, political, and economic rewards still tend to go to those whom social institutions deem intelligent (that is, "the fittest"). Social analysts who advocate this process of socioeconomic sorting in effect adopt the conservatism of nineteenth century social darwinism. They justify social inequality as a necessary condition if society wants to benefit from the resources of its brightest people. One such neoconservative, Richard Hernnstein, puts it this way:

> The ties among I.Q., occupation, and social standing make *practical sense*. The intellectual demands of engineering, for example, exceed those of ditch digging. Hence engineers are brighter, on the average. If virtually anyone is smart enough to be a ditch digger, and only half the people are smart enough to be engineers, then society is, in effect, *husbanding* its intellectual research by holding engineers to greater esteem and paying them more. The critics of testing say that the correlation between I.Q. and social class show that the I.Q. test is contaminated by the arbitrary values of our culture, giving unfair advantage to those who hold them. But it is probably no more coincidence that those values often put the bright people in the prestigious jobs. By doing so, society expresses its recognition, however imprecise, of the importance and scarcity of intellectual ability.[48] [Italics added]

Hernnstein believes that probably between 80 and 85 percent of intelligence is inherited. Thus he concludes that a person's social fate is largely a result of genetic endowment. He puts it in a syllogism:

1. If differences in mental abilities are inherited, and
2. if success requires those abilities, and
3. if earnings and prestige depend on success,
4. then social standing will be based to some extent on inherited differences among people.[49]

Hernnstein defends social class differences on the ground that they constitute a useful meritocratic process for "husbanding" (his word) human intellectual resources. He even goes so far as to suggest that prevailing social problems, such as urban poverty, may be attributed more to inborn differences than to social or environmental forces such as racism, class discrimination, and economic exploitation.

Hernnstein's theory has not gone unchallenged. His critics, including Chomsky, Bowles and Gintis, Kamin, and Kagan find much to fault in this brand of social darwinism. Some of these critics argue that intelligence tests have not overcome their inherent racial biases. Others argue that even if we accept the hypothesis that 80 percent of intelligence is hereditary, there is no reason to believe that people with better than average intelligence need a greater monetary reward for their work than do people of average or lower intelligence. Further, they argue, there is no evidence that poor people are less intelligent than rich people. Hernnstein's critics show that class status at birth (poverty or wealth) is a far greater determinant of eventual station in adult life than is intelligence. The following evidence, provided by Bowles and Gintis, typifies the assault on Hernnstein and on neoconservative ideas in general:

> Among children with identical IQ test scores at ages six and eight, those with rich, well-educated, high-status parents could expect a much higher level of schooling than those with less-favored origins. . . .
>   Only a small portion of the observed social class differences in educational attainment is related to IQ differences across social classes. . . .
>   For "high ability" students (top 25 percent as measured by a composite of tests of "general aptitude"), those of high socioeconomic background (top 25 percent as measured by a composite of family income, parents' education, and occupation) are nearly twice as likely to attend college than students of low socioeconomic background (bottom 25 percent). For "low ability" students (bottom 25 percent), those of high social background are more than four times as likely to attend college as are their low social background counterparts.[50]

Ultimately, critics of the new social darwinism see Hernnstein and his colleagues as apologists for the status quo and responsible for all the social inequities that attend it.

Just as Hernnstein's neoconservative social darwinism and I.Q. controversy seemed to be subsiding, another social theory emerged as the forerunner of neosocial darwinism. It is called Sociobiology. Edward O. Wilson, a Harvard zoologist, popularized the term with his book, *Sociobiology: A New Synthesis*. He defines Sociobiology as

> the systematic study of the biological basis of all social behavior. For the present it focuses on animal societies . . . But the discipline is also concerned with the social behavior of early man and the adaptive features of organization in the most primitive contemporary societies.[51]

From the standpoint of social problems, it is hard to understand how scientists could really expect to explain much of human conduct by looking at animal behavior. We are political beings, animals are not. Yet sociobiologists seem undaunted. Sociobiology, like eugenics, presumes that scientists can explain social behavior as the product of human genetics and biological heritage. Note, for example, Wilson's analysis of sex differences:

> In hunter-gatherer societies, men hunt and women stay at home. This strong bias persists in most agricultural and industrial societies and on that ground alone appears to have a genetic origin. . . . My own guess is that the genetic bias is intense enough to cause substantial division of labor even in the most free and egalitarian societies . . . even with identical education and equal access to all professions, men are likely to continue to play a disproportionate role in political life, business and science. But that is only a guess and, even if correct, could not be used to argue for anything less than sex-blind admission and free personal choice.[52]

Presumably, even with egalitarian admissions policies, Wilson could foresee continued unequal roles for men and women in "political life, business, and science" as natural consequences of biological reality.

As we might expect, sociobiology has found substantial support in some academic circles, not so much because of its potential race, sex, and class bias, or even because it seems an incarnation of earlier social darwinism, but because it turns the analysis of social problems into a "real science." It suggests that the social condition is largely, if not entirely, determined by biological and not social factors. Critics charge, on the other hand, that sociobiology is "scientism" not "science." Critics note that sociobiology has produced no substantive evidence of any scientific merit that any but the most basic human actions (for example, eating, sleeping, breathing) can be understood as biologically determined. Further, although sociobiologists and many of their critics would agree that the human condition reflects and depends on biological processes, the latter do not believe in the determining role of biology in most social events. Critics of sociobiology see too vast an array of cultural and other human behavior to believe that a biological science capable of explaining anything but the most trivial social events is possible. The critics thus charge that sociobiology will prove to be merely one more attempt to clothe conservative, status quo rooted social darwinism in scientific language. As one critic sums it up, by having us accept biological determinism, sociobiology would have us reject social inquiry:

> Questions of destiny, of meaning in history, or of cosmic purpose are not likely to disappear from human discourse, and there are no legitimate grounds for proscribing them. A more immediate, and perhaps more practical, objective of historical study of social and cultural affairs, however, is a revelation of the kinds of lives peoples have so far led and the circumstances under which they have come to lead them. These are the alternatives displayed by cultural differences. Now it is obviously the case that knowledge of such differences is of no practical import if human beings cannot by their own activity make choices among alternatives and pursue alternatives. If the alternatives are essentially the same, and if what we regard as human activity is only a reflex consequent upon genetic signals, with no source or result in human activity itself, then the records of human histories are of little moment and study of them can yield only illusions. To deny the reality of human activity in this sense, then, is not only to put checkreins on freedom. It stops inquiry into historical sources of human conditions. It cuts man off from his history, denies him access to his experience.[53]

From the point of view of community organizers, sociobiology, like all forms of neosocial darwinism, also denies the possibility of *making* history. It finds human action predetermined. It relegates individuals to the status of preprogrammed automatons in an unfolding of biologically ordained events. It places social change beyond our control.

THE MAKING OF A SOCIAL PROBLEM

> Forty-three citizens of New York State died at Attica Correctional Facility between September 9 and 13, 1971. Thirty-nine of that number were killed and more than 80 others were wounded by gunfire during the 15 minutes it took the State Police to retake the prison on September 13. With the exception of Indian massacres in the late 19th Century, the State Police assault which ended the four-day prison uprising was the bloodiest one-day encounter between Americans since the Civil War.[54]

The Attica prison revolt had one purpose, and that was to make New York State and America aware that prison conditions at Attica were a real problem. Although the first set of demands which the rebelling inmates made public at the time of the prison takeover included amnesty, freedom, and safe transportation to a "nonimperialistic country," when the prisoners actually got down to negotiating, they also made clear why conditions at Attica were a problem. Inmates rejected continued institutional peonage—inmates were paid only $.25–$1.00 per day for their work in the institution. Hence their demand: "STOP SLAVE LABOR." They demanded the right of political and religious expression. They demanded an end to censorship of magazines, books, and other published literature. They demanded the right to communicate with whomever they chose, and called for modernization of educational facilities. They demanded narcotics treatment programs, adequate food, more recreation time, adequate legal assistance, some Spanish-speaking doctors, an inmate grievance system, as well as an expanded work release program.

At the time of its construction, Attica was to be "an answer to charges of inhuman penal conditions." In 1931, the *New York Times* reported that Attica was "said to be the last word in modern prison construction."[55] In reality Attica resembled the typical congregate style maximum security system. The 30-foot-high grey concrete exterior wall cost one million dollars. Fourteen gun towers ringed the facility. By 1971, it held 2,243 inmates and of these more than sixty percent were from minority groups and more than seventy-five percent were from urban areas.

Most people remember Attica for the massacre that occured when state police retook the prison and, in so doing, killed 39 people (hostages and inmates alike). However, the revolt and its bloody resolution also made public the problem of prison conditions and, as a consequence, New York State established a special commission on Attica. Citizen groups became more active in demanding prison reforms. Attica became a symbol of one kind of social injustice in America.

What prisoners at Attica did is what organizers must always do: (1) create awareness of abhorrent human conditions; (2) define those conditions as problematic; (3) take action to make others aware of the problem; and (4) recommend solutions to the problem. The conditions at Attica were not new. Institutional peonage, censorship of publications, and a host of other dehumanizing practices had gone on for years. What was new was that prisoners themselves had now defined these conditions at Attica as a major social problem and were demanding attention to it.

The Process of Making a Problem

Without a consistent framework for understanding the world, an organizer can never expect to achieve much of anything. On the other hand, having a perspective or ideology through which to define social conditions and forces as problems does not necessarily translate into action either. This means that the ability to define social problems does not in itself guarantee change. A social problem has a career or definite stages of growth. If one stage supposedly leads to change, we must initially define the problem in a manner that suggests ways of building broad-based support and in a manner that implicitly suggests ways of carrying out social reform. Hence, when we speak of making a social problem we mean defining a set of conditions as a problem, selecting strategies to spread awareness of and acceptance of a particular problem definition, identifying ways of keeping knowledgeable about the problem, and creating plans to overcome the problem. These are all activities in which organizers engage.

Consciousness raising. A favorite strategy of organizers for defining social conditions as a problem is a process of dialogue called consciousness raising. Consciousness raising presumes a process of self-education by which people "develop their power to perceive critically the way they exist in the world with which they find themselves; they come to see the world not as a static reality, but as a reality in process, in transformation."[56] Consciousness raising assumes the learner can participate in the world, interact with it, and not merely exist as a subject whose duty it is to obey and adjust. Whereas the interests of elites lie in maintaining the gulf between themselves and the people whom they exploit, the interests of the oppressed, the marginal, and the discriminated against lie in their own ability to find the causes of their condition and their ability to transform it.

Consciousness raising takes many forms. Some activists have formed study groups in which members read the same book and then discuss its meaning in relation to their own lives and to society at large. Others use the consciousness raising group as a self-education forum in which the members learn about their rights, about organizing, and about models of change. Still others turn more to personal experiences as the subject matter of personal and political change. The rapid spread of women's consciousness raising groups in the 1970's typifies this type of group. Feminist activist Susan Brownmiller describes the purpose and effect of women's consciousness raising.

> Few topics, the women found, were unfruitful. Humiliations that each of them had suffered privately—from being turned down for a job with the comment, "We were looking for a man," to catcalls and wolf whistles on the street—turned out to be universal agonies. "I had always felt degraded, actually turned into an object," said one woman. "I was no longer a human being when a guy on the street would start to make those incredible animal noises at me. I never was flattered by it, I always understood that behind that whistle was a masked hostility. When we started to talk about it in the group, I discovered that every woman in the room had similar feelings. None of us knew how to cope with this street hostility. We had always had to grin and bear it. We had always been told to dress as women, to be very sexy and alluring to men, and what did it get us? Comments like "Look at the legs on that babe" and "would I like to———her."
>
> "Consciousness-raising," in which a woman's personal experience at the hands of men was analyzed as a political phenomenon, soon became a keystone of the women's liberation movement.[57]

Similar groups emerged around other interests and issues. Disability rights activists, older people, gay people, and other minority groups have all used consciousness raising as a means of clarifying issues.

Creating a New Language

Every social movement needs a way of talking about or characterizing its issues so that they can be experienced anew, with a sense of clarity and immediacy. A chief means of fulfilling this need has been language creation. Before Blacks and whites began to organize against racial discrimination, the terms "Blacks," "civil rights," and "integration," were not commonplace terms. Rather, organizers introduced them as part of their campaign to make certain conditions known as problems and to point the direction for social change. Feminists found they needed a term to characterize the shared experience and commitment of women. They subsequently spoke of "sisterhood" and coined the slogan "sisterhood is powerful." Disability rights activists needed a word to characterize discrimination, prejudice and stereotyping on the basis of disabilities, so they coined the term "handicapism." Handicapism is a "set of assumptions and practices that promote the differential and unequal treatment of people because of apparent or assumed physical, mental, or behavioral differences."[58] Similarly, organizers who are concerned with the very high number (40 percent in many major urban schools) of students, most often minority students who do not complete high school, have rejected the term "high school dropouts" as a fair way of describing the problem. That term placed the onus entirely on high schoolers. Instead, organizers prefer the term "push-outs" for that term suggests that schools and other institutional and social factors may cause certain groups of young people to leave high school. Similarly, prison abolitionists and prison reformers have come to call the criminal justice system the criminal injustice system. A group of older activist people in Philadelphia, seeking to counteract the image of older people as incompetent, inactive and dependent, adopted one word from another activist organization and formed a new group called "The Grey Panthers." Meanwhile, a group of retarded people in Oregon, sick of being referred to primarily by clinical labels, started an organization which they called "People First." Another disability rights group in the East printed a poster entitled "Label Jars, Not People."

To some people language may seem rather unimportant. "Why quibble over words?" But organizers have long recognized that words strung together as language are the basis of communication, which both reflects and shapes how people view each other and the world. Hence organizers' concern for language. Words can often provide the means by which to define issues anew and to take action.

Knowledge. The fact that organizers often state issues boldly and with great certainty should not be interpreted to mean that organizers are ideologues and therefore are basically uninterested in new knowledge. It is true that some people who call themselves organizers may be sectarian ideologues who adhere to "the party line," deny their own curiosity, and who close themselves off from new information and new analyses. But such people will always fail. For they cannot long maintain credibility either with themselves or with people around them. Every true organizer knows that in order to effectively define social problems he or she must have both an analytical framework and a willingness to apply and test the applicability of that framework to continually changing facts.

An entire chapter of this book is devoted to strategies of action research which organizers use to increase their knowledge of facts and interpretation of facts. Hence, the various aspects of action research are not discussed here. However, several examples will help demonstrate the importance that knowledge brings to the task of problem definition. The issue of fluorocarbons is a case in point. A professor at the University of California, F. Sherwood Roland, and a photochemist from Mexico City combined their research findings and learned that the earth's existence was threatened.[59] They found that two gases, trichloromonofluoromethane and dichlorodifluoromethane, which are commonly used in aerosol propellants, air conditioning, and refrigeration, were entering the earth's troposphere. This process would set up a chemical chain reaction which would eventually lead to a dramatic decomposition of the earth's ozone layer. If allowed to continue, this process of decomposition could destroy earth's biological systems. After they disclosed their findings to scientists and to the public, the major corporations which produced propellants, including DuPont, Allied Chemical, Union Carbide, Pennwalt, Kaiser Aluminum and Racon attempted to delay any action on the news by calling for and financing a three-year study of the problem. Meanwhile several federal agencies began to investigate the problem as well and confirmed the scientists' fears. Still, the government delayed in moving against the corporations that manufactured the sprays. Citizen groups, on the other hand, mobilized. Environmental groups campaigned against continued use of the gases and corporations were slowly forced to replace aerosol gases with hand pumps. It was a classic case in which organizers, in this case environmental groups, needed information in order to make their case. The knowledge had to be linked to organizing in order to overcome the inertia created by resistant special interests. The position of government and the corporations was one of placing the burden of proof on those who wanted to protect the public interest. Because the burden of proof regularly falls on organizers, they have generally accepted the responsibility of being well informed.

In some instances, securing knowledge can prove difficult, even nearly impossible. Note the following odyssey of an environmental activist in pursuit of knowledge to help the public.[60] An expert on radiation, Ernest J. Sternglass, has "long been concerned about the harmful effects of low level radiation." Thus when the Three Mile Island nuclear accident occurred in his back yard—Sternglass lives in Pittsburgh, Pennsylvania and Three Mile Island is just outside Harrisburg, Pennsylvania—he decided to investigate the effects of fallout. First, Sternglass learned from transcripts of a Nuclear Regulatory Commission meeting that radiation leaks had been greater than publicly reported. By then studying infant death rates in Harrisburg as well as in places farther away such as New York City, Ohio, upstate New York, and Maryland, he began to see clear abnormalities in Pennsylvania which seemed to follow the precise ratios that would be expected to accompany radiation contamination. To complete his analysis, Sternglass needed a bit of information which, to use his words, was "the Pennsylvania Health Department's carefully guarded data." Fortunately, Warren Prelesnik, newly appointed executive vice president for administration of the Harrisburg hospital, heard Sternglass give a speech. Prelesnik offered to help Sternglass secure the information he needed. It proved to be the key to Sternglass confirming that the cause of death was clearly related to abnormal radiation leakage. Sternglass's findings further fueled the antinuclear movement. Knowledge in this instance had been hard to come by, but once again it proved to be an important ingredient in the process of formulating social problems.

Institutions.   In order to define issues and guarantee their continued visibility, organizers create organizations devoted to the study, formulation, and reformulation of social problems. The Children's Defense Fund, the National Welfare Rights Organization, the National Tenants Organization, Public Interest Research Groups, the Grey Panthers, the Prison Research Education Action Project, the National Organization of Women, the Redistribute America Movement, ACORN, and literally hundreds of other organizations serve as the base for local, regional, and national community organizing. Many of these organizations put out newsletters, bulletins, action research reports, and pamphlets which provide information and analyses on their respective issues. In effect, organizations keep issues alive.

Becker, in his classic article on "what is a social problem," sees the institutionalization of a social problem as potentially perilous:

> Personnel of the organization devoted to the problem tend to build their lives and careers around its continued existence. They become attached to "their" problem, and

anything that threatens to make it disappear or diminish in importance is a threat. What can be said of "rule enforcers" working in organizations dedicated to controlling deviance may be applied with equal justice to the staff of any organization devoted to dealing with a social problem, even in fields such as race relations, housing, or education: "the rule enforcer faces a double problem. On the one hand, he must demonstrate to others that the problem still exists: the rules he is supposed to enforce have some point, because infractions occur. On the other hand, he must show that his attempts at enforcement are effective and worthwhile, that the evil he is supposed to deal with is in fact being dealt with adequately. Therefore, enforcement organizations, particularly when they are seeking funds, typically oscillate between two kinds of claims. First, they say that by reason of their efforts the problem they deal with is approaching solution. But in the same breath, they say the problem is perhaps worse than ever (though through no fault of their own) and requires renewed and increased effort to keep it under control."[61]

Becker's critique does not reflect the actual situation. When organizers talk of institutionalizing social problems, they do not envision themselves as enforcers, but rather as change agents. Their role is not to control "deviants." More often than not, they *are* the deviants (for example, older people, minorities, poor people, disabled people, people who are the objects of industrial pollution). Their organizations wage nearly constant battle with society's mainstream institutions. Their role is that of outsider and militant catalyst. To the extent that social movement institutions become concerned with maintaining a status quo or a static definition of social problems, they fail to effectively organize for change.

Actions, alternatives, and redefinition.   Organizing never ends. As soon as organizers achieve one objective or goal, they search for new seeds of discontent, new issues, or new analyses of old issues. Their business is always the business of pursuing ideals such as equality, justice, improved health, better living conditions, and the like. Because none of these ideals reflects or could reflect a static condition, organizers continually strive toward them. Their task is what the Chinese have called "the ongoing revolution." The organizer's process of problem definition continually calls for reassessment and redefinition.

Frequently, actions provide the vehicle by which organizers bring their current problem analyses to the point of broad public recognition. Hospital employees in New York City, Topeka, Kansas, and many other places have had strikes, and their opposite, "work-ins," to expose inadequate staffing of health facilities. Organizers against the Vietnam War used teach-ins as a kind of action and education strategy. Parents and a few professionals opened up the doors of Willowbrook institution for the retarded to Geraldo Rivera of ABC television to let the world know about the horrid conditions in that facility. The Berrigan brothers and six other antinuclear activists walked into a nuclear weapons plant in Pennsylvania where they symbolically banged hammers against warheads. Their subsequent arrest, trial, and sentencing brought national attention to the dangers of nuclear weaponry. Disabled people organized sit-ins at regional federal office buildings in order to educate the public about their movement and their chief demand, that the government enforce the disability rights antidiscrimination law which Congress had passed four years earlier. The Children's Defense Fund produced a report which exposed the national scandal that nearly two million school aged children had been excluded from school.

Besides affecting existing policies and practices, demonstrations, demands, public forums, boycotts, strikes, litigation, press conferences, action research, negotiations, and lobbying, as well as many other strategies tend to make issues public. They provide the visibility that is so essential to making a problem definition influential. It is probably safe to say that when prisoners at Attica first staged their prison takeover, few Americans knew much of anything about prison conditions. Those who had followed the writings of celebrated prisoners like George Jackson knew of prison injustices, but most people were generally unaware of such matters. The prison takeover cost America its ignorance about prison life. The Attica uprising and subsequent police assault caused America to literally stop for four long days while television and newspapers communicated the prisoners' grievances. By all accounts, the Attica rebellion was an extreme version of how an organizing action can cause people to confront facts, definitions, and reforms which they had previously not known about or ignored. Some people may look back on Attica and say little has changed but, in fact, much has changed. It is true that prisons still dehumanize prisoners, that minorities still account for most prisoners, and that prisons do not rehabilitate. But because of Attica and a host of other organizing events, many people now regard American prisons and the American justice (some call it injustice) system as deeply in need of reform. The notion that prisons rehabilitate prisoners no longer has much credibility. Similarly, the idea that prisoners surrender all rights, even the right to decent treatment, when they enter prison is no longer defensible. Attica provided a means, albeit an expensive one in lives lost, to define and redefine criminal justice issues.

NOTES

[1]Richard C. Fuller and Richard R. Myers, "The Natural History of a Social Problem," *American Sociological Review,* 6 (June, 1941), p. 320.

[2]Jessica Mitford, *Kind and Usual Punishment: The Prison Business* (New York: Knopf, 1973), p. 71.

[3]Howard S. Becker, "Introduction," in *Social Problems: A Modern Approach,* Howard S. Becker, ed. (New York: John Wiley, 1966), p. 7.

[4]Becker, "Introduction," p. 7.

[5]Becker, "Introduction," p. 7. And C. Wright Mills, *The Sociological Imagination* (New York: Oxford University Press, 1959).

[6]Mills, *Sociological Imagination,* p. 12.

[7]Jerome G. Manis, *Analyzing Social Problems* (New York: Praeger, 1976), p. 28.

[8]Manis, *Social Problems,* pp. 82–89.

[9]Mills, *Sociological Imagination,* p. 8.

[10]Mills, *Sociological Imagination,* p. 8.

[11]Mills, *Sociological Imagination,* p. 9.

[12]Kenneth Kenniston, "How Community Mental Health Stamped Out The Riots (1967–68) in *Total Institutions*, Samuel E. Wallace, ed. (New Brunswick, N.J.: Transaction Books, 1971) pp. 115–130.

[13]William Ryan, *Blaming the Victim* (New York: Vintage Books, 1963), p. 7.

[14]Ryan, *Victim*, pp. 10–11.

[15]Ryan, *Victim*, pp. 127–28.

[16]Ryan, *Victim*, p. 140.

[17]Robert Reinhold, "Public Found Hostile to Welfare as Idea, but Backs What It Does," *The New York Times*, Wednesday, August 3, 1977, pp. 1 and 49.

[18]Sheila Collins "Welfare Rights: Dignity, Justice, Adequate Income" in *Your Community and Beyond*, Julia Cheever, ed. (Palo Alto, Calif.: Page Ficklin, 1975), pp. 74 and 75.

[19]C. A. Bowers, "Emergent Ideological Characteristics of Educational Policy," *Teachers College Record*, 79, 1 (September 1977), p. 51.

[20]Bowers, "Emergent Ideological Characteristics," p. 51.

[21]Philip M. Stern, "Uncle Sam's Welfare Program for the Rich," in *Crisis in American Institutions*, 3rd ed., eds. Jerome H. Skolnick and Elliott Currie (Boston: Little Brown, 1976), p. 120.

[22]Stern, "Uncle Sam," p. 120.

[23]Stern, "Uncle Sam," p. 120.

[24]Richard Goode, *The Individual Income Tax* (Washington, DC: The Brookings Institution, 1976), p. 268.

[25]Goode, *Income Tax*, p. 249.

[26]Rolf Goetz, "The Housing Bubble," *Working Papers*, Vol. VIII, No. 1, (January/February, 1981), p. 44.

[27]Stan Steiner, "La Raza: The Mexican Americans," in *Crisis in American Institutions*, 3rd ed., eds. Jerome Skolnick and Elliott Currie (Boston: Little Brown, 1976), p. 179.

[28]Steiner, *La Raza*, p. 179.

[29]Steiner, *La Raza*, p. 179.

[30]Steiner, *La Raza*, p. 179.

[31]Steiner, *La Raza*, p. 180.

[32]Steiner, *La Raza*, P. 180.

[33]Steiner, *La Raza*, p. 181.

[34]Richard Titmus, "The Gift of Blood," in *Crisis in American Institutions*, eds., Jerome H. Skolnick and Elliott Currie (Boston: Little Brown, 1976), pp. 557–67.

[35]Daniel Zwerdling, "The Food Monopolies," in *Crisis in American Institutions*, 3rd ed., ed. Jerome H. Skolnick and Elliott Currie (Boston: Little Brown, 1976), p. 47.

[36]Zwerdling, "Food," p. 47.

[37]Jim Hightower, *Eat Your Heart Out: Food Profiteering in America* (New York: Vintage Books, 1976), p. 123.

[38]Tom Hayden, *The American Future* (Boston: South End Press, 1980), p. 171.

[39]Michael Parenti, *Power and Powerlessness* (New York: St. Martins Press, 1980), p. 190.

[40]Hayden, *American Future*, pp. 169–74.

[41]Hayden, *American Future*, pp. 125–26.

[42]Ray Rist, "Student Social Class and Teacher Expectation: The Self Fulfilling Prophecy in Ghetto Education," *Harvard Educational Review*, Vol. 40, No. 3 (August 1970), p. 425.

[43]Richard H. DeLone, *Small Futures* (New York: Harcourt, Brace, Jovanovich Inc., 1979), pp. 164–65.

[44]Thomas Szasz, *The Manufacture of Madness* (New York: Harper & Row, Pub., 1970).

[45]Szasz, *Madness*, p. xix & xxiii.

[46]Thomas Szasz, *Law, Liberty, and Psychiatry* (New York: Collier Books, 1968), p. 108.

[47]Edwin Schur, *Radical Nonintervention: Rethinking the Delinquency Problem* (Englewood Cliffs, NJ: Prentice-Hall Inc., 1973), pp. 154–55.

[48]Richard Hernnstein, "I.Q.," *The Atlantic Monthly,* 1971, p. 51.

[49]Hernnstein, "I.Q.," p. 43.

[50]Samuel Bowles and Herbert Gintis, *Schooling in Capitalist America* (New York: Basic Books, 1976) pp. 32–33.

[51]Edward O. Wilson, *Sociobiology: The New Synthesis* (Cambridge: Belknap Press, Harvard University, 1975), p. 4.

[52]Edward O. Wilson, "Human Decency is Animal," *The New York Times Magazine,* October 12, 1975, p. 50.

[53]Kenneth E. Bock, Human Nature and History: A Response to Sociobiology (New York: Columbia University Press, 1980) pp. 197–98.

[54]New York State Special Commission on Crime, *Attica* (New York: Bantam, 1972), p. xi.

[55]Commission on Crime, *Attica,* p. 15.

[56]Paulo Freire, *Pedagogy of the Oppressed* (New York: Continuum Books, 1970), p. 71.

[57]Susan Brownmiller, "Sisterhood is Powerful," in *Social Problems: Private Troubles and Public Issues,* eds. Arnold Birenbaum and Edward Sagarin (New York: Charles Scribners, 1972) pp. 577–78.

[58]Robert Bogdan and Douglas Biklen, "Handicapism," *Social Policy,* April 1977, pp. 14–19.

[59]Morton Mintz and Jerry S. Cohen, *Power Inc: Public and Private Rulers and How to Make Them Accountable* (New York: Viking, 1976), pp. 545–51.

[60]Ernest Sternglass, "The Lethal Path of T.M.I. Fallout," *The Nation,* March 7, 1981, pp. 267–69 & 272–73.

[61]Howard Becker, "Introduction," p. 13.

CHAPTER FOUR
THE ORGANIZER'S ROLE: LEADERSHIP FOR CHANGE

"DOING GOOD," CAN IT BE DONE?

Social historians generally agree that early efforts to "do good"—doing good was a turn of the century term for charitable work—enabled society's elites to control, moralize to, and keep dependent society's poor.[1] While modern day professionalism has long since forsaken moral evangelism for scientific treatment, it too perpetuates an enormous gulf between the service provider (for example, visiting nurse, social worker, lawyer, psychologist) and client. The term client itself suggests the gulf and its root, "cliens," means "to follow."

Ironically, both charity and professionalism were conceived as democratic social reforms. Thus to the extent that social historians now believe these "reforms" accomplished the opposite, that they maintained or even exacerbated social class division, we must ask: "Where did these movements go wrong?" More than that, "Does history then tell us that charitable acts, professional service, and social reform can never occur without reinforcing social inequalities?" If so, what does the future hold for community organizing?

In this chapter we will address those questions by examining the meaning and consequences of charity, professionalism, and community organizing as social roles. More specifically we will ask "What were the origins of charity?", "How did charity manifest itself?", and, "What is its legacy today?" Then we will inquire, "Why did professionalism fail to achieve its reform goals?" and "What made its institutional conventions, its science, the social beliefs of its actors antidemocratic?'' Finally, we will ask, ''What is the community organizer, a modern day charitable worker? A humanistic, reform minded professional?'', ''What can we learn from the social history of charity and professionalism that will inform community organization?'' and ''Can organizers lead the way in changes for social equality and justice?''

WHAT WENT WRONG
WITH THE CHARITY MODEL?

No one would argue with the importance of individual good will or charitableness among people. Most people embrace both the concept and practice of being charitable, of helping their neighbor. However, when charity becomes an ideological paradigm for how society deals with basic human needs (for example, health care, housing, education) as well as with social matters like inequality and injustice, it then becomes something different than individual help and sharing. Institutionalized charity bears little resemblence to personal acts of good will.

Historically, the promoters of charity, usually prominent citizens, believed that charity would preserve or reinstate independence among the downtrodden. In this view, charity could also have a negative effect. If given too liberally, it would foster dependence. If given carefully and modestly to the right recipients, it would result in independence. One of charity's leaders during the early 1900's, Josephine Shaw Lowell, warned that ''even the widow with little children, if she finds that everything is made easy for her, may lose her energy, may even, by being relieved of anxiety for them, lose her love for the children.''[2] Handouts would breed slovenliness.

> Men and women, seeing the reward offered to those who give up the struggle and sit down to be fed by others, in their time, relinquish in ceaseless labor required to keep themselves and their children from want, and they, too, fall into the ranks of those who have been ruined by almsgiving.[3]

Unless educated to proper moral beliefs,

> human beings were (thought) naturally inclined to laziness. The poor must not starve or freeze, but neither must the worker be deprived of the incentive to labor by the prospect of readily obtainable alms. Deviations from this policy would lead to degeneration in the form of a permanent pauper class, for the ''biological condition'' of individual and racial development was effort, and ''the being which is fed without expense of effort becomes a parasite, and loses powers of locomotion and initiation.'' The New York Charity Organization Society warned that ''honest employment, the work that God means every man to do, is the truest basis of relief for every person with physical ability to work,'' and ''the help which needlessly releases the poor from the necessity of providing for themselves is in violation of divine law and incurs the penalties which follow any infraction of that law.''[4]

Charity was the forerunner of welfare. Its detractors and even some of its advocates feared a "charity" problem in much the same way that some people today speak of a "welfare problem." Hence charity's architects applied to it a kind of work test.

Charitable organizations have always perceived their role not only as the conveyors of alms, but also as decision makers whose duty it was to differentiate between the worthy and unworthy. Screening out the unworthy from the worthy was one way of guarding against formation of a "beggar class." In the eyes of those who formed the early charitable associations, there were two kinds of poor: those whose impoverishment stemmed from their bad moral attitudes, their slovenliness, their lack of motivation, their poor work habits, their fondness for alcohol and so forth—the New York State Board of Charities described this group as the bulk of all paupers, who have reached that condition by idleness, improvidence, drunkenness, or by some form of vicious indulgence;[5] and those whose impoverished state was a function of ill fate. For the first group, charity was seen as providing moral renewal. One leading reformer, Father James O. S. Huntington, thought it would be a good idea if a few of those who had gone astray could find right morality again by engaging in philanthropic work themselves:

> Imagine some mighty movement that would lay hold upon the weakest and the worst and gather them up and send them forth to save their fellows, might there not be found a moral motive power that would be strong enough to lift men above themselves, above the cravings of their appetites, above their selfishness and their sin? And that is what must be sought by the new philanthropy.[6]

For the latter group, morality was less of an issue because their condition was no fault of their own. No matter how diligently and valiantly this latter group worked, a series of misfortunes befell them. It was expected that one would use all personal resources, even sink far into debt, before asking for charity. The ideal recipient was the one who, for reasons of personal dignity, disdained charity. The ideal recipient was the one who never asked for help, was never bitter, never angry, and the one who accepted fate as justifiable but who always strived to reverse it.

In this scheme, old people, children, the widowed, people with disabilities, and the sick were ideal recipients. Note, for example, how the *New York Times* described its neediest "deserving" cases. The most popular case of 1925, measured in number of donors, was that of "Two aged sisters, spinsters, once rich, but now poor, and under the death sentence of cancer." Their top competition that year was a blind mother of eight, Helen, 35 years old, struggling against the dark curtain over her eyes, with her brood too young to help and "crippled Sheila, a lame little girl of nine, who feared that no foster home would be found for a child with a twisted leg."[7] Each case bore the imprint of tragedy. Headlines told it all: "Half blind, yet she works"; "eyes fail, then mind"; "only one hand"; "two feeble sisters: too weak to work"; "tubercular"; "three orphan sisters"; "old, crippled"; "shut in"; "once they gave to others"; "Dickie, 3, left alone"; "widow working for four children"; "abused and neglected"; "a hard fate"; "Annie, the worker"; "the old hunchback."[8] The *Times'* goal was not merely pity, but also "the estimated cost of bridging the gap of distress for those in need, carrying them over until they are able once more to support themselves."[9] Like directors of charity everywhere in those early days, the *Times* editors sought to convince the public that their charity cases were not immoral freeloaders. The ideal charity case was the person of hardworking nature beset by a tragic and fateful calamity.

The notion of "worthiness" carried with it the belief that charities' clientele could, ultimately, fend for themselves if only they could exhibit the proper moral determination and self-discipline. That belief excluded the possibility that social structures, economic systems and conditions, societal prejudice, and institutional discrimination caused people's miseries. Charity, with its characteristic moral imperialism, assumed that people suffered as a result of their own failings or by fate (old age, disability, abandonment, and neglect) and not of social injustice (economic exploitation, class origin). One was to feel pity and even compassion for such people, but not anger at a system that might have caused their condition.

Of course, not even charity's proponents could fail to see the flaw in this reasoning. Typical economic fluctuations with their concomitant effect on employment and unemployment made the "laziness and poor morale" explanation of human suffering highly suspect. Bad attitudes could simply not account for all joblessness and poverty.

> The pauperism and vagrancy which they hoped to discourage through stringent relief policies were not simply expressions of individual moral perversity, but phases of labor mobility in a growing industrial economy. Those problems were real and disturbing; but benevolent stinginess could no more cope with them than could liberal or indiscriminate relief. Poverty was rooted in structural changes in American economic and social life with consequences too complex and far reaching to be affected significantly by any form of relief policy.[10]

Not surprisingly, Jane Addams, James O. S. Huntington, and others recognized the absurdity and potential cruelty of stingy relief practices which ignored economic realities.[11] Yet charitable organizations proved either unable or unwilling to resolve the obvious contradiction between the puritan betterment-and-salvation-through-work ideology and prevailing economic realities. Actually, this was only one of several major contradictions embodied in the charity model of public assistance.

As with many social institutions, charity tolerated concepts and practices which stood in direct opposition to each other. On the one hand, charity's soldiers, namely friendly visitors, promised to bring friendship to the downtrodden. However, they also brought control. The two hardly seemed compatible. Charity's architects[12] hoped for the actualization of the American dream of a single class of people equal in social participation, but its practice required unequal class position.[13] Why, after all, would anyone deliver charity to an equal? This was the reasoning of many elite donors. As Josephine Shaw Lowell put it, "Charity must be exercised toward a person in inferior circumstances to those of the benefactor. We cannot be charitable to our equals."[14] Ironically, friendly visiting achieved precisely the opposite effect from what it intended:

She (the friendly visitor) intervened in the lives of the poor by virtue of a presumptive wisdom and superiority, yet was to conceive of her charges as personal friends. In practice, the superiority ascribed to the volunteer visitor could not be reconciled with the desire to draw rich and poor together as neighbors. Charity organization was the creation of middle class Protestant Americans, denouncing rigid sectarianism in charitable affairs but inspired by an evangelical sense of mission. Immigrants and workers were not conspicuous as visitors, paid officials, or directors. In a sense, charity organization was more a closing of the ranks against a common threat than a cooperative, equalitarian association of disparate economic and ethnic groups.[15]

For those at the top end of the class ladder, charity afforded a means of doing good work, yet this selfish opportunity conflicted with the mythology that charity was a selfless act. Finally, a considerable segment of the charitable believed, as reported earlier, that they had to dispense alms carefully and only to the truly worthy or else risk promoting mendicancy. Another group, which included those who recommended cautious relief, feared that a failure to give alms would set off a destructive process, whereby the poor and downtrodden would infect the rest of society with their heinous condition: "if we do not furnish the poor with elevating influences, they will rule us by degrading ones."[16]

The institution of charity never found a way to resolve those internal conflicts. However, charitable workers, later to be called social workers and counselors, were to some extent able to escape the obvious contradiction of the early charitable role by turning to a "scientific case approach." In other words, the early twentieth century brought with it a new model of service, one more nearly professional in character. We will discuss the nature and consequences of this new model in the next section. But first, let us explore the present day legacy of the early charitable model of public assistance. Far from shedding the institution of charity, contemporary society still entertains the charity model of social service to a remarkable extent. Moreover, today's form of charity poses many of the same problems now that its predecessor did a century ago.

Despite the enormous post-World War II growth in public services, the activity of private charities has not diminished. If anything, charity's importance as a financial and social institution has expanded exponentially. Donations have risen more than 300 percent since 1961 when the annual total was 9.4 billion dollars. Nobody knows the exact number of charities—estimates range from 500,000 to 6 million (depending on the expansiveness of one's definition of charity) and include birth control clinics, colleges and universities, churches, neighborhood youth centers, junior leagues, symphonies, and "senior citizen" organizations. One hundred and fifty-nine billion dollars accrued to charities during the sixties. By 1975, annual proceeds totalled 27 billion dollars, and in 1979, charitable organizations received 39 billion dollars in contributions.[17] Americans now give over eighty million dollars per day to charity. Forty-three percent of this amount goes to religious organizations, 15% to education, 8% to civic and cultural groups, 9% to welfare, 16% to health, and 9% to other organizations. Individuals, not corporations, unions, or other organized units account for the bulk (86.5 percent) of charitable contributions.

The dollar amount involved in charity may actually be twice the thirty-nine billion dollar figure if one calculates the dollar worth of the millions of hours expended by volunteers. There is another way that charitable organizations account for a greater money flow than the total of their receipts—they and their beneficiaries enter the credit market. Vincent Fulmer, writing for *Harvard Business Review,* explains:

> Like it or not, in good times and bad our educational and charitable institutions live to a surprising degree on credit. They borrow and beg for money to accomplish their purposes. But they are by no means alone in their financial life style; the society that supports them lives blithely on credit. And to a surprising degree it gives on credit.[18]

A whole host of businesses have emerged to service the thirty-nine billion dollar charity industry. There are banks that provide loans to charitable fundraising programs as well as suppliers of canisters, posters, mailing lists, mailing services, candy, and other charity-related paraphernalia. Their earnings constitute profit for the private sector, but they are wholly or in part dependent upon the welfare of charity.

Some analysts have criticized the high administrative costs of charity—certain "charities" spend more than half their budgets on the costs of fundraising. Duplication of effort and even fraud sometimes occur.[19] Charity's toughest critics raise other questions, many of which rehash the same themes levied against turn-of-the-century charitable organizations.

Charities still find an apparent need to distinguish the worthy from the unworthy:

> Time has chipped away at Mrs. N's world and now, sitting alone and motionless before her living-room window, the 81-year-old widow fears that the last piece of the life she once led—the home that is her own—will also disappear.
>
> Mrs. N. retains the sparkling green eyes and smooth, feminine voice of her youth, and she can vividly recount the past without sign of tears. But her legs now barely support her on a journey from one room to the next, and the body that was once so agile is racked by heart disease, diabetes and continual aches and pains. . . .
>
> Mrs. N. was always an energetic woman: She went to work in a candy factory at 14, learning a craft that helped support her and her family for nearly half a century. She married young and with her husband, a truck driver, raised three sons—"good boys, not professional types, but hard workers."
>
> Time wore away at her life slowly. Mr. N. died 28 years ago, a few years before she was forced to retire, and her oldest son died of cancer 10 years ago. . . .
>
> "I was worried about my health and my house was a mess," she said, "I've never, never let my house get dirty. But what was I going to do? I had no one to help me. I was depressed, but picture how bad I would have felt if I couldn't live in my own home."[20]

Modern-day charities combine the disparate themes of hope (Easter Seals tells us: "be a miracle worker, give") and despair (Jerry Lewis declares that "his" kids will die of muscular dystrophy; the Diabetes Foundation informs us that diabetes is the number three killer). The public is also asked to help those with nonfatal conditions to help them live a "normal" life. We are shown their wheelchairs, leg braces, medical equipment (dialysis machines, injections for diabetes) so that no doubt exists about their involuntary differentness—this connotes their "worthiness" as recipients.

These portrayals of dependent, needy, worthy recipients bring a steady stream of criticism. On the matter of dependency, Judith Chamberlain, author of *On Our Own* and founder of the Boston-based Mental Patients Liberation Front, finds that charity campaigns portray "a person with one need as being totally needy."[21] Similarly, the parents of a child with hemophilia, a condition that can lead to frequent internal bleeding of the joints, particularly during a child's growth, complained about the dependence that charity encourages. Like other families with children who have hemophilia, they found themselves battling to locate money and blood donations to meet their child's expensive need for transfusions. They resented their own powerlessness and their sense of having no right to such a basic commodity, blood.

> The problem was having to be grateful. Before the first blood drive, the newspaper had declared: "The Massies are wholly dependent on blood donations from friends, neighbors, and the generosity of the community-at-large." It was true and we hated it. Nobody likes to be wholly dependent. Nobody likes to beg for charity. . . . It destroys pride and independence. The people in our society who proclaim in booming voices that private charity is the answer to preserving pride and independence are always the donors, never the recipients.[22]

The Massies' words echoed an implication of one of this culture's most familiar refrains, "I'm not a charity case."

Charity has always afforded the rich and important a means of "doing good." Father James O. S. Huntington, writing in the 1890s, saw the irony in this fact:

> Modern philanthropy fails to minister to the moral life of its beneficiaries . . . the charities of the rich are an insurance which they pay for the security of their possessions and the continuance of their gains . . . I do not mean to say that many people actually sit down to figure the thing out; but there is . . . "a soothing of their conscience and a coloring of their fears" in knowing, or having reason to believe that the poor are not quite starving.[23]

Today, politicians, popes, kings and queens, and corporations alike find charity useful to their public images. As one corporate executive has noted, charity offers "a means of regaining some respect that business has been losing recently."[24] Similarly, another top executive admitted the possible imbalance, as far as his corporation was concerned, between self-interest and service: "We feel that our gifts are helping to improve society . . . yet it's still all largely a matter of public relations."[25] When business gives its merchandise or services to people with disabilities, its generosity is rewarded by a feature newspaper photo of the gift-giving event with the familiar headline: "Aid to handicapped gives hope and cheer." In the case of a sponsored outing for poor children, the headline might read, "they had the time of their lives.'' When politicians campaign for office they invariably arrange to be seen helping or greeting the usual recipients of charity, particularly those perceived most worthy, especially older people, orphaned children, and people with disabilities. It is what one might call charity for the profit of the benefactor.

On the surface at least, charities would seem not to impede social change, because of how they respond to human suffering. They treat symptoms, not possible causes. They blame fate (bad luck), not social forces, for the human condition. Moreover, charity and fundraising tends to exaggerate the recipients' downtrodden and dependent status. However, charity's antichange stance is of an even more fundamental character. Large charities resist social change using policies that reflect the particular interests of those who dominate these organizations. When one United Way executive, for example, was asked why his organization did not fund more women's organizations, he replied:

> The only way you're going to raise money in a community like this is to have participation by top corporate executives—and not too many of them are women. I'm not sure that any of us know whether it is right for us to fund a program that is only for women. The whole issue of daycare, for instance, is one that still needs to be looked at in this community. I've always been leery that daycare could be used as a tool to make women work.[26]

On the topic of social change he remarked, ''I'm not sure United Way should be supportive of advocate programs. We are a political beast. If we fund a whole range of risky organizations, that will hurt our fundraising. United Way is striving to be representative of the whole community.''[27] By the whole community, he means the mainstream or, even more accurately, the business and government community, not poor people, not poor or even middle-class women, not those who raise strong questions about current patterns of service and nonservice, and not those who engage in controversial activities such as advocating abortion clinics and environmental causes.

In North and South Carolina, Brown Lung disease is ''controversial.'' United Way has refused to fund it.[28] The Carolina Brown Lung Association is comprised largely of textile workers and others concerned with this health condition which is attributable to working conditions in textile factories. Not coincidentally, United Way agencies in the Carolinas include representation by business executives associated with the textile industry. Giving attention to brown lung disease does not suit their self-interest. Some foundations do fund liberal causes—poverty law centers and environmental change groups for example. In general, though, charities are sensitive to the self-interest of their benefactors. Wealthy benefactors generally do not advocate social change that might upset their business interests. Robert Coles, in his book *The Privileged Ones* (Volume V of *Children of Crisis*) talks about charity and interests. He presents the case of a West Virginia mine operator:

> Her father strongly believes in private charities, as opposed to government sponsored welfare programs of various kinds. He proudly tells his wife and children that he tithes himself, as his father and grandfather did before him: 10 percent of his gross income

goes to assorted causes—the Presbyterian Church, the United Fund, a program directed at "problem children." After the mine disaster, Marjorie (his daughter) wondered out loud at the supper table whether her parents would be sending any money to the survivors of the men killed. She was told the answer immediately and abruptly: no.[29]

For the mine owner, though perhaps not to his daughter, it was obvious that miners and miners' families could not be given charity. They, after all, were not the usual, grateful alms takers. They made too many demands. They wanted too much change, too fast. They didn't accept things as they found them—at least that is how the mine owner saw it.

As long as alms takers are considered tragic victims of fate, to give them alms, and not social change, makes good sense. Helen Keller understood this well. Having overcome the handicaps of her own disabilities, she too was expected to assume the charitable role. But she chose another course:

> So long as I confine my activities to social service and the blind, they (the newspapers) compliment me extravagantly, calling me "archpriest of the sightless," "wonder woman" and "a modern miracle." But when it comes to a discussion of poverty, and I maintain that it is the result of wrong economics—that the industrial system under which we live is at the root of much of the physical deafness and blindness in the world—that is a different matter. It is laudable to give aid to the handicapped. Superficial charities make smooth the way of the prosperous; but to advocate that all human beings should have leisure and comfort, the decencies and refinements of life, is an Utopian dream, and one who seriously contemplates its realization must indeed be deaf, dumb, and blind.[30]

The dilemma, of course, is that even if the charities wanted to become more oriented towards social change, many of them believe, whether falsely or not, that fundraising depends upon appealing to people's feelings of guilt and pity. Since it is generally believed that people feel more sorry for children than adults, for example, some foundations falsely imply that their primary beneficiaries are children. This may explain why the Arthritis Foundation pays so much attention to the relatively rare condition of childhood arthritis. Two-thirds of all blind people are adults, many of them elderly, yet charity appeals frequently feature blind children. Diabetes affects older people far more frequently than younger people, yet young people are most frequently shown in fund appeals for the condition. If charities did choose an alternative approach, we must ask, "Who would contribute to a campaign which spoke of the competence and dignity of disabled people, of poor people, of older people?" and "Who would give to a cause on behalf of people who have been exploited by rent gouging or illegally dumped and poisonous industrial waste?" To be sure, some people would give to such causes and campaigns to remedy the social practices which create them. However, the recent history of charity fundraising suggests the greater saleability of pathos, pity, and dependence.

The present system of charity, in which pity and guilt are combined with high-powered hucksterism—a recent muscular dystrophy telethon was billed as "The

Greatest Show on Earth''—stands on precarious financial ground. Potential problems, such as hard economic times, poor fundraising strategies, failure to elicit enough pity, competition with more popular causes, inability to attract a top movie star sponsor can spell the end of human service programs funded by charity. They would then become available only as a privilege and not as a right. The tragic consequences of this reality can manifest themselves in families unable to pay a heating or phone bill; in children at home bleeding internally for hours, even days, because their parents cannot afford more blood or ''clotting factor''. Adults remain untrained for work and unemployed because funds are unavailable; elderly people go hungry because the homemaker services they need have been unsupported. As television commentator Phil Donahue has written, ''We don't have telethons or bike-a-thons or walk-a-thons for highways or airports; why must we resort to this loosely organized and often unsuccessful Roman circus to raise funds for our children?''[31]

The practice of funding programs by charity obviously militates against social planning. Charities for older people, people with asthma, muscular dystrophy, heart disease, cancer, mental retardation, and poor children, along with many others each compete for funds. Even so-called one-stop charities, like United Way (''Thanks to You It Works for All of Us'') compete with other charities who are not covered in the one-stop approach. While United Way officials were holding their 1979 convention in Dallas, Texas, a group of officals for 70 other charitable associations met just eight blocks away to map strategies to break up what they regarded as a United Way monopoly.[32] In Los Angeles a group called Associated In-group Donors accused the United Way of practicing restraint of trade.[33] The National Black United Fund filed suit in Washington, DC against the Civil Service Commission charging United Way and the Federal Government with violating federal antitrust laws.[34] The criticism was that United Way captured the market on payroll deductions—an effective, if sometimes intimidating fundraising technique in which business and government leaders ''allow'' their employees to tithe themselves for United Way.

The success of any given charity often depends on the appeal of a movie star, the ingenuity of a television ad, or the impact of a new fundraising gimmick. The Muscular Dystrophy Association is one of the nation's most successful fundraising operations, but the condition of muscular dystrophy affects less than 200,000 Americans. Research into the cause of muscular dystrophy is generally considered as one of the most complex in medical research and an area of research least likely to yield a breakthrough. That research is important, certainly desperately important, to the families of children who have or will contract the condition. But how do the needs posed by this condition compare to other needs in other areas and how will the competition for finite social resources be resolved? Will it be resolved by waiting to see which charity creates the most ingenious and successful fundraising gimmickery? Or by waiting to see which charity the top movie stars and sports figures will adopt as their own?

In the competitive world of charity, planning, particularly national planning, has no place. Even when United Way and the other conglomerates engage in fundraising, they fund programs in accordance with particular local political pressures. They call their work process planning, but few of their activities can truly be called social planning. Major needs of people are not assembled and analyzed. Spending plans of charities do not affect the causes of social conditions. There are no planners at the national level to assess whether one disease or condition has a greater likelihood for breakthrough treatment or rehabilitation than another. Despite the formidable size of charity nationally, it is by nature ad hoc and antiplanning.

Finally, charities organized for particular causes like cerebral palsy, blindness, older people, homeless children, or the hungry people of the world, tend to promote services which are, in William Ryan's terms, "exceptionalistic."[35] Such services, including special schools, centers, and social programs, are designed to meet the special needs of certain people who have, in effect, been driven out of or excluded from generic or mainstream services and settings in our society. These segregated services for "special" (a euphemism for surplus) groups are justified on numerous grounds such as the difficulty of changing the system or perceived gaps in the service system. Future fundraising is made easier when special services are highly visible. The cost effectiveness (in relation to money raised) of bringing specialists and special populations together also serves to propagate special programs. Interestingly, there is no research to support the segregation of such groups on an educational, therapeutic, rehabilitative, or any other basis. Moreover, separate services have never proven more cost effective. In fact, there is an inverse relationship between most segregated services and cost effectiveness. Ironically, when charities, and eventually the government create separate, "special" programs for excluded or surplus groups, they in effect perpetuate the mainstream systems' failure to provide services to those very same groups. Their actions have much the same result as those of Anglo-Saxon, protestant friendly visitors who spoke of friendship and equality for newly settled Italian immigrants. However, their actions created a social barrier so that immigrants had little or no access to mainstream social institutions.

On balance, charity, both in its historic and present-day form, has failed to achieve the ends espoused in its noblest ideals—relief with dignity, greater independence, and equality. While no one would deny that charity has relieved immediate human suffering, few would contend that it has altered the structural social conditions which cause human suffering. Moreover, despite a general agreement among scholars of early charitable activities that the charity model of service had obvious drawbacks (for example, elitism, moral domination, and social control) social critics have generally ignored the fact that the charity model's failings are still very much present today. Clearly, as long as those concerned with improving the human condition, with promoting equality, and with facilitating integration of disparate segments in society fail to recognize that the legacy of charity survives in modern day forms, they cannot possibly hope to escape its pitfalls. Rather, we must ask, knowing the past and present failures of charity, are there alternative approaches to social change? Is there any aspect of the charitable model worth salvaging (see the discussion of the organizers' role in the third section of this chapter)?

WHAT'S WRONG WITH PROFESSIONALISM?

Apart from charity, the other dominant route toward improving the human condition has been professionalism. As a social paradigm, professionalism enjoys a far greater reach today than does charity. Indeed, as noted earlier, many of the original American charitable activities (friendly visiting, establishment of neighborhood centers) evolved into professionalism. However, charity work was but a small thread in the unfolding fabric of professionalism. Where pity, magnanimity, almsgiving, and evangelism had failed, professionalism was supposed to succeed. Armed with the tool of the scientific method, professionalism promised careful analysis of the human condition, medical advances, a refined and fair legal system, and efficiently run industries. Like charity, professionalism promised greater social equality, more democracy, and an improved quality of life for all. And, like charity, professionalism sometimes achieved the opposite of its original intent.

One of the first, formal definitions of professionalism came from Abraham Flexner, author of the now famous "Flexner Report" which historians generally regard as having had a summative if not revolutionalizing (that is, professionalizing) effect on American medicine.[36] To quote one medical historian:

> He "pulled no punches" and revealed conditions no longer tolerable (in medicine) in the present century. (The report) was dramatic, and perhaps exaggerated at some points, but its author and backers (Foundation for the Advancement of Teaching) could not be accused—as a medical group might have been—of seeking selfish ends. The press took it up immediately and public opinion was aroused. State legislatures and licensing boards also responded and brought pressure to bear on medical schools to meet standards laid down in the foundation report. The outcome seemed miraculous to those not familiar with the efforts (to promote professionalism) which had finally led up to the survey.[37]

Flexner quickly won the reputation as an expert on professionalism. In a speech given before The National Conference of Charities and Corrections he outlined his criteria for professionalism.[38] First, professionals are people who engage in their chosen occupations full-time and they are thus distinguished from amateurs. Also, they are people who possess expert training as evidenced by academic degrees. But, he argued, there must be more, considerably more. The term "professional" was, in his mind, a highly prized appellation deserving careful protection:

> If there is a dancing profession, a baseball profession, an acting profession, a nursing profession, a musical profession, a literary profession, a medical profession, and a legal profession . . . (then) the term profession is too vague to be fought for. We may

as well let down the bars and permit people to call themselves professional, for no better reason than that they choose in this way to appropriate whatever of social distinction may still cling to a term obviously abused.[39]

Not surprisingly, Flexner, a champion of professionalism, proposed a tight, rigorous, even exclusionary definition. Professionals must possess more than a degree. In order to "extract the criteria" of professionalism, he decided to examine the already established professions. Historically, these included medicine, law, and preaching. First, he argued, professional activities are "essentially intellectual in character." While true professions—here he cited doctors and engineers—might engage in and use instruments associated with manual labor, the professional enterprise required above all "the thinking process." Indeed, the rise of professionalism in the latter quarter of the 19th century followed the belief that science and the scientific method—the latter was synonymous with intellectual activity—would free the individual to analyze *and* solve troubling problems. Flexner embraced this view in its entirety: "A free, resourceful, and unhampered intelligence applied to problems and seeking to understand and master theory—that is, in the first instance characteristic of a profession."[40]

Second, Flexner's professionalism simultaneously required enormous autonomy and responsibility. Because intelligence guided professionals in their analysis of problems, they were expected to exercise personal discretion in determining their actions (solutions). The professional could not hide beneath the oft-heard complaint of bureaucratic functionaries or technicians, "I was just following orders, just doing my job." By accepting intellectual freedom, the professional assumed responsibility, and therefore, risk. Autonomy had its price.

Third, professionals were expected to know things others did not know. They were supposed to keep a foot in the laboratory, an eye on appropriate journals, and the mind continually involved in the creative process. The professional who failed to regard the professional role as an ongoing process of experimentation and learning would quickly slip into degeneracy and thus beyond the boundaries of professionalism. Flexner felt that to be learned was so much a part of being professional that to call a professional learned was to be foolishly redundant.

Fourth, in addition to being intellectual, autonomous, responsible, and learned, the professional was to balance these attributes with practicality. Ultimately, the professional should act in a clear-cut, concrete way. It was the professional's duty to transform knowledge and theory into practice. Physicians study anatomy, physiology, and pharmacology in order to restore health. Architects study physics, mathematics, and design theory in order to design buildings. University professors study ideas so that they may engage in the practical undertaking of teaching.

Fifth, a profession possessed a distinct body of facts, hypotheses, and theories which were easily communicated through formalized education and apprentice programs. Flexner believed that professionals in a particular field could responsibly determine the nature of a curriculum, the length of training, and tests of competence. In deciding upon these standards, professionals tend, as Flexner puts it, "to self-organize.'' Thus, professionalism offered its members at once a brotherhood, "a caste," and a democratic institution. Because professional work is intrinsically interesting, even fascinating, "the social and personal lives of professional men [Flexner left out women] and of their families . . . tend to organize around a professional nucleus," a brotherhood.[41] "A strong class consciousness soon develops." And "though externally somewhat aristocratic in form, professions are, properly taken, highly democratic institutions."[42] They were democratic presumably because anyone with the requisite intellectual abilities could pass through the matriculation and skill test requirements. Noticeably absent from literature on professionalism was any mention of the barriers to Blacks, native Americans, and certain recent immigrants to the settings of professional socialization.

Sixth, and finally, Flexner included among professionalism's attributes altruism. How could one justify learning, responsibility, risk, intellectual creativity, and action if it were not directed toward the public interest. Flexner, like his contemporaries (Addams, Richmond, Frankfurter, and Brandeis) rejected the selfish ideology of social darwinism in favor of progressive politics. He believed in the perfectability of the human condition. He believed further that "on the whole" professional groups, more so than individuals, would respond to the body politic's needs. That is to say,

> under the pressure of public opinion, professional groups have more and more *tended* to view themselves as organs contrived for the achievement of social ends rather than as bodies formed to stand together for the assertion of rights or the protection of interests and principles. I do not wish to be understood as saying that this development is as yet by any means complete. Such is far from being the case. Organizations of teachers, doctors, and lawyers are still apt to look out, first of all, for "number one." But as time goes on it may very well come to be a mark of professional character that professional organization is explicitly and admittedly meant for the advancement of the common social interest through the professional organization. Devotion to well doing is thus more and more likely to become an accepted mark of professional activity; and . . . the pecuniary interest . . . is apt to yield . . . [43]

Modern theorists of professionalism diverge only slightly from Flexner's overall formulation of professionalism. Current definitions literally match the one Flexner presented. Where they diverge is in their evaluation of professionalism's worth.[44] Is professionalism genuinely intellectual or merely pretending to be so? Do professionals deserve nearly unbridled discretion, or have they sought autonomy without risk? Do educational hurdles and competency criteria protect the public or the self-interest of the few who have already achieved professional status? Are professions natural collegial associations or exclusionary castes which represent particular class interests? Finally, have the professions delivered on their promise to keep the public interest foremost among their objectives or have they instead concerned themselves more with "looking out for number one?"

Sociologists of the mid-and late twentieth century see most of the same characteristics that Flexner saw in professionalism, but with a far more skeptical eye.[45] Noted social historian Christopher Lasch explains the difference between modern day critics and progressive era intellectuals, not in terms of the hindsight advantage so obviously available to recent critics, but to the starry-eyed, defensive, and uncritical approach of the progressives. Even the most intellectual of the progressives, especially Jane Addams, were to a surprising extent uncritical of professionalism. Lasch believes this attitude reflected their hope, so apparent in Flexner's outlook, that science would save society's outcasts and downtrodden:

> Estrangement of intellectuals, as a class, from the dominant values of American culture [presumably he means materialism] . . . accounted for what seems to me the chief weakness of the new radicalism, its distrust not only of middle-class culture but of intellect itself. Detachment carried with it a certain defensiveness about the position of intellect [and intellectuals] in American life; and it was this defensiveness, I think, which sometimes prompted intellectuals to forsake the role of criticism and to identify themselves with what they imagined to be the laws of historical necessity and the working out of the popular will.[46]

Of course, it is equally plausible that progressives embraced scientific (that is, professional) determinism for "the public good" in part as an overreaction to the crass determinism of social darwinism. In other words, they rejected "survival of the fittest" darwinian determinism.

More recent analysts of professionalism do not share the progressives uncritical outlook.* On the surface, professionalism had not changed:

> A profession delivers esoteric services—advice or action or both. The action may be manual . . . , (yet) it need not be . . . Even when manual, the action—it is *assumed* or *claimed*—is determined by esoteric knowledge systematically formulated and applied to problems of a client.[47]

Note Hughes' introduction of the words "assumed" and "claimed." Neither he nor his colleagues of the mid and late twentieth century any longer regard professionalism's qualities as necessarily true or justified. Indeed, in varying degrees, sociologists and social historians of professionalism have come to see professionalism as potentially, if not actually, antidemocratic.

Professionals "profess to know better than others the nature of certain matters, and to know better than their clients what ails them or their affairs."[48] In essence, professionals are in the business of identifying particular areas of study and practice which they can monopolize. They develop methods for understanding a speciality area. In addition, "since the professional does profess, he asks that he be trusted. The client is not a true judge of the value of the service he receives."[49] Wilensky believes that professionalism tends to render the public dependent: "the theoretical aspects of professional knowledge and the tacit elements in both intellectual and practical knowing combine to make long training necessary and to persuade

---

*At the practical or service level, the ideology of Flexner persists nearly in its original form, but with significant modifications to recognize new consciousness about racism, sexism, and other political biases of service providers and to heighten the professional's moral responsibility to the public. The Code of Ethics of the National Association of Social Workers adopted in 1979 and implemented July 1, 1980.

the public of the mystery of the craft."[50] The public, of course, plays an important role in legitimizing a profession. The public must believe, for example, the field or specialty to be sufficiently broad so as to require intellectual creativity. If too narrow, the field could presumably be reduced to a series of easily routinized, technical (as opposed to scientific or intellectual) steps. If too broad and, therefore vague, the public might regard the specialty as being no specialty at all. Hence a particular field needs to project a seemingly self-contradictory image of broad specialization. Optometrists and dentists may have lower professional status than medical doctors because the former's tasks can be conceived of as too mechanical. By the same token, school teaching may seem overly broad, not specialized enough. Without public credibility, a professor cannot achieve "the exclusive jurisdiction necessary to professional authority."[51]

Certain specialties deserve true intellectual and scientific inquiry. Most overstate their reliance on science. Critics of professionalism realize that there is no vocation entirely void of serious inquiry and so do not criticize the concept of professionalism per se. Rather, they have questioned its glorification. They ask, for instance, "how much of a field's knowledge is legitimately esoteric? How much is made unnecessarily esoteric by virtue of the particular profession's use of jargon and other symbols of scientific inquiry?", and "How much is manufactured mystique and how much is truly scientific inquiry?" The critics find that because professionalism offers remarkable status and financial reward, certain groups aspire to create a mystique of science where science has only the most questionable validity.

By the late 1800s, nearly everyone wanted to be a professional. Nurses, educators, civil servants and politicians, business people, social workers, all coveted professional identification. Professional associations sprang up with incredible alacrity and included librarians, pharmacists, city planners, and funeral directors. They all had professional associations and considered themselves professionals before the twentieth century.[52] Even those with relatively unusual vocations like detective work sought to demonstrate special, esoteric expertise and, therefore, professionalism. Bledstein quotes Pinkerton:

> The spectacle of so vast a country as ours being even for a short time palsied, its local authorities paralyzed, its State governments powerless, and its general government almost defied, was so sudden, so universal, and so appalling, that the best judgment of our best minds were found unequal to cope with so startling and extreme an emergency.
>
>   Only the professional detective in plain clothes, infiltrating the "entire school of crime" by means of his own "quick conceptions and ready subterfuges," his own "superior intelligence" and "high moral character," could protect the constantly threatened client. "His calling," Pinkerton said of the detective, "has become a profession. . . . Few professions excel it."[53]

If professionals controlled the knowledge of literally hundreds of fields and specialties, in what position did that leave consumers? Unfortunately, it left them decidedly more dependent than before. The same professionalism which promised a new era of democracy by rationalizing politics (and rejecting spoils), which guaranteed the latest scientific medical care by throwing out medical quackery, actually disenfranchised the average citizen politically and created a health care system best characterized as a medical monopoly for doctors. Recent research shows that the American Medical Association used reform of medical education as a way to limit the number of doctors and to drastically improve the financial position of doctors (Markowitz and Rosner, 1973). Similarly, if city planning were to become a rational, even scientific process, would it not be taken out of the hands of the general populace? If assistance programs for families were to become an enterprise dominated by social theorists and "established" methods, would it not limit the involvement of volunteers in all but the most functionary levels? (for example, door-to-door solicitations, envelope stuffing, phone answering).[54] If education were to become professionalized, would it not have the effect of limiting the public's involvement in designing the content of education? Indeed, these were some of the antidemocratic effects of the professedly democratic professional reforms. Increasingly, social phenomena like poverty, child rearing, education, delinquency, and care of people with disabilities, were taken out of the hands of people in communities and neighborhoods. The emerging professions literally institutionalized these problems. Katz put it thusly:

> By the last quarter of the nineteenth century, specialized institutions were dealing with crime, poverty, disease, mental illness, juvenile delinquency, the blind, the deaf and dumb, and the ignorant. . . .
> [Today] we accept institutions and experts as inevitable, almost eternal. That, after all, is the way the world works. It is hard—almost impossible—for us to recall that they are modern inventions.[55]

The more professionals controlled particular service settings like hospitals and schools, the less involvement the public was allowed.

Even so public (in the sense that it affects everyone) an issue as sex was presumed by professionals to be their property. Some doctors claimed medical grounds for urging great moderation in sexual intercourse. In his infamous book *Functions and Disorders,* William Acton wrote, "the best mothers, wives and managers of households know little or nothing of sexual indulgence. Love of home, children, and domestic duties are the only passions they feel."[56] Similarly, Dr. John Kellogg, in his popular book, *Plain Facts for Old and Young* (1910), wrote, "it would appear that the opportunity for sensual gratification has come to be, in the world at large, the chief attraction between the sexes."[57] According to Degler, Kellogg recommended that people "should take their cue from animals, who have intercourse only for procreation and then at widely spaced intervals."[58] Obviously, these medical professionals merely mask their own moral views in the garb of scientific expertise. This became a common problem with all professionalism. Through the expansion of professionalism, everyday beliefs and prejudices took on new legitimacy and even authority.

The professionalization and ultimately the bureaucratization of government provides perhaps the best evidence of how professionalism diminishes the public's power and promotes the public's dependence. The "good government" movement promised to limit political patronage and inhibit the potentially destructive effects of a particular elite interest or power group while in office. While it may well have accomplished that goal, it also confirmed the public's marginal role in political decision making. Habermas has called this a transformation to "the technocratic model of scientized politics":

> The reduction of political power to rational administration can be conceived here only at the expense of democracy itself. If politicians were strictly subjected to objective necessity [presumably by technocratic managers], a politically functioning public could at best legitimate the administrative personnel and judge the professional qualifications of salaried officials.[59]

In other words, the public would be allowed to pass only on qualification of decision makers, not the decisions themselves. If the technocratic managers possessed adequate or standard credentials, then it would matter little which elite (political) group gained power.

This technicism, earlier called rationalism by Weber, literally took over in America. To recall Katz' finding, one could hardly imagine any other model for considering the human social condition. As Talcott Parsons put it:

> Rationality in this sense is institutional, a part of a normative pattern: it is not a mode of orientation which is simply "natural" to men. On the contrary comparative study indicates that the present degree of valuation of rationality as opposed to traditionalism is rather "unnatural" in the *sense* that it is a highly exceptional state. The fact is that we are under continual and subtle social pressures to be rationally critical, particularly of ways and means. The crushing force to us of such epithets as "stupid" and "gullible" is almost sufficient indication of this. The importance of rationality in the modern professions generally, but particularly in those important ones concerned with the development and application of science serves to emphasize its role in the society at large.[60]

Professionalism is presently dominant. This would probably cause no problem were it not for the fact that much, even most of what passes for rational or professional thought and practice at any given time in nearly every field is by definition not natural truth but rather interpretation, perspective, and even ideology put forth in the name of rational science. This fact, combined with professionalism's exclusionary attitude toward the great majority of society means that professionalism, at least if embraced uncritically, inevitably promotes particular ideas and beliefs in an antidemocratic manner.

The other major problem with professionalism, or the rationalization of society, is that while it began as radical reform—participants and critics alike have termed it progressive, liberal, even radical—its institutionalization dampened forces of change. The move to license professions was intended to protect the public. Yet, as we noted, the movement forced the public to accept veritable service monopolies, usually by design of the American Medical Association, the American Bar Association, or other similar professional associations.[61] Standardized curricula in training as well as accreditation reviews undoubtedly closed off innovation and experimentation at the margins of the emerging fields.[62] Technicism and the importance of so-called standard methods for research and practice controlled but also limited knowledge and theory. Individuals entering a professional field needed not only to learn new subject areas, but also to be socialized to their fields.[63] Virtually every prospective professional experiences the dissonance between his or her image of the profession—this is basically the public's beliefs about a profession—and the professional role itself. The two dominant responses to this dissonance are: (1) to quit, in other words change fields; or (2) to become socialized to the tasks of the profession and to project to the public the profession's image. Day to day activities of insiders rarely approximate the public's image of them. Hence the conservative demand on new recruits. Socialization to the role requires that professional participants accept the given role. In effect, enlistees in a profession learn to accept it, *not* change it.

Once initiated, professional ethics usually call on professionals to keep their complaints with individual performance and social policy inside the profession. The National Association of Social Workers' code of ethics, noted earlier, warns, "treat with respect the findings, views, and actions of colleagues and use appropriate channels to express judgment on these matters."[64] In this context, significant dissent from standard belief and practice might easily bring forth charges of unprofessionalism. To call someone unprofessional is to suggest that he or she does not belong in the profession. It is tantamount to demanding one's excommunication.

Perhaps one of the most telling signs of professional reform's conservatism has been its effect on Blacks and women. For both groups, reform meant fewer opportunities to become professionals. From 1880 to 1904, women received 4.3 percent of all M.D. degrees earned. By 1912 that percentage dropped to 3.2 percent.[65] At the same time, women's access to so-called lay medical work ended. Women midwives were, in the age of reform, replaced by doctors of obstetrics who had "a complete medical education."[66] The same fate came crashing down on aspiring Black physicians. Between 1890 and 1910, the number of Black physicians increased "from 909 to 3409; thereafter the flow stemmed."[67] As Stevens has noted, a "serious and long-term result of standardization (the essence of professionalization) was the closure of schools for Black physicians."[68] There were eight such schools in 1900. Four closed by 1914. Another closed in 1915, and a sixth shut its doors in 1923. Of the original eight, only Howard Medical School in Washington, D.C. and Meharry Medical College in Nashville, Tennessee remained. Moreover, Black students were systematically discriminated against by white schools. Stevens notes that as late as 1947, only 93 Black students were in attendance at white medical schools. Clearly, reform had a decidedly bad effect on women, Blacks, and, it almost goes without saying, on the poor.

Even in pursuing altruism, service, and the public good, professionalism encountered problems. That is not to say that reformers failed to reform, that educators failed to educate, that social workers failed to mediate family destruction, that doctors failed to treat sick people, or that lawyers failed to represent individual clients. The difficulty was in the ever-present, enormous conflict between what Flexner called the professionals' pecuniary interest and their altruism. Plainly speaking, poor people and minorities rarely received the same medical attention as the middle class and wealthy. Reformers hoped that the inherent conflict between capitalism and provision of service could be solved or ameliorated with government subsidies and entitlement programs such as aid to dependent children or medicaid. Nevertheless, the basic conservatism of professionalism is still with us. In part this is explained by the tendency of each profession to individualize problems. Medical professionals treat individual pathology. They are far less likely to investigate and treat a possible social cause such as dangerous industrial equipment. Lawyers represent individuals and their research focuses on individual factual circumstances. Until quite recently, the law was not a tool for social reform and even now it is only used by lawyers and organizers. Even today, so-called strict constructionism, and narrow case-by-case application of the law prevails as the dominant model of the legal profession. Likewise, professionalization of education has meant greater and greater individualization. This view of education has proven so dominant that some scholars (for example, Jensen, Schockley, Hernnstein) have had difficulty recognizing the full force of the social environment on whole classes of children.

Social work is a case in point. Here we can see how the "scientific method" had an overall conservative effect. In 1917, Mary Richmond published her now famous treatise, *Social Diagnosis.*[69] She provided social work with a method similar to those available in "justice (law), healing (medicine), and teaching (education)." Social diagnosis involved three stages: (1) collection of evidence from the client, the client's family, and "sources of insight outside the family group," (2) "comparing the evidence gathered from these various sources (inference)," and (3) interpreting its meaning (diagnosis). In her book, Mary Richmond argued for the unique nature of social work, defined numerous kinds of evidence, described a process for making inferences, and demonstrated the process of making diagnoses. She provided extensive, detailed interview schedules and practical investigatory techniques. Her book declared social work's science and therefore its professionalism.

While Mary Richmond spoke of the importance of social reform wedded to individual case work, her model, which became the dominant one for social work practice, mirrored the pattern of law, education, and medicine. It focused on the individual. She herself fought for better child labor laws, improved conditions in custodial institutions, and improved public sanitation. Each of these conditions affected individual cases. However, she did not support mass social legislation— indeed she was often at odds with social activists—like public relief and old age pensions because these, she felt, would harm the family unit and supercede the individual case approach which she had outlined in *Social Diagnosis.*[70] Thus, much as the charity model had done, the professional model narrowed its participants' social vision. Despite a rhetoric of *social* reform, the social diagnosis model encouraged social workers away from systemic reforms toward individual therapy and individual adjustment.

HOW IS COMMUNITY ORGANIZATION SIMILAR TO AND DIFFERENT FROM CHARITY AND PROFESSIONALISM?

When organizers become *professional* organizers, they stop organizing. They become professionals. Experiences within the American labor movement verify that fact. Who is more of an organizer, United Farm Worker Cesar Chavez or Teamster leader Frank Fitzsimmons? The person who created the national lettuce boycott, led hunger strikes, and farm laborer walkouts, or the man whose union has become a business enterprise? Even so formidable a labor leader as Samuel Gompers traded the role of organizer for that of professional leader.[57] At one point in his career he told his union members to give him complete authority for negotiations. Saul Alinsky recounted the problems of educating union organizers to become *community* organizers and thus showed how unions themselves had changed:

> Their experience was tied to a pattern of fixed points, . . . demands on wages, pensions, vacation periods . . . (between one contract and another one dealt mainly with grievance meetings over contract violations). Mass organization is a different animal, it is not housebroken. There are not fixed chronological points or definite issues.
> When labor leaders have talked about organizing the poor, their talk has been based on nostalgia, a wistful look back to the labor organizers of the C.I.O. through the great depression of the thirties. Those "labor leaders"—Powers Hapgood, Henry Johnson, and Lee Pressman, for instance—were primarily middle-class revolutionary activists to whom the C.I.O. labor organizing drive was just one of many activities. The agendas of those labor union mass meetings were 10 percent on the specific problems of that union and 90 percent speakers on the conditions and needs of the southern Okies, the Spanish Civil War, and the International Brigade, raising funds for blacks who were on trial in some southern state, demanding higher relief for the unemployed, denouncing police brutality . . . . They were radicals, and they were good at their job . . . . But they are gone now, and any resemblance between them and the present *professional* labor organizer is only in title.[71]

By the same token, when professionals turn into organizers, their professions threaten them with excommunication. An example of this is the experiences of doctors-in-training who went on strike in 1981 against what they charged were critical staffing and equipment shortages in New York City hospitals. A doctor from Harlem described the untenured professional's precarious position when he or she turns to organizing:

> House staff training is a very difficult psychological period in your life, when a lot of your future depends on how well people like you, how diplomatic you are in dealing with the director of your department and the senior physicians, and your ability—literally—to work yourself into the ground.

If you are too aggressive, too intelligent, too assertive or too political, you make a lot of problems for yourself.[72]

Another doctor-in-training reported, "we were striking for the patients, not for ourselves." Yet she reports that surgical interns were told by their professional supervisors that "if they walk, they should just keep on walking."

Organizers have little use for the main tenets of either charity or professionalism. They can ill afford either. Much of what they organize against are contained in the tenets of those philosophies. In the former, providing a basket of food to a poor family, toys to a crippled children's center, or a donation at the local blood bank cannot possibly provide any kind of long-range remediation of peoples' problems. Doing any one of these things may relieve immediate human suffering, but none of these acts accomplishes even a token amount of social change. Giving a meal will not, nor could it ever, change the social conditions which ensure that some people will always have too little food. Giving a crippled child a toy will not help that child gain acceptance in the mainstream of society. Donating blood will not alter the fact that, in America, commercial companies sell blood for a profit, even as some individuals have too little money to afford the blood they need for transfusions. In addition, giving blood can never totally remove the urgent need for a national noncommercial blood system.

Organizers, like charity workers and professionals, work with individuals. However, their work is neither to heal nor uplift. Rather, they organize. They seek to join with people who have endured exploitation and discrimination at the hands of certain social forces and social institutions. Unlike those engaged in charitable or professional work, organizers have no wealth to bestow and no treatment to confer, but they do have the ability to become effective allies with affected people.

Instead of pity for the victims, organizers feel anger at the social conditions which degrade people. The goals they choose reflect this approach. Their targets for reform are institutions, not people. General problems such as enforced segregation of juvenile delinquents in isolated routinized, stigmatizing, even brutal institutions are the organizer's concern. Medical insurance policies which systematically discriminate against people with disabilities and catapult whole families from middle-class status to poverty status nearly overnight, require an organizer's attention. Exploitation of older people by unscrupulous nursing home operators must be countered by organizing activity. The list goes on and on, but it never veers from the large issues.

The institution which Stokely Charmichael sought to change was white America. The institution he decried was racism. His scenario was change and called not for an uplifting of Black people, but a transformation of all people and complete rejection of racism:

Now we maintain that we cannot afford to be concerned about 6 per cent of the children in this country, black children, who you allow to come into white schools. We have 94 per cent who still live in shacks. We are going to be concerned about those 94 per cent. You ought to be concerned about them too. The question is are we willing to be concerned about those 94 per cent. Are we willing to be concerned about the black people who will never get to Berkeley, never get to Harvard, and cannot get an education, so you'll never get a chance to rub shoulders with them, and say, "Why, he's almost as good as we are; he's not like the others?" So the question is how can white society begin to move to see black people as human beings. I am black, therefore I am. Not that I am black and I must go to college to prove myself. I am black, therefore I am. And don't deprive me of anything and say to me that you must go to college before you gain access to X, Y, and Z. It is only a rationalization for one's suppression.[73]

To whites, Charmichael counselled "work in white neighborhoods." In short, he located the problem of Black people not with the victims (Blacks), but with those people (whites) and those institutions (white institutions including the most prestigious universities, the best hospitals, and the wealthiest corporations) which practiced discrimination.

Lest it appear that organizers forsake charity altogether, it is important to note several qualifications. Community organization, like charity, relies heavily on a spirit of volunteerism. Moreover, community organization pursues a goal identical to one that was stated by early "friendly visitors," friendship and community (for example, visions of racially integrated communities). Also, like the early charity workers, organizers feel it their obligation and to their benefit to spend hours upon hours listening closely to consumers' perspectives. However, unlike charity workers, the organizer relates those perspectives not primarily to the individual's immediate situation, but rather to structural conditions of the society and to large ideological principles (such as equality, justice, and democracy). If there is any moralizing to be done, it is directed towards society and social policies, not towards consumers.

The organizers' divergence from professionalism is no less severe. Since professionalism rests on the principle that its participants possess esoteric knowledge of enormous value to the society, professionals literally own the knowledge:

The culture of professionalism required amateurs to "trust" in the integrity of trained persons, to respect the moral authority of those whose claim to power lay in the sphere of the sacred and the charismatic. Professionals controlled the magic circle of scientific knowledge which only the few, specialized by training and indoctrination, were privileged to enter, but which all in the name of nature's universality were obligated to appreciate.[74]

Even when their vocation calls for manual activities, these activities are based upon knowledge of the field, from which consumers can benefit but not understand. The consumer, excluded from the profession's knowledge by strict professional gatekeeping (for example, formal training programs, esoteric jargon, certification requirements), is rendered dependent, even submissive. In this professional world, consumers or clients are, by design, outsiders. Organizers challenge the professional knowledge-monopoly and forced exclusion of consumers. Most notably through the strategy of action research, but also through legal advocacy, alternative plan formulation and community education, organizers take it on themselves to demystify professions. For instance, public interest research groups publish reports on nursing home conditions. A noted pediatrician-researcher turned organizer explains in lay language, along with hundreds of research citations, the hazards of nuclear energy.[75] A lawyer by the name of Ralph Nader exposes the absence of safety provisions in American automobiles. A citizen group forms to evaluate police conduct, a national task force calls for a moratorium on prison construction while another calls for accessible mass transit. In each instance, organizers invade the sanctuary of professional knowledge whether it is comprised of corporate or government nuclear scientists, automobile executives, or gerontologists. In each case, organizers refuse to grant blind faith to "professionalism." In effect, but not in so many words, they call for decentralization of so-called professional knowledge and professional power. Frequently, to the extent that community organizers become experts themselves in a professional field, their purpose is to know in order not to be fooled by professional claims *and* to help the public become more aware by translating esoteric ideas and language into lay terms.

The strategies which professionalism uses to keep consumers powerless are frequently the practices and policies which organizers attempt to change. In the human services such as education and health care, organizers demystify professional jargon which keeps consumers from a full understanding of service information. For instance, organizers commonly demand an expansion of service options from which a consumer can choose. Consumers are then able to demand to see their own case records and can refuse to provide intimate personal details about their lives unless they deem it essential. Organizers also frequently call for external, impartial monitoring of professional conduct. Consumers can then demand specific criteria on which professionals justify their decisions to serve or not serve certain clients. One organizer, a parent of a handicapped child, has written about the importance of overcoming the mystique of professionals.

The "mere parents" myths have their foundation in a collection of beliefs held by some school people that parents always know less and are less capable than professionals (because to them [professionals] a lack of professional training means a lack of objectivity and good judgment), and that parents will waste hours of the professionals' valuable time if they are allowed to participate in their children's education. This kind of thinking puts you on the receiving end of professional expertise and in a defensive posture when you try to deal with the school people. Thus, you may feel that you must argue for your ideas and requests while the professional simply passes judgment. Measured against the professionals (and by the professionals), you, the parents, are always found wanting. . . .

Most parents stand in awe of school people and systems because schools represent our childhood images of authority and mystifying expertise. We are all products of school systems and we still retain a number of childlike school behaviors based on the old rules: "Stand in line," "No gum chewing," "No talking out of turn."

The school building brings out these old feelings and behaviors in practically everyone who doesn't work in a school. School people who feel most secure in authoritarian roles tend to exploit this habitual response to shore up their status with almost everyone who is not a regular part of the system. They may use a commanding tone of voice, keep people waiting in the outer office or halls, require silence as you walk the corridors, and generally treat parents as children and intruders. They make it clear that everyone in the building has a particular place, and the parent's place is that of the child.[76]

Only by rejecting professionals' decision making monopolies can consumers begin to control their own lives. In this view, the good professional is one who is willing to share information, to learn from and respect consumers, and to act as a consultant to the consumers, with consumers sharing decision making with the professional.

Another of the organizer's criticisms of professionalism is that in its pursuit of specialization, it segments society. On the one hand, specialization encourages professionals to analyze cases not issues. As C. Wright Mills put it:

Present institutions train several types of persons—such as judges and social workers—to think in terms of "situations." Their activities and mental outlook are set within the existent norms of society; in their professional work they tend to have an occupationally trained incapacity to rise above series of "cases."[77]

On the other hand, when professionals dare to rise out of a case-bound model or to go beyond their prescribed fields to examine social issues, they face opposition, sometimes even from the public, which by now has accepted the notion that experts have legitimacy only in their specialties. The reasoning which prevails is that just as professional fields and subfields have more or less distinct boundaries, so too must the issues with which they deal. Perhaps this explains the great stir created when Dr. Benjamin Spock announced his opposition to the Vietnam War. He is a pediatrician and his antiwar activism did not fit in with the vertical model of professional careers. Professionals are expected to keep on track in their own subject area. "He should stick to what he knows something about," some thought, and "leave foreign policy to the foreign policy experts." Likewise, there was a furor, even within the civil rights movement, when Reverend Martin Luther King, Jr. declared *his* opposition to the Vietnam War. The principle at work here is that unless a person is trained and credentialed in a particular subject area, his or her words and thoughts should not be regarded with the same legitimacy and authority as those of the expert. Indeed, by speaking beyond their credentials, Spock and King broke a rule of professional conduct. Yet, their actions, like all organizing actions, encouraged others to follow suit. Organizers reject credentials and professional initiation rites as standards of legitimacy. Rather, they rely on the truthfulness of the "facts" they present *and* their ability to communicate in a compelling way with the public. If a person must demonstrate irreverence to one or another professional group in doing this, it is a small price to pay for the pursuit of justice and equality.

The above point deserves emphasis—an organizer must always place the substance of an issue (for example, injustice) foremost. Most organizers either come from or have achieved middle-class status. Hence they always face the danger that sharing a common class background with their opposition may interfere with their ability to advocate change. If they are products of the middle class they have been socialized to appear "reasonable," "to play the game," or "to get along." However, as organizers, they must not feel bound to ethical codes which warn the middle-class professional to air grievances "within the system." They must not be so accepting of others that they fear to offend by speaking out. This truth has not entirely escaped the field of social work. As Ernest Greenwood noted, all-out pursuit of professionalism could cost social work that part of its original heritage, which was social action oriented.[76]

Of course, many of the qualities good organizers need do *not* conflict with qualities possessed by professionals or even adherents of the charitable service model. If organizers expect to work with broad constituencies, they will probably embrace some equally broad philosophical principles such as democracy, equality, and justice. Noted organizers of twentieth century America have generally avoided narrow sectarian politics (for example, trotskyism, Scientology) even though they might themselves have come out of sectarian backgrounds. Here, professionalism and community organization seem to have a common attribute, commitment to a degree of nonsectarianism in how they relate to their consistuency, the public. Each seeks a broad base of support, yet each seeks that support in different directions. The professions historically have been more concerned and inclined to find their constituency in the middle and upper class. Organizers, on the other hand, generally align themselves with the condition of oppressed people and whomever else can be solicited to support poor people's interests.

Other good qualities of an organizer are essentially like those associated with effective leadership: an organized personality, a strong ego, a vision of a better world, curiosity, a facility with asking questions, a sense of humor, a better-than-average ability to communicate, and, equally important, an ability and desire to listen and analyze. In one sphere, the matter of routine, the organizer parts company with many other types of leaders. Organizing itself rarely becomes routine and, so, organizers must develop an unflappable ability to live with ambiguity. A principle organizing strategy is to do the unexpected, to throw the opposition off balance, to identify a point of vulnerability and exploit it. The specific manifestations of all this will become clearer in Part II, the chapters on organizing action.

People can organize even if they lack one or several useful organizer qualities, but one of these is clearly indispensible. Organizers must possess optimism. In order to make change, we must believe it to be possible and believe in this possibility with a passion. Fortunately this is a finding that need not be adopted on faith alone because there is clear evidence of its importance. For instance, if you were a severely disabled person living in America fifty years ago it would be hard to conceive of a time when America would begin changing its attitudes about disabilities and when public buildings would become accessible, when Congress would pass legislation which would outlaw discrimination against people with disabilities. You might have thought a person needed to be rich and possibly powerful as well, perhaps like Franklin Delano Roosevelt, to find access to America's mainstream. Yet, fifty years later, with massive pressure from disability rights activists, through litigation, demonstrations, sit-ins, lobbying, action research, and media campaigns, all of these objectives have been won or are at least on the national agenda. Without the passage of time and events to provide evidence, we would have no reason to believe change possible. We would have no reason to be optimistic about the chance of winning specific or sweeping social changes. Hence the importance of history. Some people say that history repeats itself. Others say we learn from history. If all we learn is one general principle, that things *do* change, then history will have given us a great deal. Change may happen slowly or it may lead in uncharted directions. From any particular perspective, change may even worsen the human condition (for example, industry's effect on the environment). In any case, history does tell us that change happens and that ordinary and not-so-ordinary people alike participate in those happenings. History therefore gives us reason for optimism, a quality no organizer can do without.

NOTES

[1]Roy Loubove, *The Professional Altruist* (Cambridge, MA: Harvard University Press, 1965); Willard Gaylin, Ira Glasser, Steven Marcus and David Rothman, *Doing Good* (New York: Pantheon, 1978); Burton J. Bledstein, *The Culture of Professionalism* (New York: W. W. Norton & Co., Inc., 1976).

[2]Josephine S. Lowell, *Public Relief and Private Charity* (New York: Arno 1884), p. 85.

[3]Lowell, *Public Relief.*

[4]Loubove, *Professional Altruist,* p. 8.

[5]M. Gettleman, "Charity and Social Classes in the United States I," *The American Journal of Economics,* 22, 2 (1963), p. 327.

[6]J. O. S. Huntington, "Philanthropy and Morality," in *Philanthropy and Social Progress,* eds. Jane Addams, Robert A. Woods, J. O. S. Huntington, Franklin H. Giddings and Bernard Bosenquet (New York: Thomas Y. Crowell, 1892), p. 189.

[7]*The New York Times,* January 4, 1925, Section II, p. 1, Column 8.

[8]*The New York Times,* January 4, 1925, Section II, p. 1, Column 8.

[9]*The New York Times,* December 6, 1925, Section II, p. 1, Column 1.

[10]Loubove, *Professional Altruist,* p. 9.

[11]Loubove, *Professional Altruist.*

[12]Jane Addams, *Democracy and Social Ethics* (New York: Macmillan, 1902).

[13]Gettleman, "Charity."

[14]Lowell, *Public Relief,* p. 89.

[15]Loubove, *Professional Altruist,* pp. 15–16.

[16]Loubove, *Professional Altruist,* p. 5.

[17]Carl Bakal, *Charity USA* (New York: Times Books, 1979).

[18]V. Fulmer, "Cost/Benefit Analysis in Fund Raising," *Harvard Business Review,* 51 (1973), pp. 103–110.

[19]*Syracuse Post Standard,* April 10, 1979, p. 10; Harvey Katz, *Give* (Garden City, NY: Doubleday, 1974); Bakal, *Charity USA.*

[20]*The New York Times,* December 7, 1980, p. 58.

[21]Personal interview, 1979.

[22]Robert Massie and Suzanne Massie, *Journey* (New York: Warner Books, 1976), p. 81.

[23]Huntington, "Philanthropy," pp. 190–191.

[24]N. K. Barnes, "Rethinking Corporate Charity," *Fortune,* 90 (1974), p. 171.

[25]Barnes, "Rethinking Charity," p. 171.

[26]S. S. Hubbard, "Thanks to You, It Works for Some of Us," *The Syracuse New Times,* September 26, 1979, p. 7.

[27]Hubbard, "Thanks to You," p. 7.

[28]*In These Times,* October 24–30, 1979, p. 24.

[29]Robert Coles, *Privileged Ones* (Boston: Little, Brown 1977), pp. 177–78.

[30]Philip S. Foner, ed., *Helen Keller: Her Socialist Years* (New York: International Publishers, 1967), p. 14.

[31]Phil Donohue, *My Own Story* (New York: Simon and Schuster, 1979), p. 225.

[32]*The New York Times,* May 2, 1979, Section A, p. 12.

[33]*The New York Times,* April 3, 1978, p. 1.

[34]*The New York Times,* May 2, 1979, Section A, p. 12.

[35]William Ryan, *Blaming the Victim* (New York: Vintage, 1971).

[36]Abraham Flexner, "Medical Education in the United States and Canada: A Report to the Carnegie Foundation for the Advancement of Teaching," *Bulletin,* no. 4 (New York: The Carnegie Foundation for the Advancement of Teaching, 1910).

[37]Richard H. Shryock, *Medical Licensing in America, 1650–1965* (Baltimore: The Johns Hopkins Press, 1967), pp. 62–63.

[38]Abraham Flexner, "Education for Social Work," *Proceedings of the National Conference of Charities and Corrections,* (1915), pp. 577–90.

[39]Flexner, "Education for Social Work," p. 577.

[40]Flexner, "Education for Social Work," p. 578.

[41]Flexner, "Education for Social Work," p. 580.

[42]Flexner, "Education for Social Work," p. 580.

[43]Flexner, "Education for Social Work," p. 581.

[44]Everett C. Hughes, "Professions," in *The Professions in America,* ed. Keneth S. Lynn (Boston: Houghton Mifflin, 1965), pp. 1–14. William J. Goode, "The Theoretical Limits of Professionalization," in *The Semi Professions and Their Organization: Teachers, Nurses, Social Workers* (New York: Free Press, 1969), pp. 266–313.

[45]Bledstein, *Culture;* Loubove, *Professional Altruist;* Hughes, "Professional"; Goode, "Theoretical Limits"; Carl Degler, "What Ought to Be and What Was: Women's Sexuality in the Nineteenth Century," *American Historical Review,* 74 (December, 1974), pp. 1467–1490; Morris L. Cogan, "Toward a Definition of Professions," *The Harvard Educational Review,* XXIII, 1 (1953), pp. 33–50; Harold L. Wilensky, "The Professionalization of Everyone?" *The American Journal of Sociology,* LXX, 2 (September, 1964), pp. 137–52.

[46]Christopher Lasch, *The New Radicalism in America* (New York: Knopf, 1965), p. xv.

[47]Hughes, "Professions," p. 1.

[48]Hughes, "Professions," p. 2.

[49]Hughes, "Professions," p. 2.

[50]Wilensky, "Professionalization of Everyone?" p. 150.

[51]Wilensky, "Professionalization of Everyone?" p. 150.

[52]Wilensky, "Professionalization of Everyone?"

[53]Bledstein, "Culture," p. 45.

[54]Mary E. Richmond, *Social Diagnosis* (New York: Russel Sage Foundation, 1917).

[55]Michael B. Katz, "Origins of the Institutional State," *Marxist Perspectives* (Winter, 1978), 6–22, p. 6.

[56]Degler, "What Was," p. 1478.

[57]Degler, "What Was," p. 1478.

[58]Degler, "What Was," p. 1458.

[59]Jurgen Habermas, *Toward a Rational Society* (Boston: Beacon Press, 1970), p. 68.

[60]Talcott Parsons, *Essays in Sociological Theory* (Glencoe, IL: Free Press, 1954), p. 37.

[61]Shryock, "Medical Licensing"; Bledstein, "Culture"; and Hughes, "Professions."

[62]Goode, "Theoretical Limits."

[63]Fred Davis, "Professional Socialization as Subjective Experience: The Process of Doctrinal Conversion Among Student Nurses," in *Institutions and the Person*, ed., Howard S. Becker, Blanche Geer, David Riesman, and Robert Weiss (Chicago: Aldine, 1968).

[64]Code of Ethics, adopted by the Delegate Assembly of the National Association of Social Workers, 1979 and implemented July 1, 1980. Social Work, Vol. 25, no. 3, May, 1980, pp. 184–88.

[65]Gerald E. Markowitz and David K. Rosner, "Doctors in Crisis: A Study of the Use of Medical Education Reform to Establish Modern Professional Elitism in Medicine," *American Quarterly*, 25 (March, 1973), pp. 83–107, p. 97.

[66]Barbara Ehrenreich and Deidra English, *Witches, Midwives, and Nurses: A History of Women Healers* (Old Westbury, NY: The Feminist Press, 1973), p. 27.

[67]Rosemary Stevens, *American Medicine and the Public Interest* (New Haven: Yale University Press, 1971), p. 71; See also Herbert M. Morais, *The History of the Negro in Medicine* (New York: Publishers Company, 1967).

[68]Stevens, *American Medicine*, p. 71.

[69]Richmond, *Social Diagnosis*.

[70]Muriel W. Humphrey, "Richmond, Mary Ellen," in *Notable American Women*, eds., Edward T. James, Janet Wilson James, and Paul S. Buyer (Cambridge, MA: The Belknap Press of Harvard University Press, 1971), pp. 152–54.

[71]Saul Alinsky, *Rules for Radicals* (New York: Vintage, 1971), pp. 66–67.

[72]*The New York Times*, March 26, 1981, p. B3.

[73]Stokely Charmichael, "Stokely Charmichael, Black Power," in *The Agitator in American Society*, ed., Charles W. Lomas (Englewood Cliffs, NJ: Prentice-Hall, 1968), p. 141.

[74]Bledstein, "Culture," p. 90.

[75]Helen Caldicott, *Nuclear Madness* (Boston: Autumn Press, 1978).

[76]Barbara Coyne Cutler, *Unravelling the Special Education Maze: An Action Guide for Parents* (Champaign, IL: Research Press, 1981), pp. 33 and 19.

[77]C. Wright Mills, "Power, Politics and People," ed. Irving Louis Horowitz (New York: Oxford University Press, 1963), p. 535.

[78]Ernest Greenwood, "Attributes of a Profession," *Social Work*, (July, 1957), pp. 45–55; See also Herbert Bisno, "How Social Will Social Work Be?" *Social Work*, I, 2 (April, 1956), pp. 12–18.

PART TWO
PRACTICE

How do we know when to use one organizing strategy rather than another? And, if we *can* figure which strategy to use, how much must we know about the strategy before we can employ it effectively? In Part Two, we attempt to answer both of these questions.

To answer the first question, "which organizing strategy for a particular situation," we must look back to the theoretical chapters in Part I. Herein lie a series of rules on selecting strategies. First, all strategies should be consistent with our values. Hence the importance of discovering the values upon which we base our organizing (Chapter 1). Second, we should select the strategy or strategies which are most likely to empower (Chapter 2) the group or community with whom we are organizing. In other words, we want a strategy that will work. For example, if two reasons for a group's powerlessness to improve health care services to its members are the group's lack of visibility, and therefore lack of political leverage, and its ignorance of the political and economic processes by which health planning agencies design health services delivery, then the group may naturally benefit most from use of the media, lobbying, and action research. In other words, with our understanding of how power works, we ask: "What are the reasons for people's cooperation and obedience with policies which contradict their own interests?" and "what strategies will best enable the group to exercise more control over decisions which directly affect its interests?" Third, we must ask, "Which strategies will best educate the public or other broad constituencies to our way of defining certain social issues?" (Chapter 3). Fourth, and finally, we should choose strategies which complement our particular leadership style (Chapter 4).

Even after we have examined the strategy options, we are usually left with several strategy choices from which to choose. The next stage in our decision making requires that we know something about the strategies themselves. For example, in the health care issue noted above, we might want to consider litigation. But, first, what must we know about legal advocacy in order to make a competent decision in this situation? Ideally, we should be able to distinguish between a legal and a nonlegal issue. We should even be familiar with the record of litigation in health care delivery. We should know where to find inexpensive legal assistance. We should know how to present the issue to lawyers. We should know the drawbacks of litigation as a strategy (for example, long delays and problems of achieving implementation of court victories). Similarly, if we are considering media exposure, we should know how the mass media tends to "cover" community organizing groups. We should know the media's limitations (for example, deadlines, inability to cover issues in depth, reliance on official sources for most of their information) and how to use these limitations to serve our interests. If instead we think negotiations might prove more effective or that negotiations could occur at the same time as litigation and/or media exposure, then we must know certain things about negotiating. With whom shall we negotiate? How much should we ask for at the outset? What kinds of people, what kinds of skills should be involved in our negotiating team? Should we negotiate behind closed doors or in public (for example, on television or at a public forum)? Should we prioritize our issues or should we negotiate for everything?

In each of the strategy chapters we include theoretical background on the strategies themselves. For example, the action research chapter includes a discussion on the nature of this strategy, and how it differs from traditional research methods. Of course the chapter also provides a "how-to" guide to action research as well as many examples of its application to community organizing. For those chapters on traditional organizing strategies (for example, negotiating, social protest, and community education), the theoretical background may seem more familiar and the relationship of theory to practice may be more obvious. For the newer organizing strategies such as litigation, self help, action research, and whistleblowing, background on the nature of a strategy and its place in organizing is no less essential to its effective use and certainly no less deserving of our interest. Take, for example, whistleblowing. While we can locate cases in history of people inside human service and other settings who spoke out against injustice perpetrated by their own organizations, the act of whistleblowing as a change strategy is relatively new. Thus, in the chapter on whistleblowing we define what it is, how it has been used, its limitations, its risks to those who use it, as well as methods for employing it effectively. That is to say, organizers should know more than just how to blow the whistle. We should also understand the nature of this particular strategy. Only then can we make an informed decision as to whether and when to use it. Each of the chapters in Part Two has been designed to provide enough background mixed with practical "how-to" strategy information so that organizers can truly select from among alternatives.

CHAPTER FIVE
SOCIAL PROTEST

SOCIAL PROTEST: AN AMERICAN TRADITION

It is fashionable in some circles to lament the growth of social protest as a form of political expression. "We have too much confrontation," the argument goes. "Why can't we work together?" "Why must there always be confrontation?" Those who disdain social protest are probably the people who feel adequately represented by the dominant people and institutions of society—by political leaders, by the school board, by commercial establishments, and by human service professionals. But what of the other people, the ones who have no easy access to the powerful and influential? What of the young person who found that he could not sit in a certain section of a lunch counter simply because of his skin color? Should he have kept quiet? What of the parents whose children were denied educational programs because of their disabilities? Should they not have organized? What of parents who do not have jobs, provision of day care programs, and a way to feed their children? Should they let their children starve rather than raise their voices?

Social protest has never enjoyed the same legitimacy as electoral politics, but it has always been very much a part of the American political landscape. When colonial activists dumped tea off ships in Boston harbor, they engaged in a form of social protest. In 1877, when workers in Martinsburg, West Virginia shut down the railroad yard rather than accept a second consecutive pay cut, they started one of the greatest mass strikes in our history. It was protest writ large.[1] When Rosa Parks refused to give up her bus seat to a white man in Montgomery, Alabama, she protested. And when hundreds of thousands of citizens of all ages "mobilized" in Washington, D.C. against America's war in Vietnam, protest was their strategy.

Who can doubt the importance of social protest to our current social condition? Protest has shaped, altered, challenged, and created attitudes, social policy, beliefs, and dreams. Rosa Parks' action on that Montgomery bus illustrates the meaning of protest:

> On December 1, 1955, a Negro woman, Mrs. Rosa Parks, took a seat on the Cleveland Avenue bus in Montgomery, Alabama, and refused to give it up to a white man when the bus driver demanded she do so. Mrs. Parks, long active in the NAACP, was arrested, starting a chain of events as consequential as William Lloyd Garrison's decision to publish the Liberator in 1831. Within twenty-four hours the Negro leaders of the city had gathered and proclaimed a boycott of the city buses. Seventeen thousand colored citizens organized car pools or walked back and forth to work, in rain as well as sunshine, for 381 days, rather than accept second-class status.[2]

The chain of subsequent events was impressive. A little-known minister, the Reverend Martin Luther King Jr., became one of the protest leaders. He insisted on nonviolent strategy even though his home and others were bombed. This series of protests in the form of boycotts and demonstrations led to other boycotts of segregated lunch counters and of other segregated transportation systems. It led to sit-ins, more demonstrations, "freedom rides" of blacks and whites together, and voter registration campaigns. No one could have predicted that Rosa Parks' action would have spurred such immense social protest. Her protest became a symbol of a social protest movement which then became the civil rights movement. Her action, or rather her inaction, her unwillingness to cooperate with discriminatory segregation and second-class citizen policies made real the meaning of the song, "We shall not be moved." She stood for resistance to oppression.

More than twenty-five years later, Rosa Parks' strategy was not forgotten. In New York City where the transit agency had purchased a new fleet of buses accessible to people in wheelchairs, Denise McQuade reenacted a version of the 1955 Montgomery protest. The circumstances were a bit different, but the strategy was similar. Denise McQuade is a slight woman, only 4 feet 11 inches tall. She has had a physical disability ever since she contracted polio at the age of three. The problem she faced now, at age 33, was that while New York City had purchased buses with wheelchair lifts, it had repeatedly delayed putting the lifts into operation. Denise McQuade decided to take direct action. She waited at 50th Street and Broadway for one of the new buses. When one pulled to the corner, she maneuvered her wheelchair to the door and transferred herself onto the bus stairs. She informed the driver that she intended to stay there until the transit company agreed to operate the wheelchair lift with which the bus was equipped. Her protest lasted seven hours—that's how long it took transit authorities to agree to use a key on the lift. Denise McQuade then had her first ride in a bus since she was three years old. More than that, she was living out the legacy of Rosa Parks. She was using social protest to help speed up the fight for accessible transportation.

What emerges from each account of social protest is the meaning that "getting organized" has for participants. Yes, the goals are important: to win access, to defeat segregation, to achieve greater equality. However, protesters also possess a sense of affirmation that comes with taking action, have a feeling of standing up for deeply held values, of putting oneself on the line, of taking risks for what is important. In part, the feeling is one of living out values which have been suppressed. The recollections of John Lewis, former national chairperson of the Student Nonviolent Coordinating Committee shows this to be the case. Speaking of civil rights movement goals, he said:

> We talked in terms of our goal, our dream, being the beloved community, the open society, the society that is at peace with itself. You come to the point where you forget about race and color and you see people as human beings. And we dealt a great deal with questions of means and ends. If you want to create the beloved community, create an open society, then the means, the methods, must be ones of love and peace.[3]

There is also the feeling of satisfaction that comes with having accomplished something through self-initiated efforts. Much of the almost intoxicating appeal of social protest is the feeling among participants that they can make a difference, that through collective action they can make things change. In other words, social protest is founded on the belief that people can affect their own futures. Here again, we can turn to organizers to see what social protest means. We can witness this spirit of self determination first hand. An organizing group in New York, known as the Redistribute America Movement, described its efforts to win an increase in welfare payments this way:

> We won! New York's welfare grant will go up 15% in July! And it was a long, hard struggle. We didn't win by voting. We organized ourselves and our neighbors to join RAM and used statewide pressure through coordinated local actions to fight for our rights. We organized our allies—politicians, churches, unions, and sympathetic grassroots organizations—to pressure our legislators. We got press coverage of our actions and turned the issue of welfare around—from "fraud" and "rip-offs" to the truth, that women and children were forced to live on $2.08 per person per day. It didn't happen overnight, or at our first or even second action, but we didn't give up, and we won! . . .
>
> Taking our issue "Welfare Budgets are Killing Our Children" to the legislature, we demanded a welfare grant increase. About 2000 recipients and supporters joined in a mock funeral, moving 25 legislators to support a grant increase that only 2 legislators had supported before the demo. It wasn't enough, but it was a start. . . .
>
> We hit people who supported an increase behind closed doors but wouldn't come public with their support. We took over the mike every time the target person spoke. These actions moved many of these people to publicly support the grant increase. . . .
>
> We moved every liberal legislator there was to move. The increase passed in the Assembly, but died in the Senate. Again, it wasn't enough.
>
> It was clear to us that our problem was with the conservatives . . . especially those upstate who claimed that their constituents weren't in favor of an increase. We knew they were wrong; we had to put them in a position where they couldn't deny the need for an increase, even in their counties. So we devised a new way to look at the grant increase—The Clothing Campaign.
>
> By demanding clothing grants, people's welfare grant would go up. We used

the welfare's own law which says that a catastrophe entitles you to a replacement clothing grant. Declaring inflation catastrophic, as do most Americans, we began the clothing campaign and membership drive, to fight for more money and to build RAM so we could continue to fight. . . .

To answer, "Where will the money come from?", we sponsored a picket at the Hyatt luxury hotel, recipient of a huge welfare grant tax abatement. We moved enough support to have the owner's next tax abatement (of 50 million!) DENIED!

AND WE WON THE GRANT INCREASE![4]

On one day alone the RAM group held demonstrations in 13 different cities. It followed these actions with another 17 demonstrations at welfare centers. In New York City, welfare recipients and other RAM members were arrested when they attempted to take over a welfare center. In the state capital, RAM activists paraded through the aisles and halls with a child's coffin, a graphic symbol of their plight. Each time the governor went around the state to speak on a range of issues, RAM people forced him to address the welfare issue. After all these strategies and actions, the RAM newsletter characterized the ultimate results of the struggle not as an act of a benevolent legislature, not as a human government policy, and not as a miracle. Rather, RAM linked the results with the actions. It was action, demonstrations, symbolic funerals, an office takeover, kidnapping of microphones, and simple disruption which saved the day. In the end, RAM declared the result: "We Won!"—in Spanish, "Hemos Ganado!"

Quite possibly, for some of the RAM protesters, this was a first involvement in direct action. But their demonstrations, mock funeral, office disruptions, microphone takeovers and the like were not new to America. These are the stock-in-trade of social protesters. They are strategies that have been used time and again by groups concerned with a broad range of issues. Indeed, social protesters often refer to their roots with statements like, "We borrowed this strategy from the civil rights movement (or the antiwar movement, or the feminist movement)." It is this tradition of protest and its lessons which concern us here. In the succeeding sections of this chapter we will examine principles and issues that permeate social protest movements. Specifically, we will address a series of political questions. How can those sympathetic to protest but who are not direct participants help support protest? What are the preconditions for social protest? How and on what basis should organizers select action strategies? Which strategies are best suited to which situations? What types of actions comprise this phenomenon we call social protest? And, finally, how shall we measure the success or failure of social protest?

THE ALLY'S ROLE

Social protest raises moral issues. For example, welfare demonstrations say to legislators "accept the fact that as welfare recipients we are victims, that our children need adequate clothing, that inflation has touched us cruelly, that our plight reflects on you and how you treat your fellow people." The moral issue here is society making a choice between economic comfort for all or only for some. A tenant strike or boycott says to officials, "you have failed to protect our rights as tenants against the neglect of exploitative landlords, so we are seizing control of our own fate, disobeying one law in order to have another enforced." The moral issue is one of whether human dignity is held to be a higher value than obedience to the law. Protesters of racism-in-hiring say to the public, "stand with us against racial discrimination; admit as we have that, for some, America is not yet the land of opportunity." Here we are asked to see that our country has not fulfilled its stated ideals and decide whether this situation can be allowed to continue. All of these are moral issues calculated to call on various audiences—legislators, municipal officials, the public—to take sides, to declare exactly where they stand.

Questions of morality, particularly those that ask, "Where do you stand?", evoke mixed emotions. For some, demands on public institutions elicit feelings of confusion about whether the demands are reasonable and what the implications are for other groups if one group gets its way. Some people experience fear in regard to moral issues—fear that involvement will bring great personal risk. For others, demonstrations and the moral principles they demonstrate generate excitement— excitement that people have seized the day, that people have shown a determination to shape their own future. For some, social protest evokes excitement, confusion and fear. There is excitement that it is time for change and that change has been too slow in coming through other more "legitimate" channels (for example, electoral politics, social policy/planning). Confusion exists about just how the outsider, the human service worker, the professional, the social worker or educator can be supportive. There is also fear of acting and fear of social protest's dilemma: "If I do not participate, am I collaborating with the opposition? If I do participate—that is, go on the streets and demonstrate, grab a microphone from the opposition, carry a child's casket through the halls of the legislature—will I not lose my job, or, at the very least, open myself to charges of unprofessional, disruptive conduct?"

There appear to be four recurring barriers that hold people back from becoming involved in social protest as principal participants or as allies. First, many become immobilized by their own calculations. "How can we be sure that the conditions or problems are severe enough to warrant direct action? How can we be sure that all other measures have been tried or that other less confrontational measures would not succeed? Can we determine whether social protest is the correct strategy for a particular situation? Is the risk of involvement worth the potential gains? Indeed, nearly everyone who becomes involved in social protest makes such determinations in the privacy of his or her own mind before becoming involved. Such calculations make good sense so long as they lead to informed decisions to get involved or not, and in what fashion, whether it be as an active protester or as an ally.

Second, would be protesters ask themselves whether the group with which they will be aligned in protest is sufficiently representative of their own feelings and sense of what is appropriate protest activity. As most protest participants realize, the individual has little control over the entire group. Thus in joining a protest, people may be joining a group which will engage in some activities with which they feel uncomfortable or even disagree. They may not agree with every slogan or chant of the crowd or with every demand put forward. They may even dislike the attire of some protesters. A commitment to get involved in direct action requires the same kind of commitment required when participating in other social institutions. As participants, we may not agree with all of what the group or institution does, but we decide that our level of discomfort is offset by the potential for gains associated with collective action. The point is that we each have choices to make and that to feel fearful of action groups and strategies is very understandable. To decide not to participate in such groups or events is understandable as well. We may decide that we can support the goals of one group but not its *means,* for instance. In other situations we may feel perfectly comfortable with a group's strategies and the decision to join becomes easier. Whatever the situation, it makes good sense to assess the group and the strategies it employs as well as the goals it is striving for in order to decide about personal involvement.

Third, social protest frequently challenges the very people and institutions with which protesters have some identification such as human service organizations, political parties and officials, private corporations, and long held traditions. While potential activists may see the inequities targeted for protest by organizers, they may at the same time feel modest discomfort with the challenge that protest poses to these institutions. In short, protest often requires a parting of company with some social attachments and beliefs. We must make our principal identification with the ideals embodied in a protest movement or with social institutions in their current form. What helps in making a decision of course is to see that the choice need not be between protesting (thereby giving up on social institutions with which we feel some allegience) and doing nothing (taking our social institutions in their current imperfect form or, as the slogan goes, ''love it or leave it.'') There is a third choice and that is to find a way of becoming involved or supportive of protest so that the institutions can change, reform, improve, and still exist.

Fourth, people sometimes fail to act, whether as direct participants or as allies, simply because they do not know *how* to act. This is not a new problem. Years ago, Henry David Thoreau lamented our condition of inaction:

> There are thousands who are *in opinion* opposed to slavery and to the war, who yet in effect do nothing to put an end to them; who . . . sit down with their hands in their pockets, and say that they know not what to do, and do nothing . . . .
> They will wait, well disposed, for others to remedy the evil, that they may no longer have it to regret. At most, they give only a cheap vote, and a feeble countenance and God-speed, to the right, as it goes by them.[5]

Thoreau suggested ways of action such as speaking out, refusing to pay taxes, breaking unjust laws, and going to jail. However, the options are considerably more varied even than these. No person could ever hope to act on ''all the issues.'' Today we face persistent assaults on equality and see constant economic exploitation, environmental destruction, inadequate human services for some people, and a host of other issues. No single person can ever hope to act on his or her conscience on each of these issues. Because there are so many important issues to address, we are forced to choose those on which we will act. Toward some issues we may feel sympathy but not act. On others, we may act because we have chosen to place our energy and resources where we think we can and want to make the greatest difference. In either case, we still must possess the tools for action. We must know or learn *how* to be involved.

Given that social protest has never been legitimized as a form of political expression, even though it has been recurrent and influential in America's history, it should surprise no one that people are generally ill-informed about how to participate or, for that matter, support it. In school, we learn how to vote, but not how to stand at the barricades, hand out leaflets or compose poster slogans. We learn a great deal about how legislators make laws but little about the workings of social protest groups. In a very real sense the history most of us learn in school is the history of leaders and of dominant institutions, not a history of ordinary people or of insurgent protest organizations. We certainly learn little about how social action materializes. In professional training, the formal curriculum hardly ever includes discussion of how professionals can assist or participate in social protest that may relate to their field of work.

The roles for activists are those described in the section of this chapter on social protest forms. Aside from active roles, there are other important ways that people can become involved in protest. These ways constitute the ally role. One of the most important actions that people in any position or setting can take with respect to protest is to become informed on the issues. This means reading the popular publications, but also reading the protesters' own literature. It may mean going to meetings. Many professional organizations hold teach-ins, debates, and public forums within their own organizations so as to become better informed. At the very least, this strategy of getting informed, particularly if it occurs in some institution-wide forum, serves not only to increase awareness of an issue but also legitimizes it. For example, one member of a medical school faculty recently invited a leading national advocate against nuclear power and nuclear weapons to make a presentation to the entire medical staff (doctors, nurses, social workers) on the relationship of nuclear radiation to health. While this action did not gain the notoriety that accompanies direct action—for example, an occupation of a nuclear power plant construction site,—the teach-in did contribute in a concrete way to the social change process.

A similarly low-key but nevertheless important role for allies is to speak out on issues in a manner that is consistent with the efforts of protesters. Professional groups and associations, for example, frequently issue position statements, petitions, and public declarations in which they align themselves with a protest goal, congratulate a protest, and provide supportive evidence to legitimize the goals of protest. Most such statements are formulated by ad hoc groups. For example, in the midst of struggles over the deinstitutionalization of mentally retarded people into local communities—parents and allies were protesting in state legislatures, before local community zoning boards, and in the courts to speed the provision of community living programs such as group homes and satellite apartments—over a hundred researchers, policy makers, parent leaders, and nationally known educators released a declaration known as "The Community Imperative." In it they declared that, for educational and developmental reasons, community living should be an option available to all people, irrespective of the severity of their disability. The declaration read:

The Community Imperative:
A Refutation of All Arguments in Support of Institutionalizing
Anybody Because of Mental Retardation

In the domain of Human Rights:
All people have fundamental moral and constitutional rights.
These rights must not be abrogated *merely* because a person has
a mental or physical disability.
Among these fundamental rights is the right to community living.

In the domain of Educational Programming and Human Service:
All people, as human beings, are inherently valuable.
All people can grow and develop.
All people are entitled to conditions which foster their
development.
Such conditions are optimally provided in community settings.

Therefore:
In fulfillment of fundamental human rights and
In securing optimum developmental opportunities,
All people, regardless of the severity of their disabilities,
are entitled to community living.[6]

The declaration's organizers then submitted it to leading journals, to the national news media, and to the President's Committee on Mental Retardation. They asked for and received the President's Committee's vote in support of the declaration. In a sense, this declaration was intended to say two things. First, that there is professional support for what protesters seek and second, that a vehicle is available through which professionals and other interested parties can express their allegiance with protesters and other activists.

Third, and finally, allies can provide information, consultation, and general support to protesters. Protest usually evolves from grass-root movements in which people feel discontent. An example of this is the people who lived in the Love Canal area outside of Buffalo, New York where the land on which their houses and local school were located was comprised largely of toxic wastes (see Action Research chapter). They felt enormous discontent. They demanded that officials tell them the real dangers associated with this land. Most professionals they contacted, including public health officials, local doctors, and environmental specialists simply refused or avoided helping them. However, one public health specialist did respond and this person became their ally. She provided consultation in the form of interpreting data, help in the design of a survey, and general encouragement. In other words, this specialist used the knowledge of her field to assist grass roots activists. Many professionals believe they must disdain activism or even association with activism for fear that their professional objectivity may be impaired by such an association. Ironically, they do not fear a similar contamination by allying themselves with dominant social institutions and status quo policies. Yet clearly, many professionals are discovering that in their roles as writers, as analysts of information, as interpreters of professional or scientific language and ideas, and as "authorities" on various topics, they can assist protesters in significant ways.

PRECONDITIONS FOR PROTEST

When does protest occur and under what circumstances? Who starts it? These are questions that must be answered if the place of social protest in community organizing is to be understood. Certainly the most obvious precondition is a given group's level of dissatisfaction or disaffection with some issue, policy, or condition. As Piven and Cloward suggest, people do not go to the barricades over abstract principles.[7] Protest nearly always originates in real-life circumstances that cause people to feel frustrated. In the Great Upheaval of 1877 that began in Martinsburg, West Virginia, which has been chronicled by Jeremy Brecher in his book *Strike!*, railroad workers were driven to protest by railroad officials who had lowered their wages two times in a period of eight months.[8] These workers were motivated by real, immediate circumstances. Their anger at company policies had reached such a level, and their efforts to negotiate changes in company policy had been so unsuccessful, that they chose direct action. In the prologue to his book, Brecher cites the warning of the famous French traveller to America, Alexis de Tocqueville who said, "the manufacturing aristrocracy which is growing up under our eyes is one of the harshest that ever existed in the world." De Tocqueville described some manufacturing centers where workers were being constantly asked to do a more and more narrow, circumscribed task, a miniscule piece of the total fabrication. He graphically described the worker's alienation from the end product. He also noted the enormous wealth of some manufacturing aristrocracies as measured against the considerable poverty of the mass of their workers. Such conditions posed a threat to equality and laid the foundation for protest.

Whether protest occurs in broad societal contexts as mass upheaval or as more localized action against the policies and practices of a particular institution such as a business, hospital, school, or welfare department, it always derives from frustration over actual conditions. That is, mass protest requires mass dissatisfaction, a collective sense of injustice or inequality. For example, the mass disruptions that came with the civil rights movement and in urban riots reflected real conditions that people found abhorrent. One civil rights activist described the reasons for discontent and protests in Albany, Georgia in the 1960s:

> A century after the Civil War, Black people made up two fifths of Albany's population. There was not a single Black elected or appointed official, jury member, or policeman. Blacks were barred from "whites only" city parks and swimming pools, from the town library, and from all but the lowest paid jobs. From the "colored

waiting room'' of the bus station it was eight blocks to a restaurant that served Blacks, and six miles to a "colored motel."

Such are the conditions of discontent. They are the same kind of conditions which have always fueled protest. In the earliest days of the United States, protest was not uncommon. The conditions out of which protest sprang were similar to conditions which have yielded more recent protests, namely those of economic inequality, exclusion from legitimate political processes, and social discrimination. Interestingly, we have rediscovered this history when we as a society searched our past to try to understand recent disturbances. Thus the so-called Skolnick report, produced under the direction of Jerome H. Skolnick, Director of the Task Force on Violent Aspects of Protest and Confrontation of the National Commission on the Causes and Prevention of Violence, examined the rich and often violent history of protest in America. It cited instances of class conflict in America's past:

> Appalachian farmers living in the western regions of the Eastern Seaboard states participated in civil disorder from the 1740's, when Massachusetts farmers marched on Boston in support of a land bank law, until the 1790's, when farmers and mountain men fomented the Whiskey and Fries Rebellions in Pennsylvania. The series of revolts now known as the Wars of the Regulators (North and South Carolina), the War of the New Hampshire Grants (New York-Vermont), Shay's Rebellion (Massachusetts), and the Whiskey Rebellion (Pennsylvania) were the principal actions engaged in by debtor farmers protesting half a century of economic exploitation, political exclusion, and social discrimination by the East Coast merchants, shippers, and planters who were in substantial control of the machinery of government. In state after state, civil disobedience of hated laws was followed by intimidation of, or physical attacks on, tax collectors and other law enforcers, by the closing down of courts to prevent indictments and mortgage foreclosures from being issued, by the rejection of halfway compromises proffered by Eastern legislatures, and finally by military organization to resist the state militia. Although most insurgent groups were finally defeated and dispersed by superior military force, the rebellions did not end until Jefferson's election provided access for Westerners to the political system, and new land created fresh economic opportunity. Where political and economic systems were especially rigid, as in New York's Hudson Valley, agitation and sporadic violence continued well into the nineteenth century.[9]

What can be seen in such examples is confirmation that protest is not simply subversion of a basically good political and economic system by people who believe in another system. Nor does protest arise from abstract political beliefs. A precondition for social unrest and popular upheaval, whether in the workplace, in a service setting, or in society at large, is people's perception and experiencing of immediate conditions as inequitable and intolerable. Piven and Cloward put it this way:

> People experience deprivation and oppression within a concrete setting, not as the end product of large and abstract processes, and it is the concrete experience that molds their discontent into specific grievances against specific targets. . . .
> People on relief experience the shabby waiting rooms, the overseer of the caseworker, and the dole. They do not experience American social welfare policy.

> Tenants experience the leaking ceilings and cold radiators, and they recognize the landlord. They do not recognize the banking, real estate, and construction systems.[10]

People will naturally protest their immediate conditions, but relief from the conditions they face is inevitably tied up in the larger forces that the welfare, the banking, and real estate systems represent.

Social protest geared to overcoming immediate conditions which provoke feelings of dissatisfaction and discontent can lead to cosmetic or particularistic changes in those conditions. However, they will usually not lead to fundamental changes, the kinds of changes that might make such conditions less likely to arise in future years. This points out the importance of defining social protest and the targets of protest in a manner that begins to address larger issues such as the welfare system, the banking and real estate systems, and the political system. We can call this a second condition for social protest, one that aids in implementing long range effective social protest. People need an alternative vision of how things might be, of how social systems might operate. This vision, as much as current experiences with oppression, can foment and sustain social protest.

A vision differs from an immediate need. The parents of children with disabilities who had been excluded from public schools or segregated into disabled-only schools where they could have no contact with their nondisabled peers wanted something quite obvious—integration. They also wanted a right to education. Ultimately, however, these parents would come to see that these immediate wants were inadequate goals in themselves. It is true that they were major issues of concern and, if achieved, they would represent major victories. However, parents who have become active in the disability rights movement have come to realize that denial of access to integrated education or to any education is symptomatic of larger problems namely those of stereotyping, prejudice, and discrimination toward people with disabilities. The same attitudes and policies which prohibited children with disabilities from receiving much needed education programs are the ones which have also systematically kept people with disabilities out of jobs. They have justified institutionalization of hundreds of thousands of people with disabilities and this has of course kept people with disabilities outside the social and economic mainstream. Even the seemingly responsive attitudes of society and charities toward people with disabilities have served to keep them dependent. Cultural stereotypes that portray people with disabilities as violent, sexually deviant, and incompetent compound the problems posed by exclusionary public policies. Thus parents of disabled children and disabled persons themselves have come to see and articulate the fact that their problem is not merely one of immediate conditions such as discrimination. Rather, they have envisioned a world rid of prejudice, stereotyping, and discrimination toward people with disabilities. They envision a world free of handicapism.

Parallel events occur in other social change movements. The civil rights movement is a case in point. Activists knew the complaints of Blacks. They could not sit at so-called ''whites only'' lunch counters. Blacks could not get jobs as bus drivers, firefighters, police officers, librarians, teachers, business leaders, town or city officials. Blacks could not get treatment at so-called "white" hospitals. Blacks could not use "public" restrooms unless marked "colored." The immediate enemy was Jim Crow. But for most people who became involved, the vision shone past any particular instance of discrimination to all instances of discrimination. The vision was to eradicate the barriers to equality and to overcome racism. Civil Rights leader Bernice Reagon explained her own vision this way:

> I had grown up in a society where there were very clear lines. The older I got, the more I found what those lines were. The Civil Rights Movement gave me the power to challenge *any* line that limits me. . . .
>
> Before then, I struggled within a certain context but recognized lines. Across those lines were powers that could do you in, so you just respect them and don't cross them. The Civil Rights Movement just destroyed that and said that if something puts you down, you have to fight against it.[11]

Without a vision of a better world, we have nothing. Put another way, to have vision is to have optimism. We must believe that things could be different, that the way things are is not immutable. In the words of Saul Alinsky, "optimism brings with it hope, a future with a purpose, and therefore, a will to fight for a better world. Without this optimism, there is no reason to carry on."[12] We do not require a perfect blueprint of the future in order to act against injustice, but we do need at least a sense of the better world. That sense or vision is a precondition for social protest. People need to know that there is something for which to fight.

A third factor which may foment social protest is alienation or, put more positively, the desire for community. Ask any social activist what it is like to participate in a social movement and he or she will tell you about the "sense of community," the togetherness, the solidarity. Simply put, people who feel isolated and powerless gravitate naturally toward an opportunity to experience community. Alienation refers to the loss of community, a loss of connectedness with other people who have potentially common interests and experiences. Social movements, like religion and other group situations, provide the possibility of people sharing experiences and perspectives. Through group affiliation, participants can discuss their life situations, identify those events which they have in common, create a language to describe those events—words like racism, sexism, sisterhood, sex object, tokenism, and handicapism come from social movement groups—and develop a shared vision of the future.

It has long been recognized that alientation leaves a people vulnerable to exploitation. In her book, *The Origins of Totalitarianism,* Hannah Arendt argues that people who are isolated and who thus lack relations with other individuals and groups can find a sense of belonging in movements created by elites.[13] They are vulnerable to solicitation into totalitarian movements such as the nazism of 1930s and 40s Germany. The difference of course, between mass, totalitarian movements and social movements is that social movements of the sort we describe here are democratic in nature. Participants come together out of common need. They share common experiences with injustice and a common interest in finding ways to overcome it. Through group association, they develop plans of action. Unlike totalitarian situations, the definition of common problems and solutions is not imposed from above. In group association, people ask, "What is the Black experience, the Disabled experience, the Female experience, the Welfare Recipient experience?", "What are the conditions, beliefs, and practices which would have to change in order for our lives to change?", and, "How can we create those changes through our own efforts?" Similarly, when neighborhood groups come together and organize for improved services, for protection against change forced from outside, neighbors find group identity in their past, shared experiences. As Boyte explains, "citizen activism frequently grows directly from traditional and particular group identities . . . —religious and civic traditions, ethnic ties, and family relations. In the course of struggle, people often feel deepened appreciation for their heritage, symbols, and institutions close to home."[14] All these activities are part of finding community. A social movement which fails to recognize and attend to people's need for community will shortly find itself devoid of participants.

The fourth and final precondition for social protest concerns the relation of individuals to their social environments. Some people see themselves as isolated, powerless, and inconsequential in this regard. They may resent certain policies and practices of society but fail to act on that resentment. As Thoreau put it, too many people know how to sit on their hands and wait for others to change the conditions they find abhorrent. What we discover in social protest movements is people taking responsibility for the state of the world. We see people with what has been called a social conscience. Like Thoreau, they seek to change the world not only so that others' lives will improve but so their own will improve as well. In doing this they can feel more comfortable in a more just world. From this perspective, we are all tied to and responsible for injustice. Consequently, we all have a moral obligation to acknowledge our connection with and to eradicate injustice. Thoreau says:

> If it (government injustice) is of such a nature that it requires you to be the agent of injustice to another, then, I say, break the law. Let your life be a counter friction to stop the machine. What I have to do is see, at any rate, that I do not lend myself to the wrong which I condemn.[15]

To remain silent and cooperative in the face of policies which cause injustice is to collaborate with injustice. This is essentially the position taken by Martin Luther King toward racism and by Daniel and Philip Berrigan, and Maggie Rush toward nuclear armament. People who join protest movements see themselves directly or indirectly connected with injustice and they seek to sever that tie. A. J. Muste, an important progenitor of America's recent peace movement was one of many who lived by this principle. In 1949, on the occasion of the U.S. Government's jailing of a young Quaker, Larry Gara, who had refused to register for the military draft, A. J. Muste announced his own disobedience as an act of solidarity with Larry Gara and as a source of disruption to the government:

> While not desiring anyone to take this stand who is not inwardly prepared to do so, I have done and shall continue to do all in my power to increase the movement of civil disobedience to the draft among the young and old, men and women. . . .

Since January 1, 1948, I have refused to pay Federal income taxes because I felt I had to find every possible means to divorce myself from any voluntary support of the crowning irrationality and atrocity of atomic and bacterial war. . . . I am by no means eager to go to prison; and I bear no ill will to any Federal officials or any one else. But adolescent and growing youth should not be conscripted for atomic and bacterial war. Young men like Larry Gara ought not be jailed for expressing their deepest religious convictions. . . . Whether at liberty or in prision, where Larry Gara and these young men are, I belong.[16]

Some people may argue that civil disobedience has no place in a society of laws, but this argument is of the same sort as those against social protest itself. As Alinsky has explained, where there is change there is movement and where there is movement there is friction.[17] We cannot have real change without both movement and friction. In terms of upholding and breaking the law, and knowing which to do when, advocates of social protest and, in particular, civil disobedience, point out that a just society demands just laws. Breaking laws perceived as unjust is not indicative of disrespect for laws in general. Historian Howard Zinn found that those who participated in civil disobedience as a civil rights strategy did not at the same time break other laws. In fact, crime rates in Albany, Georgia, the location of the early mass civil rights demonstrations and civil disobedience, actually declined during the time of protest.[18]

In conclusion, advocates of social protest do not want anarchy nor do they encourage people to ignore laws indiscriminately. The general rules advocates follow are to (1) break unjust laws when other less confrontational strategies have failed; (2) educate the public about why you break certain laws; and (3) break unjust laws when the positive consequences (chances of winning) outweigh the negative ones (potential for violence, chance of losing). Advocates do not believe that laws are irrelevant or that people should feel disconnected from laws. Rather, they encourage active responsibility for laws. Where laws are unjust they counsel against merely ignoring them. They point out that laws are an extension of the collective will and if they are unjust, the laws must be changed. If access to the electoral process is limited, if pluralism has failed, unjust laws must be resisted. Far from rejecting society, people through social protest embrace their connectedness to it. In social protest people express the belief that their own good, their own well-being is tied to the good and well-being of all people. Alinsky saw this as a precondition for action: "A major revolution to be won in the immediate future is the dissipation of man's illusion that his own welfare can be separate from that of all others."[19]

CHOOSING THE RIGHT FORM
OF SOCIAL PROTEST

The term "social protest" refers to myriad actions. It includes teach-ins, boycotts, sit-ins, symbolic acts, vigils, walks, work-ins, phone-ins, office takeovers, construction of barricades, mass demonstrations, distributing leaflets, "guerrilla theater,'' and strikes, to name a few strategies. Two questions confront organizers. First, what strategy should be used when? Second, how are these strategies actually carried out? In this section we will discuss the question of choosing strategies. In subsequent sections we will address the question of how they are implemented.

As with other aspects of strategy, there is no formula or stock way of predicting what strategy will work best in a particular situation. Choice of strategy must always reflect complex factors (for example, who is involved, what has been tried previously, how much time is available, number of people in the organizing group). Even if we were able to account for all the particular factors, we would still have to rely on a certain amount of creativity, and no one has yet figured out how to teach that. Therefore, not even a computer analysis of a particular situation would be able to deduce the perfect strategy. Nevertheless, despite these limitations, there are certain guidelines by which strategy selection can be guided. They cannot substitute for creativity, but go a long way toward recognizing the uniqueness with which each situation must be addressed.

Defining Issues, Goals, and Objectives

Once again we ask, "What are our issues?", "What is the focus of our concern?" No matter what strategy we select, we must first identify and prioritize the issues, policies, or practices which concern us most.

Next, we must determine what we want to achieve in both the short and long term. Short-term change usually means helping one person or a small group of people without radically challenging or altering the conditions or structure of the system which creates the problem. Long-term change addresses the systemic issues. For example, a Black news photographer was beaten by police officers when he tried to take pictures of the police's attempts to break up a party. The police charged the photographer with resisting arrest. The young man was then indicted by an all-white grand jury. His testimony and other witnesses' accounts of police misconduct were covered up by the district attorney and never properly presented to the grand jury. Local activist groups and the victim himself were faced with a choice. Should community groups pursue a short-term objective of having the charges dropped or of working out a plea bargain with the district attorney? Or, should they address larger, more systemic and long-term issues? They considered, for example, challenging the procedures for selecting grand juries and jurors in general for its systematically failed to produce juries of the victims' peers, that is, multiracial and multiclass juries. They also considered demanding a civilian review board to oversee and investigate police conduct. Furthermore, they considered bringing a civil rights complaint against the police and the district attorney's office for violating the civil rights of the photographer. The actual choice of strategies depended first on the victim's wishes and then on a variety of other considerations which we will discuss below. However, the prior consideration in this situation for these groups and for any organizing group, was to answer the question, "what are the long-term and short-term goals and objectives?"

What is Winnable?

Having identified a range of possible objectives, we must then ask what can we expect to win as well as what is possible to win. Groups that fail to determine what is possible to win will most likely sow the seeds of their own destruction. Nothing deflates a group more than a series of defeats. People want to succeed—that, after all, is why we organize. We believe that through collective action we can achieve change. Hence we must always make at least a guess about what particular objectives we are most likely to accomplish. One advocacy group, for example, had as its goal making it possible for children with disabilities to participate in their education programs, including special education, in regular neighborhood schools where they could interact with nondisabled children. However, the school district was planning to construct a new school for disabled children only. At the time, at least forty children with moderate to severe retardation were on waiting lists to get into school because of space problems. The balance of the disabled children in the district attended public school in a rented church basement.

The advocacy group had the multiple goals of getting the children on waiting lists into school programs, integrating special education into regular schools, and improving the quality of special education programs. However, the group assessed the climate for change and decided that if it were to express open opposition to the planned new separate school it would not only invoke the wrath of the district officials, it would also split the parent movement. Many parents of older children had fought long and hard for a school building to house their children's programs. Parents of children on the waiting list did not have a commitment to a new, separate school. They wanted integration if possible, but their first need was for any program. Therefore, the advocacy group selected the most winnable objective, that of getting rid of waiting lists by demanding four new special education classes in existing regular public schools. The strategy worked.

Even while construction for the new facility got under way, school district officials agreed to open two special education classes in a local school immediately. They were expanded the following year. Once the parents of the children in the integrated setting experienced the benefits of having their children in the more "normal" environment, they became staunch advocates of integration. Within seven years, all segregated programming ended because parents became more and more organized in making their demands on district officials for integration. A number of parents reported that the experience of winning something gave them a feeling of power, a feeling of being able to effect more change in the future.

Fitting the Circumstances to the Hour

Direct action frequently provokes controversy and controversy often leads to an official reaction, hopefully a shift in policy or practice. Usually, however, it is best to take direct action only after other means have been tried. These other means include negotiations, action research, use of the media, public forums, and lobbying. If these milder strategies do not provoke change, direct action should be used. Here too, however, the type of direct action should fit the circumstances of the hour. If the opposition (usually officials) has argued that the organizing group is merely a small "band of misfits," a "tiny minority," a "deviant fringe," it may make sense to hold a mass rally. Such a rally will dispel any claim that the group does not represent a broad constituency. In another situation it may be necessary and strategically wise to select a type of protest which will address the oppositions' own ideological beliefs. For example, in the case of the Redistribute America Movement campaign for welfare payment hikes, the group decided that one way to reach conservative legislators was to appeal to their sensibilities about the needs of children. The group did this by formulating demands and demonstrating outside the legislative halls for a "clothing allowance." When RAM leaders realized that some legislators were publicly afraid to express support for welfare hikes they privately supported, the group used the strategy of harassing legislators in public until they made their private views public ones. In short, their strategies were suited to the circumstances of the hours.

Utilize Skills of the Constituency

Not every group has people who are good public speakers, people who want to picket and march, people willing to go to jail in civil disobedience actions or able to dress up in theatrical garb for a symbolic act. However, each group does have members with certain skills. For example, teach-ins are popular on university campuses and in university or college towns because university-related social movements have members who are knowledgeable on the issues. Similarly, student groups use sit-ins and other forms of civil disobedience more often than other segments of the population because they have fewer outside responsibilities (for example, a family to support or a job to keep) to hold them back from confrontation politics. Likewise, office workers may use slowdowns, consumers may use boycotts, and people at home during the day may use phone-ins because these strategies use skills that they possess and which are relatively easier to use than other strategies.

Will the Action Educate?

Most actions will have a secondary effect of educating the public about an issue. A street demonstration will alert the public about an issue whether or not it achieves a policy change. It will place an issue on the public agenda. Groups often select strategies which will have maximum educational benefit as well as the greatest likelihood of effecting immediate or long-term change. If an issue has been on the national or local agenda for a long time, a group may choose a strategy aimed at refining the public's understanding of the issue. The civil rights movement used this tactic. Initially, activists organized sit-ins at lunch counters and were arrested. This strategy informed the public of the issue and the fact that Blacks were unwilling to respect racist, unconstitutional laws. Subsequently, large demonstrations informed the public of the strong, widespread support for the few who practiced civil disobedience. Meanwhile pickets of northern U.S. stores owned by the same chains (Kresge's, Woolworth's) as were picketed in the South began to build public sympathy at the national level for the struggles in southern towns and cities. In this case, there were two targets: (1) the stores, which were being asked to change their policies and (2) the public, which was asked to help pressure the stores. Similarly, "freedom rides" of blacks and whites kept public attention on policies of segregation in transportation.

One Action Leads to Another

"Sure, they protested, but they didn't really accomplish their objective." This charge is often heard. Perhaps because we live in a society that moves so fast, or perhaps because the mass media portrays life as eventful and therefore immediate, we sometimes seem to forget that change can take time, a great deal of time. Few social change efforts have taken only one action to win something. More often, change comes after a long string of actions that are loosely related. In many cases, even the organizing group cannot determine just which action, if any, had a decisive effect in forcing change. Hence the need to plan actions in sequence. Effective organizers unravel action strategies one after another, using a variety of approaches. They are always keeping the opposition guessing about what will come next, always keeping up the pressure, and always keeping one or a few key issues high on the public agenda. When one strategy seems to fall on its face, the group needs to have another ready to go. When success with a strategy causes the group to feel content, perhaps even lazy with the sweetness of success, it is time for another action. Community organizing never leads to a final resolution. One goal folds into another and one action leads to another. Even if the public and officials responded to the same type of action over and over again, which they rarely do, organizers would probably not feel satisfied with such a static approach. Part of what makes organizing so fulfilling is the creative enterprise, thinking up new strategies and making them unfold.

Actions and Values

We usually do not like to get involved in actions which are in conflict with closely held values. If we organize our values hierarchically, we can, however, sometimes make choices between values. We may, for example, simultaneously support the right of free speech and despise racism. But, what do we do when the Ku Klux Klan wants to march through town? Do we support a ban of their march and, in effect, limit their freedom of expression? Here, some people, especially civil libertarians, choose the freedom of speech value as the one that needs active support. Even though civil libertarians may not support racist values, they may feel compelled to allow others, namely the Klan, to express their racist views. The point is that organizers face similar dilemmas in value choices. This is particularly true with respect to strategies selection. We tend to feel most comfortable if we can satisfy two desires: (1) to pursue objectives we value; and (2) to pursue such objectives by means we value or, at the very least, by means that do not offend our values. Strategies which cause massive disruption of others' lives will obviously give us more pause than ones which do not. Strategies which call for disobedience of the law raise more questions than those which do not. Strategies which offend other or even our own sensibilities (for example, yelling of epithets) may cause us to stay away from protest. Similarly, strategies which lead to property destruction are not popular with most protesters in most situations. As a general rule, organizers attempt to select strategies that conform with the values of potential participants.

BASIC TYPES AND METHODS
OF SOCIAL PROTEST

Demonstrations

Demonstrations are the most well-known form of social protest. To many people, a demonstration is synonymous with social protest. In fact, however, a large number of strategies can be included under more general heading of "demonstration." These include marches, vigils, motorcades, sit-ins, phone-ins, protest meetings, takeovers, sing-ins, distributing leaflets, picketing, sit-downs, disruptions, and walkouts. Demonstrations of all types have been used successfully by diverse groups for diverse issues. Women's suffrage, civil rights groups, disability rights groups, and welfare recipients, to name just a few, have used demonstrations effectively.

Demonstrations have multiple purposes. They bring an issue to public attention and may cause officials embarrassment. Demonstrations generally elicit media attention and sometimes effect policy and practice changes immediately. They may intensify the willingness of the opposition to negotiate and/or compromise. They are a useful way of involving large numbers of people who willingly align themselves with a group. They establish the group and its issues as a "community presence" and educate the public.

There are a number of rules and principles which can be employed to enhance the probability that a demonstration will be successful. These are as follows:

1.   **Try to have each demonstration focus on a single issue.** Have a leaflet or public statement ready which presents the issue. For example, one group of feminists wanted to expose the practices of local businesses which discriminated against women. They organized a bus tour of a half dozen such organizations which they had targeted as particularly discriminatory. At each stop a member of the group acted as a tour guide, giving specific information to the group and the media on sexist practices by the organization in question. Protesters use other means of communicating their issue such as placards, posters, slogans, press releases, and speeches.

2.   **Plan the demonstration carefully.** This is best accomplished by a series of meetings involving a planning committee. In this way various aspects of the

preparation can be divided among members. Someone needs to handle the media while someone else has to recruit protest participants. Another can plan crowd control strategies. If the protest will take place early in the morning where it may be cold, bring coffee; if it is to be a long protest, organize food. This may sound like a trivial or even frivolous detail but it can make the difference in terms of holding the crowd at the protest site.

3. **Vary demonstration strategies** (sit-ins, mass gatherings, picketing, walkouts). For example, when a major university invited President Reagan's secretary of state, General Alexander Haig, to receive an honorary degree and give the graduation ceremony address, protesters who saw Secretary Haig as standing for injustice on the international and domestic fronts used multiple strategies. When Secretary Haig began his address, 100 faculty and students walked out on him. When he had completed his address, the 100 walked back in again. When the University Chancellor conferred his honorary degree, the 100 stood up and turned their backs on him. Through these multiple strategies, the 100 protesters made public their dissent with Mr. Haig, his policies, and with the honor the university gave him. The variety of strategies also enabled the group to prolong the protest.

4. **Involve the media.** Demonstrations which receive media attention have a multiplier effect. Sometimes the uniqueness of a strategy will draw media attention, as was the case with the guided tour of sexist institutions mentioned above. On other occasions, the importance of an issue will cause the media to attend the protest (for example, racial segregation in 1960's, Albany, Georgia). In still other instances, the target of a demonstration—Secretary of State Haig for example, was quite controversial and a regular newsmaker—may lure in the media. Organizing groups can increase the likelihood of media attention simply by actively soliciting media coverage for demonstrations (see chapter on the media).

5. **Have an effective means of communicating with prospective protest participants.** Groups accomplish this through public announcements to the media about protests and through newsletters, telephone chains, advertisements, leaflets, preprotest organizing meetings, and word of mouth.

6. **Select appropriate protest strategies.** The group should have a good likelihood of accomplishing particular strategies which accurately reflect its ability for continued action. On this topic, Si Kahn cautions:

> A march called to initiate a boycott is effective only if the boycott is effective. A sit-in at a lunch counter works only if it prevents the restaurant from doing business. A picket line around a plant is important as a symbol of the strike—if it keeps workers out of the plant. A picket line around the mayor's house should be used only when it represents the intention and the ability of the people to vote him out of office. . . .
>
> If a march is called in a town of 10,000 to kick off a boycott and only 35 people show up to march, it will do more harm to the boycott than to anything else.[20]

Kahn may overstate his case a bit—we can imagine for example, that a group might picket a mayor's house in order to demand a policy change or shift without being committed to getting rid of the mayor altogether—but he is absolutely correct in suggesting that organizers need to use strategies which they can accomplish successfully.

7. **Follow through.** Seasoned protest groups know how to use an event even after it is over. Organizers may make reference to past protests when negotiating with officials, as if to say, "if you do not negotiate in good faith, we could go to the streets again." Organizers write about protest to share the positive results of action. They collect news clippings and reproduce them and incorporate experiences from one protest into training and planning for future protests. Organizing groups recognize that effective protests instill in participants and in prospective participants of future demonstrations a sense of empowerment.

8. **Demonstration strategies should fit the situation.** The possibilities for types of actions are nearly endless. The important considerations here are to choose demonstration forms which are possible, enjoyable, and above all, creative. A protest against the government's transfer of funds from domestic programs to military purposes, for example, should use the circumstances created by the issue. Slogans could show the amount of food that could be purchased with the money spent on a single type of weapon or suggest that people cannot eat weapons (for example, "Let them eat missiles."). When the American Coalition for Citizens with Disabilities, the Center for Independent Living, Disabled in Action, and other disability rights groups wanted to force enactment of federal regulations necessary to implement a congressional law against disability related discrimination, they carried out simultaneous office sit-ins and encampments at Regional Federal offices across the country. This strategy caused enormous controversy because the public was not used to seeing people with disabilities in such a militant role. Certain groups like the National Federation of the Blind had used direct action before, but this series of sit-ins and encampments had an especially powerful effect because the activists vowed to stay at the offices until the regulations were signed. Their protest led to a negotiated settlement with the government, including a speed-up in finalizing the regulations.

Boycotts

The boycott is a standard tool of community organizers. It takes various forms such as tenant strikes, boycotts of stores, walkouts, stalling, refusal to pay for services, noncooperation with official functions (such as refusal of assistance to police during investigations or incidents), slow compliance, and even work-ins (a kind of reverse boycott). As with demonstrations, it is difficult to identify the exact conditions under which the boycott or a particular style of boycott will be a useful and effective strategy.

While boycotts have been a familiar type of organizing strategy, they are difficult to accomplish. In order to mount an effective boycott, there must first be something available to boycott. There must also be a constituency willing to boycott and they must believe strongly enough in such an action. If the boycott does occur, organizers and participants alike must ask if it is targeted on a sufficiently important commodity or practice (for example, rents for the landlord, government agencies' needs for cooperation, store products) that the opposition will capitulate under pressure and thus make the boycott a success.

The following are factors which should help determine whether to use the boycott as a strategy or not and what type of boycott might be effective:

1. **The first question to ask is "what is there to boycott?"** For example, even if people receive poor medical treatment at a local hospital, prospective patients are unlikely to boycott the facility unless they have an alternative health care facility available to them. Human service settings of all kinds, including schools, day care centers, clinics, and treatment programs generally do not make good boycott targets because consumers usually feel dependent on their services even if they are of less than optimal quality. Some groups, however, have used short-term boycotts of a week or two just in order to make their concerns or issues clear and compelling to the public or to officials. Longer-term boycotts work best in situations where the boycotting group has alternative ways of securing boycotted services or goods. Boycotts succeed most often when participants do not stand to pay an enormous price for their activism (for example, lose their jobs, lose their homes).

A boycott must fit the circumstances at hand. If tenants have multiple complaints about building code violations, absentee landlords who fail to make necessary repairs, skyrocketing rents, and security, their concerns may lend themselves to a rent strike. However, if it appears that most tenants will not participate over a long period of time, then the boycott should be organized to withhold a single month's payment and to put the money aside so that it can be paid at a later date. People who would not commit themselves to a protracted struggle might readily participate in a limited action designed to bring attention to a problem and apply intense pressure for a brief period. Similarly, if parents of school children believe that school officials have been unresponsive to their concerns, they may want to mount a day-long or week-long boycott during which time they could create alternative schools for their children. Such actions have been more popular than long-term boycotts against schools simply because parents rarely have the resources to maintain alternative schools for very long and because state laws require children's attendance at school.

On the other hand, some situations lend themselves to protracted boycotts. Suppose, for example, that a community development agency had been making decisions about how to spend its funds and was not involving its "community representatives" who were sitting on the Board of Directors. The "community representatives" could stage a boycott of the Board until certain demands concerning how decisions are made were met. Such an action takes few resources, makes a point, forces the agency to deal with an issue, and has a good likelihood of succeeding.

In Montgomery, Alabama, Rosa Parks' refusal to give up her bus seat led to a massive boycott by Blacks of the metropolitan bus system there. It worked. Emotions ran high, the participants were highly organized, and they created self-help alternative modes of transportation. The point is that organizers must examine constituency feelings, availability of alternatives to the service or goods boycotted, how many people must be involved in order to be effective, and the length of time over which people are willing to be involved.

2. **Identify possible reactions to a boycott.** How will the public perceive a boycott? How might the opposition attempt to beat a boycott (for example, leaving town, by calling in the police, by spreading rumors about the boycott participants)? What groups are likely to help the opposition survive a boycott? It is always best to plan for the worst possible reactions. The target must be sufficiently narrow that the boycott can have a direct impact. On the other hand, it may be possible to select the boycott site or target in such a manner that the opposition's traditional allies want the opposition to make a settlement. Si Kahn discusses this possibility in his book, *How People Get Power:*

> If a business boycotted is in the central shopping district a picket line out front will create considerable psychological pressure on other businessmen in the area. When possible, it is a good idea to boycott one of two similar stores within sight of each other, so that the man being boycotted can get a good look at his long-time customers shopping across the street.[21]

In addition, boycott organizers should develop systematic and persistent strategies for educating the public about why the boycott is important and deserves support. This should include regular updating of the boycott's progress.

3. **Boycotts are a single type of organizing action.** They do not, however, occur in isolation from other strategies. Groups that develop boycotts also use related strategies such as organizing press conferences, developing slogans and doing action research on the conditions that led up to the boycott and on the effects of the boycott. They negotiate with officials for a resolution to the problems and the boycott as well as maintain regular communication with boycott participants through newsletters and meetings. Boycott groups hold public forums related to the boycott issues, produce leaflets and buttons, list issues or demands associated with the boycott, and secure statements of support from other groups in order to organize sympathy boycotts.

Demands

When groups engage in problem definition exercises, whether through action research, interviewing each other, brainstorming and prioritizing issues, or consciousness raising, they inevitably develop a series of long-term goals and short-term objectives. It is a small step to transform these activities into demands. However, groups have varying success with their efforts to use "demands" as an effective strategy. On the surface, demands look simple and straightforward as indeed they should. The appearance of simplicity can be deceiving. There are a number of crucial factors that should enter into the process of developing demands.

1. Demands, like slogans, placards, posters, and leaflets, must communicate ideas simply and directly. This means that only basic ideas, not the complex-

ities that often stand behind them, "work" in the demand format. Thus it is important to define issues in their basic form if they are to fit successfully into this format.

2.   Decide on the purpose of the demands. Some statements of demands are more on the order of statements of belief or philosophy (for example, "we demand an end to racism"; "we demand equality"; "we demand justice"; "we demand peace") while others put forth a more specific program of action (for example, "we demand a moratorium on prison construction"; "we demand medicaid funding for abortion" or "we demand an end to medicaid funding for abortion"; "we demand active enforcement of building code violations in our neighborhood"). Some groups successfully mix the two types of demands statements by prefacing a statement of programmatic demands with a statement of principles or beliefs on which they are based. The example of a demands statement in Figure 1 combines broad principles (fair representation and participation in the political process) and programmatic requirements (systematic preparation and examination of all legislation, taking into account its effects on women).[22]

3.   Demands should use words and phrases that are vivid, easily understood, and memorable. Jargon, complex images, mixed images, hard-to-decipher data, and other information which might be acceptable forms of communication within a group of experts or highly informed people, will not do for demands. Demands must serve the broadest possible audience, always including the well-informed and the uninformed alike. After all, the purposes of demands are as diverse as their audiences. They are presented to clarify issues, to win concessions or fundamental change, and to inform the public.

Figure 1
U.S. National Women's Agenda—1975
This agenda, a list of priorities for 1976, was developed by eighty national and regional women's organizations, representing over thirty million American women. One hundred women's organizations, ranging from Girl Scouts to radical women's liberation groups, were queried by questionnaires as to their legislative and programmatic priorities for 1976. Eighty of them replied, and the items on which they agreed were incorporated into the agenda. It represents an expression of consensus not reached since the woman suffrage movement mobilized a broad spectrum of feminist organizational strength around the single issue of passage of the Nineteenth Amendment.

What is remarkable in the agenda below is not so much that consensus was reached on passage of ERA as a top priority, but that so many diverse organizations reflect a feminist awareness in a broad program for societal change.

I.   *Fair Representation and Participation in the Political Process*
Encouragement for women to run for elective office, and provision of the necessary resources for women candidates; appointment of increased numbers of women to political positions.

Provision of opportunities for women and girls to develop and exercise leadership skills; systematic preparation and examination of all legislation, taking into account its effects on women; commitment to and enforcement of equal access and affirmative action rules within political parties. . . .

II. *Equal Education and Training*

Enforcement of laws which guarantee equal access to and treatment in all educational, vocational, and athletic programs and facilities; equalization of financial aids, research opportunities and educational funds for girls and women.

Development of continuing education programs to meet the needs of varying life patterns, and to assess and give education credits for appropriate life experiences.

Increased numbers of women on faculties, administrations, and policy making bodies, at all levels of educational systems.

Incorporation of women's issues into all areas of educational curricula.

III. *Meaningful Work and Adequate Compensation*

Enforcement of legislation prohibiting discrimination at all levels of employment.

Extension of the basic workers' benefits to household workers, migrant and agricultural workers, and homemakers.

Economic and legal recognition of homemakers' work.

Recognition of pregnancy related disabilities as normal, temporary employment disabilities.

Attainment of equal pay for comparable work, that is, work frequently performed by women which is equivalent to work performed by men, but for which women receive less pay.

Review of widely used industrial designs and machinery which inhibit women's work production.

IV. *Equal Access to Economic Power*

A minimum standard of income for low income and disadvantaged persons.

Elimination of discrimination in income tax laws and the social security system, and introduction of coverage under S.S. for unpaid homemakers; elimination of discrimination against women in credit, insurance, and benefit and pension plans.

V. *Quality Child Care for All Children*

Creation of a comprehensive system of child care which includes parent involvement; child care as a tax deductible business expense.

VI. *Quality Health Care and Services*

Support for and expansion of medical and mental health services available without regard to ability to pay.

Implementation of the legal right of women to control their own reproductive systems.

Expansion of private and public health insurance to provide for women's special needs.

Increased attention to and support for research into new drugs and medical procedures which have special significance for women.

VII. *Adequate Housing*

VIII. *Just and Humane Treatment in the Criminal Justice System*

Repeal of laws which treat women and men differently within the criminal justice system; equalization of services for women and men offenders.

Achievement of expanded representation and participation of women in positions of authority in the criminal justice system.

Improved treatment of rape victims by personnel within the criminal justice system; reexamination of laws pertaining to victimless crimes.

IX. *Fair Treatment By and Equal Access to Media and the Arts*

X. *Physical Safety*

Recognition of and respect for the autonomy and dignity of the female person; recognition of rape as a violent and serious crime.

Reform of laws which make it unduly difficult to convict rapists and which place victims of rape in the role of the accused in the legal system; creation and expansion of support programs for rape victims.

XI. *Respect for the Individual*

Protection of the right to privacy of relationships between consenting adults.

Extension of all civil rights legislation to prohibit discrimination based on affectional or sexual preference.

End to prejudice and discrimination against women who wish to determine their own names.

Elimination of discrimination against women based on marital status.

Recognition that women are individuals with full rights to make the choices affecting their lives.[22]*

---

4.   If the demands statement focuses on programmatic issues (for example, enforcement of laws, how public money should be spent), then the statement's authors will want to consider what programmatic demands are realistic and which ones are winnable. Demands, like negotiating stances, can stake out an extreme or optimistic position but leave room, in the minds of organizers, for compromise. Whatever strategy is employed, the question "What is achievable?" must always be taken into account.

5.   Demands are very much like posters and other abbreviated forms of communication. As noted above, they must make points simply. In addition, demands should include only a limited number of key ideas. Some demands statements present the group's full range of principal concerns, although even here they are usually limited to ten or fifteen and are briefly stated. Demands of the programmatic kind should be sufficiently focused so that both the public and officials can seriously consider them as a package. If programmatic demands cover too much ground, they run the risk of appearing frivolous or unrealistic. At the very least, organizers should write demands so that they cannot easily be discredited by the opposition as outlandish. That does not mean that we need to compromise our goals, merely that demands, as a type of action, are best implemented in succinct units that hold together conceptually.

6.   If demands are intended for a particular agency or organization's response, they should cover only those issues on which the agency or organization has authority to act.

Symbolic Acts

Symbolic acts are perhaps the most fun of all social protest strategies because they require the greatest amount of creativity. They also pose some real risks to the organization's image. Typical symbolic acts include such things as mock awards,

---

*Excerpts from a leaflet circulated by Women's Action Alliance, New York City, in behalf of the sponsoring organizations, 1975.

mock elections, street theatre, and counter events (for example, grading the school; declaring welfare officials ineligible to serve poor people). The symbolic act calls attention, often with humor and sarcasm, to a policy or practice of need that the groups want to expose or change. Because it appears shocking or surprising, people tend to remember the symbolic act. By the same token, if a symbolic act offends the sensibilities of the intended audience (usually the public) it can have an opposite effect from the one intended. In other words, there is a danger in creating an overly bizarre or controversial symbolic act. For example, one local group wanted to protest the U.S. War in Vietnam and did so by having women participants dress in peasant clothes and cover themselves with blood. These costumed participants then lay down on the main street of their city while other participants handed out leaflets and carried protest signs. The event accomplished one of its purposes, namely to attract media attention as well as attention from passersby. Unfortunately, a few people in nearby office buildings who saw the bloodied women lying on the side-walks thought there had been an accident. Within minutes, ambulances came speed-ing into the center of the city, with their sirens blaring. The ambulance drivers became annoyed when they saw that the people were not really hurt. Many pas-sersby expressed anger at the protesters for disrupting local ambulance services.

Some principles for carrying out successful symbolic acts are as follows:

1.   One strategy noted above is the mock award. In one instance, a local peace and justice group gave an award to the person who had attended the most demonstrations sponsored by the group. The award was given to a police officer who had attended the "ceremony" to photograph and thereby intimidate people from participating. The main consideration in such award-granting is to ensure that the "mock" nature of the event is sufficiently obvious to the intended audience. The contrast between the values and beliefs of the group giving the award and the person or group receiving the award must be clear to everyone. Gene Sharp notes an example from the environmental protection field. The Boston Area Ecology Action campaign presented the Boston Edison Company with its "Polluter of the Month" award because the latter had been embroiled in charges of polluting the atmosphere with its generating plants.[23]

2.   Mock elections and mock referendums work best where they are linked to issues of inadequate representations. When groups feel that the decision-making machinery of city government, or of a corporation or other organization effectively excludes important issues and constituencies from representation, they will find mock elections and mock referendums to be extremely helpful. Again we turn to Gene Sharp for a powerful example:

> In 1963 and 1964, Civil rights groups set up "freedom registration" for any Mississippian who wanted to register, regardless of the legal restrictions which were widely used to disfranchise Negroes. (Only seven percent or 23,000 of all voting-age Negroes were legally registered to vote in regular elections at the time.) About 83,000 people did "freedom register" and cast their "freedom ballot" for governor and lieutenant governor.[24]

This strategy vividly demonstrated the effects of policies which excluded Blacks from voting. It also communicated the real possibility that people could mobilize to express their interest in voting. Within local communities and organizations, mock referendums and elections have the effect of destroying the credibility of the so-called legitimate elections, referendums, and decision making procedures. Mock referendums or elections challenge the substance of official decisions and policies, the process by which decision making happens, and the representation of constituencies involved in the decision making processes.

3. A vivid symbol must be used to communicate the significance of a symbolic act. The incident cited in the opening section of this chapter concerning the case of Denise McQuade protesting against the New York City transportation authority's failure to unlock the accessible lifts on city buses is a good example. We could imagine members of the Center for Independent Living arriving at the Authority Director's offices with hundreds of keys with the message, "We have the keys to answer the problem." In one town where deaf children had been systematically denied special programming in regular schools—instead they were sent to state-operated and private residential schools far from their home communities—a mother chose to dramatize her son's need for a local program in the regular schools. She called her school, announced that she would be coming over to register her child, and invited a news reporter and photographer to observe the event. Interestingly, what began as a symbolic act and media event won her son his programming within the week. The school district capitulated and hired a teacher for the boy. This individual effort and use of similar protest strategies by others eventually led to the creation of deaf education programs in regular schools for all deaf children in that metropolitan area. One neighborhood group that could not get the mayor to attend negotiation sessions in public held a mock hearing in which it placed a life-sized doll that looked like the mayor in a chair labeled "The Mayor."

Protesters concerned with dangers of radioactive wastes attended a shareholders meeting of a major corporation which produced radioactive wastes and which contaminated residential areas. The shareholder activists—they had bought single shares in order to gain access to the annual meeting—listened while corporate officials claimed there was no danger for families living on and nearby waste sites. Then, to challenge the officials' statements, the protesters brought in a sack of dust which they claimed was radioactive. Suddenly, the corporate officials scrambled away from the bag. The point had been made. The protesters forced the officials to admit the dangers of radioactive waste. Further, they dramatized to the public, through the media, the urgency of the situation. Through creative selection of location and strategy, the protest group made its issue vivid and powerful.

4. Another symbolic medium is theater. It works well as a strategy if the group can establish an audience. Usually this means securing media attention. The problem, of course, with media coverage of theater is that the media covers a small portion and misses the overall message. Segmenting the theatrical event into brief sections that make points which can stand alone is helpful in this regard. Symbolic theater can examine in a humorous way the vast differences which often exist between consumer and official perspectives. It is an ideal medium for exploring the feelings of consumers. For example, a theatrical parody of welfare clients' interac-

tion with welfare officials, parents' interaction with school officials over a difference of opinion about what their children need, or a resident's interaction with health officials about nearby toxic wastes, can expose the dramatic difference in perspective, interests, and concerns between the two. Theatrical presentations have an advantage over the didactic statements contained in demands and leaflets. They can communicate nuances and feelings of people's experiences with official organizations. This can prove a particularly good strategy to use with the protest group itself in order to develop a shared sense of common experience ("that's just what it's like") and an easy camaraderie about working together. The theatrical approach also effectively draws in new participants to the organizing group.

DID IT MAKE ANY DIFFERENCE?

Just as it may be fashionable in some professional circles to say that we have too much confrontation and interest group politics these days, so too it is easy for onlookers of social protest to ask rhetorically, "What difference did it make?" or to say critically, "Their approach (protest) seemed to defeat their own purpose." However, as we have seen, social protest has multiple functions, all of them important in our history as a culture, and all of them important to community organizing.

Social protest galvanizes participants. It carries with it a sense of personal involvement in change, a feeling of "putting your body on the line," that few other types of organizing strategies can even approximate. It acts as a vehicle for getting large numbers of people involved. It helps provide the sense of community that so many people desire from social movements.

Social protest puts issues on local and national agendas quickly. By the time people protest, they believe in their issues. They have a language with which to communicate their concerns. They literally force their issues onto the social policy stage. In most instances, other forms of political expression for protest constituencies' issues have been unavailable. Direct action provides immediate access.

Social protest intensifies the importance of an issue to political leaders and bureaucracies. In effect, social protest on an issue causes decision makers to respond more quickly by forcing issues higher up on a crowded issue agenda. Social protest disrupts the political calm that politicians would prefer. It forces people to take a stand.

Social protest is a demanding activity for organizing groups. It requires greater discipline than many other strategies. Organizing groups which use direct action strategies must define their issues, possess clear goals and objectives, be able to determine what goals and objectives are winnable, and know how to fit strategy to circumstances and timing. They must have a good sense of the group members' skills and abilities, be able to engage in direct action and educate the public at the same time, link one action to another in a sequence, and ensure that its action strategies are compatible with its values. Thus consideration of social protest as a strategy should force groups into careful self-reflection.

Finally, social protest does achieve change. Tremendous changes have occurred in our society. There is much greater awareness of racism, sexism, and handicapism. Integrated education (albeit still inadequate) and greater job opportunities exist for women and minorities. Consumer involvement in questioning health care practices has increased. The right to education for children and youth with disabilities has been won. These changes have occurred in part because people engaged in organized social protest. In turn, these changes encourage others toward future social protest. They suggest that change *does* occur and thus give cause for optimism.

NOTES

[1]Jeremy Brecher, *Strike* (Boston: South End Press, 1972).

[2]Sidney Lens, *Radicalism in America* (New York: T. Y. Crowell, 1966).

[3]John Lewis, in *They Should Have Served That Cup of Coffee,* ed., Dick Cluster (Boston: South End Press, 1979).

[4]"We Won!" *The Ram's Horn,* May 1981, pp. 1–3.

[5]Henry David Thoreau, "Civil Disobedience," in *Civil Disobedience,* Hugo Adam Bedan ed., (New York: Pegasus, 1969), pp. 31–32.

[6]The Center on Human Policy, "The Community Imperative," (Syracuse, New York: The Center on Human Policy, 1979).

[7]Frances Fox Piven and Richard A. Cloward, *Poor People's Movements: Why They Succeed, How They Fail* (New York: Pantheon, 1977).

[8]Brecher, *Strike,* 1972.

[9]Alexis de Tocqueville quoted in Brecher, *Strike,* p. xxi.

[10]Piven and Cloward, *Movements,* p. 20.

[11]Bernice Reagon, quoted in *They Should Have Served That Cup of Coffee: 7 Radicals Remember the 60's,* ed., Dick Cluster (Boston: South End Press, 1979), p. 23.

[12]Saul Alinsky, *Rules for Radicals* (New York: Vintage, 1971), p. 21.

[13]Hannah Arendt, *The Origins of Totalitarianism* (New York: Harcourt Brace Jovanovich, Inc., 1951).

[14]Harry C. Boyte, *The Backyard Revolution* (Philadelphia: Temple University Press), p. 9.

[15]Thoreau, "Civil Disobedience," p. 35.

[16]A. J. Muste quoted in *Peace Agitator: The Story of A. J. Muste,* ed., Nat Hentoff (New York: Macmillan, 1963), pp. 124–25.

[17]Alinsky, *Radicals,* p. 21.

[18]Howard Zinn, *Disobedience and Democracy* (New York: Vintage Books, 1968), p. 13.

[19]Zinn, *Disobedience,* p. 23.

[20]Si Kahn, *How People Get Power* (New York: McGraw-Hill, 1970), p. 81.

[21]Kahn, *People Get Power,* p. 85. See also, Si Kahn *Organizing, A Guide for Grassroots Leaders,* (New York: McGraw-Hill, 1982).

[22]Excerpts from a leaflet circulated by Women's Action Alliance, New York City, 1975, entitled *U.S. National Women's Agenda—1975,* reprinted in Gerda Lerner, *The Female Experience: An American Documentary* (Indianapolis: Bobbs-Merrill, Inc., 1977), pp. 458–62.

[23]Gene Sharp, *The Methods of Nonviolent Action* (Boston: Porter Sargent Publishers, 1973), p. 131.

[24]Sharp, *Nonviolent Action,* p. 131.

CHAPTER SIX
LEGAL ADVOCACY

THE RISE OF LAW IN
COMMUNITY ORGANIZATION*

The Supreme Court's decision in *Brown* v. *The Board of Education* (1954)[1] revolutionized American education and opened the floodgates of civil rights litigation. Segregated schooling had been deeply rooted in America. The court ordered its halt and in so doing wiped out the legal basis for all publicly sponsored racial segregation. It rejected the "separate but equal" mentality of *Plessy* v. *Ferguson* (1896).[2]

But the *Brown* v. *The Board of Education* case did not happen simply[3] nor was it an isolated event, in law or in society at large. This landmark school desegregation case grew out of a long tradition of community organizing and legal wrangling. Innumerable cases had preceded it. Levi Pearson, with the backing of a local South Carolina Chapter of the National Association for the Advancement of Colored People (NAACP), risked his farm and, therefore, his livelihood to win the right of black children, including his own, to school bus transportation. Meanwhile in Texas, when a sixty-five year old Black college president was dragged from a courtroom where he was to have served jury duty, the NAACP again took up the challenge to overcome racism. The college president won. A few years later, B. W. Steele, an Alabama railway worker was denied promotion because of a secret and fraudulent agreement between a white union, known as the Brotherhood of Fire-

---

*Certain legal terms appear throughout this chapter. These terms are defined at the end of the chapter (A Glossary of Terms). The reader may want to refer to this section before reading the other sections.

men, and the Louisville and Nashville Railroad. The NAACP challenged the company-union deal. The NAACP and its client, the black railway worker, won.

By 1950, the NAACP was winning more regularly than in earlier years, but the decisions were still narrower than what was later to be achieved in the Brown case. For example, in *Sweatt* v. *Painter* (1950), Heman Sweatt won entrance to the University of Texas Law School.[4] Previously, the state had established a new law school just for him, one with 16,000 books, 23 students, and 5 full time faculty. It was the determination of the Supreme Court that this separate school was obviously unequal to the established and well-endowed state university law school. Also in 1950, the Supreme Court abolished segregated dining car service on the Southern Railway. These decisions were narrowly drawn because none overthrew once and for all the *Plessy* v. *Ferguson* separation doctrine. For that, society had to await the famed Brown case. This string of court cases, nearly all of them created, nurtured, and fought out by the NAACP, pushed the courts closer and closer to the ultimate *Brown* decision. The NAACP organizers were often the lawyers themselves. Two such organizers were Thurgood Marshall and Charles Houston:

> Thurgood Marshall thrived under the tutelage of Charles Houston. They worked closely for only a few years, but there was an intimacy and an understanding . . . "You have to understand that we had absolutely no money at all in those days," Marshall recounts. When they were on the road, filing law suits in the court houses of the South, "Charlie would sit in my car—I had a little old, beat up '29 Ford—and type out the briefs. And he could type up a storm—faster than any secretary—and not with just two fingers going, I mean he used 'm all. We'd stay at friends' homes in those days—for free, you understand. I think the whole budget for the legal office then was maybe $8,000—that was for two lawyers and a secretary." And when they could not find the friends' home, they would put up at grimy hotels and something a little better if they could find it in the land of Jim Crow, and Houston and Marshall would jaw over bourbon about life and law far into the night . . . Where Houston was a fine writer and superb draftsman of legal briefs, Marshall was gifted with the spoken word, full of humor or fire as the occasion demanded, whether in a court room or before a packed house of overwrought black farmers in a remote church.[5]

Marshall and Houston would drive through southern states literally soliciting plaintiffs for various test cases, all having to do with discrimination toward Blacks. Marshall's notes from those days reveal the fact that he and Houston were as much organizers as lawyers. In the words of Richard Kluger (1976), Marshall was "an experienced guerrilla fighter." In South Boston, a tobacco town, Marshall wrote the following:

> School situation is terrible. Principal of elementary school is gardener and janitor for the county superintendent of schools and is a typical Uncle Tom. New addition to high school at Halifax but not equipped. Elementary school is terrible. Question of voting has not arisen because so few register. Spoke at mass meeting and stressed school questions and voting questions. Negroes in this community very lax and inactive. President of (NAACP) branch fighting almost alone.[6]

In Winston-Salem, he wrote:

> Only those negroes are permitted to register who are "alright" negroes. Others are refused. No one will bring a case on the question. Had the president of the branch . . . call a meeting of his executive committee. Stressed the point to them and told them that they should start a program to break this down. We will have to keep behind this branch. Winston-Salem negroes have money—they all work in factories and make good money. They have a bus company on the streets owned and operated by negroes. Branch should be strong. They want a speaker for mass meeting, but do not have money. Winston-Salem should be one of the main spots for the franchise (voter registration) fight.[7]

The National Association for the Advancement of Colored People had created its own legal corporation, known as the NAACP Legal Defense and Education Fund, Incorporated, in 1939 (its nickname was "the Inc. Fund"). It was not until the 1950s, however, that the NAACP won cases on a regular basis, and it was not until 1954 that the full fruits of the years of organizing were realized. In its watershed Civil Rights decision, the court outlawed separate schools by declaring that separation was inherently unequal. With those words, the legal onslaught against Jim Crow laws grew from battles and skirmishes to all out war.

The Brown decision was accompanied by growing protest movements. In 1955 Rosa Parks refused to give up her seat on a Montgomery, Alabama bus to a white passenger. She was arrested for breaking a city ordinance that called for segregated transportation. Martin Luther King, Jr. took her case to the streets. He organized a city-wide boycott of the bus system that began in December 1955. That boycott is generally regarded as the first in a flood of "direct action" protests. It was part of what has been variously called the "civil rights movement" and "the second Reconstruction." The protests and increased use of litigation after the 1954 Brown case led to the passage of the 1964 Civil Rights Act.

It was not until the 1960s that litigation became a *commonplace* weapon in community organizers' arsenals. Urban riots of the late 60s gave impetus to increased focus on the institutional quality of discrimination and economic oppression. Perhaps most important, though, was the emergence of the federal legal program, known as the Office of Economic Opportunity's Neighborhood Legal Services. Piven and Cloward believe there was a cause and effect between OEO funding and litigation's influence on welfare agencies and clients: "Lawyers know what they are paid to know, and until OEO funds became available very few knew anything about laws affecting the poor, least of all about the "poor laws.""[8] OEO funding soon outstripped all other legal aid services combined. The effects were nearly instantaneous:

> For decades reformers had lobbied unsuccessfully for legislative repeal of residence laws, man-in-the-house rules, and employable-mother rules. But, in the 1960's these foundation blocks of the "poor law" were washed away by one court (decision) after another.[9]

Basing their decision on the constitutional rights of equal protection, due process, and freedom to travel, the courts knocked down residency requirements. The Supreme Court ruled that children could not be denied welfare payments simply because their mother had relations with a man. Welfare recipients won the right to a fair hearing before the Welfare Department could cut off payments. Later, federal welfare regulations would ensure the welfare recipients' right to a fair hearing at every major decision point:

> In every state, under the federal law you are legally entitled to a fair hearing any time that: (1) a request for aid is denied; (2) a request for aid is not acted upon within forty-five days; (3) a request for aid is only partly granted; or (4) aid that you are receiving is reduced, suspended, or terminated; (5) aid is paid in the form of vendor or third party payments.[10]

Use of the law spread. The National Welfare Rights Organization published welfare rights booklets in which legal rights were translated into lay language. The Mobilization for Youth, which was the prototype for the Great Society program of the 1960's, encouraged poor people to demonstrate their awareness of their rights when negotiating with welfare officials. Welfare Rights advocates demanded tighter, more explicit regulations for welfare laws. They sought to reduce the discretionary power of welfare officials. Poor peoples' groups began to monitor welfare practices to see if they matched legal requirements.[11]

The issues to which law could be addressed also spread. In 1967, juveniles won the right to be represented by attorneys in Juvenile Court. Justice Abe Fortas outlined juvenile rights in the famous case *In Re Gault*. Included were:

> (1) timely notice of the specific charges against them; (2) notification of the right to be represented by counsel in proceedings which "may result in commitment to an institution in which the juvenile's freedom is curtailed"; (3) the right to confront and cross-examine complainants and other witnesses; and (4) adequate warning of the privilege against self-incrimination and the right to remain silent.
>
> The right to counsel was the fundamental issue in *Gault* because exercise of the right assures procedural regularity and the implementation of related principles.[12]

In Minnesota, nursing homes became the object of legal analysis. Daphne Kraus, Executive Director of Minneapolis Age and Opportunity (MAO) Center, Inc., collected sworn affidavits on nursing home abuses from older people, nursing home staff, and families whose relatives resided in nursing homes. With these documents in hand, MAO demanded new state rules and regulations for the nursing home industries. One of the new regulations was a patients' bill of rights. Another provision called for unannounced state inspections.[13] In 1979, older persons in Massachusetts went into court (*Linden* v. *King*—represented by Greater Boston Elderly Legal Service) to argue for their right to noninstitutional care and supportive services in the community.[14]

Tenants' rights became a legal issue as well. The Cambridge Tenants Organizing Committee published a handbook called Legal Tactics for Tenants. The Minnesota Tenants Union published the handbook, "If You Pay Rent, You've Got Rights Too!" Another group, Shelterforce, published a quarterly newspaper in New Jersey. One of the best known national lobbyists for tenant rights is the National Tenants Organization (NTO), based in New York City. The emergence of tenants' rights as a legal issue stems in part from the consumer rights and civil rights movements of the 50s and 60s, but also from the promise embedded in a single court decision, *Javins v. First National Realty* (1970).[15] In that case, District of Columbia Federal Circuit Court Judge J. Skelly Wright found that the relationship of urban tenant to landlord was often an unequal one:

> The inequality of bargaining power between landlord and tenant has been well documented. Tenants have very little leverage to enforce demands for better housing. Various impediments to competition in the rental housing market, such as racial and class discrimination and standardized form leases, mean that landlords place tenants in a take-it-or-leave-it situation. The increasingly severe shortage of adequate housing further increases the landlord's bargaining power.[16]

For these and a host of other reasons, Judge Wright declared the tenants' right to expect quality housing. One could expect a roof that did not leak, an apartment with heat and running water, and so on. There was, to use the court's language, a "warranty of habitability." The leased property had to be habitable, and the lease itself was to be treated as any other contract would. Also, a landlord would not be allowed to insert clauses in a contract that would exclude provisions of municipal housing codes, health standards, or other housing regulations. Even if not stated in writing, the warranty of habitability was implied.

Comparable rights were being won in health care. Not all the new-found health rights grew out of organizing efforts, but their effect was nevertheless to bolster an emerging health rights movement. A man who entered a hospital for treatment of a gunshot wound was allowed to bleed, untreated, for two hours, before being transferred to another hospital where he died shortly thereafter. The court, in the case of *New Biloxi Hospital v. Frazier*, found the hospital liable.[17] It was not permissable to make a person wait an unreasonable time for treatment. Similarly, the courts have found that "essential hospital treatment must be administered without regard to cost or ability to pay."[18] Much of the recent health rights litigation has focused on the rights of particular segments of society. Mental patients and exmental patients, for example, have carved out a major area of litigation known as mental health law. The American Bar Association now publishes a journal called the *Mental Disability Law Reporter* which reports on this new legal territory. The preeminant mental health case in the practice of this kind of law is *O'Connor v. Donaldson* (1975).[19] Kenneth Donaldson, represented by Bruce Ennis of the American Civil Liberties Union, established the right not to be incarcerated unless proven to be potentially dangerous, and the right to treatment if incarcerated.

Another segment of the population that has had a profound impact on health law is women. For example, women challenged tradition when they began to ask for the right to have their husbands participate in childbirth. While this has not yet become a legal right, for many hospitals it has become commonplace policy. Men have won access to the delivery room and participate in the childbirth process. Declaration of a legal right in this area cannot be far off.

In 1973, women won the right to have an abortion. But in 1980, women on medicaid lost the right to have medicaid pay for an abortion. This occurred when the Supreme Court upheld a federal law (the Hyde Amendment) barring medicaid payments for abortions.[20] The conflicting views of the Supreme Court Justices reveal the degree to which health care, like other human services, has been declared a political issue.

Speaking for the court majority of Stewart, Burger, White, Powell, and Rehnquist, Stewart argued that though women possessed a choice of abortion or birth, Congress had no obligation to make that choice equally accessible for poor as well as monied women:

> Although government may not place obstacles in the path of a woman's exercise of her freedom of choice, it need not remove those not of its own creation, and indigency falls within the latter category; . . . poverty, standing alone, is not a suspect classification; . . . the only requirement of equal protection is that congressional action be rationally related to a legitimate government interest. The Hyde amendment satisfies that standard since . . . it is rationally related to the legitimate governmental objective of protecting potential life.

Brennan, one of the dissenters, found the court's ruling hypocritical:

> In the abstract, of course, this choice (of birth or abortion) is hers alone . . . But the reality of the situation is that the Hyde Amendment has effectively removed this choice from the indigent woman's hands.

Marshall, equally distraught with the court's ruling, predicted dire consequences:

> They (poor women) must resort to back-alley butchers, attempt to induce an abortion themselves by crude and dangerous means, or suffer the serious medical consequences of attempting to carry the fetus to term. . . .
>
> Federal funding is thus unavailable even when severe and long-lasting health damage to the mother is a virtual certainty. Nor are federal funds available when severe health damage, or even death, will result to the fetus if it is carried to term. . . .
>
> The Court resolves the equal protection issue in this case through a relentlessly formalistic catechism. . . .
>
> The Court's decision today . . . marks a cruel blow to the most powerless members of our society.

Blackmun had a similar view:

> There is "condescension" in the court's holding "that she may go elsewhere for her abortion"; this is "disingenuous and alarming"; the government "punitively impresses upon a needy minority its own concepts of the socially desirable, the publicly acceptable, and the morally sound"; there truly is "another world" out there; the

existence of which the Court, I suspect, either chooses to ignore or fears to recognize"; the "cancer of poverty will continue to grow"; and "the lot of the poorest among us," once again and still, is not to be bettered.[21]

Stevens also dissented.

We have taken considerable space to elaborate on the abortion case, not because abortion is controversial, nor even because it is a principal example of women's law, but rather because *Harris* v. *McRae* (1980) reveals the fundamental division in the Supreme Court and among legal scholars over the issue of equality. This definitional dispute is crucial to nearly every area of public interest law. Does the court's view of "equality" assume a neutral social context? Are all people, poor and wealthy, black and white, the powerful and powerless, equally able to make informed choices? Or should the concept of equal protection be applied differentially to overcome the imbalance of the social context, an imbalance of power, status, class position, and wealth?

Also, in the late '60s and early 1970s litigation was brewing on behalf of another fledgling social movement. People with disabilities took to the streets in protest against inaccessible buildings and transportation and job discrimination. In what turned out to be landmark litigation, almost as significant in the history of disability rights as the *Brown* case was in the tradition of civil rights, parents of handicapped children initiated the first major court case to establish the right of every child, however, handicapped, to an education (*PARC* v. *Pennsylvania*, 1971).[22] The Pennsylvania Association for Retarded Citizens, thirteen parents, their thirteen children, and their public interest attorney, Thomas Gilhool, filed the PARC complaint. There was one central allegation, that handicapped children were being denied an education. The case of the first-named plaintiff was typical:

> 14. Nancy Beth Bowman, born December 12, 1950, has been assigned an intelligence quotient of approximately 55.
> 15. From 2½ to 6 years of age, Nancy Beth Bowman at her parents' expense attended private school from 9:00 A.M. to 2:00 P.M., five days a week at the Chestnut Hill Rehabilitation Center. Later, she attended the Day School of the Montgomery County Association of Retarded Children.
> 16. During this early schooling Nancy Beth Bowman learned the rudiments of reading and counting; she became toilet trained and learned table manners.
> 17. When Nancy Beth Bowman was eight years of age, the school psychologist of the Abington School District announced that she could not stay in school and recommended long term placement to her parents. Her parents have not been informed by the School District whether she was excluded or excused from the public schools.
> 18. Since her placement at the Pennhurst State School in 1960, Nancy Beth Bowman has received no educational instruction, nor is any now being provided.[23]

In a court supervised consent agreement between the plaintiffs and the State, resolution came quickly and unequivocally:

> Every retarded person between the ages of six and twenty-one shall be provided access to a free public program of education and training appropriate to his capacities as soon

as possible but in no event later than September 1, 1972 (paragraph 42 of Consent agreement, October 7th, 1971).[24]

Within a few years of the PARC decision's implementation date, the nation's state education departments were besieged by right-to-education litigation. In each case the plaintiffs prevailed. In 1974, the Washington based Children's Defense Fund declared that 2 million children had been excluded from school and that nearly half of them had been excluded because of a handicap. At the same time, state and national legislators were beginning to address special education issues as well. Congress responded to the mounting demand by disabled children and their families for equal education by enacting Public Law 94-142, the Education for All Handicapped Children Act (1975).[25] This act combined the same principles enunciated in litigation:

1. each school age child has a right to a free, appropriate education;
2. each handicapped child has the right to an individualized education plan;
3. each state must demonstrate efforts to locate unserved and underserved children;
4. child testing and assessment must be nondiscriminatory;
5. parents and their children are entitled to formal due process on matters of classification and educational placement;
6. parents are entitled to be involved in planning for their children's education;
7. parents are entitled to see their children's school records;   ·
8. education includes, where appropriate, related services, such as speech, occupational, and physical therapies; and
9. each child has the right to be served in the least restrictive environment possible (most integrated).

Public Law 94-142 and its regulations had the effect of codifying in one place the right to education litigation that had come from the grassroots of America. Henceforth, right to education litigation would focus more on enforcement, standards of quality, and/or refinement of such controversial and seemingly plastic terms as "least restrictive" and "appropriate." Public Law 94-142 cemented previous state-by-state court and legislative victories at the same time it opened the possibility of new challenges to old practices.

THE USES OF LAW IN COMMUNITY ORGANIZATION

Community organizers use the law as a tool for multiple purposes. To be sure, organizers have used the law to litigate for social policy ends. However, the uses of law extend far beyond this well-known role.

Thomas Gilhool, the attorney for retarded children in the Pennsylvania right-to-education litigation, had been involved in other areas of public interest law before coming to disability rights. He had litigated welfare rights, public housing, and civil rights cases. From this experience, he knew well the expansive role of law. In a memorandum prepared for the Pennsylvania Association for Retarded Citizens in 1969, prior to the PARC litigation, he argued that litigation could do more than settle a legal point:

> There is nothing peculiar or extraordinary about litigation as a mode of social change. It is of the same cut as the other efforts of the Association to make use of other forums to define certain issues and to secure appropriate decisions by public officials.
>
> Litigation has, inevitably, not only the function of securing a particular result, but of displaying facts and conditions clearly and precisely both before the public and before decision makers, of redefining the questions which must be answered by both. There is and should be considerable interface between litigation and the other efforts of the Association.[26]

Gilhool recognized that a lawsuit would bring media attention and consequently wake up people to a major injustice. It would establish noneducation of retarded children as a social problem, bring credibility to parent demands, and instill a sense of strength in the emerging consumer movement. Activism would be legitimized and serve as a centerpiece strategy around which other strategies could coalesce.

Indeed, the role of law extends beyond litigation itself. In community organization, law has at least five major roles.

A Philosophical Framework for Action.   All community organizers possess an ideological perspective, a framework from which their day-to-day organizing flows. Some adhere to the democratic principle that oppressed groups deserve more equal input into the political and decision making processes of the society. Some espouse a particular style of organizing such as self-help. Others base their actions on a particular goal such as legalizing or banning abortion. One group, the American Civil Liberties Union views constitutional law as its guiding framework. Hence, the ACLU can organize for such diverse groups as Nazis, communists, poor people, women, students, gays, Jews, and draft resisters.

Constitutional as well as federal, international, state, and municipal law can and does provide some organizing groups with a framework for action. While it is more common for issue oriented groups such as NAACP, NWRO, anti- and pro-abortion groups, the National Tenant Organization, and the American Coalition of Citizens with Disabilities to use the law only when it serves their interests rather than as the *central* reason for their being, certain legal principles, particularly constitutional principles, provide them with an ideological framework for practical action.

Two constitutional principles have had enormous influence within social change movements. They are "equal protection" and "due process." These two concepts, perhaps more than any others (for example, freedom of speech, freedom of travel, least restrictive alternative, privacy rights, protection from cruel and unusual punishment) have afforded organizers an ideological framework. It is difficult to think of any community organizing litigation that has not relied upon or at

least made reference to these key concepts. Equal protection is a concept outlined in
the fifth and fourteenth amendments of the constitution. The equal protection guarantee means that federal and state government must treat people equally. For instance, handicapped children cannot be denied an education when it is provided to
nonhandicapped children so long as the former can benefit from it. Similarly religious freedoms, freedom of speech, and other forms of guaranteed expression
must be available on an equal basis, irrespective of a group's or individual's status
in society. (This concept is further defined in the glossary of terms, Part III). In
Brown v. *Board of Education,* the Supreme Court found that separate schooling,
organized along racial lines, failed to respect the equal protection rights of Black
students.

The concept of due process refers to the requirement that government provide
people an opportunity to challenge or appeal a government action which will limit
their exercise of basic rights such as freedom to travel, the right to own property, or
the right to vote. In short, government must be procedurally fair. Denial of welfare
must be accompanied by the right to challenge that decision in an appeal. Denial of
education must be accompanied by due process rights. Incarceration, whether in a
mental hospital or prison must be accompanied by fair procedures, by procedural
safeguards, to protect individual rights. (Due process is further explained in the
glossary).

    Litigation.   The most obvious use of law by community organizers is litiga-
tion. Community organizers frequently use litigation in the manner outlined by
Gilhool, that is to bring attention to an issue and to help in mass mobilization. The
central purpose of "test litigation" is the establishment of public policy through
law. Certain decisions such as *Roe* v. *Wade* in the area of abortion, *Brown* v. *Board
of Education* in racial desegregation, *O'Connor* v. *Donaldson* in right-to-treatment,
In re Gault and *Morales* v. *Turman* for juvenile justice, and *Javins* v. *First National
Realty* for tenant rights, clearly become rallying points for community organization
efforts in their fields. Often what follows test litigation is grassroots organizing and
parallel litigation. These serve to win enforcement in particular localities and force
greater definition and clarity of principles outlined in the parent test cases.

    In addition to clarifying legal rights and, often, transforming privilege into
right, litigation achieves other ends. It lends authority to the organizing group and
stands out as a tangible event. Expectations are created for definitive victory and it
usually opens up official institutional structures, such as social service departments,
boards of education, and housing authorities to careful scrutiny by a process that
lawyers call "discovery." Litigation can also provide a sense of moral support to
community organization. This is particularly true when the litigation communicates
human experiences. Note, for example, the human drama and human urgency of
litigation on behalf of institutionalized retarded persons:

> The physical environment at Pennhurst (institution) is hazardous to the residents, both
> physically and psychologically (Clements, N.T., 2-59). There is often excrement and
> urine on ward floors (Roos, N.T. 1-158; Smith, Deposition at 41), and the living areas
> do not meet minimal professional standards for cleanliness (Youngberg, Deposition at

24). Outbreaks of pinworms and infectious diseases are common (M. Conley, N.T. 16-193; Lowrie, N.T. 4-153; Hedson, Deposition at 122). As Superintendent Young-berg noted: "There is not adequate space for (the residents. The living areas do) not provide privacy for those persons who can handle privacy. There does not seem to be adequate activity areas or program areas or even general activity areas within the general living area or even adequate activity program areas away from the home living area" (Deposition at 23).

The environment at Pennhurst is not only not conducive to learning new skills, but it is so poor that it contributes to losing skills already learned (Clements, N.T. 2-59). For example, Pennhurst has a toilet training program, but one who has success-fully completed the program may not be able to practice the newly learned skill, and is therefore likely to lose it (Clements, N.T. 2-36, 2-27). Moreover, most toilet areas do not have towels, soap or toilet paper, and the bathroom facilities are often filthy and in a state of disrepair. Obnoxious odors and excessive noise permeate the atmosphere at Pennhurst. Such conditions are not conducive to habilitation (Dybwad, N.T. 7-52). Moreover, the noise level in the day rooms is often so high that many residents simply stop speaking (Clements, N.T. 2-59). . . .

Injuries to residents by other residents, and through self-abuse, are common. For example, on January 8, 1975, one individual bit off three-quarters of the earlobe and part of the outer ear of another resident while the second resident was asleep (Matthews, Deposition at 83). About this same period, one resident pushed a second to the floor, resulting in the death of the second resident. . . .

In January, 1977 alone, there were 833 minor and 25 major injuries report-ed. . . .

In addition, there is some staff abuse of residents. In 1976, one resident was raped by a staff person (Ruddick, N.T. 3-115 to 3-117); one resident was badly bruised when a staff person hit him with a set of keys (Baron, Deposition at 40); another resident was thrown several feet across a room by a staff person (Ruddick, N.T. 3-113; Caranfa, N.T. 12-79); and one resident was hit by a staff person with a shackle belt.[27]

Litigation becomes an effective forum for frank, stark, even devastating revelation of the consumer's case.

Public and Consumer Education.   Just as litigation can define, clarify, and communicate issues, reference alone to legal principles and laws can also educate. Organizers have long recognized the importance of having something to offer those with whom they organize. Leadership skills, expert knowledge of the consumers' issues (for example, health care, welfare benefits, housing, education, transporta-tion, and social planning) and organizing tactics are all among the repertoire of "goods" which the organizer may bring to an affected group. Knowledge of legal rights is another skill and, often, a potential strategy.

Legal rights booklets, pamphlets, and newspapers have proven effective in issues of health care, tenant rights, welfare, education, mental health, disability rights, civil rights, women's rights, gay rights, and student rights organizing. Or-ganizing groups have translated particular federal and state laws, constitutional law, and the results of litigation (case law) into plain English. Legal rights manuals, as other organizing literature, have achieved wide circulation because they have filled a desperate need *and* because they have been prepared on a basic literacy level.

The American Civil Liberties Union has created handbooks on most key organizing issues. The ACLU series of handbooks carry such titles as: *The Rights of*

Hospital Patients (1975); *The Rights of Prisoners* (1973); *The Rights of Older Persons* (1979); *The Rights of Mental Patients* (1973); *The Rights of Mentally Retarded Persons* (1976); *The Rights of the Poor* (1974); *The Rights of Tenants* (1978); *The Rights of Gay People* (1975); and *The Rights of Women* (1973).[28] These books, like most legal handbooks for consumers, have been organized in a question and answer format.

The handbook explosion began in the 1960s:

> The community-action agencies themselves prepared handbooks in hundreds of cities and counties . . . Inner city churches produced handbooks in Cleveland and Pittsburgh. The NAACP Legal Defense and Educational Fund made up handbooks for use in some Deep South states. Civil liberties unions brought out manuals in a number of places, such as Wisconsin and District of Columbia . . . the National Urban League prepared and distributed handbooks for use in a dozen Northern states . . . in Columbus and the District of Columbia . . . handbooks were prepared by settlement houses in 1966 . . . the National Welfare Rights Organization stimulated the development of manuals in dozens of places, in part by distributing sample copies of manuals that had been prepared by various anti-poverty agencies. At one point in New York City, three different comprehensive handbooks were available; one prepared by MFY, another by the Citizen's Committee for Children, . . . and still another by the OEO sponsored Center on Social Welfare Policy and Law at Columbia University.[29]

Can tenants withhold their rent in order to win improvements? What is rent abatement? Must an emergency room treat a person who asks for help? When is a juvenile entitled to legal representation? What standards must a nursing home meet? Can older people work and still receive social security? Does a retarded adult have the right to live in the community rather than in an institution? Can the state impose residence requirements on welfare recipients? Who is eligible for vocational rehabilitation services? These are the kinds of questions usually addressed in legal rights handbooks.

The purpose of legal rights handbooks is not merely to inform people of their rights; they are an organizing tool. Knowledgeable consumers, armed with specific information, can demand their rights and resist being denied services. An informed consumer population cannot easily be dissuaded by vague and vindictive phrases such as: "We can't solve all of your problems," "That's not our responsibility," "You are not eligible," "We don't have the money," and "It's not our decision to make."

Legal handbooks inform about legal rights. Clearly, when individuals and groups can refer to a particular statute, regulation, or constitutional right upon which to base their demands, officials tend to respond differently than if these individuals were uninformed. The reason for this is that legal language, and reference to legal principles, like references to statistics and formal research, carries with it an air of authority. Edelman has noted the public's reverance for statistics:

> Statistics are so effective in shaping political support and opposition that governments quite often resort to publicizing statistics that have little or no reasonable bearing on an issue . . .[30]

The point is that statistics and other "scientific" or professional jargon conjure up images of authority. Similarly, legal jargon and, particularly, legalistic constructions, sound authoritative. Whether right or not, whether accurate or not, legal language gives an impression of correctness and precision. Not surprisingly, then, legal information couched in legal language or legal citations has proven useful to other strategies, including public education, negotiations, and monitoring.

Monitoring and Enforcement. In part one of this chapter, we mentioned Daphne Kraus and the Minneapolis Age and Opportunity Center's campaign to expose nursing home abuses. We noted that their efforts led to regulatory reforms. This type of organizing activity has been called "administrative advocacy." While it will be addressed more fully in Chapter Nine where we examine lobbying, and alternative policy formulation, one aspect of administrative advocacy, namely monitoring, deserves attention here for it is a major, though usually nonlitigative, use of the law.

As often as not, organizing begins in response to what might be termed institutional lawlessness. That is, parents file for their children's right to education when it has been illegally denied. Blacks, Chicanos, and other minorities fight business establishments when they violate civil rights acts. However, not all transgressions are met with litigation. One nonlitigative mode of enforcement is monitoring, which involves such steps as: (1) becoming informed of legal rights; (2) identification of institutional rights violations; (3) individual due process appeals; (4) notification to regulatory agencies; (5) filing formal complaints; (6) exposure to media of institutional violations; (7) holding of public forums on violations; (8) exposés through action research (described in Chapter Ten) of violations of law and regulations; and (9) independent evaluations of public policy and practice to assess whether it is consistent with laws and regulations.

To Establish a Moral Presence. The one type of legal advocacy not yet discussed is civil disobedience. In modern history organizers, including Martin Luther King, Cesar Chavez (United Farm Workers), Gandhi, Dan and Phil Berrigan, and many others, have gone to the barricades, often to seek out arrest and thereby solidify the lines of battle over social issues. In this action strategy, the "law" exists to be broken. Organizers challenge it for higher ideals.

Saul Alinsky, in his book *Rules for Radicals* (1971), discusses "Time in Jail." Going to jail was a method of building momentum and stability for a cause:

> The reaction of the status quo in jailing revolutionary leaders is in itself a tremendous contribution to the development of the Have-Not movement as well as to the personal development of the revolutionary leaders. . . .
> Jailing the revolutionary leaders and their followers performs three vital functions for the cause of the Have-Nots: (1) it is an act on the part of the status quo that in itself points up the conflict between the Haves and the Have-Nots; (2) it strengthens immeasurably the position of the revolutionary leaders with their people by surrounding the jailed leadership with an aura of martyrdom; (3) it deepens the identification of the leadership with their people since the prevalent reaction among the Have-Nots is that their leadership cares so much for them, and is so sincerely committed to the issue, that it is willing to suffer imprisonment for the cause.[31]

Traditionally, civil disobedience has been seen not as an end in itself, but as a strategy. Being jailed, therefore, has only limited short-term value in creating a moral presence and coalescence among potentially fragile coalitions. Alinsky warned against seeking out actions that would yield long jail terms. Such actions win immediate attention and sympathy but ultimately isolate activist organizers from the people with whom they organize. It should be noted though, that some outstanding organizers organized others from their jail cells.

LAW AND THE LEGAL SYSTEM

In order to use the law as a tool, whether for litigation, negotiation, monitoring, or community education, we must know at least three basic things about it. First, we must have a working familiarity with the few legal concepts which pervade public interest law. Second, we must know how to locate the key content of major statutes, regulations, and court decisions for an issue area. Third, and finally, we need to have a rudimentary knowledge of the legal system.

Major Legal Concepts

Two concepts dominate public interest litigation. Whether we speak of welfare, education, health care, housing, transportation, or any other major area of service, these concepts establish and reestablish themselves as indispensible to law reform. They are: (1) equal protection and (2) due process.[32] If we knew all there is to know about state and federal laws or an issue area and knew nothing of these two constitutional principles, we would lack the essential framework for understanding how the courts address the major human concerns of our times.

When the Supreme Court disallowed "separate but equal" segregated schooling for Blacks and Whites, in its *Brown* v. *Board of Education* decision, it did so on the grounds of equal protection. All people enjoy the same protection under law to life, liberty, and property. "Equal protection" has been the basis, along with the concept of due process, for the right of patients to be served in hospital emergency rooms, for the right of welfare applicants not to be denied payments on the basis of a residence requirement or cohabitation, for the right to education for children with disabilities, and for equal treatment of men and women under social security laws.

Of course, individuals' rights do not exist in a vacuum. All people have a guarantee to their basic constitutional rights and are protected equally under them *unless* the government (that is, government interests) has a rational reason for limiting those rights. Hardly anyone would disagree that government has a rational basis for denying or restricting freedom of movement (a liberty right) to people who commit murder. That is, government has a rationally derived interest in limiting the freedom of certain individuals. The courts have always recognized the need to balance governmental interests with citizens' individual rights.

The Courts have applied several tests to controversies which involve conflicts between government interests and individual rights. First they ask, "is the government interest a rational one?'' For example, it is generally regarded as rational to allow only those who display certain intellectual abilities to attend colleges. That policy yields unequal treatment, but it has a rational basis.

The second judicial question is, ''Is the government's interest compelling?'' If this interest were frivolous we would hardly want to forfeit individual rights. Suppose Congress passed a law which required people in Massachusetts to paint their houses pink. Suppose then that the government's only interest was that Congress thought it would be a good idea. Such a policy, which flies in the face of individual freedom of choice with respect to property and personal life decisions, fails the test of whether or not the government's interest is compelling.

Third, the government must pursue its interests in a manner which least intrudes on individual rights. Suppose, for example, that the government wanted to protect consumers from milk that is spoiled before it is purchased off the store shelves. The government would *not* be justified in the banning of all milk sales. It would also not be reasonable to deny sales by all farmers who must transport their milk long distances to market (as in *Dean Milk Co.* v. *Madison,* 1951).[33] Each of these policies would prove too drastic and too intrusive. It would, however, be within reason for the government to impose an inspection system and to demand certain standards for refrigeration and pasteurization.

The test of intrusiveness has become popular in human service litigation. It is called the concept of ''least restrictive alternative.'' The point is simply that government should pursue its interests in a manner which least conflicts with individual rights. In the Pennsylvania right-to-education case, for example, the attorneys sued and won the right for retarded children to receive their education as close to the mainstream (regular class) as possible, with appropriate support services. In short, the Court questioned the practice of exiling educationally needy retarded children to total care institutions—that kind of placement was unnecessarily drastic.

The fourth and final test for evaluating a conflict of governmental interests with individual rights concerns the group whose rights are threatened. Is there a rational reason for suggesting that a particular group should have its rights impinged upon by government? In *Brown,* the court found no rational reason to have Black children denied entrance to so-called White schools. The grouping of children by race was ''suspect.'' Similarly, unequal treatment on the basis of sex has generally been viewed as ''suspect.''

In summary, when evaluating whether a particular government policy or practice acts to unfairly deny people their individual rights, we must apply particular tests: (1) does the government have a *rational interest?* (2) is that interest *compelling?* (3) has the government pursued its interests in a manner which *least intrudes* upon individual rights? and (4) is the group whose rights are threatened rationally separated out for unequal treatment or is unequal treatment with respect to this group obviously *suspect?*

The second constitutional concept of central importance to public interest litigation is the principle of due process. The due process clauses of the 5th and 15th amendments of the United States Constitution introduce the concept. It means simply that government, federal and state, shall have clear limitations on *what* individual rights it may limit and on how it may establish its perogative to infringe upon individual rights. In fact, due process is viewed as two concepts: (1) substantive and (2) procedural due process.

Substantive due process refers to those constitutional rights that government may not infringe upon unfairly. *Black's Law Dictionary* defines substantive due process as "the constitutional guarantee that no person shall be arbitrarily deprived of his life, liberty or property; the essence of substantive due process is protection from arbitrary and unreasonable action."[34] For example, the government may not arbitrarily take someone's property or send someone before a firing squad. A person may not be summarily sent off to a total care institution without benefit of procedures by which to challenge the decision—such an action would abridge the constitutional right of liberty. Similarly, the government may not tell the individual who he or she may marry.*

Procedural due process refers to the right of individuals to be heard, to complain when their rights are being infringed upon. In other words, when government acts in a manner that will limit individual rights (for example, terminating welfare payments (property), exclusion of a child from school, confining a person to a mental hospital or juvenile detention center, denying medicaid payments) it must provide fair, impartial procedures by which the individual can test the government action. Most areas of human service law (welfare, education, public health insurance, social security, public housing, vocational rehabilitation) have established elaborate administrative remedies for the individual. The procedural requirements for these remedies are designed to escalate from the informal to the highly formal. Usually the consumer will have an opportunity to bring a dispute before an informal review by the organization administrator. If the results are unsatisfactory, the consumer may then request a formal, impartial hearing. After the hearing stages, the issue or case can usually be brought into state or federal court. Frequently, federal and state regulations spell out due process procedures for a service area.

Knowing the Area of Law

The basic constitutional principles of equal protection and due process provide a framework from which most social policy issues can be examined. These concepts inform not only litigation, but also a whole range of organizing activities (for example monitoring, negotiations, public education) which may have some legal substance. However, knowledge of due process and equal protection is not sufficient. We must also know the particular application of these concepts to specific issue areas. For this, we must turn to case law. We must be aware of particular statutes and regulations in our field of interest.

Consider, for example, racism and school financing, an issue around which

---

*Note: The term "due process rights" is a broader term than "substantive due process," and refers to any rights for which due process has been deemed (by the courts) necessary.

communities have organized repeatedly. How does the concept of equal protection apply here? An explanation of its application was afforded by *San Antonio School District* v. *Rodriguez* (1972).[35] Larson and McDonald describe the findings of case law:

> If school financing inequities are so patent, why are they not unconstitutional under the Fourteenth Amendment?
>
> In 1972, in *San Antonio School District* v. *Rodriguez*, the Supreme Court, in a 5–4 decision, held that school financing inequities do not violate the Fourteenth Amendment's guarantee of equal protection of the laws. The inequities in San Antonio were typical. The poorest school district, which was 96 percent minority, had an average property value for taxation per student of $6,000; at a property tax rate of $1.05 per $100 of property, the school district raised only $26 for the education of each student. The wealthiest school district, which was 19 percent minority, had an average property value for taxation per student of $49,000; at lower property tax rate of only $0.85 per $100 of property, this wealthy school district raised $333 for the education of each student. With the addition of state and federal funds (more federal funds usually go to poor districts than to wealthy districts), the poor district could spend only $356 per student as compared to $594 per student in the wealthy district. Based upon these financing disparities, poor and minority parents alleged that the use of local property taxes was discriminatory and unconstitutional under the Fourteenth Amendment.
>
> Not so, replied the Supreme Court. Although the Court conceded that "substantial disparities exist," it held that it could not review the case under the strict standard and review usually applied to distinctions which disadvantage minorities, because the disparities were not *intentionally* discriminatory on grounds of race. Applying the more lenient rational-basis standard of review, the Supreme Court held that the disparities were rational primarily in view of this country's long tradition of local control of schools, and that "some inequality" was not a sufficient basis for striking down the financing system.[36]

As in the area of educational finance and racism, organizers who take on such issues as welfare, institutional care and deinstitutionalization, housing, and health care must familiarize themselves with the milestones of case law in the area.

Similarly, we must know applicable regulations and statutes. Organizers who specialize on issues of community development will want to know precisely the regulations for the federal community development laws. Organizers for quality housing will want to know local housing codes, code enforcement mechanisms, the impact of Title VI of the 1964 Civil Rights Act (which allows for the cut-off of federal funds to agencies which practice discrimination), and the state laws as they relate to rent abatement (the tenant's right to pay part but not all of a rent if certain services are not provided). Organizers in the area of welfare will want to know how a local social service department can be forced to dispense funds. They will also want to know which services are mandated and which are discretionary. They will need to ask, "what are the regulations with respect to work tests?" In other words, must prospective welfare recipients demonstrate their willingness to work if offered a job? On matters of health care, one must know who may see a client's medical folder and what the mandated citizen participation is on Health Service Agencies (the regional health planning bodies). Other relevant questions are, "Can an older persons receive both Supplemental Security Income and Medicaid?" and "What rights do nursing home residents have to participate in activities outside the nursing home?" Answers to those questions can be found in statutes and regulations.

As was noted above, legal rights handbooks have proven to be an extraordinarily valuable tool for organizers. Indeed, the practice of translating professional, esoteric information into lay language for consumers, a process that amounts to demystification of "professional" knowledge, is a prime organizing activity in itself. Examples of legal information translated into consumer terms are provided in the chapter on action research. Once in the hands of consumers, this information takes on a dynamic dimension. Consumers begin to challenge bureaucratic delays, monitor state plans, call for due process hearings, and hold teach-ins to spread the word. With their new found confidence, they can dare to select strategies that would be unthinkable without a working knowledge of service laws and regulations that affect the area in which they are organizing.

How does one find out about laws, regulations, and case law? Most counties have courthouses with law libraries that are open for public use. However, few organizers will want to become expert in poring through the *U.S. Code* (federal statutes), the *U.S. Code Annotated* (another compilation of federal laws), the numerous texts on state laws, the *Federal Register* (where federal regulations are first published), or the *Code of Federal Regulations* (CFR) where regulations are systematically compiled. Tracking down case law can be even more exhausting.[37] While there are digests such as *West's Decennial Digest* (organized by topics), *West's Modern Federal Practice Digest, Black's Law Dictionary* (a dictionary of legal and law-related terms), and *Words and Phrases* (which gives court citations related to key legal phrases or principles, research of case law is convoluted and time consuming.[38] However, one index is essential. *Shepard's Citations* provides information on when cases are affirmed, reversed, and cited.[39] These Shepard's booklets are published to cover both federal and state court decisions. Thus lawyers use the phrase "shepardize a case" to refer to the process of following how a court ruling and, therefore, a legal principle, has fared in case law. Actual case law is found in volumes organized by court level and jurisdiction—for example *U.S. Reports* (Supreme Court cases), *West's Federal Reporter* (Federal Circuit Court cases) and *Southeastern Reporter* (state appeals court decisions for the Southeast Region of the U.S.).[40]

Actually, most organizers rely on Legal Services attorneys and paralegal staff, Legal Aid Societies, and special legal centers to work collaboratively on organizing litigation, legal handbooks, consumer education programs, and other law-related strategies. For their own legal education, organizers need not "shepardize" cases and scrutinize text after text of laws and amendments. The latest federal laws and regulations can usually be secured from Congresspersons and state legislators. Concise reviews of major areas of law are contained in the professional legal journals such as the Legal Services Corporation's *Clearinghouse Review,* and the major law reviews.[41] These can be found in law school libraries.

The Legal System

It is now probably self-evident how the legal system is organized. At the federal level, there is the United States Supreme Court, the Federal Circuit Court of Appeals, and the Federal District Courts. Cases with issues involving actual or perceived violations of federal statutes and the federal Constitution can be brought to federal court. Cases that involve both federal and state issues may be brought to either federal or state court, though a federal district court (the first level in the federal system) may initially remand a case to state court. The states do not have uniform court systems. Some states have three levels of state courts while others have two. Invariably, a state will have at least one trial level court and one appeals level court (often two). Federal courts can hear appeals from state courts.

Lawyers must determine when and where to "bring a case." Should an action be filed in state or federal court, and before what judge? While there are some general rules to follow—federal issues should be addressed in federal court and state issues in state court—most public interest cases involve state and federal issues. Consequently, lawyers are faced with a sometimes difficult choice and, so, they "shop" for judges and courts. Their decision may be guided by the following questions and concerns:

—In what court and with what judge are the chances of prevailing (winning) greatest?

—State action can sometimes prove more expeditious.

—If there are strong state statute issues involved, a remedy in a state court should be sought.

—If there are compelling federal or constitutional issues, federal district court would seem a better place to initiate a case.

—State court decisions will have authority only in the state in which they are developed. Federal decisions have pervasive authority nationally and mandatory authority in their jurisdiction (district or circuit depending on whether a district or circuit court gives the decision). U.S. Supreme Court decisions have mandatory authority nationally.

—Federal court decisions often achieve greater visibility and greater prestige than state court decisions.

DILEMMAS OF LEGAL STRATEGIES

Hardly anyone would question the law's enormous impact on social movements in America. For instance, *In re Gault* (1967) revolutionized juveniles' rights.[42] It turned an entirely discretionary proceeding into an adversarial one. *O'Connor* v. *Donaldson* (1975) put sharp limits on the authority of the state and institutional psychiatry.[43] *Wyatt* v. *Stickney* (1972) provided the legal basis (through application of the least restrictive alternative principle) for deinstitutionalization of retarded persons. *Javins* v. *First National Realty Corporation* (1970) spelled out tenant rights and challenged powerful landlords.[44] *Brown* v. *Board of Education* (1954) challenged the existence of separate schools for Blacks and whites and, in the

TABLE 1   Federal Judicial Circuits and Districts

FEDERAL CIRCUITS	FEDERAL DISTRICTS
District of Columbia	District of Columbia
First	Maine, Massachusetts, New Hampshire, Puerto Rico, Rhode Island
Second	Connecticut, eastern New York, northern New York, southern New York, western New York, Vermont
Third	Delaware, New Jersey, eastern Pennsylvania, middle Pennsylvania, western Pennsylvania, the Virgin Islands
Fourth	Maryland, eastern North Carolina, middle North Carolina, western North Carolina, eastern South Carolina, western South Carolina, eastern Virginia, northern West Virginia, southern West Virginia
Fifth	middle Alabama, northern Alabama, southern Alabama, Canal Zone, northern Florida, southern Florida, middle Georgia, northern Georgia, southern Georgia, eastern Louisiana, western Louisiana, northern Mississippi, southern Mississippi, northern Texas, southern Texas, western Texas
Sixth	eastern Kentucky, western Kentucky, eastern Michigan, western Michigan, northern Ohio, southern Ohio, eastern Tennessee, middle Tennessee, western Tennessee
Seventh	eastern Illinois, northern Illinois, southern Illinois, northern Indiana, southern Indiana, eastern Wisconsin, western Wisconsin
Eighth	eastern Arkansas, western Arkansas, northern Iowa, southern Iowa, Minnesota, eastern Missouri, western Missouri, Nebraska, North Dakota, South Dakota
Ninth	Alaska, Arizona, northern California, southern California, Hawaii, Idaho, Montana, Nevada, Oregon, Territory of Guam, eastern Washington, western Washington
Tenth	Colorado, Kansas, New Mexico, eastern Oklahoma, western Oklahoma, northern Oklahoma, Utah, Wyoming

FIGURE 1   Origins of the Law

Federal	Constitution	Statutes/Laws	Regulations	Supreme Court Appeals Court District Court Administrative Mechanisms
State	Constitution	Statutes/Laws	Regulations	State Court System Administrative Mechanisms
Local	Charter	Ordinances	Regulations	Municipal Courts Administrative Mechanisms

process, unleashed a massive legal assault by consumers on governments and corporations which previously had had little pressure to answer to consumer interests. Despite the law's obvious influence, it has equally obvious limitations. It poses several difficult dilemmas for community organization. First, there is concern that since law is a highly specialized profession, heavy reliance on legal strategies merely trades one form of consumer powerlessness for another. What difference is there, we might ask, between being dependent on lawyers and being dependent on other power brokers, such as health care professionals, educators, or psychiatrists? Organizers who use the law answer this challenge in two ways. On the one hand, organizers have used law in a manner that demystifies not only public policy but also the legal process itself. The flood of consumer law handbooks bears witness to this fact. On the other hand, organizers have been willing, even anxious, to use legal tools themselves if they promised to yield systemic change. In part, the dependency issue has been obviated by the reality, at least in some instances, that organizers and consumer groups have been able to enlist attorneys as consultants or aids rather than as leaders.

Second, numerous issues and problems simply cannot be addressed in a legal framework. The courts, for example, have been willing only to establish quantifiable, minimum standards in most areas of social and human services. This has been true in housing, transportation, education, vocational training, and other areas as well. The issue of quality public education, for instance, can be addressed only in the most superficial ways. Courts are willing to assert that all children are entitled to equal treatment in terms of teacher certification requirements and length of the school day, but *not* in terms of teacher performance, and rarely in terms of class size. The courts have argued that since professional educators disagree on such matters, the courts will not presume to know what makes for the best quality education. Similarly, certain practices which seem discriminatory have not been challengeable in court. For example, corporations which manufacture drugs are permitted to enlist poor people, people who have few, if any, ways in which to earn money, to serve as human subjects in drug tests. Since being poor in America does not constitute, in and of itself, a suspect classification, exploitation of poor persons who lack economic opportunities is "legal," if morally repugnant. Therefore law, while constantly in flux, has clear limitations in terms of what it covers. For some organizers, and for many attorneys, this reality merely creates a challenge to develop creative rationales and new test cases for expanding legal thinking in ways that will further consumer interests.

Third, organizers who use the law know what attorneys know. Litigation can prove expensive, time consuming, and even dangerous. The primary danger is not that a suite may be lost, but that an unfavorable decision will create "bad law." In other words, a negative decision for the plaintiffs, as in *San Antonio School Board v. Rodriguez*, for example, can have the effect of legitimizing what a community organization group perceives as an unfair discriminatory practice. In the Rodriguez case, the courts, in effect, put their stamp of approval on existing financing methods for so-called poor and wealthy school districts. A decision such as this merely confirms the fact that while law should be viewed as a potentially useful strategy, it should not be viewed as a guarantee that justice, in the eyes of the organizer and his or her constitutents, will prevail. In other words, the legal system does not approach issues in an unbiased manner. The law and its method, as the cases cited earlier surely demonstrate, respond to the ideology of individuals and historical times. The former Supreme Court Justice William O. Douglas put it this way:

> Not long after my appointment, Hughes made a statement to me which at the time was shattering but which over the years turned out to be true: "Justice Douglas, you must remember one thing. At the constitutional level where we work, 90 percent of any decision is emotional. The rational part of us supplies the reasons for supporting our predilections."
>
> I had thought of the law in terms of Moses—principles chiseled in granite. I knew judges had predilections. I knew that their moods as well as their minds were ingredients of their decisions. But I had never been willing to admit to myself that the "gut" reaction of a judge at the level of constitutional adjudications, dealing with the vagaries of due process, freedom of speech and the like, was the main ingredient of his decision. The admission of it destroyed in my mind some of the reverence of the immutable principles. But they were supplied by constitutions written by people in conventions, not by judges. Judges are after all, not creative figures; they represent ideological schools of thought that are highly competitive. No judge at the level I speak of was neutral. The Constitution is not neutral (1980).[46]

GLOSSARY OF LEGAL TERMS*

Abstention Doctrine: If a lawsuit can be decided on the basis of state law, a federal court will usually refuse to hear the case and will instead remand the case to the appropriate state courts.

Act: A law passed by a municipal, county, or federal legislature. Synonym for statute.

Amicus Curiae: The term means literally "friend of the court." Frequently, in public interest or landmark litigation, major national associations or interest groups will enter a brief to the court as amicus curiae. Such organizations, while having no direct legal interest in the case, have substantial interest in the issue. An amicus group may reveal to the court its perspectives on the issues at hand, expert knowledge related to those issues, as well as legal arguments of relevance to the issues. Litigants frequently will solicit organizational involvement in a case in order to demonstrate to the court significant national support for its point of view. In a number of landmark lawsuits, amicus briefs have been filed not only by public interest or special interest groups or organizations, but also by the United States Department of Justice.

Appeal: An application by either side in a lawsuit to a higher court for review, reversal, or modification of a lower court decision. The appeals court may rule either on the lower court's interpretation of law or on the manner in which the lower court conducted the case.

Bill: A proposed law, one not yet passed by a legislature.

Bill of Rights: The first ten amendments of the United States Constitution. The first

---

*This glossary is adapted from an earlier draft which appeared in S. Taylor and D. Biklen, *Understanding the Law* (Syracuse: Human Policy Press, 1980) by permission of the authors. I am indebted to Steve Taylor for his work as the principal author of the glossary upon which this one is based.

amendment provides for freedom of religion, freedom of speech, freedom of the press, the people's right to assemble, and the right to petition government for a redress of grievances. Other amendments include: due process rights and equal protection, prohibition of cruel and unusual punishment, states rights, and other important rights.

Brief: A written statement of legal and factual arguments in a case.

Capacity: The ability to take in information and make decisions, in other words, the ability to exercise one's rights. Also refers to one's ability to sue or to be sued. People lack capacity when they are minors by age or for some other reason adjudicated as unable to understand and utilize information, make decisions, or participate in legal proceedings. The term capacity is one of three major elements in the concept of consent.

Case: A controversy before the court.

Case Law: As distinct from statutes and regulations, this refers to the legal findings which have accumulated through years of court decisions. In preparing legal arguments, attorneys look both to statutes and regulations, as well as to the accumulated body of case law.

Cause of Action: Civil litigation requires a damaged party, somebody who has been legally "wronged." A legal wrong is considered a cause of action, something a court can consider and rule upon.

Certiorari: The writ of certiorari is the Supreme Court's device for determining whether or not it will hear a case from the lower courts. When the United States Supreme Court denies "cert," it refuses to hear a case. In "granting cert" the Supreme Court agrees to hear arguments.

Civil Action: This refers to all legal cases other than criminal ones.

Civil Rights: Congress passed federal laws protecting the rights of citizens just after the Civil War and also in 1957 and 1964. These rights acts reiterate individual rights outlined in the United States Constitution and specifically prohibit discrimination based upon race, color, age, and religion.

Class: This refers to a group of people in a like situation.

Class Action: A law suit brought by one or more individuals on behalf of themselves and all others similarly situated. Court decisions in a class action affect all members of the class, not just the named plaintiffs.

Common Law: This refers to customs, habits, traditions, as well as court decisions concerning government conduct and individual rights. Distinct from legislative law.

Complaint: A statement of claims before the court which has the effect of initiating a case.

Conclusions of Law: The legal arguments upon which a judge bases his or her decision(s) in a case.

Consent: Informed, capable, and voluntary agreement of a person to a given activity or procedure, such as medical treatment, a scientific experiment, or contract. Three conditions must be met before informed consent is given: (1) the person must be capable of understanding circumstances and factors surrounding a particular consent decision; (2) information relevant to the decision must be forthrightly and intelligibly provided to the person; (3) the person must be free to give or withhold consent voluntarily.

Consent Agreement (also called Consent Judgment or Consent Decree):   A court certified agreement between the two opposing parties in a suit. If agreement seems possible between two sides in a court case, the judge may ask the attorneys to develop a draft agreement. The effect of such an agreement is to obviate the need for further litigation. Another advantage of a consent agreement, from the perspective of the participants, is that the outcome is decided through negotiation rather than by a judge. The parties therefore, avoid the risk of receiving an unfavorable ruling.

Contempt: A deliberate act of interference, usually with Congress or a court. Contempt may also refer to failure to implement a mandated court decision. In such situations a court may punish an individual or group for failure to adhere to its judgments.

Constitutional Rights: Any right guaranteed by the United States Constitution or the constitution in the state in which a person resides. Liberty rights, due process, and equal protection rights are among those guaranteed by the United States Constitution.

Criminal Law: Any law which defines crimes. Criminal action as distinct from civil action refers to legal procedings having to do with individual behavior which contradicts legal limits.

Cruel and Unusual Punishment: The eighth amendment of the United States Constitution holds "excessive bail shall not be required nor excessive fines imposed, nor cruel and unusual punishment inflicted." Attorneys have made the argument in lawsuits involving the mentally retarded, the mentally ill, juvenile delinquents, and others who have been incarcerated in institutions, that certain prevailing institutional conditions constitute violations of the individual's right to be protected against cruel and unusual punishment.

Damage Action: Any litigation in which an individual or a group requests monetary compensation for a loss or injury. Compensatory damages refer to monetary rewards to compensate one for the amount of loss. Punitive damages refer to monetary rewards extracted as punishment for a particularly awful violation.

Declaratory Relief: This phrase refers to the courts legal findings as to the rights of plaintiffs in a law suit.

Defendant: The party against whom a law suit is filed.

Discovery: The process of gathering information in which each party in a law suit engages. There are several types of discovery: (1) depositions to obtain oral testimony; (2) interrogatories to obtain written answers to specific questions; (3) documents and materials; (4) requests for admissions—that the opposing party admit the truth of certain statements or objective facts. During the discovery phase of litigation, attorneys for one side frequently request information possessed by the other side.

Due Process: The fifth amendment of the United States Constitution declares, "nor shall any person be . . . deprived of life, liberty, or property without due process of law." The fourteenth amendment of the United States Constitution reads, "nor shall any state deprive any person of life, liberty, or property, without due process of law . . ." Thus the United States Constitution guarantees that individuals shall have the right to question any incursions upon their rights to life, liberty and property. This is commonly referred to as substantive due process. Procedural due process refers to the fairness of procedures involved in any action that deprives people of their rights. Numerous decisions in welfare cases, education cases, and institution cases, for example, mandate that individuals be given careful, procedural due process with respect to administrative decisions regarding these services and practices.

Equal Protection: The fourteenth amendment of the United States Constitution holds that "no state shall . . . deny to any person within its jurisdiction equal protection of the laws." People may be subjected to unequal treatment only if the state can demonstrate a rational basis or compelling interest for such treatment. The concept of equal protection has been central to much social change litigation.

Evidence: Testimony by witnesses, submission of records, documents, and other information to substantiate a position put forward in the courtroom. The courts have extensive rules and principles which determine whether particular evidence is admissible in the courtroom or relevant to the issues at hand.

Exhaustion of Administrative Remedies: It is frequently the case that both state and federal courts will refuse to hear a case until the individual or groups have posed their complaints before established administrative review processes within the bureaucracy with which they have a difference. Courts may, however, waive the "exhaustion of administrative remedies" rule at their own discretion. This is particularly common in civil rights cases and in cases which involve constitutional issues.

Federal Register: The publication in which the executive branch of the federal government publishes rules and regulations pertaining to federal laws.

Findings of Fact: The court's determination of fact in a case. Distinct from findings of law.

Guardian ad Litem: A guardian, for purposes of litigation, appointed by the court to represent the interests of the person lacking capacity.

Habeas Corpus: A court order requiring that a person held by the police be brought forward so that charges may be presented or dropped.

Injunctive Relief: That part of an order in which a court demands or bars particular actions. This part of a court order remedies violations of law.

Jurisdiction: Ability of a court to hear and decide a suit.

Least Restrictive Alternative: The principle that government should pursue its interests in a manner that least intrudes upon individual rights (for example, life, liberty, property, pursuit of happiness). This concept has been particularly important to litigation involving disabled persons and older persons. It has been argued, for example, that in providing services for older persons and people with disabilities, the government may overly intrude upon the lives of these groups when it forces them to receive services in a restricted environment such as a nursing home or mental hospital, when those same services might be made available through generic, community-based service centers.

Mandamus: A court order requiring a private corporation or government to carry out its legally required duty. For example, if a local agency were required by law to dispense certain welfare funds and refused to do so, attorneys might seek a writ of mandamus from the court to compel the agency to live up to its legally required duties.

Moot: A moot case involves a dispute which has already been resolved and for which a legal decision will have no practical effect. Even if a particular dispute has been resolved, and thus rendered moot, it may still be tried and ruled upon by the court if it involves a recurring controversy.

Motion: A request by either party for a particular action by the court (for example, motion for change in the venue, motion for dismissal).

Opinion: The text of a judge's decision.

Order: A judge's ruling.

Ordinance: A city, town, or county law.

Public Law (P.L.):   The term for a federal law. P.L. 93-203 refers to the 203rd law passed by the 93rd Congress.

Party: The plaintiff or defendant in a law suit.

Pleadings: Legal briefs, affidavits, and other documents submitted to a court prior to oral arguments.

Precedent: A previous court decision which raises similar issues of law and which may therefore have authority in a current case. Courts may or may not recognize a precedent as authoritative depending upon factual differences and the jurisdiction in which the previous case was decided. A previous decision by a court of the same level (for example, district court) in another jurisdiction will have persuasive, but not mandatory authority. A Supreme Court decision has mandatory authority over lower court decisions.

Preliminary Injunction: A temporary restraining order. A form of injunctive relief in which the court temporarily prohibits a party from taking a particular action pending a final court ruling.

Privacy Right: While not specifically guaranteed in the United States Constitution, the notion of liberty is presumed to imply the individual's right to have personal privacy (family relations, individual choices) protected against unnecessary and unwarranted government intrusions.

Pursuit of Happiness: A term used in constitutional law cases, which refers to the individual's right to enter into contracts, make personal decisions, enjoy family life, and so forth.

Relief: A court's determination to redress grievances (that is, violations of rights, injuries). The court's findings and orders; remedies for legal wrongs.

Remand: A court order returning a case to a lower court for further action consistent with the higher court's findings.

Respondent: The party who must respond to an appeal. The appellee.

Separation of Powers: The principles that government includes three separate branches: the legislature; the executive branch; the judiciary. One branch may not assume the duties and responsibilities of another branch.

Shall/May: The term "shall" connotes mandatory action, as stated in law or court decisions. The term "may" connotes individual discretion.

Sovereign Immunity: The notion that governments may go about their business within reasonable limits, without opening themselves to the possibility of being sued. The courts have recently limited the immunity of local or municipal governments. Municipalities may be held liable for unconstitutional acts if they are aware that their actions are unconstitutional.

Special Master: A person appointed by a court to watch over and/or implement the court's decision. In the Pennsylvania right-to-education lawsuit, for example, Judge Broderick appointed a Special Master to monitor and, in effect, insure the implementation of the court's complex order.

Standing to Sue: A person's right to seek redress of grievances. Certain organizations, such as the Sierra Club, an environmental public interest group, have sought and won standing to sue on behalf of particular interests of the citizenry. If a governmental action has sufficient effect on an individual, he or she is justified in seeking redress of grievances from governmental action. A term used in relation to civil rights cases.

State's Rights: The tenth amendment of the United States Constitution reads: "the powers not delegated to the United States by the Constitution, nor prohibited by it to the states, are reserved to the states respectively, or to the people." "State's Rights" refers to the rights reserved to the states by the tenth amendment of the U.S. Constitution.

Statute: A state or federal law.

Statute of Limitations: A law which specifies the period of time in which a law suit must be brought after an alleged violation of rights under the law.

Stay: A court order postponing implementation of a court ruling pending future legal action, usually an appeal.

Stipulation: Any agreement between the parties in a law suit that narrows the facts and points of contention.

Summary Judgment: A court ruling on the legal issues in a case or an aspect of a case, where the court finds no real dispute over facts.

Supremacy Clause: The principle that the United States Constitution and federal laws have authority over state and municipal constitutions and laws. This principle is articulated in Article 6 of the United States Constitution.

Test Case: This term can mean one of two things: (1) A case chosen from among numerous similar cases before the court to go to trial first, the outcome of which will be applied to the other pending cases; (2) a case put forward by plaintiffs to establish a breakthrough in legal rights.

Tort: A civil wrong for which an individual seeks damages. Must involve violation of duty owed to the individual (for example, privacy rights).

Verdict: A jury's decision in a case.

Warranty: A statement as to the quality of what is being transacted in a contract.

Writ: A court order requiring a particular action.

NOTES

[1]*Brown* v. *Board of Education of Topeka,* 347 U.S. 483 (1954).

[2]*Plessy* v. *Ferguson,* 163 U.S. 537.

[3]Richard Kluger has written an excellent history of *Brown* and related cases. See Richard Kluger, *Simple Justice: The History of Brown v. Board of Education and Black America's Struggle for Equality* (New York: Knopf, 1976).

[4]*Sweatt* v. *Painter,* 339 U.S. 629 (1950).

[5]Kluger, *Simple Justice,* p. 198.

[6]Kluger, *Simple Justice,* p. 199.

[7]Kluger, *Simple Justice,* p. 199.

[8]Frances Fox Piven and Richard A. Cloward, *Regulating the Poor: The Functions of Public Welfare* (New York: Vintage Books, 1971), p. 306.

[9]Piven and Cloward, *Regulating,* p. 306.

[10]Sylvia Law, *The Rights of the Poor* (New York: Avon, 1974), p. 72.

[11]Piven and Cloward, *Regulating.*

[12]Anthony M. Platt, *The Child Savers* (Chicago: University of Chicago Press, 1969).

[13]Linda Horn and Elma Griesel, *Nursing Homes: A Citizens' Action Guide* (Boston: Beacon Press, 1977).

[14]*Clearinghouse Review,* September 1979, p. 364.

[15]*Javins* v. *First National Realty Corporation,* 428 F 2d 1071, 1082 (D.C. Circuit), cert denied, 400 U.S. 925 (1970).

[16]*Javins* v. *First National Realty Corporation.*

[17]George J. Annas, *The Rights of Hospital Patients* (New York: Avon Books, 1975), p. 38.

[18]Annas, *Hospital Patients,* p. 49; *New Biloxi Hospital* v. *Frazier,* 245 Miss. 185, 146 S 2d 882 (1962).

[19]*O'Connor* v. *Donaldson,* 422 U.S. 563 (1975).

[20]*Harris (Patricia R.)* v. *McRae (Cora) et al.* (No. 79-1268), June 30, 1980.

[21]*Harris* v. *McRae,* June 30, 1980.

[22]*Pennsylvania Association for Retarded Children (PARC)* v. *Pennsylvania,* 334 F Supp. 1257, 1259 (E.D. Pa., 1971).

[23]*PARC* v. *Pennsylvania, 1971.*

[24]*PARC* v. *Pennsylvania,* 1971, paragraph 42 of the Consent Agreement.

[25]Public Law 94-142, The Education for All Handicapped Children Act, 1975.

[26]Gilhool in Leopold Lippman and Ignacy Goldberg, *Right to Education* (New York: Teachers College Press, 1973).

[27]*Halderman* v. *Pennhurst State School and Hospital,* 446 F Supp. 1295, 1978.

[28]Geroge J. Annas, *The Rights of Hospital Patients* (New York: Avon Books, 1975); Richard E. Blumberg and James R. Grow, *The Rights of Tenants* (New York: Avon Books, 1978); E. Boggan, Marilyn G. Haft, Charles Lister, and John P. Rupp, *The Rights of Gay People* (New York: Avon Books, 1975); Robert N. Brown, with Clifford D. Allo, Alan D. Freeman, and Gordon W. Netzorg, *The Rights of Old People* (New York: Avon Books, 1979); Bruce Ennis and Loren Siegel, *The Rights of Mental Patients* (New York: Avon Books, 1973); Paul R. Friedman, *The Rights of Mentally Retarded Persons* (New York: Avon Books, 1976); Richard E. Larson and Loughlin McDonald, *The Rights of Racial Minorities* (New York: Avon Books, 1980); Sylvia Law, *The Rights of the Poor;* Susan D. Ross, *The Rights of Women* (New York: Avon Books, 1973); and David Rudofsky, *The Rights of Prisoners* (New York: Avon Books, 1973).

[29]Piven and Cloward, *Regulating,* p. 301.

[30]Murray Edelman, "Language, Myth, and Rhetoric," *Society,* July/August, 1975.

[31]Saul Alinsky, *Rules for Radicals* (New York: Vintage, 1972), p. 15.

[32]For one of the best, most comprehensive, and most used law dictionaries refer to Henry Campbell Black, *Black's Law Dictionary*, 5th edition, rev., rev. eds. Publishers Editorial Staff (St. Paul, MN: West Publishing Co., 1979). This book provides concise definitions of major and minor legal principles.

[33]*Dean Milk Co.* v. *Madison*, 1951.

[34]Black, *Dictionary*, p. 1281.

[35]*San Antonio Independent School District* v. *Rodriguez*, 411 U.S. 1 (1972).

[36]Larson and MacDonald, *Racial Minorities*, p. 105.

[37]*Code of Federal Regulations* (Washington, D.C.: U.S. Government Printing Office, dated by volume); *United States Code* (Washington, D.C.: U.S. Government Printing Office, dated by volume); *United States Code Annotated* (USCA) (St. Paul, MN: West Publishing Co., 1591–present).

[38]*Eighth Decennial Digest* (St. Paul, MN: West Publishing Co., 1977); *Modern Federal Practice Digest* (St. Paul, MN: West Publishing Co., 197); Henry Campbell Black, *Black's Law Dictionary*, 5th ed., rev. eds. Publishers Editorial Staff (St. Paul, MN: West Publishing Co., 1979); *Words and Phrases*, Vol. 46 (St. Paul, MN: West Publishing Co., 1970).

[39]*Shepard's Federal Citations* (Colorado Springs, CO: Shepard's Inc., 1972).

[40]*United States Reports* (Washington, DC: U.S. Government Printing Office, 1806–present); *Federal Reporter* (St. Paul, MN: West Publishing Co., 1925–present); *Southeastern Reporter* (St. Paul, MN: West Publishing Co., 1939–present).

[41]*Clearinghouse Review*.

[42]*In re Gault*, 1967.

[43]*O'Connor* v. *Donaldson*, 1975.

[44]*Wyatt* v. *Stickney*, 325 F. Supp. 781 (M.D. Ala. 1971); *Javins* v. *First National Realty*, 1970.

[45]*Brown* v. *Board of Education*, 1954.

[46]William O. Douglas, ''An Intimate Memoir of the Brethren,'' *New York Times Magazine Section*, September 21, 1980, p. 80.

CHAPTER SEVEN
COMMUNITY
EDUCATION:
USING THE MEDIA

NATURE OF THE MEDIA

Politicians, citizen groups, and social commentators alike criticize popular media, particularly television, for manipulating and shaping public perceptions, attitudes, and even actions. Ever since Vance Packard and Joe McGinnis published their respective books, *The Hidden Persuaders* and *The Selling of the President,* the public has been wary of television's power to manipulate.[1] However, there is still considerable confusion about just what effect the media has on individuals. While some people warn against the dangers of mass media, we are compelled to ask, "What are those dangers?" and "How powerful is the media?" In answering these questions we can address the question that most concerns us: "*Can* community organizers use the media as an instrument of change?" If the answer to that question is yes, then the specifics of *how* it can best be used by organizers must be considered and explored.

From the promotional "blurbs" to a major critique of American television, we learn that "ninety-five percent of American homes have at least one television set which is on more than six hours a day"; that "crimes shown on television are being committed on the streets"; that "college entrance exam scores have dropped severely"; that "at least 85,000 acts of violence occur every night in America on TV." Finally, the book jacket of the critique warns, "television affects every aspect of American life."[2] Other critics have charged that television network news promotes leftwing and liberal views. Still others charge the media with a corporate or an establishment bias. As one group of researchers note, television has been criticized for producing a deterioration in aesthetic tastes and general cultural standards, nullifying hard-won social gains, leading to conformity, operating in the interests of political and economic interests, maintaining the status quo, diminishing the power and habit of critical thinking, concentrating on the trivial and the sensational, and for standing in the way of the development of a truly participating democracy.[3]

Certainly there can be no doubt about television's presence. Seventy-five percent of the American public derive most of their "news" from television. Fifty percent of the public receive all of their news from television.[4]*

Ironically, despite all the concern about television's manipulative powers, television has extremely limited capacity to alter attitudes on specific issues or personalities. For example, television advertisements have almost no influence on who people vote for in a presidential election.[5] In addition, television news has no more power to persuade voters than do newspapers.[6] Similarly, studies of television shows' attitudinal effects suggest that they have almost no impact at all on viewers' prejudices.

The reasons for television's failure to achieve manipulation or, even, substantial influence on specific issues and attitudes are quite predictable. On the one hand, the media as a whole, not just television, do a poor job of presenting information. In this respect, television clearly fails more often and more deeply than newspapers. TV coverage of presidential campaigns, for example, becomes an all too stereotyped collage of candidates descending and ascending planes, speaking to crowds, shaking hands with factory workers, and riding in open cars along crowd-lined streets. The commentary on these scenarios zeroes in on crowd size and the latest public opinion poll. The only issue of concern is who will win. As one commentator has noted, presidential politics are reduced to a gladiatorial battle in campaigns. The competition is more important than issues. Indeed, one rarely hears anything about issues.

The second reason for television's inability to control or shape attitudes has to do with the audience itself, which filters what it watches and will seriously consider. Hartmann and Husband explain the problem this way:

> People select what they read and what they view and tend to avoid communications that they find uncongenial. They are also selective in what they perceive and what they remember. Where the "message" clashes with existing attitudes or beliefs it is typically the existing outlook that remains intact, while the "message" is rejected, or distorted to fit the outlook. A study of viewers' reactions to a programme in an ITV series, *The Nature of Prejudice,* carried out in 1967 found that prejudiced viewers evaded the intended anti-prejudice message by a variety of means, ranging from becoming hostile towards the interviewer (who was opposed to prejudice) to finding in the programme confirmation of their own views.[7]

---

*Much of this chapter has been devoted to a discussion of television since television is the dominant media type in America. However, other media such as posters, newspapers, and "alternative newspapers" will also be discussed.

The media tend to "change" attitudes when viewers are motivated toward or otherwise predisposed to change. The latter occurs when viewers do not hold strong views on an issue, or where the "change" occurs in a direction which reconfirms already existing attitudes.

In general, the media have only marginal ability to change specific attitudes, both because they do not provide very good or substantive information on issues and because the public filters what it will read, watch, or contemplate. While the media may do poorly when it comes to changing *specific* attitudes or predispositions, they nevertheless do influence the *overall* way in which we think about issues and events. Time and again, television and other news media have proven incapable of offering up an electoral victory to a particular candidate or of even predicting who would win this or that election. However, in a much more profound, far reaching way, television does guide our lives and define our *notion* of politics. Electronic media news treats the public as a consumer of television's view of the world. It defines politics as the politics of leaders. Viewers can choose a Republican or Democrat. In television's version of politics, social movements enjoy a status barely above that of crime. Similarly, the mass media define power as something that a few individuals own. Television does not suggest that one class of people may enjoy power at the expense of another class. Further, television and newspapers legitimate the status quo by limiting audiences' viewing and reading choices to events and interpretations that are fully consonant with the prevailing institutional order. The media, for example, define crime as most devastating when perpetrated against the upper class. The murder of a white opera singer is front page news. The murder of a poor Black is back page news. As one commentator suggests, consumer sovereignty is taken as the equivalent to freedom: " 'If you don't like TV, turn it off,' 'If you don't like cars, don't drive them.' 'If you don't like it here, go back to Russia.' 'If you don't like Crest, buy Gleem.' "[8] In short, the mass media reflect their corporate context. They largely teach corporate values (for example, all problems have an easy solution that can be bought; and *existing consumer choices represent the universe of serious or legitimate choices available*).

To summarize, the mass media has, paradoxically, both a profound and insignificant effect on viewers' attitudes. On the one hand, the mass media tend to define politics, power, social problems, and other critical social phenomena narrowly and in accordance with dominant corporate social values. Once freedom has been harnessed, the media provide a series of choices. And within these choices the media seem rather ineffective as great manipulators—although one wants to ask, "Is there enough difference between choices to really expect television or any other mass medium to be able to shape attitudes on them?"

The message here for community organizers is sobering. First, organizers can expect that mass media will view them and their issues as marginal, deviant, and not in the preordained set of legitimate choices. Second, organizers can expect a difficult time of gaining meaningful access to corporate controlled media. Third, community organizers will find that access to the media may do little to increase their ability to communicate to large numbers of people. Fourth, organizers may by necessity have to limit their goal to achieving modest shifts in the media's definition of what are legitimate ideas. For example, the civil rights movement, feminist movement, antinuclear movement, and other social movements have forced the media to redefine its definition of racism, sexism, and nuclear threat. However, these movements have not caused the media to ask many serious questions of the current social, institutional order in America, or even to draw a relationship between various kinds of prejudices, economic interests, corporate social costs, and other social conditions.

In the following pages of this chapter, we will examine the relationship of political leadership to the media, how the nature of the media influences media behavior, the manner in which the mass media imposes on us an antichange vision of the world, how the media respond to social change movements. We will also explore purposes for which organizers can use the media and discuss practical media skills which every organizer needs to know.

Government Control
over Media News

Media news occupies a unique position in American culture. For many people, the mass media news provides a continual flow of events and analyses that constitute reality. The media news decides what is newsworthy, what deserves attention, what story is most important, and when a story has run its course. In the words of Daniel Boorstin:

> Every American knows the anticipation with which he picks up his morning newspaper at breakfast or opens his evening paper before dinner, or listens to the newscasts every hour on the hour as he drives across country, or watches his favorite commentator on television interpret the events of the day. Many enterprising Americans are now at work to help us satisfy these expectations. Many might be put out of work if we should suddenly moderate our expectations. But it is we who keep them in business and demand that they fill our consciousness with novelties, that they play God for us.[9]

In other words, because news exists only when reported, those who determine what is news, what to report, and how much to report exercise an extraordinary power over the American psyche.

Government leaders have understood this truth ever since F.D.R. adopted radio as his medium to communicate with the people. Prior to F.D.R.'s fireside chats and radio speeches, no President had used radio effectively, and television had not yet been invented. Along with toothpaste, cigar, and cigarette ads, Roosevelt plied radio to win the hearts of the American people. Over fifty million people heard most of his speeches. Each time he spoke, he reached out to his audience with the endearing introductory words, "my friends."[10] F.D.R. orchestrated his media events. He spent days preparing his seemingly conversational speeches and then delivered them flawlessly. He knew the value of acting well. Indeed, he became a kind of media news director. For example, when he realized the enormous power of radio to reach millions of people almost instantaneously, he altered how he treated newspaper and radio correspondents. David Halberstam, author of *The Powers That Be,* recounts this particular story. The order of press cars in presidential caravans in those days was based on circulation. First came the wire service correspondents' car, then the special correspondents for the *New York Times* and other prestigious papers or columns, and third the radio network correspondents. One day, at the radio correspondent's prodding, F.D.R.'s assistant, Steve Early, changed the order:

> As they (the correspondents) all rushed to their cars Daly and Smith (radio correspondents) found Walter Trohan (newspaper correspondent) in the second car. "You son of a bitch," Trohan told Daly, "this is our car." Not any more, it wasn't. Daly summoned Early who forced the Chicago Tribune and The New York Times to car three. When Felix Belair (newspaper correspondent) complained mildly to Early later, the press secretary apologized, "It's not that we like them better," he said. Radio had arrived.[11]

F.D.R. realized that in his role as newsmaker he could shape or even control much of what went out over the news wires. Thus if a reporter failed to report as he wanted, F.D.R. could cut off that newsperson from briefing or newsbreak. This practice continues today. Official agencies engage in news management by determining the official statistics that they will release. They strategically "leak" reports or documents, "float trial balloons," and grant special access to "friendly" reporters. When the then *New York Times* correspondent, James Wooten, wrote a story critical of President Carter's leadership abilities and growing morale problem in the White House, Wooten found himself out in the cold.[12] Henceforth, top White House aides refused to talk to Wooten. When the White House wanted something in the *Times,* Presidential aides called certain "friendly" correspondents directly. Wooten was given only official press notices. Wooten realized that his own usefulness as a reporter at the White House deteriorated from the minute his front page critical article appeared. By the end of that year the *New York Times* withdrew him from the White House beat. As a fellow *Times* White House correspondent put it, "The *Times* tends to be institutionally reluctant to bait presidents. It takes the attitude that after all, he's the president, for God's sake."[13] In fact, White House correspondents, like other reporters who must depend largely on official press releases and highly orchestrated "news," are, as Michael Massing puts it, like animals in a "cage, where they subsist largely on scraps fed them."[14]

Most presidents have tried to exercise influence over the media directly, not only by giving "exclusives" to preferred correspondents or by denying interviews to the likes of Wooten, but also by demanding that editors comply with a particular approach to the news. In 1963, President John Kennedy tried to have the *New York Times* editor remove David Halberstam from Vietnam war reporting. Halberstam's news had apparently been too critical of Kennedy's policies.[15] When CBS' Morley Safer prepared a television story which showed American troops setting fire to Vietnamese villages, President Lyndon Johnson reportedly called the CBS president and complained, "Frank (Stanton), are you trying to fuck me? . . . this is your President, and yesterday your boys (Safer) shat on the American flag."[16] In the early 1970s, President Richard Nixon went to court to try and stop publication of the *Pentagon Papers*.

During this same period, the late 1960s and early 1970s, government agencies, including the Central Intelligence Agency (CIA), The Federal Bureau of Investigation (FBI), and the Internal Revenue Service (IRS) used illegal methods to destroy the so-called alternative press, mainly radical newspapers and magazines, which were growing at an unprecedented rate and reaching literally millions of Americans on issues of race relations, the Vietnam War, feminism, and a host of other issues. The CIA instigated an IRS review of the national political magazine *Ramparts* to discover its list of contributors. Much to the chagrin of the CIA, the contributors turned out *not* to be foreign subversives as the CIA hoped to prove: "Far from being financed by any hostile power abroad, the people who were putting out these papers were, actually using their lunch money. . . ."[17] Nevertheless, the CIA continued to view the alternative press as a threat. One member of the CIA special project (code named Resistance) on underground media wrote in 1968:

> A modern phenomenon which has evolved in the last three or four years is the vast growth of the Underground Press. Underground means of mass communication utilized to avoid suppression by legal authority and/or attribution is not new to this age, but its volume is and the apparent freedom and ease in which filth, slanderous and libelous statements, and what appear to be almost treasonous anti-establishment propaganda is allowed to circulate is difficult to rationalize.[18]

The FBI found a way to shut down several underground papers. It convinced advertisers such as major record companies and local businesses to withdraw their advertising. In one instance, the FBI sent an anonymous letter to underground newspapers and antiwar groups charging that the legitimate social movement and antiwar group known as Liberation News Service (LNS) was an FBI front organization.[19] Ironically, the government used such illegal and antidemocratic strategies against an alternative press which it considered a threat to democracy.

In reality, it is not just the White House and national security agencies that exercise control over the news. Government agencies and leaders in general try to shape and determine how the media report news. One analyst of news media, Jason Epstein, believes that this phenomenon has become so commonplace that there now exists a virtual symbiosis between government and the press. Despite frequent complaints by politicians that the media has fabricated a story or blown something out of proportion, to a surprising extent the media and government cooperate with each other. According to this view, the mass media's adversary role is mythical.[20] Even the most well known of exposés, Watergate, it is argued, came to the news media largely through government leaks and official government channels (court proceedings and congressional investigations). Often times the symbiotic relationship of reporters to government operates in more subtle but no less measured ways. Note, for example, the recollections of one reporter:

Conventional news sources, especially in government, struck me as being sophisticated about the give-and-take with reporters. Press spokesmen and public relations men are often former reporters, who adopt a tone of "we are all in this together" and try to seem frank or even irreverent in their off-the-record comments. In this way they can influence the "angle" or the "slant" of a story—the way it is handled and the general impression it creates—rather than its substance, which is often beyond their control. They attempt to influence the reporter during the stage before "the story" has congealed in his mind, when he is casting about for a central, organizing conception. If his lead sentence begins "The decline in unemployment . . ." instead of "The rise in inflation . . . ," they have succeeded in their task. Some press spokesmen hoard big stories and dispense them to reporters who write favorably; but that strategy can backfire, because reporters are sensitive to favoritism and, in my experience, tend to be cliquish rather than competitive. Outright manipulation may be less effective than the establishment of a certain amicable familiarity over a long period of daily contact. After a year or so on a single beat, reporters tend insensibly to adopt the viewpoint of the people about whom they write. They develop sympathy for the complexities of the mayor's job, the pressures on the police commissioners, and the lack of room for maneuver in the welfare department . . . (For example) the veteran crime reporters who dominate the press rooms in most police headquarters develop a symbiotic relationship with the police. In Newark there were four tough old reporters who had done more time in headquarters than most of the cops. They knew everyone of importance on the force: they drank with cops, played poker with cops, and adopted the cops' view of crime. They never wrote about police brutality.[21]

Media Management's Censorship of the News

The mass media is big business. Put another way, major media outlets, like the *New York Times,* CBS, ABC, NBC, *Time, Newsweek,* and the *Washington Post* are corporations. As such, the news they produce is not immune to the interests and values of their corporate owners. Take for example *Time* magazine's coverage of China's war with Japan during World War II. *Time's* correspondent in China, Theodore White, sent the home office report after report of Chiang Kai-shek's ineffective leadership, his inflexibility, and his inability or unwillingness to see that his government was falling apart in front of his own eyes. *Time* owner Henry Luce, and his editors rewrote White's submissions or scrapped them altogether in favor of glorifying Chiang's cause and abilities. Halberstam reports that White posted a sign in his Chunking office, "Any resemblance to what is written here and what is printed in *Time* magazine is purely coincidental."[22] In 1945, White wrote his publisher, (Luce) an angry last complaint:

If Time Inc. adopts the policy of unquestioningly, unconditionally supporting (Chiang's) hand, we will be doing a monstrous disservice to millions of American readers and to the Chinese whose personal concern this is. . . . We hope that you will select facts in an impartial, judicious manner warranted by the enormous dimensions of this tragedy.[23]

But *Time* did not change its position. After Chiang's government fell and Mao and the Communists took over, *Time* painted an equally unrealistic picture of that regime, one that was as outrageously slanderous as its Chiang coverage had been unbelievably romantic.

In any number of major media stories we find evidence of media management's efforts to soft-pedal or even kill a story which threatens prevailing norms and beliefs. During the McCarthy era when Senator Joe McCarthy intimidated the nation with his witch hunt tactics, accusing hundreds of people of being communists or communist sympathizers, major media corporations handled McCarthy gingerly. Similarly, in the mid-1970s when Daniel Schorr, then news reporter for CBS, obtained a leaked copy of the House of Representatives report on covert and illegal CIA activities, CBS backed away from making the report public. Schorr was placed in the awkward position of holding the report up in front of the television cameras but not being allowed by the network to disclose its full contents. When Schorr realized CBS was determined to help Congress suppress the controversial report, he gave it to an established alternative news weekly, *The Village Voice*, which published it. CBS reacted swiftly by taking Schorr off the air. It later forced him to resign.[24] Needless to say, there was no outcry of "unfair" from other media outlets or even from the ranks of Schorr's fellow reporters. After all, Schorr had refused to follow the rules, one of which is to comply with management's wishes. Schorr ended up in the same place Theodore White did, out of a job. It was one more instance in which the mass media defined its role as playing it safe. As David Halberstam theorizes, there seem to be two essential reasons why the mass media tend to avoid frontal challenges to institutional and social norms:

> There is an unwritten law of American Journalism that states that the greater and more powerful the platform, the more carefully it must be used and the more closely it must adhere to the norms of American society, particularly the norms of the American government; . . . (Television, Robert MacNeil wrote in *The People Machine*, acts as a cheering section for the side that has already won.) Part of this is born out of (1) a need for respectability and a desire for legitimacy and a fear of disturbing the status quo, and part of it is born out of (2) a very healthy sense that if the platform (media position in society) is that powerful, personal opinions are almost dangerous, that no one journalist should be that powerful.[25]

With this reasoning (the power-of-the-platform reasoning) television navigates a narrow course, avoiding controversial exposés and issues until they are somehow no longer controversial but, rather, more or less palatable. Hence, CBS and Edward R. Murrow waited until 1954 before airing a report critical of Joseph McCarthy. In 1976, CBS refused to publish the leaked report on the C.I.A.

Corporate leadership of major media outlets obviously cannot order their reporters to give a particular slant to their stories or to espouse certain corporate values. Fortunately, there seems little evidence that media owners fire reporters for writing something that challenges the owners' values. Nevertheless, reporters seem to go through a socialization process in the workplace whereby they learn to "toe the line." Warren Breed has called this phenomenon "social control in the newsroom."[26] Owners or editors need not fire recalcitrant reporters. Rather, they need merely ignore deviant stories, hand controversial stories to reporters whom they trust, or consign troublesome reporters to unwanted beats, the best known of which Breed calls "the Chinese torture of the newsroom," obituaries.[27] Many reporters will tend to conform because they feel a sense of obligation to their employers for having hired, taught them, or as Breed puts it, "stood up for them" in controversy.[28] Reporters who want to make it big (get their own byline, get on page one, become an editor) learn to produce stories that fit the mold. Reporters may also be motivated by a fear that if they write from a deviant perspective, an editor may accuse them of the worst offense in reporting, namely bias. Each of these considerations creates a powerful incentive for reporters to provide the public with a narrow and rather conformist picture of what we call "the news."

The Media's Stylized Picture of America

The pure entertainment part of the mass media embodies many of the same characteristics as the news side. Television entertainment tends toward a highly stylized, even stereotypical vision of America. This stylized vision does essentially what news media do, that is it narrows and defines the public's sense of reality, the nature of social conditions, and viable solutions to problems. Note, for example, how the media deals with difference, with social change, with corporate ideals, and with viewer emotions in day-to-day programing.

Television treats difference (for example, poverty, homosexuality, aging) romantically, as a vehicle for humor, individualistically, or not at all. Situation comedies portray poverty in a romantic, humorous light. Productions that deal with human tragedy tend to treat genuine differences as individual problems with individual solutions. Even when television ventures out to deal with controversial topics such as racism, prejudice is often shown as laughable. The audience is largely protected from the painful hurt and suffering that attend real-life prejudice. In more realistic shows, we usually learn that social problems and personal differences rarely can ever be solved adequately.[29]

American television entertainment sugar-coats America's vision of reality. It has actually been unwilling to show the blue-collar workplace and, therefore, work itself. Violence is sanitized so as to excite viewers but never depress them. TV violence happens hundreds of times each evening without the viewer ever seeing real blood, believable pain, or credible suffering. Violence and sex dominate the media for the purpose of viewer titillation, not the presentation of realistic actions or emotions. This occurred even in the much touted television production of Alex Haley's *Roots*. According to Mankiewicz and Swerdlow:

> *Roots* did make whites more aware, undoubtedly, of the historical burden blacks must live with; but its impact in this was overshadowed, it seems by the titillation provided by its violence and its violent sex scenes. . . .

For whatever else it demonstrated, it left the message that a lot of stars and a lot of violence in a well-made production will produce and hold an enormous audience.[30]

Many consumer groups such as older persons organizations, poor people, and people with disabilities find the media more determined to portray them as despondent, incompetent, sometimes irresponsible, and piteable than as people who have suffered at the hands of systematic discrimination, prejudice, and exploitation. This is evident, for example, in the media's treatment of people with disabilities. Mass culture portrays people with disabilities as alternately cute or child-like (for example, Disney's portrayal of dwarfs in Snow White); potentially violent (for example, news stories frequently note the intellect and former mental patient status of people who commit crimes); movies relate ugliness and disability to evil deeds (as in the case of Captain Hook in *Peter Pan,* Dr. Strangelove, Ahab in *Moby Dick*); often incompetent (for example, Mr. Magoo, the silly near-blind character who bumps and stumbles through life, mistaking fire hydrants for people, narrowly escaping disaster at every turn, and always surviving by fate rather than personal skill or competence; or political cartoons on the blind leading the blind); objects of scorn (for example, comic strips use disabilities as curse words—''stupid idiot,'' ''moron,'' ''dumb'' and ''crazy''); as dependent recipients of society's good will (see chapter 4 for an extended discussion of charity's effects). In short, the mass media embodies all of the prejudices and stereotypes of society. The media, just as society at large, tends to discredit the legitimacy of people with disabilities as well as other marginal groups by fitting them into one of these stereotypes. Even when the media does recognize the legitimacy of a marginal person, they often do so in a manner that suggests the person is unusual, or even extraordinary—not like most other such people.

Kenneth Jernigan, president of the militant National Federation of the Blind, once told a story of how the media like to treat blind people as interesting oddities, as if to say they make interesting feature stories, rather than hard news. At a National Federation convention in Chicago, a reporter used all her film on a display of mechanical aids and gadgets. She literally ignored the political organizing purpose of the conference. When Jernigan accused her of promoting a distorted and stereotyped view of blind people, she countered weakly, ''My editor told me to do it, so that's the way it has to be.''[31] At another meeting, National Federation members came together to plan strategies to combat job discrimination, refusals by airlines to let blind people ride, ''refusals by hotels to let us stay, refusal by society to let us in, and refusal by social service agencies to let us out.'' But instead of political action, the reporter asked to take pictures and write a story on blind bowlers and seeing eye dogs.[32] Subsequently, hundreds of blind people (Federation members) demonstrated in the streets against the National Accreditation Council for Agencies Serving the Blind and Visually Handicapped for its policies. The National Federation believed that these policies perpetuated second-class citizenship for blind people and complained against the Board for its refusal to give more than token representation to blind people on it. The *Chicago Tribune* ignored the demonstration altogether. Instead of covering the first national demonstration ever by blind people, the paper carried two feature stories on blindness, one entitled "Busy blind man finds time to help children," and another captioned, "Blind, he directs music in city school."[33] Apparently, the media did not yet regard disabled activists as legitimate newsmakers. The media's framework for treating blind people was one which considered them interesting oddities—in this case, as people who were unusual because they were breaking the usual perceived mold of being an incompetent and dependent blind person.

Failure to cover the National Federation demonstration was a phenomenon that one analyst has called "blackout as social control" and that another has called the "threshold of legitimacy" test.[34] Whatever we call it, the news media's ability to determine what will be news constitutes a very real kind of authority over the public's ability to grapple with issues. Merton and Lazarsfeld put it this way:

> To the extent that the media of mass communication have an influence upon their audiences, it has stemmed not only from what is said but, more significantly, from what is not said. For these media not only continue to affirm the *status quo* but, in the same measure, they fail to raise essential questions about the structure of society. Hence, by leading toward conformism and by providing little basis for a critical appraisal of society, the commercially sponsored mass media indirectly but effectively restrain the cogent development of a genuinely critical outlook.[35]

The basic approach of television entertainment, like television news, has been to treat its audience as consumers rather than as producers, change agents, or thinkers. Here too, television provides the audience a particular type of package. Advertisements portray men and women consuming. Television quiz shows portray people consuming. Situation comedies trivialize and romanticize individual conflicts as well as big social problems. Here too, television treats the audience as a consumer, for it provides a solution to each problem it raises (that is, the proverbial "Hollywood ending"). Even the television news "magazines" suggest that the answer to problems its reporters uncover is simply available—if you will—consumable. These shows tend to portray problems as isolated abuses rather than as related problems associated with such structural conditions as prejudice, corporate exploitation, and enforced poverty. The television consumer learns that for most such problems there is usually a good and relatively simple solution near at hand in the form of a better policy, a technological breakthrough, or a consumable item. If the problem portrayed is political in nature, the television show usually suggests that it be resolved by political leaders, not grass-roots organizing.

Stewart Ewen suggests that the mass media of the 1950's created a "consumerized universe" in which the individual's role was to believe that freedom meant freedom of choice between consumable goods.[36] This is basically the same conclusion which Gitlin draws concerning media news. Ewen seems to speak to organizers when he writes:

> Once again, the definition proffered by a "freedom-loving" political ideology was one in which to produce one's own world was subversive (except where it was

legitimized by the do-it-yourself industry); to assert the idea that a community might control its own destiny was "communistic."[37]

The Media and Social Movements

The mass media treats social protest in the same manner that it handles crime. They tend to focus almost exclusively on the decorum of protesters and change agents, that is, "Was there violence? If so, how much? How big were the crowds?" The substance of a movement becomes obscured when attention is given to such details. On student protesters, Gitlin notes, "When dissidents were (portrayed as) 'muttering,' 'rolled up in sleeping bags,' 'bearded,' disheveled, and at the same time planning massive illegality (demonstrations), they themselves became the issue."[38] This occurred in a protest against Chase Manhattan Bank for its policy of granting loans to the racist South African government. A *New York Times* article covered the substance of the issue (Students for a Democratic Society protesting the Bank's lending policies) in several paragraphs but gave top billing to arrests. As Gitlin notes:

> There was no mention of the bank's attempt to enjoin the demonstration or to prohibit the distribution of buttons, leaflets, and research papers. No word appeared of SDS's research into the decisiveness of the role of American banks in keeping the Voerwoerd [South African leader at the time] regime afloat after the Sharpeville massacre. What was most distinctly newsworthy was sharp clash and arrests.[39]

In part, the media's reluctance to treat protest seriously may reflect its stereotyped view of marginal groups (see previous section on the media's stylized picture of America) or its need to simplify issues and to communicate quickly and at a basic level. The evening news lasts only 22 minutes; the rest is advertisements. As Walter Cronkite once noted, all the text for an evening news show could be fit on one page of the *New York Times*. Hence, for television at least, complex, deep stories simply are not possible. For newspapers, complexity also poses problems. Reporters have limited space and inflexible deadlines and generally lack expertise on most of the hundreds of stories they handle in a given year. Hence they find themselves searching for a familiar framework, a few "good quotes," and some controversy.

The media's coverage of school bussing and of urban rights both demonstrate an unfailing ability and penchant to produce a distorted picture of events in the world. The inherent problem is television's and, increasingly, the newspapers' need to supply entertainment. As Swerdlow and Mankiewicz argue, most cities in which bussing has been tried have not experienced violence. Boston and Louisville gained national attention because they did have a few violent incidents. Without violence or a threat of it—here the media can report that despite rumors of violence none surfaced—television will not cover the story:

> Since news is part of the entertainment medium, it must be entertaining. And a peaceful bus ride is simply not entertaining. What is entertaining is a shrieking con-

frontation between blacks and whites, preferrably with the shiny helmets of the National Guard for additional "color" and the threat of street violence.[40]

For precisely the same reasons, television and other news media failed in their coverage of urban riots. Mankiewicz and Swerdlow charge that even the confrontation was inaccurately portrayed:

> Where, for example, were the reports of courage and integrity, of blacks saving blacks and whites alike, of false arrests and police brutality? Those were occurrences as widespread and important as fires and lootings—but they were absent from the screen, and from, therefore, the audience's knowledge.[41]

More importantly, where was the discussion of prejudice, exploitation, and human degradation that led to the riots? And where was middle-class Harlem, which exists, but which television viewers never saw? Through television, all Harlem, indeed the Black community, became one mass of violent looters and arsonists.

Another explanation for the media's preference for violent and exciting events, as contrasted with the probing of more substantively important processes, is that the *event* fits the medium. News media, whether television, newspapers, or radio perpetually need stories and they must be able to communicate these stories succinctly in "one shot." Thus the media tend to prefer "good quotes" to good substance, "good visual material" to unexciting but important processes (for example, meetings), and "good violence" to everyday, normal occurrences—hence the old adage "Bad news is good news." In terms of media coverage of ghetto life, for example, it favors the event to the everyday reality:

> The news media are predisposed to handling discreet events—a court case, a riot, a speech—which can readily be fitted to the time schedules of their production process. Realities which are not independent, 'on off' occurrences, but which are evolving, interdependent conditions and processes—like ghetto existence, poor education, exploitation on racial grounds—are not suited to the format imposed on realities by news media's routinized processes of news collection and treatment.[42]

Graham Murdock calls this approach to news an event-orientation. Long-term and slowly evolving information has little appeal when placed next to quick and eventful happenings. Thus Murdock suggests that a coup or assassination attempt makes better news than a long, drawn-out guerrilla war.[43] By the same token, a picture of a demonstrator and a policeman fighting makes better news than a largely uneventful peace march or than a long-term social movement strategy of building a coalition for one type of reform or another.

It is the bias of the media to cover the eventful and violent. Like it or not, reporters find themselves passing up substance for entertainment. Indeed, many reporters realize full well that officials and social movement groups alike now make it their regular business to draw media attention with event-oriented strategies. Whereas officials have ready access to the media—they do not need as many theatrics—those people whom Goldenberg calls resource-poor have very little access.[44] This latter group, whatever its cause, must sing for its supper. Dean Calbreath cites media coverage of the Ku Klux Klan as an example of how the media gets "tricked" into coverage of violence and symbols of violence rather than issue content:

> There is a legitimate story lurking behind all this swastika-bedecked grandstanding: the Klan's philosophy is unfortunately gaining acceptance in the United States. The fact that Tom Metzger, grand dragon of a little band of San Diego Klanners, could get 33,000 votes in a congressional race there last November, or that Harold Covington, a Nazi leader in North Carolina, could win 56,000 votes in an election bid for attorney general last May, bears witness to that fact. The psychological, economic, and sociopolitical factors that lead people so casually to accept violence-prone bigots as political figures badly need to be probed.
>
> Unfortunately, however, those are difficult subjects, too complex to be covered by reporters working on a story or two of breaking news per day, so we resort to going after the cheap but easy tale of a dozen or so fanatics marching down Main Street and spewing out racial hatred. We get good quotes that way, and a safe, sexy story, but we often wind up becoming nothing less than flacks for the Jeff Murrays and Rickey Coopers [Ku Klux Klan organizers] of this world.[45]

While Calbreath can claim that he and others have been tricked or duped and forced by circumstances to cover violence above issues, the reality seems to be that the news industry itself, with its bias towards treating social movements of all kinds as deviant and its pressures to be entertaining and fast-paced, defines good news as news which confirms prevailing values. As a result, we often see us-versus-them situations portrayed, whether the Klan or protesting welfare recipients are involved. Issues become personified when the media make celebrities out of movement leaders. The social movement itself is then left largely unexplained. Perceptions of violence are maximized while an understanding of the regular, long-term processes of life is not promoted in any way.

The media's need for simplicity and immediacy leads it to personify issues. An issue is best and perhaps most easily presented if it has a celebrity or two on which to rest. Whether this tendency toward portraying personalities reflects the media's peculiar need to make issues vivid, to entertain, or perhaps to ignore and play down the existence of popular social movements, the phenomenon surfaces even when no celebrities seem to exist; that is, the media creates them. This happened in the late 1960s when students protested at Columbia University. The news media selected Mark Rudd, of Students for a Democratic Society, as a media celebrity. As one editor at the *New York Times* recalls, several long feature stories on the overall protest movement were rejected at the *Times* in favor of a feature on Rudd.[46] Gitlin believes that leaders who appear as media celebrities such as Rudd, Stokely Charmichael, Abbie Hoffman, and Jesse Jackson have media value because the media can present them as deviants. On the other hand, they also have media legitimacy because they are perceived as having positions of authority in social movements. Thus the media casts certain leaders into the conflicting roles of movement authorities and of individual celebrities or performers. Not surprisingly, then, news that has been cast with celebrities at center stage portrays an event more as the product of a few stars than of a social *movement*.

People who deal regularly with the media quickly learn to capsulize their issues into a series of standard phrases and slogans. The important thing, if one wants coverage, is to speak in succinct one-liners and "quotable quotes," even at the expense of trivializing an issue. This explains why political candidates seem generally to voice platitudes and slogans rather than complex ideas. Complicated ideas do not conform with the mass media's desire to report events in simple, entertaining terms.

ACTION THROUGH MEDIA

The mass media's nature and its slant toward social movements suggests one thing—organizers should approach the media with trepidation. No organizer can afford to ignore the potential pitfalls associated with media exposure. On the other hand, any group which desires to influence or educate the public needs extensive media exposure. There is no avoiding the obvious fact that mass media reach more people more often than any other form of communication. Rather than turn our back on the media by charging it with decadent pandering to images of violence and sex, with gross misrepresentation of reality, and with prejudice toward unofficial and nonelite groups, we need to plan carefully how best to use the media and how best to avoid being done in by it.

The preceding analysis of the media suggests several key principles which should guide community organizers' media activities:

1. Organizers should not expect to communicate complex, detailed, or noneventful information through the mass media. Given the mass media's nature and biases, our goal should be merely to introduce new issues before the public eye.
2. Organizers should make issues as clear and as exciting or entertaining as possible.
3. Community organizations should plan media events carefully, with an eye to overcoming the media's tendency to black out the activities of marginal groups or to treat them as they would crime.
4. Community organization should use alternative media such as newsletters, alternative newspapers, and pamphlets, and not only the mass media, to communicate with and expand its own ranks.

Types of Communication

The term media is a broad one. It includes diverse forms of communication such as books, films, newspapers, television, and radio. The media of communication include some forms which are particularly well suited to the activity of community organizing. What follows is a brief description of such strategies. The so-called media event (for example, a demonstration or press conference) will be more extensively examined in the next section.

Letter writing. We generally think of letter writing as a particularly passive way of taking action. However, as we noted in the preface to this book, it often is anything but passive. Letter writing *can* prove to be an effective, even provocative strategy. It takes numerous forms: open letters to local and national newspapers (letters are among the most read sections of newspapers);[47] leaflets; skywriting; letter-bulletins; letters of support to groups that share your interests; letters of complaint; letters to officials as a means of creating a record; letters of complaint with carbon copies sent to your attorney or another authority whom the recipient fears; publication of letters written by your opposition which will lend credibility to your concerns; and letter writing campaigns (usually designed to demonstrate broad based support for a particular position).

The purposes of letter writing vary considerably. In some instances, organizers write letters-to-the-editor in order to communicate with the public, or perhaps to expose an official action which the organizing group opposes. Other letters may have the effect of putting officials on notice that an organizing group expects change to occur. A letter that carries a carbon copy notice at the bottom may be designed to intimidate an official into action. Skywriting may put an idea in the public's mind (for example, "Vote for Proposition 20" or "Support Quality Daycare"). Some groups send out letter-bulletins to announce a major organizing victory. Others rely on letters as a strategy for fundraising.

Public hearings and fact-finding forums. Community organizing groups have always used the neighborhood meeting, the fact-finding meeting, town meetings, community polls, teach-ins and question and answer sessions as effective means of getting issue exposure. This strategy has the advantage of both communicating and clarifying needs. At the same time, fact finding or fact disclosing, like letter writing, is an action. Whatever its particular form, the public hearing communicates a sense of community concern for an issue. Official public hearings provide a good forum for community groups to focus attention on their issues. But in some instances, particularly where community groups find that official forums do not adequately address the organizers' agendas, community groups may decide to create their own public forums. These have been called Peoples' Hearings, Ad Hoc Hearings, and other similar names. In either format, organizers need to prepare for the event. Preparation includes: specifying issues to be covered; getting on the agenda (if it is an official hearing); knowing the audience and on what points it might prove receptive; gathering specific evidence in the form of statistics, case examples, laws, and quotations to substantiate specific points; having recommendations to offer; anticipating questions from the panel; having multiple written copies of testimony; making sure people know how to get to the hearing place; giving testimony in an energetic, emotional fashion; and being prepared to give the key elements of testimony to the news media in separate interviews.

Pamphlets, booklets and slideshows. Tom Paine's art of pamphleteering lives. Despite the enormous influence of the mass media in shaping and limiting what we see and consider, other media are available to community groups. As noted in the chapter on "Legal Advocacy," during the 1960s community groups began to publish and distribute thousands of legal rights booklets for consumers. Now, consumer guides proliferate on virtually every imaginable issue. Some are resource guides, replete with addresses of community services, costs, hours, and types of services available. Others put public policy and statutes in lay language. Still others explain how consumers can locate services, qualify for services, and protect themselves against official misconduct (for example, police brutality, school exclusion). Some booklets and slideshows introduce an alternative approach to solving community needs. For example, organizing groups have developed slideshows on prison abolition, school integration, health care, deinstitutionalization, birth control, and a variety of other issues. The best such materials cover a single issue, communicate in easy to understand English, provide information on how consumers can take action individually and in groups, are inexpensive or free, are easily available to large groups of people, and do not rely on sophisticated audio-visual equipment (for example, synchronized slide tape equipment).

Posters. Social protest movements have always produced posters. Most are handwritten posters prepared for the picket line. Others qualify as poster art. Both communicate a simple idea visually. Neither can communicate a complex idea or even much information to substantiate an idea. However, the political poster, with all its limitations, communicates vividly and effectively to large audiences.

Clearly, some groups find it easier than others to communicate their ideas via posters. Some ideas do not lend themselves to the poster medium. However, if a movement or issue can be communicated in a single word or several words, or in a simple image, it can be communicated by a poster. The general rule of thumb for poster preparation is that the audience should be able to have near instant recognition of a poster's meaning and content from a distance of at least fifteen feet away. This means that poster art cannot include much text. The best posters are those which rely heavily on a single strong visual image.

Advertisements. Social change advertisements communicate issues, reveal group support for an issue or perspective, and build additional support for a position (since many political advertisements include a coupon for donations). Some such advertisements resemble poster art, but often include two to six paragraphs of brief text which explain the theme of the artwork. Other advertisements are essentially petitions. They include a brief position statement and hundreds of signers' names. In another form, advertisements act as open letters to officials or to the public on a particular issue. Unless a community organizing group has specifically raised funds to support an advertising campaign, it will usually circulate a proposed statement and request signers to contribute five or ten dollars toward the cost of advertising space.

Other forms of advertisement include "bus cards" (poster-style ads which can be placed, for a modest charge, on buses and trains), billboards, and public service advertisements. Public service ads (PSA's) are usually promotional announcements for organizations and events. A group can often enlist a local radio or television station to prepare the PSA but the local group must write the script. The best way to learn how to do a PSA is to watch them on television and listen to them on radio.

Talk shows and feature stories.   While we tend to think of television news, the "hard" news story in newspapers, and radio's hourly news as the principal media outlets for organizing issues, the fact of the matter is that so-called soft news occupies an enormous place in the media. Most television and radio stations sponsor several regular talk shows. Similarly, newspapers increasingly have extensive feature and opinion sections. Both electronic and print feature outlets have an unending need for fresh stories. Thus organizing groups usually find it quite simple to call up a moderator or reporter and gain access. Such "soft" news outlets offer several advantages over hard news media. First, talk shows and news features are often much longer than the average hard news story. A talk show can last for half an hour or an hour, as opposed to the usual minute-and-a-half hard news story. Similarly, newspapers can devote a four-part series of in-depth articles on a feature story as opposed to the standard ten- to twenty-column-inch "hard news" story. Community groups have found that they can communicate a good deal of evidence and more complex issues and arguments in this format. Even uneventful but nevertheless important, information (for example, a story about absentee landlords or about the practice of banks denying mortgages to homeowners in poor areas also called redlining) "works" in the feature format. Also, organizers tend to use the feature medium as a way of following up on an issue that is no longer hot "news." In addition, community groups sometimes employ the feature story or talk show as a way of bringing attention to a model program or practice, thereby setting an example for officials and organizations to follow. It can act as a kind of rate-setting strategy.

Preparation for the soft news medium should include at least the following considerations: a clear sense of the issue or issues to be communicated; statistical, legal, and other information related to the topic, anticipation of interviewers' and audience questions; a ready stock of vivid one-line statements to communicate key issues; contrasts between model policies and practices with problematic ones; identification of effective interviewees; role-playing in advance of the interview; and identification of newspaper writers and talk show hosts who will tend to be sympathetic to the organizing cause.

Media Exposure

Todd Gitlin has produced one of the more exhaustive analyses of media and social movement interaction in his book *The Whole World is Watching*. In it he argues that organizers demonstrate naivete in their dealings with the press. Organizers, he contends, frequently seem curiously unmindful of the media's basic penchant to promote dominant social values such as the legitimacy of corporate power, respecting government secrecy clothed in a language of national security and legitimizing the high status and authority of technocratic experts. The press also generally accedes to authorized agencies' claims that they and they alone should be allowed to make social reforms, gives authority and respectability to social and political elites, and perpetuates the notion that individualism is a higher social good than social or community development. Moreover, Gitlin shows that organizers often seem somewhat caught off balance by the media's tendency to trivialize the purposes of social protest groups, to discredit social change efforts, and to focus on violence or the lack of it (for example, "the protest was unmarred by violence") as the central issue in any social protest. While organizers cannot possibly hope to alter the basically conservative nature of the mass media, they can play a much more effective role simply by preparing for media exposure. These strategies are discussed below.

Organization.   The news media will tend not to treat individuals seriously— individuals will generally be ignored as "oddballs" or deviants—unless of course they are perceived as experts or as members of and representatives of organizations. Clearly, members of dominant organizations enjoy easier access to the mass media than do marginal or social change groups. Nevertheless, group affiliation of any kind, even of a movement organization, goes a long way toward establishing legitimacy in the eyes of the media. Also, once an organization builds a reputation as an authority on an issue or set of issues, each subsequent effort to gain access to this media (for example, press conference, demonstration, public forum, interview on a controversial topic) becomes easier. In short, the organization image lowers the access threshold. Finally, the organization provides people with mechanisms by which they can present an issue or event to the media. Community organizations can provide the location for press conferences, stationery and phones to contact the press, and information centers for research needed to document press releases.

Define issues.   As noted earlier, the press plays a substantial role in defining what is and is not an issue. Thus it was that during the riots of 1967, violence and looting in Harlem was an issue, but heroism and bravery in Harlem was not. During the early days of the Reagan Administration, tens of thousands of demonstrators descended on Washington to protest the Reagan policy in El Salvador. Much of the national media attention went to showing films of gay people's groups and communist groups—these were a small number among the demonstrators—presumably because these groups were perceived as the most deviant and therefore the most entertaining. The point here is identical to that made time and again above—the media defined the issue as being the protesters themselves as much as the policy conflict their demonstration symbolized. One strategy to make issues clearer is to actually define issues succinctly and in every day nonjargon language. Organizing groups need to define their issues clearly and simply. Only then can issues be articulated in simple posters, advertisements, and statements to the press. News reporters want, above all, "good quotes" and an easily intelligible story. Organizers cannot depend on the media to distill complex stories into simple ones. The organizers themselves must package their ideas in an easily understood and communicated form.

Define goals and objectives.   Once organizers have clarified their issues, they can then map out their media goals (For example, which point does the organizing group want to emphasize in the ensuing year or decade?). Some groups use the mass media as a vehicle to portray a new image of activism that of competence and determination. In such instances, the particular issues around which media campaigns revolve may be less important than the frequency of events. For example, when the Grey Panthers lobby for an end to forced retirement or when disabled citizens hold sit-ins to force the federal government to implement the nondiscrimination clause of the Rehabilitation Act, each projects a clear policy message. But perhaps more important in each case, consumers being to create a new forceful image for themselves which challenges the usual media images of dependency, incompetence, and defeat. To the extent that groups can establish the dual purpose of long-range image creation and specific policy change, failure on the immediate public policy level does not render the act of media engagement null and void.

A group should articulate its viewpoint simply and clearly. It is virtually impossible and almost always self-defeating to try and communicate more than a single, simple point in one media event.

Plan to control the issue.   The mass media have tremendous demands on them to perpetuate dominant social values, to report stories quickly, to fit stories into limited space, to produce a story which the public can immediately understand, and to entertain its readership. These constraints dominate news reporting. They were demonstrated at one parent-power conference. Over two hundred parents met one Saturday to receive legal and organizing training on how to establish and protect educational rights for disabled children. At midday, the parents held a press conference. Their purpose was to make their existence as an organization known, to recruit additional parents to their cause, to educate the public to the educational discrimination encountered by disabled children, to create an image of activism before the public, and to put school district officials on notice that they could no longer trample on the rights of disabled children. Simply put, the intended message was parent-power for children's rights. As the reporters asked one parent interviewee why the group had gathered, she explained the kinds of problems children with disabilities faced in the public schools (for example, exclusion, inaccessible buildings, unnecessary forced segregation from nondisabled children). She spoke expansively of the new parent militancy. One reporter then asked, "Tell me, what was it like to give birth to a disabled child. What were your feelings at the time?" Caught off guard, the parent told of her initial guilt feelings, of tensions which arose between her and her husband, and of her own early depression that her child was not the perfect baby for whom she had planned. The rights message was lost. Immediately after the press conference, the parents began to wonder why the reporter had asked the question. Then they worriedly asked themselves would that highly personal segment appear on the six o'clock news. They could almost predict the answer. The discussion of feelings of guilt, of familial tensions and of depression fit the all-too-common stereotypical image of the disabled. It was a story the media was used to handling. It was a story that the public would take in and then let pass with a sigh and perhaps a brief comment, "Thank God that didn't happen to me," or "Poor woman." At six that night when the conference organizers sat down to watch the news what they saw was a woman being asked about her private feelings. The message of rights and of challenging discrimination was lost and never appeared on the television screen. Back in the editing room, the station had put personal human interest before social politics.

Initially, the conference organizers blamed the reporter and then the television station for missing the point of their organizing-for-rights gathering. However, as the days passed, the organizers began to ask, "How could we have avoided that?" After watching numerous news broadcasts they began to see that most polished politicians and organizers knew how to handle similar situations. It became obvious to them that in order to control the message—which meant guaranteeing their central message, no matter what happened in the editing room—they needed to know two things. First, they had to know how to say the same thing in at least ten different ways. Second, they needed to know how to turn any question around such that it could be answered with one of the ten prepared responses. To the reporter's question above, the parent might have answered, "Oh, I am so glad you asked that question because the truth is that while it took me some time to adjust to the fact that my child has a disability, our greatest problem proved to be the discrimination and neglect he experienced at the hands of our public education system. We pay school taxes like everyone else, yet our child has fewer rights than other children. We are here today to say 'Our children do have rights. And we will not be denied.' "

Make the issue or event newsworthy.   As long as the accessibility threshold for marginal or social change groups to the media is high, organizing groups will need to know how to make a case for the newsworthiness of issues. As noted earlier, newsworthiness is measured by the degree to which it embodies: conflict or controversy; eventful substance; simplicity and "packageability" or recognition quality; support in some authoritative circles (for example, intellectuals, experts, formal organizations); exclusivity or novelty; a subject that affects a large group of people; a subject that is entertaining; a large geographic area (that is, metropolitan area, state, region, or nation); or an issue that the public considers legitimate.

Increasingly, the media may not perceive an issue as legitimate until organizers, through repeated media strategies that attend carefully to the criteria of newsworthiness, make it legitimate. In some cases, a turn of events renders an issue more legitimate. Note, for example, the remarkable change in how the media handled nuclear power protests and concerns after the Three Mile Island accident as opposed to before it:

> Predictably, the 1979 disaster at Three Mile Island altered the prevailing frame. Three Mile Island shook the nation's elites; it was the Tet of the nuclear power industry.

Reporters now began calling up antinuclear-power groups, asking for information about reactor safety. Academically certified experts close to the movement, like Dr. John Gofman of the University of California at Berkeley and the onetime General Electric engineers, became quasi-legitimate sources, and were now cited frequently in the press giving their balancing statements against claims by Metropolitan Edison (the operators of Three Mile Island), Babcock & Wilcox (the builders of the plant), and even, though more rarely, the Nuclear Regulatory Commission (NRC). Reporters felt that they were being lied to by officials and business executives, and were saying or strongly implying so. Walter Cronkite referred one night to "the Harrisburg syndrome." The networks were reporting information leaked from within the NRC, showing how little the official regulatory agency had known about what was happening in Pennsylvania.[48]

This change in tone and content did not last forever—before too long the media returned to treating government pronouncements on the topic far more seriously than the critics'. Massive protests were clearly downplayed in contrast to official government actions. Media attention again focused more on protester decorum and the weather at each protest than on the substantive issues. However, with Three Mile Island, nuclear power achieved legitimacy as a serious, controversial issue that it had not previously enjoyed.

Knowing the opposing view.   The first media threshold for organizers is access. In order to communicate through the mass media, access must first be gained. Having achieved that—techniques for achieving media access are discussed in the next and final section of this chapter—organizers have multiple goals to achieve the most central among them being broad-based community education. The mass media provides a wonderful vehicle to reach large numbers of people quickly. In most situations, we can hope only to raise an issue, to expand the range of issues before the public eye, to spark a question. We must attempt to accomplish this while at the same time trying to defend ourselves against being discredited at the hands of the mass media. Thus we need an offensive strategy—communicate an issue or position—and a defensive one, namely to predict and answer in advance the discrediting charges of the media and one's opposition.

In most situations, organizers can forecast the kinds of remarks and criticisms that are aimed at discrediting their perspectives and actions. If a social change group pickets a speech of a leading official, it can expect to be charged with "inhibiting free speech" or with being "afraid to hear what so-and-so has to say." If a group seeks social reform of some kind (for example, public ownership of energy, deinstitutionalization of older people from nursing homes, tax reform) it must expect and be ready to counter charges of being "unrealistic," of promoting communism, or of favoring proposals too costly for taxpayers. If the group's goal is truly to educate the broadest possible constituency to its point of view, then the group needs to counter such charges almost before they arise. The group can, for example, demonstrate its realism by demonstrating that its goals can be achieved through practical steps, that its alternative plan costs less (cost data are essential in such instances), that the proposed plan or perspective has its roots in a long tradition of ideas and practices commonly accepted in society, and that the position has broad-based support in terms of the political and class backgrounds of people who have already identified themselves with it. The Civil Rights movement, for example, built a mass movement nationally for desegregation by finding advocates in all walks of life and of all political persuasions, by emphasizing the long tradition of respect for equality in America in the Constitution, in the abolition of slavery, in America's melting pot rhetoric, and by identifying civil rights as an essentially democratic pursuit. Ultimately, the organizers' effectiveness will be measured in terms of their ability to outmaneuver their opposition and to speak directly and compellingly to their audience, the public.

MEETING THE PRESS

Social change groups can develop specific strategies to overcome the major problems they encounter with the mass media. To summarize, those major problems are as follows:

*discrediting of their perspectives by portraying them as deviants.
*difficulties in gaining media exposure.
*misrepresentation in the media.
*relative powerlessness in contrast to the media forum enjoyed by officials and other elites.
*difficulty in overcoming the media's tendency to treat social change groups in stereotypic ways.
*relative inexperience in dealing with the mass media.

The actual occasions in which community organizers interact with the media cover an enormous range of possibilities, including protest marches, civil disobedience (for example when protesters chain themselves to government property, sit-ins), community forums, press conferences, and talk shows, among others. As a general rule though, if organizers know how to set up and run a press conference, they can handle any media situation effectively. Thus we conclude this chapter with descriptions of practical skills for meeting the press:

Issues. Organizing groups must define their issues clearly. Otherwise, the media or the opposition will define the issues for them. It is well worth the time to use numerous meetings to define values, goals, and objectives so that when spokespersons go before the cameras and microphones, they know how to articulate the group's issues.

Single, Simple Focus. Because the mass media tend not to communicate complex ideas, particularly those of social change groups, organizers must decide on a single, simple focus.

Ten Ways. The best way to protect against having media coverage diverge from the group's central theme is to have at least ten different ways of communicating the single core message. Organizers and media spokespersons should develop examples, key phrases, and anecdotes to express the single theme.

Newsworthiness. There is no checklist for guaranteeing what will and will not be newsworthy. Establishing newsworthiness is to some extent a creative skill, though clearly, we can identify certain standard approaches to the problem. Unless they become our everyday routine, certain events such as the filing of a lawsuit, a public demonstration, civil disobedience, awards ceremonies (for example, human rights award), disclosures of an action research study usually garner news media attention. Basically, organizers should try to emphasize an event's uniqueness, importance, interest to large numbers of people, its controversy and timeliness.

Media Outlets. Officials generally find that the mass media seek them out for news. Even so, officials have an established apparatus for contacting and communicating with the media. Organizers, far more than officials, must actively pursue the media in order to win exposure. They must watch television commentators, listen to radio news reporters, and read newspaper articles to see how particular reporters cover social movement issues. They must develop lists of media outlets (television and radio stations, newspapers, wire services), their addresses, and phone numbers, along with the names of those reporters whom they believe will write the best stories. In many instances, groups are able to establish friendships with news reporters and editors and thus can expect more positive media treatment than would otherwise be expected.

Timing. Sometimes organizers can time a news event in order to maximize media coverage. A press conference held at ten or eleven in the morning will probably not conflict with official press conferences and media events and, it will thus be more likely to receive coverage. Similarly, news events on Saturdays and Sundays invariably receive more coverage than those which occur on weekdays, because weekends are a ''slow'' news time. Of course, many news events must be timed in coordination with other occurrences (for example, with a legislative vote on some official action) in order to maximize their newsworthiness.

Making a Case for Coverage. When a community organization calls a press conference or announces a media event, it should provide enough information to whet the media's appetite, but not so much that it obviates the media's need to attend the event. Information provided in advance should include: the nature of the issue or event, its time, place, and why it is important (that is, newsworthy).

FIGURE I
Sample Press Release
Metropolitan Action Coalition
Child Care Emergency Cited
June 4, 1982
For Immediate Release
Contact Person: Marion Roberts

Metropolitan Action Coalition (MAC) issued a report today blasting the County for its failure to fund infant day care programs.

In a 92-page report entitled *Child Care Emergency,* MAC charges the County with dragging its heels on creating inexpensive, quality day care programs for infants aged 2 to 18 months. The group cites inadequate funding, bureaucratic red tape and disinterest as the causes behind the problem.

According to MAC officials, the report demonstrates that the County should immediately fund infant child care programs to serve 300 infants this year. And, the report notes, "a conservative estimate suggests we will need child care services for an additional 50 infants each year for the next five years."

"Five years of officials' promises of new programs have resulted in no new infant program being started," declared MAC leader Allison Evans today. "Three hundred working parents are forced to leave their children with neighbors, with siblings, and with untrained help every day," she charged.

"As long as County officials keep delaying, our community risks the chance of a real tragedy. Children's lives are at stake."

The report made public today for the first time statistics which place Metro city in the bottom ten percent of similar sized cities for child care services to infants.

Members of the Metropolitan Action Coalition will meet with County officials later this week to explore ways of implementing the findings. Study spokesperson Ryan O'Neal expressed his hope that the immediate crisis would be discussed in the County legislature before the current session adjourns.

Fifteen area child care centers as well as seven neighborhood organizations comprise the Metropolitan Action Coalition. The group formed three years ago to address what members called "the common interests of children and parents." The group advocates for greater support for child care programs and other programs to assist working families.

Two thousand copies of *Child Care Emergency* have been distributed to local churchs and civic organizations today. The Interreligious Council funded the study which took six months to complete.

–30–

Press Release.   Each time a group holds a press conference or plans a media event, other than a "spontaneous" event where a prepared statement would be inappropriate, it should be ready to distribute a press release. These can be sent to newspapers as long as their arrival time is coordinated with the timing of the press conference or event. A press release should include the name of the organization responsible for the release, a contact person for the media to call, a date, time of release, and the statement itself. All press releases should have short paragraphs (ideally no longer than four or five lines each). The first paragraph, preferably a single sentence, should state the central issue and the basic information. Reporters refer to the basic information as the five "W's"; who, what, when, why, and where. At the bottom of each page should be number -15- or -30- which is journalism jargon for "the end." A good press release includes several types of information including, for example, quotations, statistics, and references to public policy or particular laws. The press release, like a press conference, should focus on a single issue. The most important information should appear in the first part of the release (in case a news reporter prints it verbatim and cuts off a section). The release should be written in a way that it may be cut at any point without losing its meaning. Background information about the group releasing the statement should appear toward the end of the text.

Stars.   Not everyone can perform well before the media. A group would do well to identify which of its members have or could have a good media presence.

These personalities then become the organization's spokespersons. Attention then must be given to developing a basic message for the media person to communicate (see issues section above). Most organizations will want to develop several types of spokespersons including consumer leaders, charismatic public speakers, and well-known or credentialed experts. Each has a particular value. Consumers can communicate a sense of "reality" and "credibility" about an issue that "just another expert" cannot. An expert, on the other hand, can lend an air of technical legitimacy to an issue that a consumer or so-called layperson cannot. A charismatic leader will symbolize a social movement's strength and competence.

Entertainment.   Make the news exciting. Media outlets want news that will entertain. Rather than lament the media's resistance to treating serious issues with the "seriousness they deserve," organizers would do well to discover means of making serious issues exciting and thus newsworthy. For the individual interviewer this means having a ready store of what reporters call "good quotes." Short, pithy statements, delivered in staccato fashion, make good news, whether in newspapers or on television.

At the event level, the group should try to design an event so that it has some character. Often this can be accomplished through staging. Recall, for example, the symbolic acts cited in the previous chapter. When a feminist group wanted to draw attention to corporations and institutions which practiced job discrimination against women, the group hired a tour bus and invited the media on a guided tour of sexist organizations. At each stop, the group held a mini-press conference in which it outlined the corporation's or institution's specific discriminatory practices and their extent. Similarly, when two out of three political candidates for mayor refused to attend a question and answer forum sponsored by a militant, urban neighborhood improvement group, the group placed large mannequins in the empty chairs of the absent officials and then later led the media to the candidates' homes, where they tacked a list of demands to their front doors. Such symbolic events have an entertainment value but, more than that, they leave the viewer with a vivid image by which to remember an issue. In other words, what is entertaining tends also be to interesting, and, occasionally, compelling.

Role Play.   If you ask people experienced in giving press conferences how they prepared for them, they will invariably tell you that they go over and over the press conference or media event before it happens. They prepare good quotations in their minds and think about all the possible questions the media may ask. They try to predict what the opposition will say if it gets interviewed. They also try to think about how best to speak to their audience and the public. Finally, they try to have a few good facts and examples ready to "prove" their point. Experienced organizers can do all of this in their heads almost instantaneously. Those who are uninitiated to the process will probably want to prepare by role-playing the press conference. A few of the group's members can play the role of reporters and the interviewees can play themselves. Other group members can watch and analyze the enactment. After practicing the event, the observers and actors can discuss the degree to which the questions are realistic representations of what the media is likely to ask and whether the answers are focused and powerful enough.

Winning. Media events, like most organizing actions, are contests. Will the social change group succeed in winning the initiative, in having its perspective reach its audience? All too often, organizing groups find their message trivialized, discredited, ignored, and distorted. Certainly no social group can or should expect to achieve its media goals consistently. In addition to the above itemized media skills and strategies, organizers should consider one additional factor when embarking on a media event: will the planned event enhance the group's image as an effective, successful change agent? To put it in a slightly different way, the organizing group should avoid placing itself in situations where it will be trivialized and discredited or in situations where it will appear to be a mere complainant to "legitimate" authority. Several strategies will help accomplish this end. First, the organizing group can establish and publicize its own objectives by which to evaluate the success of its events (for example, to have 100 people protest an official policy; to have 10 leading experts condemn a government action, to force officials to respond to an issue). Second, hold occasional press conferences to announce victories (for example, a negotiated settlement of a dispute; inauguration of a long sought new program or policy). Third, organize media events to unvail recommendations, alternative budgets, blueprints for reform, and action research findings. And fourth, organize media exposure on issues for which the group believes a breakthrough is imminent.

NOTES

[1]Vance Packard, *The Hidden Persuaders* (New York: Pocket Books, 1957); Joe McGinnis, *The Selling of the President, 1968* (New York: Pocket Books, 1970).

[2]Frank Mankiewicz and Joel Swerdlow, *Remote Control* (New York: Ballantine, 1978).

[3]James D. Halloran, Philip Elliott, and Graham Murdock, *Demonstrations and Communication: A Case Study* (Baltimore: Penguin, 1970).

[4]Mankiewicz and Swerdlow, *Remote Control*, p. 94.

[5]Thomas E. Patterson and Robert D. McClure, *The Unseeing Eye* (New York: Putnam's, 1976), p. 18.

[6]Patterson and McClure, *Eye*, p. 18.

[7]Paul R. Harmann and Charles Husband, "The Mass Media and Racial Conflict," in *Sociology of Mass Communication*, ed., Denis McQuail (Baltimore: Penguin, 1972), p. 437.

[8]Todd Gitlin, "Media Sociology," *Theory and Society*, 6 (November, 1978), p. 245.

[9]Daniel J. Boorstein, *The Image: A Guide to Pseudo-Events in America* (New York: Harper & Row Pub., 1961), p. 9.

[10]David Halberstam, *The Powers That Be* (New York: Dell, 1979), pp. 27 & 29.

[11]Halberstam, *The Powers*, p. 31.

[12]Michael Massing, "Reshuffling the White House Press Pack," *Columbia Journalism Review*, March/April, 1981, pp. 36–40.

[13]Massing, "White House Press," p. 38.

[14]Massing, "White House Press," p. 39.

[15]Todd Gitlin, *The Whole World Is Watching* (Berkeley: University of California Press, 1980), p. 275.

[16]Gitlin, *Whole World*, p. 276.

[17]Angus MacKenzie, "Sabotaging the Dissident Press," *Columbia Journalism Review*, March/April, 1981, p. 25.

[18]MacKenzie, "Sabotaging," p. 60.

[19]MacKenzie, "Sabotaging," p. 60.

[20]See, for example: Tom Bethel, "The Myth of an Adversary Press," *Harper's Magazine*, January 1977, pp. 33–40 and; Edward Jay Epstein, *Between Fact and Fiction: The Problem of Journalism* (New York: Vintage Books, 1975).

[21]Robert Dainton, "Writing News and Telling Stories," *Daedalus*, 104, Spring 1975, p. 183.

[22]Halberstam, *The Powers*, p. 116.

[23]Halberstam, *The Powers*, p. 121.

[24]Daniel Schorr, *Clearing the Air* (New York: Berkeley Medallion Books, 1978).

[25]Halberstam, *The Powers*, p. 198.

[26]Warren Breed, "Social Control in the Newsroom: A Functional Analysis," *Social Forces*, 33, (May, 1975), pp. 326–335.

[27]Breed, "Social Control," p. 330.

[28]Breed, "Social Control," p. 330.

[29]Todd Gitlin, "Prime Time Ideology: The Herpmanic Process in Television Entertainment," *Social Problems*, 26, 3 (February, 1979), p. 262.

[30]Mankiewicz and Swerdlow, *Remote Control*, p. 162.

[31]Kenneth Jernigan, *Blindness: Is the Public Against Us*. An address delivered at the Banquet of the Annual Convention of the National Federation of the Blind, Chicago, July 3, 1975, pp. 4–5.

[32]Jernigan, *Blindness*, pp. 4–5.

[33]Jernigan, *Blindness*, pp. 5 and 6.

[34]Monica B. Morris, "Newspapers and the New Feminists: Black Out or Social Control?" *Journalism Quarterly*, 50, 1973, pp. 37–43; Todd Gitlin, *Whole World*.

[35]Paul F. Lazarsfeld and Robert K. Merton, quoted in Monica Morris, "Black Out," pp. 40–41.

[36]Stuart Ewen, *Captains of Consciousness* (New York: McGraw-Hill, 1976), p. 211.

[37]Ewen, *Captains*, p. 211.

[38]Gitlin, *Whole World*, p. 70.

[39]Gitlin, *Whole World*, p. 42.

[40]Mankiewicz and Swerdlow, *Remote Control*, p. 91–92.

[41]Mankiewicz and Swerdlow, *Remote Control*, p. 141.

[42]Paul G. Hartmann and Charles Husband, *Racism and the Mass Media* (Totowa, NJ: Rowman and Littlefield, 1974), p. 157.

[43]Murdock's views are discussed in Stanley Cohen and Jock Young, eds., *The Manufacture of News* (Beverly Hills: Sage Publications, Inc., 1973), p. 99.

[44]Edie N. Goldenberg, *Making the Papers* (Lexington, MA: Lexington Books, 1975), p. 145.

[45]Dean Calbreath, "Kovering the Klan," *Columbia Journalism Review*, March/April, 1981, p. 45.

[46]Gitlin, *Whole World*, p. 153.

[47]Fergus M. Bordeurich, "Supermodulating the Newspaper," *Columbia Journalism Review*, September/October, 1977, pp. 23–30.

[48]Gitlin, *Whole World*.

CHAPTER EIGHT
SELF-HELP

OUR VOICE IS NEW

They lined up in the aisles on either side of the auditorium, each waiting for a turn at one of the two microphones. "I'm sick of living in a group home," one young woman complained. "Nobody ever asked me if I wanted to live with them (the other people in the group home). I want my own apartment."

A middle-aged man at the microphone across the hall began to speak almost as soon as she completed her statement. "I want to get out of the institution," he told the audience. "They didn't want us to come here today. They don't let us do anything. They think we're dumb, but we're not. They're okay I guess, but they should let us do our own thing."

"Yeah," several people in the audience offered. A few clapped. The next person to speak said he was disgusted with conditions in the sheltered workshops. "They don't pay us enough," he charged.

"How much do you get?" I asked.

"Too little. They give me four dollars a week."

"How many hours a week do you work?" I asked.

"I work every day from 8:30 to 4:30," he said. At that point the woman who had invited me to speak on community organizing strategies stood up and offered some of her own thoughts. "I get paid $4.00 a week too. And I know I do as much work as people in factories. But they tell me I can't work in a factory. They tell me I'm not strong enough. I don't believe that. And another thing I don't like. Why do they have to call it 'the sheltered workshop'? Why can't they call it a factory or something?"

As each person spoke, I listened. What I was hearing was first-hand testimony of people whom society rarely hears—retarded adults who had serious complaints about treatment they receive at the hands of human service professionals as well as society at large.

"What should we call our group?" one man asked. "I don't like being called retarded. I'm a person." Later that night a small group of the conference participants would meet to discuss possible names for their group. They would consider acronyms like "CHARGE," "CHANGE," and "SHAPE."

The next person to stand at the microphone, a middle-aged man, dressed in a shirt, tie, and suit, spoke for people who had not come. "Our friends weren't allowed to come. The director (of another sheltered workshop) told them they couldn't come. He said they couldn't talk to you. He said they couldn't be part of our group. They should be allowed to come. They need help. I think we should complain to the government." Again there were cheers from the audience.

This man was followed by a woman whose comments brought some light-hearted laughter. She raised an issue that was more on the order of a personal trouble than a public issue. "Can you tell my roommate to stop talking too much at night? She keeps me up. And I don't like it."

Several of those who testified told of bad treatment they had received in institutions. One woman reported that she had spent sixteen years in an institution. "They told me I could never make it outside. They said I would eat too much. They told me I would get fat. But I think I look alright, don't you?" There was laughter and then applause.

"I think you look great," I said.

"That's the problem," she continued, speaking slowly and deliberately, "they didn't believe in me. They held me back. I proved I could make it. But why should we have to prove anything. We're people too. We have feelings. We can learn."

This group of over 150 adults, labeled mentally retarded, had gathered in Winnepeg, Manitoba to get organized. The participants had a few professional human service workers who assisted them in getting organized, but it was the participants themselves who set the agenda and did the talking. This was a consumer conference, and an exciting one at that. I had spoken to many consumer groups about organizing strategies, but never to a group of people labeled retarded. At first, the thought of communicating with people who were defined as having limited communication and thinking ability made me apprehensive. How should *I* communicate? Should I speak more slowly than usual? Should I use simple words? Would the audience get bored easily?

As it turned out, the experience was thoroughly enjoyable. I talked about power, about getting organized, and about specific strategies, including how to define issues, developing demands, negotiating, using the mass media for public education and political pressure, and demonstrations. I read from autobiographical statements of other retarded people who I and my co-workers had interviewed previously. In their statements we could see many of the same issues that concerned the Winnepeg group: low pay, limited choice in housing, and institutionalization, to name a few. They came to the microphones for over an hour, stating one issue after another.

Several years earlier, the People First organization had been founded by retarded people in Oregon. Nearly a decade earlier a group of people labeled retarded had issued a set of demands at a conference in Malmo, Sweden. Like so many other groups in society, retarded people were getting organized.

Three months after the Winnepeg meeting, several retarded adults from an Austrian sheltered workshop attended a meeting of the advisory committee to the International Year of Disabled Persons, the United Nations Center on Social Development and Humanitarian Affairs. One of the three spoke for the group:

> I speak in the name of persons with mental retardation.
> We are people first and only secondly, handicapped.
> We wish to speak for our rights and let other people know that we exist.
> We want to explain to our fellow human beings that we can live and work in the community.
> We want to show that we have rights and responsibilities like other people.
> Our voice is new.
> We must first learn to speak.
> And we ask everyone to learn to understand our voices.
> We need people who teach us to speak. People who believe in us.
> Mentally retarded persons do not want to live in terrible institutions.
> We want to live in the community.
> Please help all persons who are mentally retarded, especially those who are multi- and most severely handicapped, not only next year, but always.
> Thanks for listening.[1]

These ideas had grown out of self-help groups in Austria, but they could just as easily have been drafted by the group in Canada or by similar groups such as People First and Rights Now (a Boston-based organization of developmentally disabled persons).

Self-help represents an exciting development in self-determination. But is it community organizing? Do self-help groups make social change or do they merely provide a forum for personal change? If they are social change oriented, what role do they afford professionals? These are some of the many questions being asked about the ever growing number and types of self-help organizations nationally.

Gartner and Riessman, two scholars of self-help and co-directors of the National Self-Help Clearing House, see this movement as a burgeoning phenomenon. "Self-help has become newly central," they tell us, "to some 15 million Americans involved in over 500,000 groups."[2] What makes these groups unique from many other social change and political action organizations is their membership. Self-help refers to groups developed and controlled by affected people themselves, by consumers and by victims. They are, by their nature, committed to self-determination. Professionals and nonclients or nonconsumers can assist and even belong to self-help groups, but their role is always different than in traditional professional organizations and indeed than in many neighborhood groups, political action groups, and public interest lobbies. On the other hand, self-help groups come in such diverse forms that they cannot be described as one type. There are several types, and only a few of these have any meaningful bearing on social change efforts. In this chapter, we will look briefly at the diverse forms of self-help, define the type of self-help that promotes social change, describe the basic attributes of self-help organizing groups, and explore problems, dilemmas, and opportunities of self-help as an organizing strategy.

SELF-HELP DEFINED

Just as self-help groups vary in purpose, composition, working style, longevity, political ideology, structure, and tactics, so too do definitions of self-help. One frequently cited definition seems to take in most types of self-help groups, though for our purposes this definition may be somewhat too narrow or purist. According to Katz and Bender,

> self-help groups are voluntary, small group structures for mutual aid and the accomplishment of a special purpose. They are usually formed by peers who have come together for mutual assistance in satisfying a common need, overcoming a common handicap or life-disrupting problem, and bringing about desired social and/or personal change. The initiators and members of such groups perceive that their needs are not, or cannot be, met by or through existing social institutions. Self-help groups emphasize face-to-face social interactions and the assumption of personal responsibility by members. They often provide material assistance, as well as emotional support; they are frequently ''cause''-oriented, and promulgate an ideology or values through which members may attain an enhanced sense of personal identity.[3]

Given our interest in organizing, this definition is not entirely adequate. The limitation of self-help to small group activity seems unnecessarily narrow. Many self-help organizations involve a core group in face-to-face encounters and operate as small groups. However, at the same time they build large followings through publications programs, newsletters, fundraising events, political campaigns, and even coalition building. Further, while the American experience with self-help has been dominated by single issue organizations (for example alcoholics anonymous, welfare rights, women's health), many of the more social change oriented self-help organizations share certain common ideological beliefs, frequently join in coalitions with each other, and consciously seek to expand beyond their single issue image and character.

Janice Perlman has developed one of the most exhaustive analyses of self-help action groups.[4] She does not use the term ''self-help'' but rather calls such organizations ''grass roots groups.'' One of the lessons of the 1960s organizing, she tells us, is that people need local involvement with issues that affect their immediate lives if they are to remain involved and organized. She and others, most notably Piven and Cloward, believe that too much emphasis on national agendas by such groups as the National Welfare Rights Organization leave the grass roots ill prepared for the long social change struggle.[5] She describes grass roots groups organizations as using such diverse strategies as self-help, service provision, electoral politics, coalition building, boycotts, and demonstrations. They are community based, independent, and composed of members who desire to act on their own behalf. Perlman excludes government created organizations such as the current government sponsored independent living centers, the former model cities programs, and government initiated rape crises programs. Also excluded by her definition are groups that have a primarily national focus. Perlman cites two such groups, the NAACP and the League of Women Voters, presumably because these organizations set national priorities and agendas which local chapters implement. Perlman's definition of grass roots organizing also excludes advocacy organizations (for example, Nader-style public interest research groups, legal aide and legal services, the Children's Defense Fund, and the Center on Human Policy) which act on behalf of others and include many professional staff, albeit often working alongside consumers. In terms of activities, Perlman sees grass roots groups engaged in ways that are entirely consonant with, though perhaps more outwardly focused than the self-help model envisioned by Katz and Bender:

> They focus collective action on their own social, economic, and physical welfare through (1) demands directed at the public and private institutions controlling selected goods and services, (2) electoral strategies to take over the institutions, and/or (3) initiating alternative arrangements to cope with the needs of the population that those institutions fail to meet.[6]

Clearly, Perlman describes one type of self-help group rather than the whole of self-help. She focuses only on those which seek broad social change, either on one issue or on a range of issues. The key factors which characterize these groups are consumer leadership and control and local or regional organization.

The full range of self-help group characteristics is extensive. Lists of such characteristics have been developed by Katz and Bender, Gartner and Reissman, Killilia, and others.[7] Self-help characteristics typically include the following:

1. Self-help groups are initiated by people who perceive a shared problem.
2. People involved in self-help value their own personal participation.
3. The self-help group provides each member with a ''reference group.''
4. Self-help members share a common ideological perspective, and a common definition of issues.
5. Self-help groups sometimes define themselves as social movements.
6. People involved in self-help usually believe that dominant social institutions are not responding to their needs effectively or sensitively.
7. Most self-help groups have negative feelings about professionalism.
8. Self-help organizations serve as alternatives to traditional, formal organizations.
9. Self-help groups minimize hierarchy and maximize decision making by consensus.
10. While professionals may sometimes participate in self-help movements, consumers retain control.

11. Self-help organizations engage in consciousness raising, rap sessions, criticism, self-criticism, and similar strategies for refining and evolving a shared analysis of issues and strategies.

12. The majority of self-help organizations, especially those developed on an ad hoc basis to meet events or crises (for example, earthquake, proposed urban development project, nuclear plant siting) are short-lived.

13. Self-help groups tend to demonstrate new relationships between those who receive service and the caregivers, thus causing traditional professional-dominated organizations to alter their ways of relating to consumers.

14. Self-help groups generally create an atmosphere where members can give emotional as well as material support to each other.

15. Self-help participants feel more powerful as a result of their involvement in the group.

16. For many participants, self-help affiliation provides a sense of belonging, a sense of community, and for some, a substitute for the often absent extended family.

17. Self-help groups tend to operate on modest budgets.

18. Self-help groups resist bureaucratization.

19. Self-help groups may promote individual and/or social change.

20. Self-help organizations tend to have strong strategies, whether explicit or not, for socializing new members to the group.

If Gartner and Reissman's estimate of the number of self-help groups nationally is anywhere near accurate (a half million), the phenomenon of self-help may be exceedingly important indeed. Gartner and Reissman suggest that the growth of self-help reflects, in part at least, the growth of the service society. Self-help groups spring up to challenge inequalities in the provision of services. They tend to provide services more economically and more flexibly (that is, at the times when consumers most need them, in local neighborhoods). Gartner and Reissman cite four factors which relate closely to the growing concern with and interest in self-help style human services.[8] First, self-help, they argue, has an antibureaucratic ethos. It responds to a growing populist trend. Second, "self-help approaches are appropriate for a wide range of constituencies, such as women, youth, the aged. . . ." Third, self-help works for people with chronic illnesses, a very large segment of the population. Fourth, self-help activities cause traditional human services to become more responsive to the needs of their clients. Perhaps the best way to understand the nature and diversity of self-help groups is by looking briefly at a few of them.

The center for independent living. CIL was begun by several physically disabled students at the University of California, Berkeley. The group's purpose was to force reforms within the University to make it more accessible to disabled students, which meant breaking down architectural barriers such as long flights of stairs. It also meant challenging attitudes which excluded disabled students from admittance to college and to the full range of college activities. Since its inception in 1972, the Center for Independent Living has become a multipurpose center that provides services and engages in social change. CIL occupies a former automobile dealership, a very accessible, single level building. The auto repair building is now used for repairing wheelchairs and designing prototypes of high technology, highly practical wheelchairs. More than half of the 100-plus staff are people with disabilities, including cerebral palsy, deafness, blindness, physical impairments, and mental retardation. The staff provide disabled adults and families of disabled children with assistance in securing transportation, education rights, medical insurance, accessible housing, and consciousness raising. CIL has transformed the Berkeley, California area into one of the most disability-rights-conscious communities in America. This self-help organization has been featured on television programs such as *Sixty Minutes*. Moreover, CIL has led many of the disability rights political actions nationally. It is involved in litigation to promote the right to integrated education for severely disabled students. CIL was one of the groups, along with the American Coalition of Citizens with Disabilities, which organized sit-ins at regional Health, Education and Welfare Offices around the country that forced the federal bureaucracy to implement Section 504 of the 1973 Rehabilitation Act, the anti-discrimination clause.

Alcoholics Anonymous.   AA was founded in 1935. From an initially small group, Alcoholics Anonymous has grown to be one of the largest self-help movements in the world. It is certainly one of the most written about and most highly regarded. AA is evangelistic and conservative in nature. The group calls on individuals to admit their alcoholism as a problem, to admit that they are weak and cannot change themselves, and to find their salvation in God and AA. The organization is avowedly apolitical and single-issue focused. Current membership estimates vary, but it appears that AA counts its membership at over a half million people who belong to more than 25,000 chapters. The approach and ideology of AA comes through in its two guiding statements of principle, the ''twelve steps'' and ''twelve traditions.''

Twelve Suggested Steps of Alcoholics Anonymous

1. We admitted we were powerless over alcohol—that our lives had become unmanageable.
2. Came to believe that a Power greater than ourselves could restore us to sanity.
3. Made a decision to turn our will and our lives over to the care of God as we understood him.
4. Made a searching and fearless moral inventory of ourselves.
5. Admitted to God, to ourselves and to another human being the exact nature of our wrongs.
6. Were entirely ready to have God remove all these defects of character.
7. Humbly asked Him to remove our shortcomings.
8. Made a list of all persons we had harmed, and became willing to make amends to them all.
9. Made direct amends to such people wherever possible, except when to do so would injure them or others.
10. Continued to take personal inventory and when we were wrong promptly admitted it.

11. Sought through prayer and meditation to improve our conscious contact with God, as we understood Him, praying only for knowledge of His will for us and the power to carry that out.
12. Having had a spiritual awakening as the result of these steps, we tried to carry this message to alcoholics, and to practice these principles in all our affairs.

The Twelve Traditions of Alcoholics Anonymous

1. Our common welfare should come first; personal recovery depends upon AA unity.
2. For our group purpose there is but one ultimate authority—a loving God as He may express Himself in our group conscience. Our leaders are but trusted servants; they do not govern.
3. The only requirement for AA membership is a desire to stop drinking.
4. Each group should be autonomous except in matters affecting other groups or AA as a whole.
5. Each group has but one primary purpose—to carry its message to the alcoholic who still suffers.
6. An AA group ought never endorse, finance or lend the AA name to any related facility or outside enterprise, lest problems of money, property, and prestige divert us from our primary purpose.
7. Every AA group ought to be fully self-supporting, declining outside contributions.
8. Alcoholics Anonymous should remain forever nonprofessional, but our service centers may employ special workers.
9. AA, as such, ought never be organized; but we may create service boards or committees directly responsible to those they serve.
10. Alcoholics Anonymous has no opinion on outside issues; hence the AA name ought never be drawn into public controversy.
11. Our public relations policy is based on attraction rather than promotion; we need always maintain personal anonymity at the level of press, radio and films.
12. Anonymity is the spiritual foundation of all our traditions, ever reminding us to place principles before personalities.[9]

However effective AA is on the personal level (that is, helping a person overcome alcoholism), as a model for political organizing, it is a self-contradictory mixture of isolationism and movement building. It disavows political involvement or the linking of social issues. It encourages participants to see themselves as weak and powerless. It is without question exceedingly authoritarian in style of operation. On the other hand, AA uses many of the strategies most often associated with social-change-oriented self-help groups. Thus, we can learn much from AA about community organization. These strategies include: (1) use of a statement of guiding principles; (2) consciousness raising groups or rap sessions; (3) support networks; (4) self reliance; (5) promotion of a group identity rather than individual aggrandizement; (6) self disclosure; (7) shared ideology; (8) commitment to long term involvement; (9) local organization; and (10) dissemination of its ideas through an extensive publications program.

Mexican American Self-Help (MASH).   MASH is a group of Mexican American prisoners at the McNeil Island Penitentiary in the state of Washington. The group publishes a self-help magazine called *La Raza*. Its purpose is self-education, identification with the Chicano tradition, analysis of prejudice and discrimination toward Chicanos, political organizing, poetic expression, promotion of Chicano identity, and social exchange. Begun in 1968 MASH quickly became an unusual phenomenon in the prison context. Its contributors, Chicano prisoners, publish strong, politically charged tracts. Under the title, "La Causa, Brown Power Will Prevail," for example, Tomas A. Trejo writes:

> In this generation a new history was born that was to echo all over the world, and brought to this nation of American a self respect of strong determination that measures far beyond the expectations of all others, for the rebirth of the children of the sun surfaced and showed its pride by being called a "Chicano," for it has been over a hundred and twenty years since the invisible chains of rightful living were first put forth. . . .
>
> We will overcome all barriers that stand in front or in our way, for La Raza Nueva will reclaim its pasado in true humanistic ways, for the value of life is a priceless item, let us join together en unidad . . . and support La Causa, . . . as . . . proud Brown Chicanos.[10]

In humorous understatement, the MASH publication carries the following statement on its credits page: "The opinions expressed herein are not necessarily those of the Bureau of Prisons or of the McNeil Island Penitentiary Administration." In fact, La Palabra levels harsh criticism against the prison system, the criminal justice system, and the mass media for how it treats and portrays Chicanos.

The Boston Women's Health Book Collective.   This collective began as a group of women interested in consciousness raising. The group's focus was on the male-dominated medical profession. In the member's own words,

> In the beginning we called ourselves, "the doctor's group." We had all experienced similar feelings of frustration and anger toward specific doctors and the medical maze in general, and initially we wanted to do something about those doctors who were condescending, paternalistic, judgmental and noninformative.[11]

However, the group soon realized that its concerns went beyond the medical profession. They were concerned about themselves, what they knew and did not know about their own bodies, and what society conditioned them to feel about themselves as women. They were also concerned about changing both the condition of women and the condition of society, particularly in regards to how society thinks about and treats women. Initially, the group members began to write papers and do research. Through these activities they shared experiences and information. They talked about their anger at particular medical practices. They talked about birth control and examined their own values toward themselves. They studied breast cancer and methods of self-examination. They taught each other about menstruation, menopause, infections such as cystitis and nonspecific vaginitis, childbearing and childbirth, abortion, and self-defense. They warned each other about what to expect in particular clinics and from particular medical personnel. They learned how to be supportive to each other. Eventually they put their thoughts together in a book entitled, *Our Bodies, Ourselves,* which they published through the New England Free Press. It became an immediate, enormous seller. In fact, so many people wanted copies that it became a problem for the New England Free Press to meet the demand. The Boston Women's Health Book Collective then entered into an arrangement with the commercial publisher Simon and Schuster for publication and the book subsequently became a best seller for several years. It is a book that helped to transform women's awareness of their own bodies and the medical profession's attitudes toward women.

The names of self-help organizations reveal their incredible diversity in purpose: Disabled in Action, Gam-Anon, Synanon, Phobia Self-Help Groups, La Leche League, Gray Panthers, Friends and Relatives of Institutionalized Aged, Caesarian Support, Education and Concern (C/Sec), and the Mental Health Liberation Front. While they have many qualities in common, they also have profound differences—only some of them have a strong commitment to social change. Katz and Bender have developed a typology which goes a long way toward differentiating the major types of self-help organizations.[12] They identify four basic types: (1) Self-fulfillment or personal growth groups which have personal therapy as their primary purpose; (2) social advocacy groups such as Disabled in Action, welfare rights groups, the Redistribute America Movement, and the Carolina Brown Lung Association; (3) groups whose primary focus is the creation of alternative living patterns (for example, women's liberation, and gay liberation groups); and (4) intentional communities which provide refuge to people whom society considers deviant, including drug users, alcoholics, and ex-convicts. Obviously each of these groups has the potential to effect some measure of social change, if even incidentally. However, those groups which fall primarily into the second and third categories have the greatest potential for promoting social change. Self-actualization and self-fulfillment groups are by their nature focused on the individual and not on social structure or, even, social conditions and are consequently unlikely to have much effect on society. Similarly, the groups in the last category, the ones Katz and Bender label "outcasts" or rock bottom groups tend to accomplish the reverse of social change. That is, these groups frequently confirm socially dominant values by encouraging members to accept the social definition of themselves as "sick," "incapable," or "scum." These groups expect the individual to confess his or wrongs and to follow the group's prescription for achieving self change. As the case of Alcoholics Anonymous suggests, many of these groups specifically shun social change or political involvements outside the group's immediate issue area.

In the next section of this chapter we will narrow our examination of self-help groups to focus on the qualities of social change self-help or, to use Katz and Bender's typology, social advocacy self-help groups. The questions we will consider are, "What are the key characteristics of self-help organizing groups?" "How do these groups effect change?" and "How do these groups differ from more inwardly directed self-help groups?"

ATTRIBUTES OF SELF-HELP
ACTION GROUPS

Who We Are: Consciousness
Raising

Virtually every self-help action group uses consciousness raising or some facsimile thereof to define its ideology. Disabled in Action, women's groups, parent action groups, rape crisis groups, and the Gray Panthers all use consciousness raising. Through group sharing, the members explore their past experiences with social institutions and people outside their own group, their attitudes toward each other and themselves, their economic position, their political beliefs, their aspirations, and their values. Through group meetings, members examine their history and try to understand and explain their current position. They ask: "Are the experiences we have had unique to each of us or do we share common experiences?", "What is the source of our sense of powerlessness?", "Do we have experiences and resources within our own group to overcome societally imposed barriers to equality and self-determination?", "Who are our natural allies?", "How should we create social change?", "How can we support each other?"

A common declaration that we hear as a result of self-help consciousness raising is that the group will define its own condition and that the group will develop itself. In one way or another, self-help groups reject efforts by officials and the dominant society to define their needs or the methods for meeting those needs. Self-help groups express distrust of outside help as dependence building, unless of course that help has been asked for or demanded by the self-help organization. The words of Tony Palacios, a member of the Mexican American Self Help group show this attitude:

"GENTE"

WHO ARE WE? THEY ASK, WHAT ARE OUR PROBLEMS? WHERE DOES IT HURT? WHAT CAN WE SAY? HOW CAN WE EXPLAIN THAT THEY ARE OUR PROBLEM. THAT THEIR [sic] THE ONES THAT MAKE IT HURT. AND ON TOP OF ALL THIS THEY SAY THAT THEY WANT TO HELP, (sin vaselina) WITH BETTER EDUCATION, BETTER LIVING CONDITIONS, BETTER, BETTER, AND MORE VAGUE PROMISES . . .
NO! WE ARE THE ONES THAT WILL BETTER THINGS. WE ARE THE ONES THAT CAN HELP EACH OTHER, BECAUSE WE KNOW ABOUT US. WE ARE A PROUD PEOPLE AND CHARITY IS NOT READILY ACCEPTED. WE WILL HELP EACH OTHER BY BETTERING OURSELVES, YOURSELF! SO DO SOMETHING WITH YOURSELF, AND THE IMPROVEMENT WILL REFLECT ON US . . .

UNIDOS![13]

We will define ourselves. We will help ourselves. Those are common themes of self-help consciousness raising.

Self-help groups also use consciousness raising to examine social stereotypes toward its members, for example toward Chicanos, toward women, toward gays, toward people with disabilities, toward Blacks, and toward old people. For example, old people in America face powerful, if contradictory stereotypes. Simone de Beauvoir argues that whether through positive imagery (that is, making older people exceptional) or by degradation (for example, infantilization of old people), society sets older people apart from the mainstream:

> The puerile image of themselves that society offers the aged is that of the white-haired and venerable sage, rich in experience, planing high above the common state of mankind. The counter-part of the first image is that of the old fool in his dotage, a laughing stock for children. In any case, either by virtue or by their degradation, they stand outside humanity. The world, therefore, need feel no scruple in refusing them the minimum of support which is considered necessary for living like a human being.[14]

Consciousness raising provides the vehicle to examine these stereotypes and to develop evidence that the group need not accept the social definition of incompetence, exceptionality or differentness. Maggie Kuhn, a founder of the Gray Panthers sees consciousness raising as an avenue to organization and empowerment. She suggests that by looking back at one's life experiences, an older person can see quite plainly that life has been a process of development, not disintegration. She believes that consciousness raising offers the opportunity to realize that each of us possesses knowledge and, therefore, the ability to contribute meaningfully to improving our own condition through political action. Like deBeauvoir, she rejects the dominant social stereotypes: "We have been so completely brainwashed by society that we devalue experience and consider it no longer useful."[15] Through consciousness raising, the individual experience becomes political. Consciousnesss raising "is an important way to move toward relating our personal lives and our personal experience and competence to the public political sphere of life."[16]

Some self-help groups choose certain books and articles written by other people who identify themselves in the same manner as the self-help group members (for example, feminists, gays, disability rights activists). With the article or book as a common base of experience, the self-help groups then ask themselves, "Have we had experiences like those in the readings?" Alternatively, one or several members may describe an experience which can then be analyzed by the group. Older people may ask, for example, "Are we treated like children?", "Are Golden Age clubs 'glorified playpens'?" as Maggie Kuhn calls them. "Why do professionals not ask us what we want?" "Why are so many of these social services geared to segregating older people from the rest of society (for example, elderly housing, senior centers, nursing homes)?"

Self-help consciousness raising provides a forum in which members can explore those aspects of their condition which may be unique from other groups in society. Women will discuss aspects of sexism. Blacks will examine racism. Older people will explore ageism. Again, we turn to Maggie Kuhn who tells us that through consciousness raising old people discover that society has taught them to regard "old age as a plague—to be denied or hidden. The fact that it is so traumatic for many old people to admit their age is an indication of the way we have been conditioned to hate our true selves, to reject our own bodies and the passage of time. . . ."[17] Only by confronting the social definition and our own acceptance of it, however subconsciously, can we challenge it. Kuhn calls on old people to embrace themselves and their age, to recognize their worth and their strength, and to fight for power, authority, and influence.[18]

Consciousness raising looks easier from a distance than it really is. Groups which use consciousness raising find that, perhaps more than any other aspect of group activity, consciousness raising is intense and difficult, but enormously rewarding. Some retrospective comments of the Boston Women's Health Book Collective show this to be the case: "Coming together to do something about our lives was scary. It was admitting that we were not completely satisfied with the lives we were leading."[19] Some wondered if their new-found commitment to the women's movement and possibly, peer pressure would force them to "weaken our ties with our men, children, jobs, life styles . . . lose control over our lives."[20] While the fear turned out to be unfounded—they decided or understood later that no one could force them to change something they did not want to change—it was nevertheless a real feeling. It takes courage to share personal experiences and fears. It takes courage to expose ourselves. However, these fears must be weighed against the potential rewards. The Boston Women's Health Book Collective sought the reward of personal and political growth.

> What we do want to do is reclaim the human qualities culturally labelled "male" and integrate them with the human qualities that have been seen as "female" so that we can all be fuller human beings. . . .
> We want . . . to create a cultural environment where all qualities can come out in all people.[21]

Note the similarity of this goal to the equally humanizing mission put forth by Maggie Kuhn: ". . . if we join old people to fight the system that denies the value of old age, if we can open up new life styles . . . then we are working for the survival of society as a whole."[22]

Dissecting the Consumer Context

Self-help groups make it their business to criticize the institutions and service networks which provide services that they need. Some self-help groups create their own alternative services as a means of forcing change in the dominant social institutions. However, many self-help groups choose not to create their own services but rather attempt to force changes in those which exist. To accomplish this, self-help groups analyze their needs, the dominant service settings, and their complaints with these service settings.

Parents of handicapped children have been among the most active of constituencies to create self-help advocacy groups. They have defined their needs: individual education plans for their children, as much integration as appropriate for their disabled children alongside nondisabled children in public schools, the right to a free, appropriate public education, essential related services such as speech therapy, occupational therapy, and physical therapy, equal protection (meaning as many hours in school as the typical child, equal access to public school transportation, extracurricular activities, and so forth), due process rights so that parents can question school district decisions about child classification and child placement, access to their children's school records, parent involvement in development of the individual education plans, periodic review of children's evaluations and placements, comprehensive service options, and an end to racially and culturally biased testing procedures. Indeed, parent self-help groups have won all of those provisions through organizing at the local, regional, and national levels.

Initially, parent advocacy groups like local Associations for Retarded Citizens and ad hoc parent groups found that school districts were frequently reluctant to establish the programs parents wanted. Schools seemed to have standard strategies for putting parents off. But through newsletters, consciousness raising groups, and books, parents communicated with each other and compared notes. They discovered that what was happening in one school in Massachusetts was also happening in California and in Alabama. The refrains were all too familiar: "We're sorry, Mrs Jones, we just do not have a program for your child"; "We'd like to create a program, but we just don't have the money"; "We're here to provide educational programs not babysitting"; "If we provide a program for your child, we'll have to provide one for everyone"; "We have a thousand children to consider; we cannot spend all our time on your child"; "If we create a program for your child, we'll have to cut out a program for someone else"; "We just don't have the trained staff to deal with your child." Such comments angered parents, but anger was not enough to create change. Parents realized that they needed skills to respond. Self-help organizations provided the forums where they could develop those skills.

First, parents realize that they need to know more precisely what their children need. This, in turn, means that parents have to give each other an education in special education terminology. They have to learn how to assess their children's current skill level. They have to become informed about various exemplary service approaches available nationally so that they can lobby for them locally. Parents of deaf children have to know whether to ask for total communication or an oral approach. Parents of visually impaired children learn to ask for large type textbooks, for tape recorders in the classroom, and for magnifying devices. They have to know about the kinds of teaching aids that might help their children before it is too late. It helps to know the basic components of an adequate program for children with particular disabilities. In order to do this, parents hold self-help training conferences and create classes for each other in which they take turns sharing information. They invite professional consultants to answer their questions.

Parents who belong to self-help groups can enter the school system prepared. They can describe in specific terms what their children need, whether it be a prevocational program or mobility training. Of course, the knowledge that parents of handicapped children need is different from the knowledge that other self-help groups need, but all require some specific information in order to negotiate effectively with a system they perceive as having failed them. The Women's Health Book Collective, for example, developed a checklist showing what women need in a doctor. Thus women can evaluate whether a doctor can meet their particular needs. Antinuclear power groups learn enough about the industry's problems to advocate effectively. Mental patients learn about psychotropic drugs and their potential danger. Each group becomes expert on issues that affect it.

Second, parents of handicapped children, like other self-help groups, have learned to examine their sense of self in relation to the specific institutions with which they most often conflict. Recall that Barbara Cutler describes this sense of self as that of a school child.[23] Betty Pieper characterizes it as a fumbling neophyte caught off guard. She describes her reactions to school officials (who seemed unable to face up to the fact that her son needed and had a right to a full and quality educational program) as one of constantly being caught short, and of not having the right come-back phrase ready. However, she decided to persevere: "No matter how uncomfortable or embarrassed I felt at any one given moment, I was learning to stick it out . . . so that I would best know how to counter the situation when it arose again."[24] Many self-help groups use role playing and other assertiveness training techniques to counter feelings of powerlessness and vulnerability that so often accompany the consumer's interaction with professional service systems.

Even rather benevolent professionals or benevolent human service organizations can make consumers feel isolated and intimidated. This feeling of powerlessness may come from the consumer's personal insecurity, but more likely it reflects the power of the context. Unless a consumer has previously experienced a setting, it is unfamiliar territory. Consumers may not know a setting's special language or rules, the key questions to ask, or who wields the most authority. Thus they may not know quite how to establish themselves on a more powerful footing. An individual professional may be kind to a consumer and may put a consumer at ease, but even this does not render the consumer the professional's peer when it comes to exercising power. As we noted in the fourth chapter, the very nature of professionalism disenfranchises consumers from certain information, and often from the shaping of decisions. On the other hand, self-help movements have put pressure on professionals to reform. They call on professionals to make key information easily understandable, to ensure that consumers make the major decisions, and to be accountable to consumers for their actions. In questioning professionalism, self-help consumers empower themselves. That was essentially what Betty Pieper did when she decided to persevere, to "stick it out," to "counter the situation when it arose again."

Third, parents of handicapped children, like others who have sought to change human service and other social institutions, ask, "On what legal or moral basis can we demand change?" Parents of handicapped children respond, "Our children are, first of all children, just like any other children." Since they *can* learn and develop, albeit sometimes at a different rate, through different means, or ultimately to a different level than nondisabled students, they have a moral claim to educational services. On legal grounds, too, they must have education. Children with disabilities enjoy the same constitutional rights to equal protection and due process that other children enjoy. Furthermore, children with disabilities are entitled under various state and federal laws to additional services and provisions. Thus parents come together in self-help groups to educate themselves about their children's legal and moral rights, to learn how to read laws and regulations, to learn how to distinguish between legal and nonlegal issues. They secure copies of laws and regulations and carry them into school board meetings and conferences with school principals, as if to say, "We know our rights."

Fourth, parents share and train each other in advocacy skills. Parents who have jobs in the news media, tell other parents how to hold a press conference. Labor negotiators who have children with disabilities tell other parents their strategies of effective negotiations. Those who like to give speeches share their skills at speech-giving with other interested parents. Parents continually help each other to develop greater skills with which to challenge the system's standard operating procedures. It is not uncommon to find that most self-help groups have a skills building curriculum that has been self-developed or adopted from a similar group.

Consumer Control

A dominant theme in self-help groups is consumer power and consumer control. Some self-help groups operate their own services and for these there is no question of consumer control. By definition they operate services that are consumer initiated and therefore consumer controlled. Other self-help groups seek to change the manner in which professional services are dispensed. They seek consumer involvement and, often, consumer dominance. Hence, Maggie Kuhn of the Gray Panthers asks why old people do not get to decide what services they need and what services they will receive. Parents of children with disabilities want and have won the right to veto child placements with which they disagree, at least until they have had the opportunity of a lengthy due process appeal. Consumer groups want consumer dominance on boards of directors not only of health care facilities, but of corporations and a whole range of government and private agencies.

For some groups, but certainly not all, consumer control means economic self-reliance. It means avoiding federal and foundation funding that has strings attached. In the words of Mimi Silber, a member of the board of directors of Delancey Street, an organization run by community people, ex-drug addicts, and ex-prisoners, self-reliance ensures independence and self-respect. "We can't take foundation money," she explains, "because it's critical to Delancey's program of self-reliance that our people know they're really needed, that the money they bring in from the moving company and the terrarium business is crucial to keep us going."[25] According to Silber, the acceptance of foundation support is tantamount to turning self-help into dependency. Not all self-help groups take this hard line toward outside contributions, but they all value self-reliance at one level or another. They all seek some measure of consumer control whether it be total control in a self-help operated alternative, majority control on boards of directors, consumer veto power over treatment approaches, or some combination of these.

Judi Chamberlain, a member of the Mental Patients Liberation Front, a self-help group for ex-mental patients, believes that consumers must reject many systems-initiated consumer involvement activities as nothing more than co-optation. Tokenism, which is the involvement of a single or even several consumers in decision making meetings, does little to change the nature of decision making or the decisions themselves. When isolated consumers join professionally top-heavy boards, they feel intimidated and outnumbered. Instead of feeling empowered, token consumer board members feel inadequate, bitter, and disillusioned. Thus Chamberlain argues that the only true alternative "is one in which all basic decision-making power is in the hands of those the facility exists to serve." Patient ward meetings where patients can air complaints and suggestions do not constitute alternatives. They are, rather, avenues for communication at best and window-dressing for continued professional dominance at worst.

Wherever you go in the world of self-help, you find concern for consumer control. Operation Bootstrap in California began with the ethic of self-determination: "We can do it ourselves." James Farmer had predicted that if all the Black workers in America had great job skills, white America would still find ways of keeping Blacks from equality in the workplace and in the Board rooms. Hence the need for self-help economic development. Lou Smith, one of the founders of Operation Bootstrap, a Black inner-city organization founded in the wake of the Watts riots in Los Angeles was visited by three of the top leaders in the Mattel toy manufacturing company.[26] Rather than saying, "We want to build a Mattel factory here in Watts to help give employment to Black workers and we want you to help us," the Mattel officials said they would give Operation Bootstrap money for a project of Bootstrap design. Operation Bootstrap could pick its own idea, consistent with the fact that Mattel was a toy manufacturer, and develop it. Mattel would provide the capital for the project in the form of a grant (Operation Bootstrap did not resist the gift) and Operation Bootstrap would own the factory. It would also pick the workers and train them for the job. A decision was made to manufacture a Black doll, the Nancy Doll. In this way, Operation Bootstrap developed from self-help job training to self-help business. Through self-help group control came the understanding that if something went wrong in the business, that is if the overhead was too high, if production fell off, if sales failed to reach hoped-for levels, the leaders of Operation Bootstrap had to examine themselves and their own strategies for flaws.

Personal Change

A lesson of Operation Bootstrap is that people can change themselves and, in the process, their place. Lou Smith found that in the initial years of Operation Bootstrap's doll business, management had a tendency to hire people who "looked like" management people and to hire assembly line workers who "looked like" workers. This bias created a division of labor that nearly jeopardized the self-help ethic inherent in the Bootstrap model. In an attempt to remedy the situation, the company began to experiment with moving people from "the floor" to the offices and from the office to the floor. Thus all the participants experienced the freedom to try something new, to learn about the other side of the business, to be informed about how decisions in one part of the business affected life in another area. People became more productive and there arose a more tightly knit sense of community. Lou Smith summarized the experience this way:

> I found out that when you allow people to grow, you grow. Versus trying to drive people to grow. You're only going to drive me as far up that tree as you made it uncomfortable for me underneath, and if you ain't careful I'm liable to get mad and drop right off the tree and kick your ass.[27]

In other words, self-help means sharing a sense of responsibility for what happens and working to see that things happen as you want them to. It therefore means growing personally.

Political change groups, no less than personal change groups such as the therapy-oriented Alcoholics Anonymous, Weight Watchers, and Debtors Anonymous, value and promote personal change. A key step to personal change is reckoning with personal behavior. Members of child abuser support groups learn to say, "I abuse my children; I don't like myself for it; I want to change." At Alcoholics Anonymous, people learn to say, "We admit that we are powerless over alcohol—that our lives are unmanageable." At Narcotics Anonymous they say, "Very simply, an addict is a man or woman whose life is controlled by drugs. We are people in the grip of a continuing and progressive illness whose ends are always the same: jails, institutions and death."[28] The single requirement for membership in NA is a commitment to change, a desire to arrest the craving for drugs, to want recovery. In politically charged groups, those that seek to change society's definition and treatment of them, there are similar statements: "I am the parent of a child with a disability and I demand for my child what every child needs, basic rights"; "I am disabled and my biggest handicap is society's attitudes toward me!"; "I am old and a full member of society"; "I am Black and beautiful"; "I am a woman; sisterhood is powerful." The principal similarity between political change and personal change self-help groups is their affirmation of a group identity. Differences exist in the approach to that identity. Many of the personal change groups seek to *admit* their identification in order to change it, in other words, to face it and defeat it. Social change groups say, on the other hand, we embrace our definition of ourselves and call on society to recognize and value us, as old people, as women, as minorities, as people with disabilities. Thus the personal change of the political self-help group members is in the direction of positively identifying with the group and in articulating a set of values which he or she may not have previously held or had the strength or skills to espouse.

The personal change element makes self-help tailor-made to be an organizing model. People join the group, express their commitment to a common ideological perspective, provide support to other group members, form networks for support even after their intense involvement may have passed, and in the case of political change groups, use the group as a base from which to influence public policy and practice in major social institutions. Parents influence schools, women influence health care practices, and disabled people demand accessibility. The group provides a forum where members can share ideas and test out new directions. Here, they can analyze and develop strategies. Perhaps most important, self-help groups place a premium on participation. Thus members learn to try new roles and to express their values. They also learn to role-play difficult encounters, run meetings, give speeches, set up press conferences, do research, and learn to raise money, either through solicitations or through self-help group initiated businesses. In other words, self-help groups act as training grounds where new members can not only adopt new ideological perspectives, but also where they can develop organizing skills. Both these types of personal change make it possible for self-help groups to influence the shape of society.

Challenging the Professions

Self-help groups pose their greatest challenge to professionalism and to professional human services such as education, health care, day care, disability oriented rehabilitation services, welfare programs, older persons programs, and correctional programs. Various analysts of self-help have tried to catalogue the contrasting styles of self-help and professional practice.[29] The principal differences between self-help's approach to service and the traditional professional model are portrayed in Figure 1.

Two of the most profound challenges self-help poses for professional practice are its demand for information sharing and a breaking-down of status and power differences between the served and their servers. Taking the issue of information first, self-help groups generally educate themselves, as noted above, in basic aspects of the issue with which they are concerned. This is true whether the issue is health care, education rights, or approaches to habilitation. Thus it comes as no surprise that women have been teaching other women how to examine themselves, that parents of handicapped children have been teaching each other how to spot learning difficulties and how to ameliorate them, that people with disabilities have been teaching each other about health insurance and architectural barrier-free design, and that older persons have been learning the truth about the aging process. Social change oriented self-help groups believe consumers deserve all the facts. The best way to participate in human services as a consumer is by being fully informed. Note, for example, the advice given by the Women's Health Book Collective to women concerning what they should expect in the way of information from their doctor:

WHAT TO EXPECT FROM YOUR DOCTOR

1. An accurate diagnosis of your condition, healthy or otherwise, at your request.
2. Results and meaning of any tests or examinations performed by him or by others at his direction, as soon as they are available.
3. Indications for treatment, varieties and alternatives, pros and cons of particular treatments in the opinion of other experts, as well as the doctor's own preference and the reasons for it.
4. Answers to your questions about any examination or procedure he may perform,

FIGURE 1*

PROFESSIONAL MODEL	SELF-HELP MODEL
1. Professionals develop a body of knowledge which they control; they decide when and how to communicate parts of this knowledge to consumers.	1. Self-help members seek to popularize professional information; they encourage questioning of the body of knowledge; they may develop alternative information which includes and values personal experiences.
2. Professionals encourage a distinct separation between the professional group and clients. This may be accomplished by adoption of professional uniforms and titles, by causing clients to wait for services, by licensing exams, by prohibiting clients from joining professional associations and similar strategies.	2. Self-help groups attempt to dispense with the trappings of professional authority and to build a sense of community.
3. Professionals regard consumers as their clients.	3. Self-help groups regard the providers and consumers of services as being of equal status. Self-help groups believe that the term consumer (rather than client) more accurately reflects the role of the person seeking services because it implies a clear requirement for accountability on the part of the professional.
4. Professional services are controlled by professionally dominated boards and other forms of leadership.	4. Self-help groups are controlled by the membership; further, self-help groups support consumer controlled services of all kinds, whether self-help or otherwise.
5. Professionals tend to adopt an ideological perspective that combines a reverence for professionally dominated science and for the rightfulness of selling human services.	5. Self-help groups develop shared ideologies which question professionally dominated science, which generally espouse equality, and which value the provision of human services at no or modest cost.
6. Professionals prefer monitoring of the profession internally, by peer review.	6. Self-help groups demand accountability of service provider to the persons served.
7. Professional services generally view the client as the passive recipient of services.	7. Self-help groups encourage the consumer to be intensely involved as a participant in the service.
8. Professionals enjoy higher status than most of their clients.	8. Self-help groups encourage members to see themselves as being of equal status with each other and with professionals in traditional settings.
9. Professionals provide the definition of the clients' problem as well as its solution.	9. Self-help members participate in defining the problem and its solution.
10. Organized hierarchically. Encourages authoritarian decision making.	10. Organized horizontally. Encourages decision making by democratic consensus.
11. Supports the status quo.	11. Supports social change.

12. Pathology oriented.	12. Holistic orientation; sees personal difficulties rooted in both personal development and social context.
13. Seeks individualistic solutions.	13. Encourages individual or personal change as well as systemic change.
14. Adheres to structured routines for providing services and carries them out in a dispassionate fashion.	14. Tends to shun routinization and other forms of bureaucratization and alienation. Favors individualization, spontaneity, and passion.
15. Encourages consumer dependency.	15. Promotes self reliance.

*Note: This figure presents a typology of professional and self-help practice and belief. Obviously, no single self-help organization or professional setting will possess or practice all of these qualities in this form. Rather, these statements reveal some of the basic assumptions and practices which tend to characterize and differentiate the professional and self-help approaches.

in advance of or at any time during the performance of it. Stopping any examination or procedure at any moment, at your request.

5. Complete information about purpose, content and known effects of all drugs prescribed or administered, including possible risks, side-effects and contra-indications, especially of any combination of drugs.

6. Willingness to accept and wait for a second medical opinion before performing any elective surgery which involves alteration or removal of any organ or body part.

7. Answers to your questions about your body or your general physical health and functioning, in addition to any particular condition. Or, encouragement to seek these answers from another source.[30]

According to this prescription, consumers have a right to information about their condition as well as treatment options—the assumption being that what the doctor may consider reasonable or preferred, the patient (consumer) may not. Though it may threaten the doctor who has been used to enjoying a certain authority, the Women's Health Book Collective encourages women to question the doctor's information, to seek a second and third opinion. In other words, the self-help group encourages women to regard doctors as hired consultants whose duty it is to serve the consumer on the consumer's terms.

Community-building also strikes at the heart of professional practice, which frequently promotes alienation of provider and consumer. Since self-help groups encourage members to learn information about services and, in many instances, how to serve, lines between server and served become literally indistinguishable. Self-help groups generally dispense with the trappings of authority (for example, professional titles, white coats and other uniforms, crowded waiting rooms, and secluded professional offices) as well as authority itself. The idea is to question authority, not revere it. When the consumer becomes provider and the provider the consumer, both groups become one and both become aware of and committed to finding solutions to problems together. This approach replaces the hierarchical pattern of organization found in most professional settings with a horizontal, consensus-building, sharing model. In this system, participants are more likely to be respected for their ideas than their position. The goal for those providing service is service, not profit. And the outcome of the service setting does not rest with providers, but with all of the participants in the setting.

In some instances, the challenge to professionalism goes as far as questioning professional knowledge itself. Note, for example, Judi Chamberlain's plan for people with problems of living (people labeled as having mental or psychiatric difficulties):

> Real change is impossible in a system that continues to transform people into mental patients, whether the system is "community based" or not. Only by providing alternatives in which people help one another will we break the cycle in which we strip troubled people of their humanity and then turn from them in fear. Only by reaching out to one another, by replacing professional "expertise" with human concern and psychiatric labelling with the recognition of our shared humanity, will we create the opportunity for all of us to change and develop.[31]

Is the answer to psychiatric abuse (dehumanization of patients through labelling, drugging, stigmatization, and incarceration) to be found in patient-controlled, community support efforts? Chamberlain says yes. She calls for dealing with people's emotional problems in the communities where they live without control and name-calling (that is, labelling, calling people "sick"). She does not envision an absence of services, but sees alternative services arising such as crisis centers, drop-in centers, rape centers, group homes, and other supportive living programs.

Chamberlain's message is not that self-help groups do not reject all professional information. Rather, self-help groups challenge the notion that professionals own certain bodies of information. Second, self-help groups build community by forming groups and coalitions to seek out professionally held information, by liberating that information, or, in the case of particularly complex information, by securing explanations of it. Third, self-help groups ask whether, and to what extent, professional practices reflect objective findings and humanizing values and to what extent they merely reflect certain distributions of power interests. Using the issue of human services delivery, the question arises as to why so many of them are offered in segregated settings, in senior centers, in rehabilitation centers, in special disabled-only schools, and in large, isolated psychiatric hospitals and centers. Why do professionals so often segregate their clients from the rest of society? Do they have a justification? Are segregated services more humane? Are they more conducive to recovery? Do people like the segregation or is it merely a convenience for specialists? Is it just one more means to stigmatize the particular population being served? Does segregation confrim the differentness, isolation, alienation, and feeling of powerlessness of consumers? The Mental Patients Liberation Front, parent advocacy groups representing children with disabilities, the Gray Panthers, and many other groups have raised these questions over and over again. They demand that professionals acknowledge their historic as well as current role in segregating and rendering more powerless the people they "serve." The call for community-building is basically a call to fight against professionally enforced separation, isolation, and powerlessness.

As a final note on the aprofessional nature of self-help, we should examine what this practice means for the professional who wants to support self-help movements. Indeed, many professionals support the principles underlying self-help such as dissolution of status differences, popularization of knowledge, accountability to consumers, intense consumer involvement, and consumer control of services. Is there a progressive role for professionals in self-help groups? Yes and no. On the one hand, professionals can probably have their most important impact in professional circles rather than in self-help settings. That is, professionals can help consumers gain access to professional information and can lobby within professional circles for accountability to consumers. They can change their own style of service in order to minimize status differences between providers and consumers. Professionals can support social change proposals of self-help groups.

Within self-help groups, professionals may have a more difficult time. However, the evidence of current practice suggests that professionals *can* have a role in self-help if they are willing to accept the conditions set by self-help groups for professional involvement. Professionals must look to self-help members for definition of their role because the latter will undoubtedly regard the former with a certain wariness. Self-help members will define the professional as a consultant not a leader, not a decision maker, and certainly not *the* decision maker. Self-help groups expect professionals to learn how to listen. They expect professionals to be willing to learn the self-help organization's perspectives, values, and knowledge. Moreover, professionals must be prepared to have much of their world constantly attacked and maligned because self-help groups have substantial and deep criticisms for traditional professional practice. Above all, professionals cannot expect self-help groups to regard them with any special awe, to feel extraordinarily grateful for their involvement, or to assume a dependence on them. Self-help groups, after all, believe in and practice self-reliance. They will welcome allies, but at the same time shun charity. They will also accept advice if they have sought it, but will certainly reject paternalism.

THE LIMITS OF SELF-HELP

Self-help has its limits. It may be popular—witness the burgeoning numbers of people who count themselves as self-helpers—and it may be effective—why else would professionals be getting on the self-help bandwagon? But it has limitations. In this section of the chapter we will examine the most glaring problems which beset particular self-help groups and those which characterize self-help groups in general. Further, we will examine whether or not there may be ways for self-help groups to overcome their apparent limitations.

Personal and Political Change:
A Difficult Balancing Act

The diversity of self-help group missions makes it hard to define self-help as a unified movement. On the one hand, groups like Alcoholics Anonymous deal exclusively with the realm of individual change. These groups say to the individual, "Admit your problem, admit your failings, open yourself to change, use the self-help group network to resist recidivism." On the other hand, we find welfare rights groups and other political change self-help movements demanding change in social systems. While these groups espouse a philosophy of personal change (becoming personally politicized) it is subsidiary to the central mission of political change. This is shown, for example, in the stated goals of a welfare rights activist in Milwaukee:

> Now hear me good. Poor people have a right to welfare. Poor people have a right to life, not just to look forward to death and life after death, or to look forward to somebody coming down out of the sky and giving you a beautiful life later. We have a right to live decently as dignified human beings today.
> When I see money being wasted—sending men to the moon to play golf, dumping nerve gas in the ocean, burning potatoes, killing off hogs, mutilating them, just getting rid of them—and then I see hungry and raggedy children running around, this is the kind of country that we live in, and this is what just burns me up. I feel the only way changes will be made, especially in the welfare system, is through poor people, welfare people, organizing and raising a lot of hell . . . which is all we can do.[32]

What is the correct approach, personal change or political action? Are both possible simultaneously?

Self-help groups, like community organizers, can probably never answer this question satisfactorily. In part, the question is difficult because the answer keeps changing. Some situations demand personal change. Dependence on drugs and alcohol are such situations. Other situations such as the systematic denial of education to children with disabilities, require systemic changes in ideology, policy, and practice. To be sure, both types of situations call for some of both types of change. The problem of alcoholism, for example, is probably attributable to certain *social conditions* such as Madison Avenue's selling of alcoholic beverages and the common equation of drinking with socializing or the socially promoted belief that people need drinks to escape the pressures of their problems. Similarly, parents who want educational rights for their children need to develop a *personal belief* in the equal rights of their children. Further, they must prepare themselves to challenge one of the most hallowed institutions in society, the public school system. As we noted earlier, this involves transforming their attitudes about their own roles as consumers and their relationship to schools.

Clearly, any self-help group that emphasizes personal change at the expense of political change, or vice versa, limits its potential to effect social change. A political change oriented group that fails to build self-reliance through personal change will ultimately fail to sustain itself over the long run and will fail to win credibility in the larger society. The key is to strike a balance, depending of course on the particular conditions at hand, between personal and political change. Charles Hampden-Turner discusses this dilemma, and the San Francisco based self-help group Delancey Street's way of resolving it, in his book *Sane Asylum*. The dilemma is how to distinguish between

> . . . individual responsibility versus social causation. The dilemma has always been that telling the truths about how the social system creates social problems can exacerbate the problems themselves by excusing criminal behavior and by dignifying every ugly tempered lay-about with a political definition. "Some nut pisses on a bus—and says he's doing it in protest against Western society's repression of his private parts." (quotation from John Maher, one of the moving forces behind the success of the Delancey Street Foundation). . . .
>
> John argues that convicts and addicts *are* indeed the products of social pressures. . . .
>
> [Yet] while it may be "scientifically" true that criminals are principally to blame for their own condition, it is nevertheless necessary for them to accept responsibility for their condition if the chain of causation is to be broken. They must say to themselves, "I failed to survive with dignity. I colluded in my own oppression. From now on we will be stronger than the forces that victimize us."[33]

We can always blame "the system"—that is easy. But if all we do is point an accusing finger at "the system" and large social forces for causing our individual condition, then part of what we accomplish is virtual vindication of personal responsibility. It is not that blaming the system is wrong. Rather, it is simply inadequate. But neither can we merely take personal responsibility, however important that may be. Personal reform will not in itself remove the social conditions which oppress people. For that we need political change. Delancey Street's Maher suggests a middle ground, one that combines personal reform with political militancy: take stock of yourself first, become personally stronger, in order to join the struggle for social change.

Service Versus Advocacy

Advocacy is "an independent movement of consumers and their allies to monitor and change human service agencies."[34] The question is whether people can provide services and serve as advocates at the same time. Self-help groups face essentially two types of problems vis-a-vis service and advocacy. Groups whose primary focus is social advocacy may find that they have created a conflict of interest if they become model service providers, that is, how do you advocate for change within your own service setting? The second type of problem, which does not involve a conflict of interest, arises in those self-help groups which seek to effect social change by demonstrating markedly innovative alternative service models. These groups hope to foment change by example. Their problem arises when the alternatives they advocate begin to take on some of the very characteristics of traditional service settings (bureaucratic procedures, alienation, status differential between members, entrenched practices, and resistance to change) which the alternatives were created to overcome.

Conflicts of interest have always created problems for advocates. Could Ralph Nader have been so outspoken and effective an advocate for the redesign of American automobiles if he had been an employee of General Motors? Probably not. At least, he would have had to weigh the very real possibility that speaking out might have cost him his job. Similarly, would it be right to ask the staff of an alternative, self-help operated day care center to advocate for certain program changes needed by particular children in the setting? Would a consumer-run job training program welcome advocacy by its own staff for major changes in how the organization is structured? Quality services should always build in strategies for ensuring self-criticism. However, such practices are elements of good service, not advocacy. It would seem that there is a real benefit, namely independence, which comes when advocacy is not involved in service provision. Independence makes criticism easier.

The second type of conflict between advocacy and service occurs in those self-help groups whose alternative services become "established." Many self-help groups, notably rape crisis centers, consumer operated mental health drop in centers, and drug addiction programs, have a short life, often no more than five years. For such groups, entrenchment and bureaucratization do not have time to set in. However some alternative services do become established. This happens because they present a real alternative to professionally operated services and are then viewed as less threatening and less controlling. They may then gain a reputation for being effective and find that their consumer roles expand beyond the modest means of the initial service group. One response to this growth is to give in to bureaucratization and routinization. With a surfeit of consumers, some alternative services lose their personal, intense style. The group then begins to feel worse about turning people away than about the lower quality of service being provided.

Some alternative organizations never experience the problem of a consumer glut, but do experience other difficulties. Some simply lose their initial rush of enthusiasm and become less spontaneous and less creative. Some find that time creates unique problems. Members who helped found the group can come to constitute an old guard, "the authorities." Typically, the "old timers" take on more and more administrative and "leadership" duties while the newer participants keep in touch with the actual provision of service. This kind of division of labor can create misunderstandings, a distrust between administrators ("they don't do it the way we used to") and practitioners ("they've forgotten what it's really like"). Other groups become established, grow to a certain size and then become consumed by the difficulties of organizational survival—"where can we find financial support next?" All of these factors can create an atmosphere in which creativity, innovation, and enthusiasm give way to organization maintenance, routinization, and entrenchment.

What are the solutions? Is self-help doomed to conflict with advocacy? Can self-help never sustain a spirit of growth, creativity, and change over the long run? In response to the first question, the experiences of the Center for Independent Living, the Delancey Street Foundation, and other groups suggest certain principles which seem to make it possible for self-help groups to operate services and be involved in advocacy simultaneously:

COMBINING ADVOCACY AND SERVICE

1. To the extent that the group operates self-help as a kind of consciousness raising counterpart to rehabilitation, its purpose should never be lost or left unstated, namely to help members become personally strong in order that they may advocate for social change.
2. Groups which provide direct services such as health care or school programs should establish such consumer operated services as separate entities, carried out by separate members, from advocacy projects of the self help group.
3. Advocacy groups should establish model alternative services only for the purpose of demonstrating their viability; typically, advocacy groups will establish and operate such a service for two years and then "turn it over" or "spin it off" to another service provider group.
4. Advocacy groups which also operate some direct services may encourage advocacy within its services by external advocacy groups.
5. Some advocacy groups avoid operating services, but do operate income generating businesses, the proceeds of which help support the membership and its advocacy work (for example, The Delancey Street Foundation).

Guarding against bureaucratization, routinization, and waning activism in self-help operated alternative services may prove more difficult than separating advocacy from direct service. As in the case of social advocacy oriented groups, the experience of self-help groups themselves suggest certain precautions:

KEEPING INNOVATION IN THE ALTERNATIVE

1. Ensure a regular rotation of roles, with opportunities for "old timers" and newcomers to share in every aspect of the service setting (as in the case of Operation Bootstrap).
2. Develop new projects, new themes, and other new directions on a regular basis (perhaps annually).
3. Establish a series of forums in which members have opportunities to express their ideas, especially their criticism. Many groups use encounter sessions, "games," rap sessions, and staff meetings for this purpose.
4. Develop economic self-reliance so that the group does not become consumed by systems maintenance (grant writing).
5. Reward innovation by writing about it, talking about it, giving it public attention, and integrating it into the service.
6. Serve new groups of people.
7. Encourage the creation of loosely federated alternative self-help groups rather than allow the original self-help group to become too large. Smaller size (less than 100, but usually not less than 25) helps ensure democratic decision making.
8. Seek external evaluation by another alternative, politically similar group.

Going Beyond Single Issue Self-Help

There is a famous story in China about an old, crippled man. The Committee of Concerned Asian Scholars heard the story during its visit to the People's Republic of China and other groups of visiting Americans subsequently heard the same story. The story goes like this: An elderly crippled man living in the country did little work during the course of his life. Work in rural China means walking up lots of steps, carrying heavy loads, stooping over in the fields, and laboring hard. For the great majority of people it means manual labor. When the cultural revolution came and people began assessing the nature of work and the importance of having everyone in China involved in national development work, the old man rethought his own situation. Should he work? Certainly he wanted to work. He decided to try. He gathered various scraps of wood and metal and made them into turnip graters. These were particularly useful items in his section of China, for there turnips were a common crop and a regular part of each person's diet. He made several thousand turnip graters. The lesson, for the Chinese who tell this story, is relatively simple: people feel better about themselves and are viewed in a better light when they participate. "Before, everyone had pitied him and called him useless, but now they say, 'A useless person took useless material and turned it into wealth. Now he feels so much better.' "[35] For those of us concerned with self-help as an organizing strategy, the story communicates another message as well. By making turnip graters this man, old and crippled, joined a community-wide self-help movement, a movement to develop a commune and a country. He did not join the Chinese equivalent of the Gray Panthers or Disabled in Action. Indeed, China did not have such organizations for him to join. Instead, he joined a mainstream self-help movement.

Self-help in China and in Europe generally follows the pattern exemplified by this man who made turnip graters. People do not create specialty groups, single issue self-help groups, or groups characterized by their membership's label (for example, old, female, disabled, poor). Because human services are not organized along separatist lines, and because people share an ideological commitment to seeking universal rather than exceptional solutions to social problems, self-help groups in many European countries and in China tend to organize across broad constituencies.

America's single issue approach to self-help has some obvious problems. First, single issue self-help groups tend to define social issues in a parochial fashion. Thus a group of older people may seek to challenge social stereotypes, discrimination in housing, forced segregation, dehumanizing institutionalization, inflation, and inadequate medical treatment without ever recognizing or acknowledging that its issues are precisely the same ones which confront poor people as well as people with disabilities. Similarly, any self-help group which deals with issues of racism and fails to make a connection between racism, sexism, ageism, and handicapism fails to see the logical relationship of "its" condition to the oppression of others. Narrow, single-issue analysis tends to see one group's problems in isolation from others. In addition, single-issue analysis usually misses the underlying social and economic causes of those problems. Second, single-issue groups often fail to make alliances or coalitions with groups whose interests they share. Often they lack a political structure or political network through which to join forces. As long as self-help organizations develop their ideological positions apart from one another, they will continue to put themselves in the position of not sharing a common perspective from which to address broad economic and political injustice. Third, when self-help groups focus on single issues they may even compete with each other for external funding, community acceptance, media attention, and political dominance. Fourth, and finally, even if self-help groups effect changes in particular human service areas (or, more likely, in particular human service settings or over particular public policies and practices), as long as they work on single issues they are unlikely to effect broad social change.

Despite what we have just said, self-help groups have not been totally oblivious to the need for political coalitions and ideological communion. When the American Coalition of Citizens with Disabilities, comprised of members who belong to local chapters of Disabled in Action, the Center for Independent Living, and other disability rights advocacy groups, sponsored sit-ins at regional offices of the Health, Education, and Welfare Department, they sought and received support from an extraordinary range of nondisability related self-help groups, including the Black Panthers. Similarly, Delancey Street, a self-help movement comprised of ex-convicts and ex-drug addicts that follows the usual self-help model—depend on self-reliance not welfare and government grants; work hard; create support groups and rap sessions, and reject any use of drugs and criminality—embraces alliances with other political change self-help movements. Delancey Street has a long history of coalition building with such diverse groups as construction unions, women's groups, the Prisoner's Union, the United Farm Workers, the Urban League, the gay liberation movement, antiwar groups, as well as with non-self-help political groups such as the Black Caucus, and supportive individual politicians.[36] These alliances have helped Delancey Street develop one of the more politically sophisticated ideological foundations of self-help groups. It has also yielded practical political benefits. When the San Francisco political establishment tried to force Delancey Street out of one San Francisco's wealthiest neighborhoods, Pacific Heights, Delancey Street had the broadest possible alliances, including community groups, a few politicians, and high priced attorneys who volunteered their services. Delancey Street eventually had to move from the former United Arab Republic consulate building which it had rented, but it still remained in the neighborhood. Delancey Street strategists and allies purchased another large Pacific Heights residence, this one formerly owned by the Soviet Union.

The question of course is not whether a single or even a few self-help groups can aid other self-help groups or build coalitions, but whether self-help as a model of organizing can overcome the powerful tendency to focus on single issues which tends to perpetuate a splintering of groups that potentially have shared political interests. This problem is partly ideological. Can self-help groups find ideological unity? It is also partly organizational. Can self-help groups develop political networks through which to act together?

If self-help groups can respond affirmatively to these two questions, they may have more than transitory, single issue effects. In short, two things must happen. First, self-help groups must increase their aggressiveness in forming a national political action network. Obviously those self-help groups which view their issues as having systemic political and economic causes will join. Those groups that regard social advocacy as a legitimate and important strategy will join as well. Second, politically active self-help groups must commit themselves to developing a shared ideological outlook. Sidel and Sidel have suggested that in the absence of a common ideological base, self-help groups will merely help people cope and will probably continue to be exceedingly short lived: "the pattern of rise and fall of small groups is evidence that without some common purpose to keep them going, the groups cannot be sustained by isolated special interests and special purposes."[37] Such a shared set of goals, or common political ideology, would undoubtedly incorporate certain beliefs which can already be observed in existing social advocacy self help groups. These include a commitment to diminishing professionalism and professional power, a belief in democratic decision making within service settings, neighborhood organizations, and government planning and policy circles. Other beliefs held in common are support for consumer control of services, development of self, and a commitment to redistribution of wealth and resources (including services) in order to achieve not only equality of opportunity but also equality.

Perhaps the point on which ideological unity may flounder will be the last one mentioned, that of commitment to greater economic equality. While it is clear that economics is at the root of many of the problems that self-help groups address, most of these groups have had an easier time reforming professional practices and styles of human relationships than they have had in confronting major economic institutions of the society. If self-help groups are to develop a meaningful national movement, a commitment to work toward a shared political plank or platform on economic issues must be included. It is in this domain that self-help groups have deep, common interests and can therefore have a potentially enormous impact.

Co-optation

Much has been made of the self-help movement's influence on professional practice, and rightfully so. Self-help groups have forced greater accountability where it might least have been expected—in the medical profession, for instance. Self-help groups have proven that in many areas of human services, consumers can serve themselves as well or better than professionals can. Moreover, self-help groups have succeeded in exposing the fact that much of what passes for professional expertise and professional knowledge is, in fact, nothing more than professional ideology. For example, gay groups have challenged the psychiatric profession's definition of homosexuality as a sickness, as a form of mental illness. Recall that the American Psychiatric Association actually removed homosexuality from its list of mental disorders. However even as self-help has grown more legitimate and influential, so too has it become a frequent target of co-optation.

As noted earlier, some self-help groups have become dependent on government and foundation funding. In the rush to meet their own expectations for change and consumers' needs for alternatives to traditional settings, many self-help groups turned to external grant funds. The problem with grant money is that it is "soft."—

it comes and goes. Groups find that as grant money dries up, the scramble to secure alternative funding sources consumes more and more of the group's creative energies. In this situation, groups sometimes even change their mission and principal activities in order to keep the funding flowing and the organization afloat.

Other self-help groups have encountered an opposite problem which is, in a sense, too much funding. We have already discussed the problems that self-help groups encounter when they become too large: bureaucracy sets in along with routinization, hierarchical organization, a dwindling of internal democracy, and alienation of members to the group. Another related problem arises when government agencies and foundations adopt and fund a self-help model. Such has been the case for rape crisis centers, child advocacy services, and with independent living programs. In each instance, the original self-help model suffered. Part of the problem is that government bureaucracies like self-help but want a "safe" version of it. They do not want to fund trouble making or underwrite political upheaval. Moreover, once governments and foundations attach money to self-help ideas, professionals attempt to move in and recreate a professionally controlled version of the self-help model. The national networks of protection and advocacy programs and Independent Living Centers are cases in point. Congress developed these programs and centers as part of the Developmental Disabilities and Bill of Rights Act and the Rehabilitation Act amendments of 1978. Congress, however, did not put self-help advocacy and independent living funds directly in the hands of consumers. Ever since the original Community Action Projects of the 1960's, which produced considerable political upheaval, the federal government has taken pains to keep community development funds firmly in the control of the political establishment (that is, Governors' or Mayors' offices). That is currently the case with Protection and Advocacy Systems and Independent Living funding as well. The funds were distributed to individual governors who established a variety of programs, most of which include professional staff and some consumers, but few of which are in any way consumer controlled. These are what might be termed "safe," politically quiet groups that borrow the self-help image but that do not adhere to the central principles of self-help. They represent self-help co-opted.

Still another pattern of co-optation is that which occurs when government uses self-help groups as an excuse for failing to provide basic human services. This occurred in the 1950s when parents of retarded children created private school programs for their disabled children who had been systematically denied public education. The parents found that the private self-help schools, often operated by local Associations for Retarded Children, cerebral palsy associations, and groups of parents of children with Down's syndrome, acted as safety valves for the public schools. Pressure on the public schools to create programs were lessened by the existence of nonpublic schools, albeit the latter sometimes failed to measure up to public school standards in terms of quality of school facilities, certification of teachers, transportation services, and extracurricular activities. Similarly, several analysts of self-help movements fear that in looking for ways of minimizing or cutting back on the ever growing costs of human services, government may use self-help models as a convenient, cheap, way of meeting the public's needs for services. As Ann Withorn warns, "most of these self-help service efforts can be legitimately viewed as methods by which the established medical, mental health, and social work professions get people to provide services to themselves that the professionals won't or can't provide."[38] Gartner and Riessman add an additional caveat. They suggest that while self-help may prove a convenient "substitute or cost cutting device" for expensive professional services, it may also further intensify the difference in human service quality offered to the poor and the wealthy: "there is another danger here, namely, that the poor will be given only self-help, and the rich given the professional services as well."[39]

Each potential form of co-optation, namely (1) subversion of-self help by encouraging financial dependence on government and foundation grants, (2) professionalization of the idea and language of self-help, and (3) budget cutting and societal irresponsibility, threatens self-help's effectiveness as a tool for social change. Self-help groups would do well to guard against them:

STRATEGIES AGAINST CO-OPTATION

1. Avoid dependency on single source government or foundation funding; diversify funding sources; develop self-reliant funding.
2. Criticize adoption of self-help models by government agencies if they do not ensure consumer control and self determination; self-help groups possess diverse qualities, but in one respect they all converge: all true self-help groups are created and controlled by consumers.
3. Create self-help groups as "alternatives" and not substitutes for the right to publicly funded basic human services.
4. Continue to lobby for expanded publicly supported human service programs.
5. Resist cooperation with government agencies and policies that use self-help programs as substitutes for publicly funded and provided programs.
6. Educate the public about the differences between self-help services and groups and those that use the self-help image but actually continue to pursue professional control.

Is Professionalism the Correct Target?

Self-help has emerged on the American scene just when society has been shifting from a goods-producing economy to a service-oriented economy. As a phenomenon it has grown at a seemingly fast rate along with the very human services it so harshly criticizes. Self-help articulates an alternative mode of service, an alternative work style, and an alternative locus of control for this newly dominant economic orientation of service provision. Indeed, its greatest challenge has been to the autonomy and authority of professionalism. While part of the challenge has been unassailable (for example, the demand that consumers have a right to be informed before they agree to professional treatment of one kind or another; the right to see one's own records; the right to ask questions about treatment options; and the value of consumer involvement in the treatment process, for example, in natural child birth), self-help's critique of professionalism does raise some difficult questions.

For example, do self-help groups go too far in their criticisms of professionalsm? Is there no role for professional science, for example? Is professionalism really *the* central problem that social change groups should address or are there other even more troublesome issues to confront?

In response to the first question, there are, in the main, two answers. The self-help movement certainly rejects professional style—sometimes referred to as technicism. However, self-help particularly social advocacy self-help groups, do not entirely reject professionalism's technology. Rather they seek only to deprofessionalize technology by bringing it under the scrutiny and control of consumers.

Deprofessionalization is where the self-help movement faces a critical turning point. If it defines professionalism as the chief problem, it may ultimately change only professional style and decorum but not the relative powerlessness of consumers to define the shape of major services in the emerging service society. It is becoming increasingly clear that the antithesis of consumer control is *not* professional control. That is, professionals deliver services that are no longer principally of their own design. However much they may willingly embrace prevailing trends professionals could not change the current direction in human service delivery by merely changing their own style of providing those services. Increasingly, the shape of human services and, indeed, of certain product sectors of the society which self-help movements address (for example, the food industry) comes from the major corporate conglomerates. In medicine, this means more sophisticated equipment to diagnose and combat diseases, which is highly profitable to the medical industry. At the same time it pays only lip service to the need for controlling industrially created health hazards (for example, petrochemical industry toxic wastes, nuclear wastes) which may cause the diseases to occur. Barbara Ehrenreich tells us, for example, that the problems with medicine are not only that it downgrades or represses the simple function of human caring, "but that there is little accountability, even by medical professionals (and certainly not by government regulatory bodies) of the multinational corporate and conglomerate manufactures of the things—chemical and electronic—that define medical practice."[40] In neonatal care for example, premature, extremely low weight babies now receive treatments from incredibly expensive life support systems—some babies weighing as little as one pound are living—the effects of which will simply not be known for years to come. Ehrenreich calls for more than a change in treatment practices:

> A good starting point would be for physicians to confess publicly their loss of power to the medi-products industry, to admit that they have been repeatedly bamboozled by the purveyors of shiny instrument consoles and cleverly packaged pills (all of which inflate the cost of medical care) and promise to act in the future a little more like "professionals" ought to act—more thoughtful, more caring, more capable of critical judgment. Then, as a second step, let them humbly offer to join with us in the struggle against the disease producers that threaten our communities and our children—the petrochemical industry, the nuclear power and weapons industry.[41]

Similarly, in the food industry, while self-help groups may push for less dependence on pesticides, less use of antibiotics in chicken production, greater reliance on organic fertilizers, and less factory-style production of meat, the fact of the matter is that individual farmers have not really *chosen* their strategies from among alternatives. That is, the problem is not one simply of philosophy and style. The takeover of the food industry by a few corporations has forced farmers into the corporate style. Self-help must therefore address not only professionalization, but also what supports it, namely profiteering by increasingly concentrated industries.

The criticism that self-help must seek control of technology and not mere deprofessionalization of style in how we deliver technology actually suggests a basis for self-help social advocacy coalitions. It suggests the common interests, for example, between health care self-help groups and spontaneous, ad hoc community self-help groups that spring up to resist toxic waste and nuclear power sites. It suggests the commonality of interests between environmental groups and food co-ops, between disability rights groups and groups that seek consumer control of corporate boards of directors (for example, the wheelchair industry and the bus industry are dominated by only three corporations each, and both industries suffer in terms of innovation, pricing, and quality from lack of competition). It suggests the shared interests of older persons self-help groups which seek to change societal stereotypes of older people and community groups which seek to develop community controlled media (such as television and newspapers). It also suggests the natural alliance between self-help groups which seek community ownership of industry and those groups that want to improve the quality of the environment. Such alliances may well provide self-help groups with the ideological basis they need to form a national social movement.

NOTES

[1]Statement presented in German by one of three persons with mental retardation from a Viennese sheltered workshop. Statement presented to the Advisory Committee of International Year of Disabled Persons on behalf of the International League of Societies for the Mentally Handicapped.

[2]Alan Gartner and Frank Riessman, "Lots of Helping Hands," *The New York Times,* February 19, 1980, p. A23.

[3]Alfred H. Katz and Eugene I. Bender (eds.), *The Strength in Us* (New York: New Viewpoints, 1976), p. 9.

[4]Janice E. Perlman, "Grassrooting the System," *Social Policy,* Vol. 7, No. 2, September/October 1976, pp. 4–20.

[5]Francis Fox Piven and Richard A. Cloward, *Poor People's Movements: Why They Succeed and How They Fail* (New York: Pantheon, 1977).

[6]Perlman, "Grassrooting," *Social Policy,* p. 7.

[7]Katz and Bender, *The Strength in Us,* 1976; Alan Gartner and Frank Riessman, *Self-Help in Human Services* (San Francisco: Jossey-Bass, 1979); Marie Killilea, "Mutual Help Organizations: Interpretations in the Literature," in *Support Systems and Mutual Help: Multidisciplinary Explorations,* Gerald Caplan and Marie Killilea, eds., (New York: Grune and Stratton, 1976), pp. 37–94.

[8]Gartner and Riessman, *Human Services,* 1979, p. 7.

[9]Alcoholics Anonymous World Service, Inc., *Twelve Steps and Twelve Traditions,* (New York: Alcoholics Anonymous, 1953), pp. 5–13.

[10]Thomas A. Trejo, "The Birth of a New Symbol," *La Palabra* (McNeil Island Penitentiary, McNeil Island, Washington), November/December, 1973, p. 24.

[11]The Boston Women's Health Collective, *Our Bodies, Ourselves* (New York: Simon and Schuster, 1971), p. 1.

[12]Katz and Bender, *Strength*, pp. 37–38.

[13]Tony Palacios, "Gente," *La Palabra*, Nov/Dec, 1973, p. 7.

[14]Simone de Beauvoir quoted in Paul Klegman, *Senior Power* (San Francisco: Glide Publications, 1974), p. 31.

[15]Maggie Kuhn, "Grass-Roots Gray Power," in *Senior Power*, Paul Kelgman (San Francisco: Glide Publications, 1974), p. 169.

[16]Kuhn, "Gray Power," p. 169.

[17]Kuhn, "Gray Power," p. 171.

[18]Kuhn, "Gray Power," p. 171.

[19]Boston Women's Health Book Collective, *Our Bodies, Ourselves*, p. 5.

[20]Boston Women's Health Book Collective, *Our Bodies, Ourselves*, p. 5.

[21]Boston Women's Health Book Collective, *Our Bodies, Ourselves*, p. 6.

[22]Kuhn, "Gray Power, p. 171.

[23]Barbara Coyne Cutler, *Unraveling the Special Education Maze* (Champaign, IL: Research Press, 1981), p. 33.

[24]Elizabeth Pieper, *Sticks and Stones* (Syracuse, NY: Human Policy Press, 1977), p. 30.

[25]Grover Sales, *John Maher of Delancey Street: A Guide to Peaceful Revolution in America* (New York: W. W. Norton & Co., Inc. 1976), p. 107.

[26]Lou Smith, "Operation Bootstrap," in *The Strength in Us*, eds., Alfred H. Katz and Eugene I. Bender (New York: New Viewpoints, 1976), p. 139–150.

[27]Smith, "Bootstrap," p. 149.

[28]Gartner and Riessman, *Self-Help*, p. 80.

[29]Nathan Hurvitz, "Characteristics of Orthodox (Professional) Psychotherapy and Self Help Group Therapy Compared," presented at seventy-sixth Annual Convention of the American Psychological Association, San Francisco, CA, September 1, 1968, reprinted in Frank Riessman, "How Does Self Help Work," *Social Policy*, September/October, 1976, p. 44; Riessman, "Self Help," p. 45; Charles Hampden-Turner, *Sane Asylum* (New York: Morrow, 1977), pp. 281–291.

[30]Women's Health Book Collective, *Our Bodies, Ourselves*, p. 255.

[31]Judi Chamberlain, *On Our Own* (New York: Hawthorne, 1978), p. 220.

[32]Mildred Calvert, "Welfare Rights and the Welfare System," in *Welfare Mothers Speak Out*, eds., Thomas H. Tarantino and Dismas Becker (Milwaukee County Welfare Rights Organization (New York: W. W. Norton & Co., Inc., 1972), pp. 29–30.

[33]Charles Hampden-Turner, *Sane Asylum*, p. 67.

[34]Douglas Biklen, "Advocacy Comes of Age," *Exceptional Children*, March, 1976, p. 310.

[35]Committee of Concerned Asian Scholars, *Inside the People's Republic* (New York: Vintage, 1971), p. 43.

[36]Grover Sales, *Maher*, p. 60.

[37] Victor Sidel and Ruth Sidel, "Beyond Coping," *Social Policy*, September/October, 1976, p. 69.

[38]Ann Withorn, "Helping Ourselves: The Limits and Potential of Self-Help," *Social Policy*, November/December, 1980, p. 23.

[39]Gartner and Riessman, *Self-Help*, p. 3.

[40]Barbara Ehrenreich, "Letter to the Editor," *Social Policy*, May/June, 1981, p. 64.

[41]Ehrenreich, "Letter," pp. 64–65.

CHAPTER NINE
NEGOTIATIONS
AND LOBBYING

INTRODUCTION

On the evening before sitting down to write this chapter, I met with a group of parents of children with disabilities. Their children had problems such as autism, learning disabilities, severe mental retardation, and physical impairments. These parents had come together to form a parent advocacy network through which they intended to fight for education rights and quality education programming for their sons and daughters.

At that meeting, one parent said something which I have come to expect at such organizing sessions. She remarked, ''All last year, my son needed a particular kind of educational teaching machine. But except for two weeks at the beginning of the year, it was broken. The resource teacher told me that the school did not have enough money to get it fixed. I kept asking about it, but nothing was done. And I began to feel like a troublemaker. I didn't know if I should keep questioning the teacher about it. I didn't want to jeopardize my good relationship with the teacher. If she got mad at me, I didn't want her to take out her anger on my son. I know I don't want to compromise my son's education, but I don't know what to do.''

It was a familiar refrain—''I didn't want to jeopardize my good relation-ship.'' But how good could that relationship be if the parent could not openly speak her mind? The fact that this parent feels she cannot disclose her feelings to the teacher should tell us something about her predicament. Should she carry her complaints up the chain of command to the principal, to the superintendent, to the school board? Should she organize other parents who have similar problems and frustrations?

I have often heard parents in similar circumstances say, "I don't want to get into an adversarial relationship with them (administrators). I would rather work *with* them." Obviously, it is easier to work collaboratively than to have conflicts with people. That is, it is easier psychologically. We feel less anxiety when working together. In point of fact however, even when consumers and service providers (or citizens and officials) "work together" they are usually negotiating. After all, their interests are never precisely alike. Their perspectives on issues are never precisely the same. The resource teacher, for example, was worried about the limited school budget; and she may have been afraid to carry the parent's demands to her superiors. The parent cared most about her son's education. This is a natural setting for negotiating differences.

As long as the parent keeps quiet, she leaves the fate of her son's education entirely in the hands of school officials. Moreover she accepts, however reluctantly, an unequal, less powerful position in her dealings with the schools.

We all find ourselves in situations where we are vulnerable to other people's decision making. However, we need not be immobilized. Each of the action strategies (for example, demonstrations, legal action, action research, use of the media) outlined in this book offers ways to achieve greater control over our destinies. One such tool is the art of negotiating. Virtually anyone can learn to negotiate his or her interests effectively. Negotiations do not cost a lot of money. They need not always produce an adversarial relationship between citizens and officials, though they may. Perhaps most important, consumers need to recognize that officials use negotiation strategies all the time, whether the consumers like it or not. Thus the only question for consumers is whether they intend to remain ignorant of negotiating strategies and therefore lose consistently by default, or whether they will learn to be effective negotiators.

DISPUTE RESOLUTION

One of the ways people settle disputes is by going to court. We take our complaints to an administrative hearing officer, a judge, or a jury. The actual process for this kind of negotiation is not much different than the strategies of everyday negotiation which we will discuss shortly. The principal difference between legally resolved disputes and everyday negotiations is in the actors. When we take a conflict to court, the negotiations are handed over to others, namely lawyers. The lawyer is supposed to consult the client—indeed, allow the client to make key substantitive decisions about how to proceed in the case—yet the actual negotiating is done by lawyers.

In his now classic article on the alienating effect of formal legal systems, Nils Christie suggests that the courts, in effect, wrest power and an important psychological and social experience from the affected parties in a dispute or conflict.[1] His examples refer to criminal disputes (robberies, violent crimes), though his analysis applies just as well to civil disputes. In criminal disputes, the alienation of parties involved appears greatest. Both of the principal parties, the victim and victimizer, are represented by attorneys. The victim has almost no role at all because the state presumably is acting in the victim's interests. Here too there is cause for skepticism. The state, after all, collects any fines and exerts punishments. Victims do not—they have no role at all, save as spectators. Even in civil disputes, the principal participants may feel frustrated and left out by the formal legal system. Their ability to influence negotiations diminishes at each stage of the legal process. Christie attributes this loss of power to the formal structures of the law and to the professional role assumed by lawyers:

> Lawyers are particularly good at stealing conflicts. They are trained for it. They are trained to prevent and solve conflicts. They are socialized into a sub-culture with a surprisingly high agreement concerning interpretation of norms, and regarding what sort of information can be accepted as relevant in each case. Many among us have, as laymen, experienced the sad moments of truth when our lawyers tell us that our best arguments in our fight against our neighbour are without any legal relevance whatsoever and that we for God's sake ought to keep quiet about them in court. Instead they pick out arguments we might find irrelevant or even wrong to use.[3]

In short, the legal system, like all professional structures, circumscribes the role and, therefore, the power of nonprofessionals.

Some communities have recently begun experiments with alternative approaches to dispute settlement. They have established conflict resolution centers, places where people can discuss and presumably settle their differences. Some of these programs take the form of scaled-down legal forums in which the parties in dispute, often represented by attorneys, present their concerns to a third party, another lawyer or trained arbitrator who considers the evidence and issues a decision.[4]

In such systems, either party may later take the conflict to court, but usually both parties seek the more informal dispute settlement approach because it is quicker, less encumbered by legal rules, and less costly. Other dispute resolution centers do not involve the legal profession. Here, lay people form community conflict centers or programs in which people or groups can air their problems before a neutral panel or arbitrator. The chief advantage of this kind of system seems to be that the affected people actually participate in solving their own disputes. This is a kind of community organization which, unlike traditional professional structures, empowers consumers or other affected groups.

A third type of conflict resolution might be termed the "ad hoc approach." Even in highly professionalized urban culture, most people and groups resolve their conflicts through ad hoc negotiations. That is, when people have conflicting interests they create a forum (for example, a meeting, a public debate, a public hearing) in which to resolve or accommodate their differences. There are no set rules for such events, though the participants may make rules. Usually, these ad hoc negotiation sessions are one-time affairs. The same group of people may never meet together again once the dispute has been resolved.

Since dispute resolution most frequently takes the form of ad hoc negotiations for community organizers and their constituencies, we will concentrate in the following section of this chapter on describing negotiation strategies and considerations most applicable to such informal settings.

THE NEGOTIATION PROCESS:
GETTING READY

Identify, prioritize, clarify.   What are our issues? How many objectives can we reasonably expect to achieve in a single negotiating sequence? Which are long-range goals? Which are short-term objectives? These are questions that we can answer only in relation to specific circumstances. There are no textbook recommendations to rely on when it comes to identifying issues, prioritizing them, and deciding how much to put forward at one time. Most groups meet for hours on end, often for several days or over several months to clarify issues. Once identified, the group can prioritize them. This requires at least the following considerations: (1) Which are most winnable? Our objective is to win, not merely to look good; (2) Which are most important? There is little purpose in negotiating for trivial gains; (3) Which are most efficiently achieved by negotiations and which by other strategies (for example, litigation, media exposure, action research, self-help, demonstrations)? (4) How much negotiating time will be required for each issue or sub-issue? (5) Do we have the necessary knowledge on each issue?

It usually helps to brainstorm issues. In brainstorming, group members call out issues and record these on a blackboard or on large pieces of newsprint paper. Members of the group then can each prioritize them privately. Next, each group member shares how he or she prioritized the items and states the basis for the priorities. A group may go through this process several times before it achieves consensus on specific negotiation goals. While such a process of issue identification and prioritization can take time, the group must agree on its goals at the outset.

Gather evidence.   Has our particular issue ever been taken up by another group? We must find out. This means gathering evidence on how successful it was. If there were problems with the issue elsewhere, we should be prepared on how to respond to those criticisms. Are there statistics available which support our point of view? Numbers always add to the persuasive effect of a claim. Are there statutes and regulations which cast a favorable light on the goals? We need to read and analyze relevant reports and other documents. When we locate any evidence that runs counter to our objectives, we must not simply pass over it; we must find evidence and arguments to counter it. Above all, we need to know how to communicate our issues in human terms. If, for example, our goal is to close down abusive nursing homes, then we must tell the world, including those officials with whom we negotiate, the stark realities of life in such facilities. We must be able to describe the filth, the bedsores, the forced feeding, the use of tranquilizers to quiet those who speak out, the medicaid ripoffs and unnutritious diets. We must document and expose how such practices harm actual victims. Above all, we must make our case compelling on a human level?

Creating the agenda. It would seem that the upper hand in negotiations belongs to the officials who have something to give up, something to change, something we want. However, that is not necessarily the case. The effective negotiator or negotiation team frequently captures a dominant position by using effective strategies. One such strategy is agenda setting. Who defines the key issues for discussion? Who decides in what order to discuss them? Finally, who decides how to structure negotiations? One relatively recent example of negotiating strategy involved the seemingly bizarre wrangling that went on for weeks between the United States and North Vietnam over the shape of the table that they would use for their negotiations to end the Vietnam war. In fact, it was not bizarre at all. These were seasoned negotiators, testing each other out, each trying to gain the upper hand, a bit more control over the proceedings, a psychological edge that might later lead to a substantive edge. Most negotiations by community advocacy groups never focus on such things as table size, but they frequently do start off with disagreement over who may participate in the negotiations. Officials frequently try to limit and control who and how many people may negotiate for the organizing group. Another issue that almost always requires mutual acceptance is the agenda. Hence we should develop our preferred agenda of issues prior to the actual negotiating session. Through this strategy we can focus issues to suit our interests, exclude issues that do not concern us or which will divert us, and seize the initiative in negotiations rather than assuming a defensive posture. By making the agenda ours, we make the negotiations ours.

Ground rules. In more formalized negotiations we may want to plan ground rules. Shall we demand the right to keep a recorded transcript of the proceedings? Shall we keep minutes? It is dangerous to allow the other side to keep the minutes, simply because each side has a tendency to cast itself in the most favorable light. How long will each session last? Do the negotiators want to agree ahead of time not to talk to the media during certain phases of the negotiations or on certain topics? The organizing group may want to consider making such a proposal.

Choosing a team. Match numbers with numbers. There is nothing worse than going into a negotiation session alone or even in a group of two or three when the other side has a dozen or more. In such a situation it is hard to feel anything other than besieged. It is probably best not to negotiate at all if the opposition has more than five or six negotiators. Ideally both sides will have a small negotiating team, usually between two and five. The team should be representative of its constituencies, that is there should always be people present who are affected by the issue at hand, such as consumers and victims. The team should also have diverse skills or knowledge. One of the negotiators may be a storehouse of information while another may know how to put the information together in a convincing argument. It pays to openly discuss the particular strengths and weaknesses that different people will bring to the negotiation process. Groups which use negotiation as a favored strategy will have the additional incentive to use each session as an opportunity to train members of its group in negotiation skills.

I once participated in a negotiation session in which our group wanted to win the right to a full day of educational programming for over a thousand mentally retarded youngsters at a large institution. More than 60 percent of the children received no education at all despite the fact that the institution was called a state school. Of the remaining 40 percent, only a fraction received more than an hour of education each day. We did not expect the negotiations to succeed. In fact, we intended to file suit or go to the media in behalf of these children. First, though, we wanted to be able to say that we had met with the responsible officials and had received no satisfaction. We knew what their defense would be. The parents had heard it many times over: "There is not enough money and there are not enough teachers." We wanted to be able to say publicly that we had used every possible effort to win a negotiated settlement. We felt that if we could demonstrate that we had done everything, including face-to-face negotiating to resolve our dispute, that our pleas to the Governor and our plan to litigate would be more popular. We felt that the State would send in a sizeable team to negotiate. We expected an assistant commissioner, the institution director, the facility's top educator, the State's education director, the facility's chief physician, the director of children's services, a social worker, and a psychologist. We had the same numbers as the other side and had the same credentials. We also had people who could speak to any issue that arose, which gave us credibility. Our choice of the team, while large, was right. The negotiations were a stand-off. When the state refused to make any firm commitment to upgrade its educational practices, we felt free to go public with the issue.

Strengths and weaknesses.   What are our strong points? Is the opposition afraid we may stir up public furor in the media? Are politicians anxious to have our votes? Does the opposition believe we can win at litigation or other strategies and therefore desire to negotiate a settlement? We need to assess our strengths. At the same time we must know our points of vulnerability. How might the opposition discredit our cause? We need to consider our weakest links and plan to protect against exploitation of these potential weaknesses. For instance, community organizers frequently find themselves accused of being outsiders, professional trouble makers, radicals, communists. We can safely predict those charges will arise again and again when negotiations get acrimonious. But, we can protect against such charges. We can involve politically diverse members, develop evidence of the deep local roots of our demands, and marshall evidence that whenever there has been turmoil or trouble associated with the negotiations the opposition has fomented it.

Have a plan.   We noted earlier the importance of creating an agenda and ground rules for the negotiations. These are items presented to the opposition at the outset. In addition, however, negotiators need their own internal plan for how best to win the objectives. This means deciding ahead of time:

1. which points to raise first;
2. when to introduce compromises;
3. when to call for delays;
4. how to relate to the media and to the constituency for whom we organize;
5. who among the negotiating team will say what;
6. the style for negotiating—firm, humorous, plaintive, angry . . .;
7. complementary organizing strategies to accompany negotiations; and
8. strategies to ensure that negotiated agreements actually get implemented.

Negotiate with the right people. I have been in negotiation sessions in which we negotiated for several hours before it became clear that the people with whom we were negotiating did not have the authority to meet our demands. It almost goes without saying that there is no point in negotiating with people who cannot deliver on the negotiations. Thus, as a preliminary action to negotiations, we need to find out who has the authority to respond meaningfully to our concerns. Typically, large bureaucracies send public relations specialists and lower level bureaucrats to negotiate. These people rarely have the power to make decisions or to present more than a single formal proposal. Rather, their role is to act as a messenger for top officials or perhaps as a buffer, to keep the top officials from having to negotiate personally. This strategy enables officials to avoid giving legitimacy to the organizing group's demands. The best strategy in this situation is to expose the officials' refusal to face the group personally. Never negotiate, unless it is with people empowered to respond to the group's concerns.

Know the Audience

Even when they take place in dark, out-of-the-way smoke-filled rooms, negotiations have audiences greater in number than the participants on hand. We need to recognize that every negotiation has its constituencies. These usually include groups and individuals who will be immediately affected by the outcome. Another constituency may be the media and another, the public. Those officials who are watching the group's activities, not so much out of any immediate concern but to assess the group's strength and its potential influence on other issues and constituencies in the future are also an audience. Given all of these diverse audiences, we need to ask ourselves, "How will our negotiations influence how each of these groups perceives us?" It may be possible and advisable to tailor certain negotiation strategies to win the support of one or several of these groups. When special interest groups such as disability rights groups, older persons' action organizations, and neighborhood improvement associations negotiate with public officials, they rely heavily on their ability to win over the public to their side. Their ability to win concessions from political leaders corresponds directly to the officials' perception of the group's public support.

Role Play

Most of the anxiety people feel in negotiation sessions comes from not knowing precisely what the other side will say or how they will try to catch their opponents off guard. Fortunately, in most situations we can predict what the opposition will say and even how they will say it. An easy way to discover the other side's approach is to try to act out its parts—in other words, role play. Divide the group into two groups, the community organizers and the officials. Appoint specific roles to each of the participants. Next, briefly decide, in a line or two, the key argument and tone for each negotiator—then begin. Negotiate. What we find is that by acting out the parts of our side as well as of the other side, we discover how the opposition will attempt to beat us. At the same time, the vividness of the role play forces us to examine our own position and the manner in which we intend to present it. It helps to have an audience for the role play. The audience can take notes throughout and provide a critique of the arguments and negotiation style when completed. Which arguments seem to work? Which seem weak, trivial, or implausible? Have we left out any powerful evidence? Is our timing right?

Actors in the role play frequently become so involved that it almost seems like the real thing. In fact, we recently made a videotape of just such a negotiation role play. When we used the videotape for training sessions around the country, even though we introduced the videotape as a role play, members of our audiences would often asked us, "How did you get that official to willingly participate in the filming?" Of course, we had not. The official was a fellow organizer but he so captured the role people expect an official to play that he looked like the real thing.

Hope for the Best;
Prepare for the Worst

No matter how much we plan ahead, no matter how skilled we are in the best negotiating tactics, we need to remember that we do not, by ourselves, control the outcome. We need optimism to begin the process, but need realism to succeed. The best arguments do not always prevail nor do the best interests. Part of knowing how to negotiate effectively is learning how to accept setbacks while at the same time maintaining enough optimism to begin again.

NEGOTIATIONS

Stating the Issues

By the time negotiations begin, the issues are usually clear. However, we need to remember that most negotiations involve lengthy give-and-take discussions in which two sides slowly move toward a mutual position that each can live with. Imagine, for example, a neighborhood group in a downtown urban area that is negotiating with city officials over where to locate a trash-burning steam plant. City and county officials argue that the plant should be constructed adjacent to the group's neighborhood. "It will be clean and innoffensive. It will provide lower cost power," the officials argue. City residents in this poor district fear a safety and health hazard that will come with having garbage transported through their streets. Further, they ask, how can the plant operate without any stench? They negotiate. Now, actually, the neighborhood has multiple concerns: safety of children who play near the streets where garbage trucks enter and leave, possible odiforous fumes from the plant, and general disruption of the neighborhood. Should the group present all of its concerns at once? Should it prioritize these concerns?

First, the number of issues should be limited to the important ones. The focus should then be placed on those that have some likelihood of succeeding in the negotiations. Prioritize the issues. Which are most important, which less so? Obviously, even if city and county officials found a way of cordoning off the garbage truck traffic so that neighborhood children could play in peace, the neighborhood would not want or agree to the garbage plant. The basic issue is the plant itself. The neighbors do not want it because they regard it as a potential blight on the neighborhood. It would therefore be a major error to get sidetracked into lengthy planning on how to protect the children's safety. That concern is a subissue, merely one of many arguments against the garbage burning facility. Essentially, the neighborhood needs to highlight its central issue and subordinate all other issues to it.

Second, after prioritizing issues and stating the top issue, negotiators must communicate the lead issues compellingly. How will failure to negotiate a settlement affect the community's future? How will it affect individual families and individual people? Negotiators enter the fray with the attitude that they must not only state their issues, but that they must ultimately either sell or impose them. In addition to using statistics, models, laws, supporting statements by sympathetic officials and/or experts and legitimizing documentation, negotiators have a central obligation to render their cause human. The issues must be compelling on a human level.

Third, compromise. Give in on lesser issues so that the opposition will feel better able to compromise themselves. It is important to not appear uncompromising. This helps to avoid allowing any negotiating point to seem too rigid and inflexible. Know where it is possible to empathize with the opposition without compromising a major point. At all costs, negotiators should do everything possible to keep positions from becoming rigid at the outset. This means trying to find areas of commonality, issues that lend themselves to compromise, and a way of presenting issues that clearly points out chief concerns, but that also gives an impression of not being entirely inflexible. Occasionally, we hear negotiators say, "We'll consider any reasonable proposal," or "Everything is negotiable:" While this is not always true, negotiators say such things because they want to create the impression that they are open-minded. This strategy wins support outside the negotiations and creates a climate that facilitates compromise on the other side of the negotiating table.

Fourth, negotiators may have in mind the destruction of a current policy or practice, but they find it to their advantage to portray themselves as tradition-conscious, constructive, progressive-minded people. Groups usually accomplish this image-building by identifying certain traditions in public policy and practice in which to locate their proposal. In other words, they try to say, "Our proposal reflects long held values and proposes strategies that, over the years, have always proven effective." Further, effective negotiators usually point to existing policies and practices in other communities or settings which bear resemblance to those proposed—though of course negotiators always promise improvements over any existing models—as evidence of their proposal's practicality.

Style

Once we issue an ultimatum, our maneuverability is limited. If we make too many ultimatums, no one will take us seriously. If we make ultimatums too early in the negotiating process, we run the risk of angering the opposition needlessly. If we make an ultimatum which the opposition cannot meet, we put ourselves in the position of having to back down. This is hard and it causes us to lose face. We feel as if we have failed. It is far better to negotiate toward a resolution than to feel we have "compromised on something we said could not be compromised." If this happens, we appear to ourselves and perhaps to others as if we have "sold out."

Ultimatums are a form of communication. They combine with many other types of communication used in negotiations to comprise what we might call negotiating style or technique. No one can tell another person just how to use particular techniques because so much of negotiating is subjective decision making. At a certain point, an ultimatum may be just what is needed to scare the other side into a settlement, or as a statement of exasperation, or to cut off negotiations. It takes a certain amount of intuition to know the best point at which to act. However, at the same time, we can identify a few broad principles concerning negotiating style.

First, there are boundaries for ultimatums. They should be used as infrequently as possible, and only for a calculated purpose. Even though we often regard certain issues or positions as nonnegotiable, it rarely benefits a cause to look inflexible. The "love it or leave it" approach to negotiating makes dialogue difficult. We are better off using phrases like "we believe these principles are essential to our interests," or "without this point, we are unable to see how our interests can be met," or "this is a central concern to us."

Second, we should not contradict ourselves. Negotiating groups have a difficult time honoring this principle, particularly in the heat of discussions. With several people involved on either side, it is easy to make a mistake, to say something that contradicts an earlier claim, demand, or statement. Obviously, the other side can use such contradictions to fuel their own arguments. They may say, "You don't seem to know what you want," or "You keep changing your positions, how do you expect us to believe you?"

Third, do not call people names. Stick to the issues. Ad hominem arguments, ones which direct anger and frustration at individuals, only add to the rancor of the negotiations and divert attention away from the important issues. Pettiness of any kind usually backfires. For one thing, the opposition can call public attention to our use of such tactics as name-calling. For another, name-calling on our part may evoke similar behavior on the other side. It is better, as a rule, to avoid any name-calling and ad hominem arguments. After all, the goal of negotiations is to win, not to impugn or harm the opposition.

Fourth, we should not make careless threats. The worst threats of all are those on which we cannot follow through. An opposition group usually has enough experience in negotiations and administrative work to know when a group can deliver or not on its threats. Empty threats merely dissipate the group's credibility. School teachers, parents, and administrators all know that the minute their constituencies (for example, children or subordinates) perceive that they are the objects of meaningless warnings, they cease to view the parent or administrator as a serious leader.

Fifth, be determined. Negotiations take time and patience. Those who negotiate effectively know how to wait for their victories. Negotiators, like organizers, need to be of the frame of mind that change occurs slowly and erratically. A setback now may only set the stage for a greater stride forward later. What is important is that we demonstrate commitment over the long period of negotiations. Only then do we create the impression that we will not fade away, that the opposition will have to reckon with us sooner or later.

Sixth, know how to keep secrets. Specifically, in the early stages of negotiations we must never divulge more than the situation requires. We usually know certain things about the opposition and its position that it would rather we did not know, but it is just as important how we use that information as that we know it in the first place. We are under no obligation to share everything we know with the opposition. As long as our goal is to win, we should use information carefully and sparingly. For example, suppose we are negotiating with banks over redlining, the practice of denying mortgage money to residents of particular neighborhoods. Should we tell the opposition that we have informants in several banks and that we thereby have countless documents which reveal the specific nature of redlining by certain banks? Or, are we better off keeping the opposition in suspense, not certain of what information we actually have? Clearly, the latter course of action puts us in greater control. We can negotiate for a time and then discredit certain positions taken by the banks by providing clear evidence of wrongdoing. As long as we have a store of information to disclose at appropriate moments, the opposition is kept guessing. Surprise is on our side. At the same time, we may want to be careful how this data is presented so that we do not jeopardize the jobs of informants.

Seventh, use stalling tactics when necessary. "We will consider it." "We will show it to our members." "We will research it." These are all familiar phrases designed for one thing, to stall the opposition, to buy time. Frequently time is needed to let tensions build or, for that matter, to let tensions cool. Sometimes time is necessary to develop a new set of negotiating strategies or to secure additional evidence upon which to buttress our cause. Whatever the reason, stalling meets the need.

Eighth, use emotion—fear, anger, frustration, compassion, excitement.

These emotions have a place in negotiations. As with other tactics, we need to do more than use them or show them. We need to use them for a purpose, at the right time, and toward the right end. A calculated walk-out makes a point as does a fit of anger or an outburst of frustration. But a steady stream of venom, or humor, or fear, or any single emotion has little effect. Emotion must be used to draw attention to a point, to dramatize something. In this vein, I am reminded of a story told to me by a former social welfare director. A child welfare official was negotiating with a child-caring agency over its license to operate in the State of Michigan. At a certain point in the negotiations—actually it was more like a hearing—the official said, "Could you tell me about the case of T. Wilson?" The agency representative obliged. The agency had arranged for adoption of the 11-year-old boy by a family. In the course of describing the case, the agency representative explained, "For personal reasons the family asked that the boy's name be changed from Thomas to James." When the child welfare official heard this he could not believe it. He looked at the agency official carefully and said, softly, "Excuse me, could you repeat that?" "Yes," the agency person replied, "for personal reasons the family wanted the youth's name changed from Thomas to James. So we complied." The child welfare official became livid. He turned red. He raised his fist in the air and slammed it down on the table. Then, in a ferocious voice, he yelled, "You mean you changed the boy's name, just like a dog?" There it was. The child welfare official had found a very human way of demonstrating his concern over this agency's operation. To dramatize the point, he yelled in full rage.

Ninth, expect threats, criticisms, and even insults. No one likes to have other people yelling at him or her. The best strategy is to rise above such attacks and stay cool. The other side does not have to like us; it must simply reconcile itself to compromising with us. The worst possible responses to verbal outbursts from the opposition are uncontrolled outbursts from us—sarcasm, name-calling, and sniping. The minute we begin to make fun of or in any fashion ridicule the opposition we make agreement on the issues perilously difficult. On the other hand, bad behavior by the other side can serve our ends. If negotiations break down or if they linger on for a protracted period, careful documentation of bad behavior of the opposition may be used to garner popular support for our position. The best response to accusations and insults is one of patient discussion of the issues.

Tenth, never lie. Negotiators, like public relations specialists, find themselves bending evidence, selecting words to avoid saying other words, and generally doing everything within legal and moral propriety to put the best light on their interests. But we must never lie or even appear to lie. Deceit of any kind, particularly if intentional, can totally discredit our position and destroy popular support for our position. If we ever give the opposition justification for saying, "They fabricated the evidence," "They knowingly misled the public," or "They lied in order to promote their own interests," we contribute to our own demise.

Eleventh, watch the time. Negotiation takes time. But so does makework. Some groups fear negotiations because the process sometimes deteriorates into meaningless task forces which issue reports that sit on office shelves and influence nothing—in other words, makework. Therefore we need to communicate to the opposition early on that we expect progress. We need to show a spirit of compromise, while at the same time we need to communicate to the opposition our expectation that they reciprocate in kind, and in reasonable time. We need to set some kind of general time limit that will be a guidepost as to whether progress has occurred.

Know the Opposition

Negotiations take place in stages. Participants usually begin with general statements. They want to size up the opposition. They then present their first negotiating position, which is usually their strongest. However, it would be a mistake to think of either the opposition or their arguments as monolithic. Like any group, the opposition represents multiple interests and presents diverse personalities and styles of negotiating. Our task is to know the opposition in order to negotiate with it.

Negotiators possess or adopt every possible personality style. Some cultivate hostility. Others try to persuade with patronizing altruism, saying "I care as much about your interests as you do." For still others, negotiations offer a forum in which to try and dominate or compete with others. Some envision themselves as seasoned traders locked in a zero-sum game, each side giving a little bit from their fixed resources. Some operate like detectives, searching for the other side's weakest link. Others take on the role of prosecuting attorney whose role it is to tear down the opposition point by point until it concedes to the opposition's point of view. Some seem more interested in public relations and use the negotiations as a stepping stone to media access. Much of their negotiating goes on outside the conference room, in front of the television cameras, reporters' pads and newcasters' microphones. Others use the aura of professionalism to impose their will—"You do not have enough information on which to make the decisions that we are forced to make. Everyone will be a lot better off if you would leave these matters to the professionals who are trained and experienced in dealing with them."

By consciously analyzing the negotiating styles of the opposition as well as observing them, and talking to people who have seen them negotiate before, we can prepare a style or styles of response. Usually a negotiation team displays multiple styles. It chooses these styles in order to react to or account for different styles of the opposing side. One member of the team may have responsibility for challenging the accuracy of the other side's statements. Another may play a counterpoint to the professional role. This person would have facts and figures to back up the lead negotiator's points or would challenge the opponents' assertions. Still another would act as the lead negotiator, ready at all times to respond effectively to the particular styles of the opposition.

Above all, we should not allow the opposition's style—which may itself be a strategy—to dictate our style. Our goal is to win and to realize this goal we must approach the opposition with a high degree of self-consciousness, aware of how our arguments and style will affect the other side. We know not to force the opposition's hand. Also, we know that since the opposition, like our own negotiation team, is not entirely of one mind or style, we can try and find a sympathetic hearing with the most sympathetic voice of the opposition and then try to generalize gains made with one negotiator to the group. In some cases we may be able to develop specific lines of reasoning that will appeal to the opposition. There may be a way of convincing them that we all have something to gain, if for different reasons, from a settlement such as the one we seek. Thus, for example, human service officials may accept a program model that departs from standard operating procedures if they believe the new model will result in fiscal savings, greater harmony with consumer groups, and positive publicity. It may even help to reveal to the opposition that our group has different perspectives on an issue. We sometimes call this "the tough guy/soft guy routine." One of the group's negotiators begins the negotiations with a hardline approach by appearing very aggressive, greedy, and intransigent. Then a second negotiator plays a more conciliatory role: "Let's not get polarized. Why don't we put our heads together and recognize that we will all be better off if we can come to a reasonable agreement. We don't want to push you up against the wall. All we want to do is improve. . . ." The opposition sees that the second person is easier to deal with than the first. Not surprisingly then, the opposition may begin to feel the second offer is indeed reasonable.

Another element of style is something we might call body language. For instance, if the opposition looks down and mumbles, this usually reveals uncertainty. Similarly, if the other side appears overly formal, this most likely reflects an unwillingness to compromise. On the other hand, backslapping and overly solicitous behavior may be designed to make the negotiator feel like a child in the face of his or her parent.

Most groups will use space and physical design as a negotiating tool. The opposition gives itself luxurious chairs and expects the other side to sit on folding chairs. Sometimes one group of negotiators will put themselves at a large table while requiring members of the other side to sit in seats off to the side. Here I am reminded of an agency director who had his desk positioned at the far end of a long (perhaps thirty feet) room. He positioned himself at a huge leather chair between the desk and a picture window. In the late afternoon, when the sun would set behind his desk, a person entering the room to talk or negotiate for something, would immediately feel exposed. Here you would stand, in full open view of this man who was but a large silhouette behind a broad stately desk. It was an imposing and intimidating setting. Whether conscious or not—and it is hard to believe this could be anything but conscious—this man's use of space placed his visitors at an immediate, unstated disadvantage.

Know the Opposition's Motivation

What are the opposition's interest? What are they trying to protect or expand? These are questions of power (see Chapter 2). Power exists wherever people cooperate or obey. Thus the key to understanding particular distributions or power is our ability to fathom the reasons why people cooperate and obey in particular circumstances. In other words, what motivates peoples' actions? What are their interests? Are they trying to protect or expand their ability to make decisions in certain aspects of community or agency life? Are they interested in keeping consumers dependent? Do they seek after status and money?

Each group has its needs. Community development officials may want the bulk of redevelopment and capital construction funds to subsidize big business. They may want this as a means of ensuring business contributions to the mayor's political campaign. They may view business as the greatest supporter of urban stability and, therefore, worthy of rewards. Or they may believe that investments in businesses will generate more jobs than money simply dispersed to assist poor people in rehabilitating and purchasing homes. Similarly, human services executives may fear public attention and notoriety for their programs because the latter can make them a liability to the political leaders for whom they work. Also, public exposure increases their need to be accountable for their actions to the public. Public employees generally want to maintain an air of calm and control. If there is controversy, they want to have the appearance of being in complete control of its outcome.

"I would rather negotiate than litigate."—so say many administrators. If they have a sense that they are on shaky legal ground or that litigation will cost a good deal of money, administrators may opt for a negotiated settlement. As noted earlier, litigation, unlike negotiation, places decision making power in the hands of a third party, the courts. Unless they believe that the court's position will mimic their own, most administrators would rather retain some control over the decision making process.

On occasion, we may be able to demonstrate that the opposition would be better off negotiating and, indeed, capitulating than facing public embarrassment. That is, if administrators or officials believe their position unpopular with the public, they will seek conciliation behind closed doors. In these situations, organizers can use the threat of public exposure as an inducement to negotiate: "We don't want to go public on this, but if you refuse to respond meaningfully to our demands, our hand will be forced."

In some cases the point of vulnerability for the opposition may be peculiar to the setting, issue, or people involved. For example, politicians and public officials who hold appointed positions and are, therefore, beholden to the politicians who appointed them, generally want to avoid controversy, particularly if arguing publicly will alienate one of their large constituencies. Thus, for instance, older people, a sizeable voting bloc, can often force politicians and public officials to negotiate on issues such as emergency heating allowances, additional public housing, or expanded mass transit. Elected officials would rather negotiate and appear as if they are taking a responsible or reasonable leadership position on behalf of older constituents than appear to be the older person's enemy. Quiet negotiations appeal to the politician or public office holder because such negotiations keep them out of the limelight. Also, if negotiations occur out of the public eye, then these same officials retain greater ability to manage their public image. Instead of having their positions and, hence, their image, forged in the public consciousness through highly visible controversy, they can tell the public, through press releases, campaign literature and the like, what their positions on issues are and why the public should continue supporting them.

Other Considerations

Take notes throughout negotiations. They can prove extremely fruitful at later stages when it comes time to compare and contrast different proposals or to analyze the opposition's reasoning.

Make sure that, during the negotiations, points of agreement are recorded as they are reached. Also, both sides should agree on means of evaluating actual implementation of settlement.

Be careful with language. Our own choice of words reveals much on how we think about an issue. When a youth advocacy project advocates for school reforms to alter student absenteeism and noncompletion rates, it may choose to speak of school pushouts rather than school dropouts. By making the issue one of "policies and practices which force youngsters out of school," the youth advocates put their opposition on the defensive. Similarly, groups which want to promote mainstreaming of students with disabilities into regular schools where they can interact with nondisabled students characterize their goal as integration versus segregation— again a choice of language that puts the opposition on the defensive.

Involve new people in negotiations. We can read about it, practice it, observe it, and worry about it, but the very best way to develop skills as a negotiator is through practice. Therefore, groups frequently include at least one newcomer to the activity in each negotiation effort. Aside from its obvious value as a training device, the presence of novices to the negotiation team helps protect the group against unhealthy isolation from criticism. A new person can bring new insights concerning the team's performance as well as new knowledge and strategies.

Finally, do not be put off with age-old tricks. The refrains of these are familiar and responses are easy enough to conjure up:

Official Cool Outs	*Possible Responses*
"That's a good idea, but our Board of Directors will never buy it."	"If you do not have the power to negotiate reasonable solutions to our differences perhaps we should be negotiating with your board."
"We agree with you in principle but we have to be practical."	"Are you saying that you agree with our goals but are simply unwilling to implement them?"
"You must be patient. Change takes time. You can't expect miracles overnight."	"What you call miracles are to us basic amenities—food, shelter, a decent education. Let's get back to specifics. It's alright for you to talk about time, but you don't face the problems we do."
"Even if we wanted to, we couldn't. We just don't have the money."	"That sounds awfully familiar. There was enough money to put up a skywalk downtown to aid the department stores, there was enough money to remodel the

Official Cool Outs	*Possible Responses*
	mayor's office, and enough for an airport parking garage to serve people wealthy enough to fly, but meanwhile you tell us there is not enough for the few crying needs we have."
"You are looking out for your interests, but we have to be concerned about the public interests."	"We are part of the public too. 'The Public Interest' is for us all, not just for the powerful."
"It's a good idea, but the union will never go for it."	"They have never seen a specific proposal on this. Don't blame the union for your own resistance."
"How can we be sure this will work even if we do agree to try it?"	"You can't. But it has been tried successfully before. And if it does not work, we can always change back."
"If you knew as much about this as we do, you would know that it cannot work."	"We don't buy that 'we're the experts, trust us' line. If there is something you think we do not understand, explain it to us clearly. Frankly, we already know enough to know that you have been hiding information from us rather than giving it to us straight."
"What you are asking for is a major change. We will have to study it. That will take time."	"We don't mind your studying the question, but we do mind stalling. Let's agree now on how long the study will take. Our experts tell us it should take no more than a week if you have knowledgeable people."
"We are willing to give this serious consideration. What we would like to do is establish a task force to review it and make recommendations. We would like several of your members to participate on that task force.	"We cannot agree to form any committee until you agree to our basic demands. Then, if there is to be an implementation committee, we must have equal representation on it."
"You are being too emotional about this."	"Of course we are emotional; this affects us deeply."
"Your demands are completely unrealistic."	"If they are so unrealistic why have they worked so well in five other cities? And why are they recommended by so many citizens and experts? Perhaps you are out of touch with reality. Or, perhaps reality has passed you by."
"If we let you get your way, we will be participating in policies that will harm everyone concerned. We cannot do that in good conscience.	"Don't you see? Just the opposite will happen. You will get credit for implementing a successful policy, for showing flexibility, for listening to the ordinary citizen."
"I know you hate me, but don't use other people and their issues to get at me."	"We have no interest in hurting you or your reputation. All we care about is how you respond to the issues at hand."

Know Your Constituency

If you do not like talking and listening to people, you can never be an organizer. Good organizers are willing to spend a lot of time talking with their constituencies, learning their issues, getting advice, and trying out ideas. Moreover, while an organizer can never live up to every group member's expectations, if he or she at least communicates effectively and often with the group, trust will likely develop.

Negotiators always have diverse constituencies. Some group members dislike confrontation of any kind and may regard negotiations as too confrontational, too adversarial. They may fear losing previous gains. On the other end of the spectrum, some group members usually feel that to negotiate is to sell out. To them, negotiation means compromise, and some people cannot accept compromise. Others respect and revere the opposition and wonder why you need to negotiate at all. Still others, hardened realists, see negotiations as one of many means to win some modest gains. They endorse negotiations fully.

The negotiator's constituency cannot possibly know all of the details and bargains that occur in the negotiating room. They therefore cannot possibly have quite the same perspective on negotiations as that of the negotiator. Thus they may not express as much support for the negotiator as he or she wants. It is not uncommon for negotiators to become embittered when they sense a lack of support. They feel caught between an inflexible opposition and a constituency that does not appreciate the difficulty of the struggle. In other words, the negotiator's constituency and opposition want their own way, and the negotiator feels trapped between them.

Because of the nature of the negotiation process, problems with a constituency are probably inevitable. Negotiators can only *try* to prevent them and *try* to deal with them as they arise. They probably cannot be eradicated altogether. Here are some useful strategies: negotiators should try not to be surprised if a member of the constituency "bad mouths" the negotiation team or a particular aspect of a negotiation package; negotiators should consciously maintain lines of communication with the constituency through press conferences, newsletters, special update meetings, and queries on issues; negotiators should work on building public support during negotiations; negotiators must be willing to lead, to make hard decisions, even if they will incur some resistance from within the constituency; negotiators must recognize that things they say and write will become public, and often will be misrepresented, misunderstood, or misinterpreted; negotiators should try to make only the most general commitments to the constituency, otherwise the constituency will develop expectations that cannot possibly be fulfilled; negotiators should encourage consensus building and unification in the constituency so as to make negotiations easier, and do not make any private "deals" with the opposition—these have a way of becoming public and such private agreements set the negotiator above the constituency.

Follow Up

Just as negotiations require planning and preparation, they also require follow-up. How often have we heard the complaint, "We won, but nothing has changed." Actually, negotiators can take specific measures to help ensure that a negotiated settlement get implemented:

1. Put the settlement or agreement in writing. Confirm it in correspondence with the opposition.
2. Publicize the agreement through press conferences, action bulletins, newsletters, etc.
3. Hold training sessions for the constituency on what the agreement means in practical terms.
4. Establish a timetable for implementation.
5. Formulate strategies to implement a settlement if the opposition fails to uphold the agreement (for example, demonstrations, boycotts, litigation).
6. Establish a means of monitoring and reporting on implementation.
7. Encourage the news media to do follow-up stories on implementation.
8. Invite outside experts to evaluate progress toward implementation.
9. Hold conferences, public hearings or similar forums to evaluate implementation.
10. Congratulate the opposition for successful implementation.

LOBBYING

Unlike negotiators, lobbyists do not confront their opposition directly. Rather, they deal with them through intermediaries, legislators, and the media. While lobbyists employ many of the same principles as negotiators—indeed their work is a type of negotiating—they practice a trade that has some unique characteristics. In a kind of informal sense, lobbying resembles litigation or arbitration. Lester Milbrath puts it this way: "Lobbying is the stimulation and transmission of a communication, by someone other than a citizen acting on his own behalf, directed at a governmental decision-maker with the hope of influencing his decision."[6] That is, lobbyists make their arguments to a third party, the legislator. We measure the lobbyists' effectiveness by the legislation they instigate or impede. The legislation is, in effect, a decision as to whose interests have prevailed, much like a court decision or an arbitrator's decree.[7]

Many principles inherent in negotiating also apply to lobbying. Lobbyists, for example, must know their constituency and its interests. They are, after all, intermediaries between the constituency and the legislative body, whose duty it is to translate constituency concerns into practical policies and programs. Clearly, lobbyists must prioritize and articulate issues. It is their job to bring issues to legislators' attention, to help shape the public agenda. Lobbyists gather evidence to support their agenda. They develop a plan for lobbying, construct defenses for arguments against their proposals, and try to locate sympathetic legislators. They also look for ways of convincing the unsympathetic (that is, they know the opposition), accept the fact that change occurs slowly, and demonstrate a willingness to compromise. They find ways of communicating the human import of their proposals (for example, how will it affect a single family) and communicate regularly and effectively with their constituency.

What makes lobbyists different from typical negotiators is the context in which they work. They need not convince or compel the opposition. Rather, they must convince a third party, namely legislators. More likely than not, lobbyists will not even try to lobby certain legislators if they believe them to be unalterably opposed to their cause. They need only win a majority.

In addition to those strategies which lobbyists share with the typical negotiator, they employ some which are unique to their style of negotiation. The following strategies are among those most commonly associated with lobbying:

1. *Location.* Lobbyists must locate themselves near the legislators whom they attempt to influence. Some organizations may locate their office far from the legislature but then hire representatives (lawyers, professional lobbyists, former legislators) who live and work near the legislature.

2. *Special Expertise.* Ideally, lobbyists should be informed on the issues about which they lobby. However, lobbyists generally agree that it is far more important for them to be expert about the legislative process and how to gain access to it than to be an expert on the substantive issues. This conclusion seems to be supported by the fact that many ex-legislators have gone into business as lobbyists. They know the legislative process, the personalities involved, and the form in which to articulate issues.

3. *Staff Support.* Lobbyists actually draft legislation. Their role, much like legislative staff, is to provide support for legislators. They not only state the constituency's concerns and place them on the public agenda, they also develop documentation to support those concerns, write actual draft legislation, and solicit support for the legislation among a broad range of legislators.

4. *Language.* Lobbyists must concern themselves even more than other types of negotiators with the language they use to characterize the causes they represent. Thus, for example, groups favoring abortion believe they can find greater support for their position (even win support from those who do not personally support abortion) by calling it a pro-choice position. Similarly, anti-abortion groups presumably hope to have their definition of the issue prevail when they call their cause pro-life—they thus accuse the opposition of a pro-death stance. Those who want pollution controls lobbied for the "Clean Air Act." That term, "clean air" was enormously popular. What legislator would want to be known for being against clean air? When lobbyists developed an act to mandate educational programming for children with disabilities, they might have encountered more resistance had they labelled their efforts "The federal mandate to educate handicapped children." States historically do not like mandates. The actual title of the law, "The Education for All Handicapped Children Act," had a more positive ring to it. Using the same reasoning, lobbyists may refuse to use the language of the opposition. Thus when the American Civil Liberties Union fought enactment of the Criminal Code Reform

Act because it objected to aspects of the proposed law which it felt would violate individual liberties—criticism was that it would give the government excessive power to curb protests and intimidate protest leaders—it constantly referred to the legislation as S-1. The term S-1, which stands for Senate Bill 1, has no positive connotations to it.

5. *Vote Watching.* Lobbyists can exert pressure on legislators by bringing their voting record to public attention. Thus many special interest groups keep track of legislators' voting records on certain issues and then develop ratings of legislators based on how they voted on key issues. The idea behind this is that legislators are generally concerned about keeping in good favor with their electorate. If politicians believe that a particular vote may jeopardize a significant portion of their constituency, they may change their vote.

6. *Surveys.* Lobbyists frequently poll their membership as well as the general population to find evidence that may sway a legislator.

7. *Advertisements, Awards, and Other Media Events.* Politicians receive countless awards from local interest groups. In some instances these awards reflect a group's appreciation for a legislator's voting record on some issues or for sponsorship of an issue. In other cases, groups give awards to politicians in hopes that the politician will then feel committed to working for the group's interests. Some groups endorse political candidates. Lobbyists and lobbies (the organizations for which lobbyists work) occasionally place full-page advertisements in newspapers and magazines to explain their position, to enlist contributions, to elicit public support, and to place legislators on notice that the issue they represent is on the public conscience. This is all part of the strategy to place an issue on the public agenda.

8. *Public Pressure.* Mailgrams, telephone calls, sending busloads of constituents to the legislatures to lobby all have a single purpose, that of pressuring legislators on an issue. Some legislators claim these face-to-face meetings with constituents and letter writing campaigns do little to sway their votes. They argue that such strategies simply reveal which groups are better organized and financed, not which groups represent the most people or what in the legislator's mind is right. On the other hand, there is no evidence that these strategies harm a cause and they may actually help. Many groups, ranging from pro- and anti-abortion forces, civil rights groups, environmentalists, and medical professionals use these strategies. The basic approach here is one of demonstrating a sizeable vocal concern.

9. *Action Packets.* Lobbyists must concern themselves both with politicians and grass roots support. Their greatest source of persuasion with politicians is either the monied interests they represent (something few public interest groups have in great supply) and/or the voter sympathies they can claim.[8] Thus lobbyists work with their organizations to develop packets on how to organize local groups, how to start local issue campaigns, how to engage in local fundraising, and how to organize fact sheets on the issues that concern them. National organizations generally develop a national strategy (for example, passage of the Clean Air Act; a campaign to pass the Civil Rights Act) that includes petition drives, public forums, lobbying of legisla-

tors, letter writing campaigns, appearances of advocates on radio and television talk shows, and distribution of fact sheets and background statements. Through each of these mediums, groups stress statistics (who is affected by the issue, what are the costs involved), the proposed model legislation, how the legislation will help individuals, and the dangers that may arise if the legislature fails to act positively on the group's agenda.

10. *Coalition Building.* A few exceptional lobbies have been inordinately influential on their own, without the assistance of other groups and constituencies. The so-called "China lobby," which worked for years to persuade the U.S. Congress that failure to support the Taiwan government of Chiang Kai-shek was tantamount to aiding and abetting the communists, (i.e., The People's Republic of China) was such an exception. Similarly, the Israeli lobby has had enormous influence over U.S. foreign policy. Another influential single issue group is the National Rifle Association which opposes any form of gun control. Despite the success of these few single-issue interest groups, most such groups find it expedient to join forces with diverse other special interests, even when it requires compromises, in order to win support. Thus national and local organizations engage in coalition building. For instance, peace groups join with civil rights organizations, unions and church organizations to lobby for reduced military expenditures and greater domestic programs. Indeed, legislators have criticized single issue groups for their narrowness. Partly because their numbers are smaller than broad based coalitions and partly because they tend to be more inflexible on the issues than are coalitions, politicians apparently feel free to challenge their legitimacy. Politicians know quite well that as a general rule, the public does not assess legislators' performance on the basis of how he or she voted in a single issue area. Lobbyists and legislators generally agree that political power or the legislator's perception of political power plays a major role in legislative decision making. Thus the issue is not so much whether a group adheres to single issue or coalition politics. Rather, the issue is whether the group possesses sufficient political force, usually measured in numbers and wealth, to make its case persuasive.

NOTES

[1]Nils Christie, "Conflicts as property," *The British Journal of Criminology,* vol. 17, no. 1, January 1977, pp. 1–15.

[2]Christie, "Conflicts," p. 3.

[3]Christie, "Conflicts," p. 4.

[4]James Feron, "Law Offices Become Courtroom for Small Civil Suits," *The New York Times,* February 25, 1980.

[5]Despite its popularity as an action strategy in community organizing, surprisingly few practical resources exist on the topic. Readers interested in theoretical and practical perspectives on negotiations may want to explore literature on collective bargaining (union/employer negotiations). While collective bargaining tend to be a more formalized process than the negotiations model discussed here, this literature comes closest to addressing the topic of negotiations as a social change activity. See, for example, Richard E. Walton and Robert B. McKersie, *A Behavioral Theory of Labor Negotiations* (New York: McGraw-Hill); Terence F. Connors, *Problems in Local Union Collective Bargaining* (Detroit, MI:

UAW Education Department, Solidarity House, N.D.); and Thomas A. Kochan, *Collective Bargaining and Industrial Relations* (Homewood, IL: Irwin-Dorsey, 1980). For a more general treatment of negotiations, see I. William Zartman (ed.), *The Negotiation Process: Theories and Applications* (Beverly Hills: Sage Publications, Inc., 1978) and *The Art of Negotiation Newsletter*, 230 Park Avenue, New York, NY 10169.

[6]Lester W. Milbrath, *The Washington Lobbyists* (Chicago: Rand McNally, 1963), p. 8.

[7]For case studies of lobbying efforts see Norma J. Ornstein and Shirley Elder, *Interest Groups, Lobbying and Policymaking* (Washington, D.C.: Congressional Quarterly Press, 1978) and Jeffrey M. Berry, *Lobbying for the People: The Political Behavior of Public Interest Groups* (Princeton, NJ: Princeton University Press, 1977).

[8]Most lobbyists do not represent the average citizen. Instead, most represent major corporations, banks, public institutions, foreign governments, and truly moneyed interests. See for example: Russell Warren Howe and Sarah Hays Trott, *The Power Peddlers: How Lobbyists Mold America's Foreign Policy* (Garden City, NY: Doubleday and Company, 1977) and Mark J. Green, *The Other Government: The Unseen Power of Washington Lawyers* (New York, NY: W. W. Norton & Co., Inc., 1978).

CHAPTER TEN
ACTION RESEARCH

THE MANY FACES OF ACTION RESEARCH

Surplus Children

Kenneth Wooden set out across the country to investigate services for unwanted, delinquent, homeless, retarded, and other "surplus" children. The results of his investigation revealed a scandalous situation. He found, among other things, a national practice of "shipping" children from one state to another. Here is how he tells it:

Interstate Commerce of Children:
There is in this country a mushrooming multi-million-dollar industry that thrives on the interstate commerce of dependent and neglected children. In air terminals across the land, these children, over 15,000 in number, usually poor, of minority background and rejected by local private child-care facilities, stand with their state guardians, waiting to travel hundreds, even thousands of miles away from family and friends: Virginia sends them to Idaho; Idaho sends them to Virginia; Arizona ships them to Texas, California and Colorado; Colorado sends them to Arizona. Alaska sends it legal wards to five different states. In all, I have found twenty-eight states who admit to interstate commerce of children. Theoretically, the youngsters' destinations are private treatment centers where they will have a home and care. In reality, this care amounts to that given to cattle or a precious commodity, assuring the continuation of a profit-making scheme.[1]

Wooden described in detail this system and its treatment of children. In some instances youngsters were kept in private residential centers for a cost of three to four dollars per day, yet states paid the agencies twenty-three dollars per day. In some so-called "residential settings" children were fed potatoes, bread and other starches as a total diet. Some were denied any educational services for years at a time, and some found themselves locked in isolation cells or subjected to noxious "treatments." Wooden's account was one of several that led to congressional investigations, further exposés on television, most notably by CBS's *Sixty Minutes,* and to litigation aimed at putting a stop to interstate commerce of children. While there is no way of knowing the precise impact of Wooden's report, it clearly contributed to a growing movement to change America's treatment of children.

Drugged Children

In 1975, between 500,000 and 1,000,000 school age children were receiving "amphetamine type drugs and other psycho-stimulants by prescription."[2] In 1969, a New York physician, Arnold Hutschnecker, recommended a national screening program to predict which youngsters would become delinquents. He proposed this plan despite the inability of scientists to predict which children would or would not become delinquent. Also, during the early 1970s numerous special education experts suggested that fully as many as 40 percent of all school children possessed learning disabilities. These are some of the startling facts revealed in Peter Schrag and Diane Divoky's shocking exposé, *The Myth of the Hyperactive Child.* The book shows how learning disabilities, while a well-intentioned concept, has taken on the characteristics of a growth industry. The people who profit from it are often not the children whom the movement purports to serve.

This study along with several television reports and a growing parent consciousness raised serious questions about what initially seemed to be an unstoppable, potentially dangerous therapeutic juggernaut.

Blood Banks

Robert Massie, Sr.'s son has hemophilia. The cost of providing transfusions for Robert, Jr. are enormous, from ten to twenty thousand dollars per year. When AHF Fraction became available to help control the bleeding of people with hemophilia, the Massies were hopeful. A *Wall Street Journal* article read, "Medical researchers believe that they are coming close to controlling hemophilia." But upon researching the politics behind AHF, Robert Massie, Sr. found that despite the fact that AHF Fraction research had been funded principally by the Red Cross and the National Institute of Health (a federal agency supported by taxpayers), the "miracle medicine" would be sold at exorbitant rates by commerical drug manufactures. Thus the miracle of science would fail to reach poor people and those without adequate medical insurance. In the words of Robert Massie, Sr., "Even today the daily shot still is not widely available because it costs too much. The hemophiliacs continue to bleed."[3] Robert and Suzanne Massie tell their story in their action research-autobiography, *Journey.* As a result of this and similar exposés some states passed catastrophic illness insurance coverage to protect children.

Nursing Homes

In 1964, Mary Adelaide Mendelson began a job that, ten years later, led to a major book exposing the nursing home industry. *Tender Loving Greed* rocked the nursing home industry.[4] Ms. Mendelson uncovered nursing home operator families that owned the pharmacies from which their nursing homes purchased drugs at exorbitant rates. She reported on one operator who filed a tax write-off for an elaborate sprinkler system when in fact all that had been installed were the nozzles for such a system, a cruel ruse perpetrated on the elderly patients who resided in the home. She exposed the relationship of medical doctors to the success of some nursing homes: "When the (Four Seasons Nursing Home) chain was going to build a nursing home in a community, it got local doctors to invest in the operation, so their referrals would add to the return on their own investment."[5] She also discovered that nursing homes were sometimes sold and resold repeatedly among family members to inflate the "worth" of a home, thus making them eligible for higher medicaid and medicare reimbursements.

Mary Adelaide Mendelson's research paved the way for congressional and state investigation of the nursing home industry. Her book became a kind of citizens' guide to understanding nursing home abuses.

Famous Writers, Undertakers, and Prison Wardens

When Jessica Mitford investigated the highly successful Famous Writers School, a mail order correspondence learn-to-be-a-writer program, she had no expectation that the School would be forced into bankruptcy two years after her exposé hit the newsstands. (A decade later it was to make a comeback.) Among other things, she discovered that students rarely if ever had their writing analyzed by a famous writer. Noted authors like Bennett Cerf, Rod Serling, and the others were merely window dressing, whose role it was to promote the school. She also learned that the school profitted enormously from its students' high dropout rate. In the words of Famous Writer Phyllis McGinley, " 'We couldn't make any money if all the students finished.' "[6] Jessica Mitford also found that in 1966, when total earnings reached $28,000,000—they would reach $48,000,000 by 1969—one-third, or $10,000,000 was spent on advertising, selling the school to prospective students. After publishing her humorous but devastating article, "Let Us Now Appraise Famous Writers," in *Atlantic Monthly*, Jessica Mitford learned from a letter to the editor that comments on students' papers were actually stored on the corporate computer. Instructors would read the papers and then identify by a number code the criticism paragraphs to be incorporated into letters to the students. Meanwhile, students believed that they were being treated individually and personally by famous writers.

Jessica Mitford's fame has spread with each of her biting critiques of American institutions. Her book, *The American Way of Death*, exposed the funeral business. *Kind and Usual Punishment* unveiled prisons in a way that left abuses of the corrections industry naked.

ACTION RESEARCH DEFINED

Mendelson, Wooden, Mitford, Schrag and Divoky, and the Massies practice a common trade, action research. It is an action strategy that, as these cited examples demonstrate, can transform a public's consciousness. In contrast to the thousands upon thousands of government and academic studies which often end up on someone's shelf, gathering dust, influencing little, action research calls out, even to those who might rather not hear, for attention, for recognition, and for action. When done well, action research reports take on a life of their own, playing on the consciences of policy makers, buoying up those with problems, crying out for change.

In recent years, research in general has come under harsh criticism for its apparent failure to effectively address public policy needs. In their book, *Useable Knowledge: Social Science and Social Problem Solving,* Lindblom and Cohen cite a study which indicates that policy makers cannot point to particular studies which directly caused them to make particular decisions.[7] In defense of research, or what Lindblom and Cohen call professional social inquiry, they suggest that research may have a major, if unheralded, impact on the long-range shape of policy:

> It may be that the principal impact of policy-oriented studies, say, on inflation, race conflict, deviance, or foreign policy—including those specifically designed to advise a specific policy maker at a particular time—is through their contribution to a cumulating set of incentives (study upon study with like results) for a general reconsideration by policy makers of their decision-making framework, their operating political or social philosophy, or their ideology.[8]

In other words, when researchers amass enough evidence, in study after study, they can topple a whole way of thinking, but it is a slow process. This may suggest a bias among policy makers, that they are more comfortable with the traditional and accepted than the new and controversial. It also probably reflects certain other characteristics of traditional policy research and its sponsors.

The way we define social research clearly limits what policy makers consider legitimate and influential. While at first glance social research seems to include a broad range of activities, traditional social research is, in fact, defined narrowly. It does not include what we call action research. Again, we turn to Lindblom and Cohen for a description of what social research entails. They distinguish "professional social inquiry" from general academic (social science) research in that professional social inquiry is not designed to extend theory, to find causal explanations for social phenomena or to relate present investigations to an extensive body of preexisting research literature. Lindblom and Cohen define professional social inquiry or what we call policy research as research which uses social science methodology, which is carried out by professionals, and which seeks to be authoritative.[9] As we will see, action research differs from traditional policy research on all three counts. The examples they give for professional social inquiry are:

> evaluation studies carried out in profit-making firms; opinion research in commercial survey organizations; university-trained policy; analysts working in government of-

fices; newspaper and TV reporters specialized in some aspect of social science germane to their beats; development and dissemination work aimed at solving social problems carried out in specialized R & D "laboratories" in education or mental health.[10]

In contrast, action research need not be carried out by such established groups or traditionally trained professionals. It need not and often does not follow the strictures of social science methodology. Additionally, action research values influence more than authoritativeness.

In addition to challenging conventions of who may do policy research, how policy research is done, and to what end, action research does not subscribe to the notion that research is or should be independent and neutral. In this respect it resembles policy research. All research, whether traditional policy research or action research, reflects particular interests. The very choice of problems to study indicates research's political nature. To the extent that the definition of any set of objective phenomena as a social problem reflects particular viewpoints and interests, study of that problem also reflects those or opposing interests. We could, after all, choose to study something else. Interests, whether for or against, make something "worth" studying. In the words of Lindblom and Cohen, policy research fits into an active, not passive or neutral context:

> PSI (Professional Social Inquiry) would perhaps appropriately aspire to serve a nonpartisan user if policy were made by a hypothetical policy maker pursuing the "public interest." But policy is actually made not by a policy maker but by interaction among a plurality of partisans. Each participant in the interaction, as noted above, needs information specialized to his partisan role in it.[11]

The tendency for traditional research is to represent dominant social interests or the interests of its sponsors. This can be seen in evaluation research sponsored by the Department of Housing and Urban Development on community development block grants. The well-known Brookings Institute received nearly two million dollars to examine this program. Critics charge that the Brookings studies understated controversial findings, focused more on issues of process than of substance (for example, who are the program's big winners? who does the program not help?), and found what it wanted to find. As one Brookings study co-author put it, "The general style of the Brookings reports was to make no waves, probably because the data wasn't good enough, but also because of the bias toward the New Federalism (a Nixon presidency strategy) and decentralization."[12]

The atmosphere in which researchers do their work is hardly neutral. As long as policy research understates the controversial, ignores the substantive, and holds to conventional beliefs it may seem neutral enough. It is a different matter, however, scientists, or anyone else for that matter, use research for action. We note (see chapter on whistle-blowing) for example, the ostracism faced by Drs. Gofman and Tamplin when their research led them to challenge the Atomic Energy Commission and industry standards for exposure to radiation. In their book entitled *Poisoned Power,* Gofman and Tamplin charge that exposure of the population to "permissible" radiation levels could lead to 32,000 additional cancer deaths a year and hundreds of thousands of increased miscarriages and deaths at birth.[13] That finding has won them only retribution:

> The Gofman-Tamplin findings were considered "heresy" by the AEC. Within months the responses came. The head of the NCRP (National Council on Radiation Protection) completely rejected their conclusions. In a well documented pattern of both petty and substantial harassment, the AEC had their staff "reassigned" and refused to pay them for days spent at meetings where they might be testifying about AEC laxity on the radiation-protection front. Meanwhile, other AEC staff were paid for attendance at meetings where they gave the correct "line" on radiation dangers—no problem.[14]

That kind of reaction by official agency personnel is not unfamiliar to action researchers. As Ralph Nader notes, "For many years, the industry (chemical industry) ridiculed the suggestion that synthetics might pose health hazards."[15] The petrochemical industry's critics were romantics who lacked scientific data to back them up. Today, as the damaging evidence accumulates, the critics are being taken more and more seriously.

Action researchers recognize that in the final analysis only their accuracy can defend their integrity. At the outset of any research project, they of course make a decision about what is worth studying. Action researchers, like all social researchers, work on problems which are bascially located in a political context. However, once they have chosen their focus for study, action researchers take pains to report their findings accurately. One action researcher, whose work involved preparing reports of mental hospitals and mental retardation institutions for community groups and legal services corporations which were developing litigation to protect the rights of institutional inmates, speaks to the issue of accuracy in this way:

> These reports are not intended to yield an "objective" view of a facility, if "objective" means devoting equal attention to the positive and negative aspects of a facility. Institutional brochures, press releases, public statements always paint a positive picture of the setting. As a monitoring strategy, descriptive reports should be oriented to violations of legal and moral rights—things that are seldom reported and that need to be changed. Given this orientation, the observer should report his or her observations as honestly, completely, and objectively as possible.[16]

Similarly, action researcher Jessica Mitford perceives accuracy as inviolable and objectivity as more a matter of theatrics. She suggests a special benefit (in terms of social change value) in projecting an air of objectivity or neutrality around the research findings:

> Accuracy is essential, not only to the integrity of your work but to avoid actionable defamation. It can be ruinous to try to tailor the evidence to fit your preconceptions, or to let your point of view impede the search for facts.
>   But I do try to cultivate the appearance of objectivity, mainly through the technique of understatement, avoidance where possible of editorial comment, above

all letting the undertakers, or the Spock prosecutors, or the prison administrators pillory themselves through their own pronouncements.[17]

Just as action research challenges traditional notions about "value-neutral research" it also challenges many other conventions. Therein lies both its controversy and appeal. Action research, as its name suggests, links research to action. It has the professed purpose of promoting dissent and fomenting change. Often, it reveals needs and issues that have heretofore remained unstudied or even masked. It brings accountability to major social institutions that might prefer no monitoring at all. Financially, it is considerably less expensive than traditional policy research. Unlike conventional policy research, action research involves consumers and non-professionals as well as so-called professionals. Doctors, scientists, social workers, service consumers, and interested citizens alike can use it. In contrast to the wanderlust quality of so much social research, action research invariably has a specific focus both in terms of topic and future change orientation. It asks questions of consequence to certain groups in the population. It combines multiple types of data sources. It demystifies obscure and hard-to-understand information. It usually makes waves, and it is frequently both dramatic and humorous.

The Subjects of Action Research

Dan Wakefield once wrote an article for the *Atlantic Monthly* about his mentor at Columbia University, the famous radical sociologist C. Wright Mills. Mills was a sociologist who spoke in common-sense terms about important social concerns. In *Sociological Imagination* he unveiled the simple and powerful distinction between private troubles and public issues. In *Power Elite* he presented an extraordinarily controversial (for its time) exposé of the symbiotic and antidemocratic relationship of wealth, status, and power. His other works, particularly *Listen, Yankee* and *White Collar* were no less influential. Where most sociologists studied the vulnerable and presumably deviant (that is, poor people, minorities), Mills studied issues of poverty and oppression by looking at middle class and elite groups. In his personal account, Dan Wakefield describes a memorable scene, one that deserves repeating.

Mills always encouraged his students to take on important research topics, ones that would not only analyze but also influence the world. He disdained the trivial. He implored all to "take it big," as if to say, "Take important subjects and do them in a major way." The incident Wakefield recounts makes the issue plain:

He told me about attending a party of Columbia graduate students in sociology, and his account of it seemed to sum up the relations he had reached with his scholarly profession:
    "I simply sat in a chair in a corner," he said, "and one by one these guys would come up to me, sort of like approaching the pariah—curiosity stuff. They were guys working on their Ph.D.'s, you see, and after they'd introduced themselves I'd ask, 'What are you working on?' It would always be something like 'The Impact of Work-Play Relationships Among Lower Income Families on the South Side of the

Block on 112th Street Between Amsterdam and Broadway.' And then I would ask—''
Mills paused, leaned forward, and in his most contemptuous voice, boomed:
"WHY?"
        He was working himself then on The Causes of World War III, a subject he
considered worthy of the attention of "a full-grown man."[18]

Like C. Wright Mills, action researchers believe in asking questions of consequence. They ask how many millions of children have been excluded from schooling. They ask why America operates large, self-contained, and remarkably abusive
institutions for vulnerable people. They ask how toxic chemical dumps will affect
the health of their neighbors. They ask whether prisons protect or endanger society.
And they ask who benefits most from community development funds. Each action
research study cited in this chapter confirms the simple fact that action researchers
waste no time on the trivial and inconsequential. They choose important and immediate concerns.

        The case of action researchers at Love Canal demonstrates this fact. Love
Canal is a section of the Buffalo, Niagara Falls area where Hooker Chemical
Company dumped chemical wastes, including the dangerous carcinogen dioxin. At
the time, during World War II, the country did not yet have standards for disposing
of toxic wastes. Chemical companies routinely used vacant properties and water-
ways to get rid of potentially hazardous materials. At Love Canal, Hooker deposited
several hundred tons of waste. In 1976 families whose homes were located on the
old dumpsite, something they did not know, began to see chemical seepage into
their basements. The residents' first response was to try to pump the black sludge-
like material out of their drain pipes with sump pumps. The Health Department told
them that that was against the law. Yet the families learned through a newspaper
investigation that the chemicals were also hazardous to their health, particularly to
the health of children and pregnant women. They were getting mixed messages.
Mokhiber and Shen report that one Niagara County Health Department official
warned the families: (1) not to pump the chemical sludge out of their homes; (2) to
wait for the officials to take corrective action; and (3) to keep children away from
the material.[19] Meanwhile, Hooker Chemical officials avoided commenting on the
situation.[20] The families became frantic. They were at once besieged by toxic
chemicals in their homes and by official inaction and contradiction in the community.

        It was not long before the various official study groups looking into the Love
Canal situation began to turn up uncontrovertible and altogether unsettling evidence. Mokhiber and Shen summarize some of those initial findings:

> Surveys begun by the New York State Department of Health (DOH) in the spring
> found that 95 percent of the homes in the first ring of those constructed around the
> canal were contaminated by chemicals. The EPA determined in May that the toxic
> vapors in the basements presented "a serious health threat." What's more, people
> living near the former dumpsite were experiencing as many as 3.5 times the expected
> number of miscarriages, as well as a disproportionate number of birth defects and

spontaneous abortions. The state found that the women who suffered miscarriages had lived at the canal an average of about 18.5 years—7 years longer than the average for women who didn't miscarry.[21]

The families wanted out of their homes at Love Canal, but few had money enough to walk away from them, however dangerous. They formed the Love Canal Homeowners Association, the primary purpose of which was to force state agencies to admit to the hazard and to finance a full scale evacuation of families in the area. But the State was unwilling to buy up the homes of more than the 100 closest families to the Love Canal dumpsite. The State Health Commissioner did call for all young children and pregnant women to leave the area immediately.

But what was to happen to the rest of the families? Would they be forgotten? Would they be forced, by virtue of their modest economic means, to live on in the midst of a chemical wasteland? The national news media were, by now, focusing considerable attention on how the Love Canal situation would be resolved and recognized its importance as a precedent-setting case. It was but the first of what promised to become an explosion of confrontations across the country between citizens and industrial, chemical and nuclear waste polluters.

The families relied largely on their own resources. The Love Canal Homeowners Association became their organizing vehicle. They steeled themselves for a long and bitter struggle with official agencies that seemed determined to minimize the costs involved in confronting the problem. There were too many instances of official foot-dragging and avoidance for the homeowners to feel confident that the officials would handle the chemical waste situation competently. According to Murray Levine, a State University professsor who studied the controversy, the homeowners were distrustful when the governor announced, even before the State Health Study was completed, that only 100 homes would be purchased and evacuated.[22] Although the governor did say the State would take further action if test results showed dangers in other area homes, the families were already skeptical since officials had previously given them double messages about how dangerous the chemicals were. Moreover, the parents were angry that school officials did not move immediately to close an elementary school that had been built on the Love Canal site. However, they were most upset that state officials seemed unwilling to admit that many families who lived away from the dumpsite were as sick as those literally on top of it. Professor Levine tells the story: "Lois Gibbs lived a number of streets away, but ever since her son Michael started to go to school, he had been ill. He had bladder difficulties, and epilepsy, both illnesses which could have been caused by toxic chemicals, according to . . . Niagara Gazette stories."[23] Mrs. Gibbs' first reaction was to try to have her son transferred to another school. When the school board refused on the grounds that it could not provide special treatment to her child, she began a petition drive among neighbors to close down the school. "She was soon overwhelmed with the tales of illness she was hearing, not only among those who lived directly on the canal, but among those who lived several blocks away as well."[24] Unlike professional researchers, Mrs. Gibbs had no training in research methods. But like the best researchers, she let the data speak for itself:

> Mrs. Gibbs recalls coming home from a meeting and sitting in her kitchen at 2:00 AM, puzzling about what to do. . . . She took out her notebook and began putting pins in a street map to indicate the location of homes with ill family members. Much to her surprise the pins clustered in several wavering lines, and in the southwest corner of the map. The next day she showed the map to some old time Love Canal residents who told her the illnesses clustered along the pathway of underground drainage ditches, called swales, that ran off the canal. One area, the southwest corner, had been swampy land that had been filled in by developers.[25]

The family researchers, led by Mrs. Gibbs, found little support for their findings when they took them to the Health Department. However, they did find a receptive ear in Dr. Beverly Paigen at Roswell Park Memorial Hospital. With the doctor's assistance, the Homeowners Association did a complete and systematic survey of the community's health problems. The results confirmed the more informally gathered results of Homeowner Association President Gibbs. The health problems were greatest along the drainage lines and in wet areas:

> Women living in wet areas reported three times as many miscarriages as they had had before moving to the canal area. These miscarriages constituted 25 percent of all pregnancies in wet-area women. The survey determined that nine of the sixteen children—56 percent of the children—born to women living at wet areas of the canal from 1974 to 1978 had birth defects. The survey also found increased risks of nervous-system problems, respiratory disorders and urinary illness for families living in the wet-area homes.[26]

With accurate information in hand, the parents had ammunition for their press conferences, letters to the editor, public debates, and public speeches. Eventually, health officials accepted the families' "swale theory." Action research had carried the day. Largely through a community's own organizing, including exemplary action research, what began as an issue of considerable consequence to a few hundred families became a matter of consequence to communities everywhere.

ACTION RESEARCH STRATEGIES

By Their Own Petard

In the book *Whistle Blowing,* Ralph Nader and his colleagues describe with seeming delight the possibility of judging official or institutional practice by its own standards. They call this strategy "by their own petard." Jessica Mitford seems to mean the same thing when she speaks of allowing officials to pillory themselves. Whatever we call it, it is a strategy that is certain to anger those against whom it is applied. However, it is also guaranteed to make a point.

Action researchers like using this strategy because it obviates the need to create elaborate justifications for alternative standards. Moreover, if a point can be made simply by using standards that the opposition itself professes, the problem of having our standards rejected or discredited is avoided. Perhaps most importantly, official standards often provide a stark contrast to action research findings and thus help to dramatize the issue.

In one of our own action research projects, in which we sought evidence on the extent and nature of human abuse in retardation and mental health institutions, we used this strategy extensively. Our group of twenty-five teachers, social planners, and sociologists divided up into groups of two and three to carry out three day observational forays into the institutions. We went to the directors' offices as well as the back wards. We heard official explanations and saw day-to-day realities. We spoke with consumers and treatment staff alike. By the time we returned from our rounds of observation, each researcher had brought back between thirty and fifty pages of notes detailing statistical information, conversations, and incidents observed. Included in the "raw data" were some official standards against which we could measure our findings.

At one institution we picked up an official brochure. It described the institution to the public and, apparently, to the parents and families of current and prospective residents. The institution was described presumably as officials believed it should be described. On the cover was a picture of two adults, probably parents, and a young boy, most likely their son, with suitcase in hand, walking toward the institution's main entrance. It was a picture of parents bringing their child to the institution. Inside the brochure were pictures of sparkling facilities and of attentive staff interactions with residents. It presented a promising vision of life on the inside. The text of the brochure was no less glowing, though perhaps somewhat defensive:

> For none is it [the institution] a dungeon of oblivion and neglect, walled up against the rest of the world. Rather it is a place of devotion and dedication which draws upon the good will, resources and services of society and, in turn, contributes to the benefit and welfare of that same society.[27]

The brochure, and particularly this statement, in Nader's word was the official "petard." It stood in the starkest contrast to the reality we recorded in observational notes. At this same institution, we found some residents locked in isolation cells. One emaciated woman whom we observed and photographed was tied to a bed, held down by a restraining sheet. She had been so restrained for eleven years, according to staff accounts. In one room, staff showed us the residents' "death packs," fresh dresses and suits laying in waiting for when the residents would die. Outside the institutional buildings we were shown a burial area comprised of circular headstones lying flat on the ground with numbers on each. When someone dies at this institution, the staff bring out the post-hole digger and dig a cylindrical grave. At this same institution, in the infant nursery, we observed groups of severely disabled youngsters lying on mats on the floor. We observed no systematic programming for them. In a subsequent study of the infant nurseries, another researcher found that if babies of 25 pounds had not yet learned to walk they were transferred to an infirmary where they were kept bedridden, never again to be exposed to an opportunity to walk. These and other observations of institutional life, measured against official claims (for example, "for none is it a dungeon of oblivion and neglect"), formed the core of a series of action research reports designed to discredit institutions as an appropriate placement for children.[28] Those reports became the basis for forming a national center to promote service alternatives to institutions.[29] That data was later used in a position paper on the question of deinstitutionalization which served as an organizing tool nationally.[30]

To cite one more example of the "by their own petard" strategy of standard-setting and action research monitoring, note the case of a national survey undertaken by the National Committee for Citizens in Education. This group, which includes professionals in the field of education and consumers of educational services (parents and students), has long advocated a variety of consumer rights reforms in education. It is perhaps best known for its pivotal role in helping to formulate and pass the Family Rights and Privacy Act (also called the Buckley Amendment after its chief sponsor, former Senator James Buckley), which gives students the right to see their own public school files. More recently, NCCE joined with Ohio State University to survey how well school districts were meeting their obligation under federal special education laws to involve parents in planning their children's "individual education program." In a survey of parents, they found numerous areas of noncompliance. By law, school districts were supposed to prepare the individual education plan *with* parents. That was the official standard. However, 52 percent of the parents responding to the survey said that the plan was completed by the school officials before the parents ever arrived to "participate." Federal law required that the plan include specific information about how much time a child with a disability would spend in a regular classroom with nondisabled classmates—another official standard. Yet thirty percent of the respondents said their children's individual education plans did *not* include this information. Perhaps most important of all, the law provides that school districts must inform parents of their right to formally appeal the results of an evaluation of their children. Again, many officials failed to live up to the official standard. More than half of the families participating in the study reported not being informed of their right to appeal an evaluation. NCCE disclosed the preliminary results of its national action research on parent involvement in individual education plans simultaneously through a press release and testimony before members of the House (Congress) Subcommittee on Select Education.

Clearly, the "by their own petard" strategy of standard setting makes action research more appealing to the public than might otherwise be the case. In adopting official standards, action researchers give their research an immediate air of respectability. They align their work with legitimate authority. At the same time, in accepting or at least giving the appearance of accepting official standards, action researchers seem to be saying, "we do not argue with the system's goals, we only argue with its results." That stance immediately places officials on the defensive. Do they or do they not believe in their own standards? Have they lied to the public? If they have lied to the public, can they be trusted in the future? If they have failed to adhere to one set of official standards, does this mean they have failed in other areas as well? Once even a single official action is in question, it suddenly becomes more legitimate and less radical for action researchers to ask other questions. Even if there is no evidence of additional misconduct, action researchers find they can ask questions which, had they been asked previously, would have seemed unfair, disrespectful, and perhaps characteristic of a witch-hunt.

Finally, the "by their own petard" strategy puts officials in the role of deviants. By not meeting their own standards they fail to meet the standards they have told the public it should expect. Measured by their own yardstick, officials have only two defenses. One is that they can admit the problem and accept the action researchers' or anyone else's recommendations for change. Their second defense is to discredit the study by other means. Common discrediting strategies include personal attacks on the researchers (for example, labelling them as disgruntled employees with a vendetta), finding fault with a single fact in the study and using this as an excuse for questioning its complete accuracy, and suggesting that the action researchers do not have professional training. Other strategies used are asserting that the action researchers have employed a faulty research methodology, suggesting that the action researchers could not possibly have all the evidence (and that "all the evidence" can only be garnered by years of expert experience in the field or by access to confidential data), and claiming that the action researchers have not taken into account recent organizational changes which make the action researchers' findings no longer valid. Ideally, the action researcher will be prepared for such ploys. In fact, we can often respond to such criticisms even before they surface by stating the researchers' credentials, by having the methodology certified by an expert, by identifying all the evidence, and by requesting all other evidence be provided by the appropriate officials.

Consumers Speak

Action researchers use standard kinds of research data such as answers to survey questions, statistics, government and private study reports, policy memoranda, and observational notes. However, action researchers legitimize the consumer's perspective as data to a far greater extent than most formal or so-called policy research. Action researchers let consumers speak.

When the Washington, D.C.-based Children's Defense Fund, a kind of professional lobby for children's interests and rights, announced its national study of Children Out of School in America (school exclusion and school dropouts), the nation was shocked by the report's statistical data. The Children's Defense Fund announced that two million children in America did not attend schools. The reasons were numerous. Schools were telling poor children that if they could not pay for their books they could not attend. Some were excluding pregnant teenagers as bad influences. Others felt they had no obligation to educate disabled students. Some children were found to be working to support their families, thus making it also impossible for them to attend school. Others never made it to school because they had no way of getting there. Still others found that the school was unwilling to provide bilingual education; hence, they had no way of participating effectively in schools. These latter children either dropped out or were pushed out.

The two-million exclusion figure shocked policy makers, educators, legislators, and citizens because it contradicted our belief that all children are being provided an education. Indeed, if education was compulsory, why were so many children not compelled to attend school? Statistics, official memoranda, government studies, and answers to survey questions told only part of the story. To really understand the nature of the school exclusion issue and its implications for children and their families, we need to hear from the consumers themselves. The Children's Defense Fund understood this fact. It gives us case after case of individual description and testimony. Here are a few examples:

Theresa, 12

Theresa Engler, a 12-year-old black girl from one of Boston's poorest neighborhoods, had been absent from school. No one took much notice of Theresa's absence of several days in October. In November, her teacher reported that she had returned to school but had been absent quite often for weeks thereafter. She had never spoken with her about the absences, or whether the girl was in danger of failing because of them. "There's no time," her teacher said, "I've got twenty-six Theresas.". . .

Theresa's grandmother knew what was wrong. "She won't go because she's ashamed that we ain't got anything, in the way of material things I mean." . . .

"She used to like to talk in class. But then the teacher started to ask the children about their homes and their families, and what it was like outside of school. She knew they'd get around to her and she'd have to tell them about this house, and the street, and us too. She must have got scared, or ashamed, . . . She couldn't do it. I think that's when she stopped going."[32]

Kenny, 14

Kenny is a 14-year-old black child in Canton, Mississippi. The last time he was in school was in the 3rd grade. The reason: he is partially sighted. He is a quiet, sensitive child, shy and often hesitant because of his handicap. His teachers had little sympathy for him. One slapped him on the head when he didn't move out of her way fast enough. Another told his mother that she "didn't have the time or the patience to teach him." When a third teacher teased Kenny and called him "a fool," his mother took him out of school. "I asked the principal and the teacher who had struck Kenny why they didn't have the time to teach him." No justifiable answer was given. . . .

"I want the school to prepare a class or program to meet Kenny's needs without making him embarrassed. Most of all I want him to have an education so that he will be able to get a job to support himself. I don't know what he's going to do when I'm no longer with him."[33]

Maxine, 14

Maxine Dolan is 14 and has an eight-month-old son. . . .

She . . . wants to return to the school that suspended her when they learned she was pregnant and that remains unwilling to let her return on the grounds that she now represents a dangerous influence to other girls. "What do they think I'm going to do in that school—teach everybody to make babies? They think all us girls don't want anything but just to get pregnant. They think that's all we're doing, making babies." . . .

"I'm his mama and there nothing I'd rather be, but I'm still sorry that they made me leave the school, even if I did make a mistake. My baby would be better off if they let me go back, but all they can think about is that there ain't no mama going to school."[34]

Since action researchers consider the public their audience, consumer perspectives go a long way toward popularizing otherwise dry material. For example, when investigative reporter and action researcher Betty Medsger set out to write an article on the wheelchair industry, she made sure to gather first-hand testimony from wheelchair users along with the industry's own reports, statistics, and promotional claims, as well as government reports and memoranda. In her article entitled, "The Most Captive Consumer," she confirmed the findings of an earlier action research report by the Disability Rights Center and claims made by the activist Center for Independent Living in California.[35] She found substantial evidence that just a few companies monopolized wheelchair sales in America, that basic wheelchair design had remained stagnant for over thirty years, that many wheelchair products were unreliable and prone to breakdowns, that consumers had difficulty securing spare parts, and that the government was dragging its feet in dealing with these problems. She introduced the issue by recounting the experiences of one wheelchair user, George Mason. Mason, an assistant attorney general in Michigan read about an electric wheelchair designed for outdoor travel and purchased one. His problems then began. The first difficulty he experienced with the new wheelchair was traumatic indeed—the right wheel feel off, and he fell out. The chair tipped over and fell on top of him. Acid from the battery which powered the chair got on his clothes. Fortunately, some people nearby were able to help him and he was not seriously injured, only shaken. Then,

three months after the wheel fell off, the repaired chair carried Mason part way across a busy Lansing intersection only to stall in the middle of traffic. Several frightening minutes passed before a passerby pushed the chair off the road. Mason concluded his Remarkable Mark 20 was expensive, unreliable, and dangerous. To continue to use it, he thought, would be suicidal—so he stopped.[36]

No "scientific findings" could make the issue of danger and unreliability more vivid. Mason's case, after all, provided the action researcher with ideal empirical (observable) data. Medsger then provides another case to definitively illustrate the plight of wheelchair users:

James May, former executive director of the Paralyzed Veterans of America and now director of testing and utilization for the Veterans Administration, has a virtual fleet of E&J chairs—four in all. May's oldest chair is no longer functional, so he cannibalizes it for parts to repair his remaining chairs. "One of my chairs is always in a state of disrepair,'' he says. ''Recently I had one chair out getting repaired. It took 196 days to get it fixed. Within that time, my second chair broke down twice. One day it broke in the office. It took two or three weeks to get it repaired.''[37]

The consumer perspective also provides action researchers with a way of making assertions and conclusions which, if made by the researchers themselves, would seem biased and, therefore, less credible. Note, for example, how Betty Medsger handles the issue of innovation in the wheelchair industry. She amasses compelling evidence showing that monopolistic practices and government inaction permit the industry to get by with almost no innovation. The wheelchair industry spends proportionally far less on research and development than do other industries. Again, it is the consumer perspective which legitimizes Medsger's analysis:

> Becky Heinrichs, a thirty-one-year-old secretary in Bakersfield, California, a paraplegic since birth, is puzzled by this lack of innovation. ''I've sat in my wheelchair and watched men walk on the moon. I know science was able to do that. I know it has developed strong, new light materials. Why is the wheelchair I'm sitting in like the one I sat in as a child?''[38]

As some of the examples cited above reveal, consumer accounts can often establish a sense of urgency that other data cannot. The reason for this may be that the public has become inured to body counts and other statistical reports of bad news. Or it may be that unless we see the reality of people living day-to-day social problems we become isolated (social scientists use the term alienated) from them. Action researchers avoid this problem altogether by giving us consumer accounts. In her book, *Tender Loving Greed,* Mary Adelaide Mendelson offers such data. At one point, for example, Mendelson gives us the verbatim notes of an elderly woman who was upset by conditions she found in a nursing home. It was a case of older people using their own words to report the treatment, or rather the mistreatment, of older people:

> This tactic was used on me in Cleveland in 1970, after I had met with a group of senior citizens who had been organized into a government-financed project to reach out to elderly people. The group had extended its contacts into a nursing home, and its members did not like what they had found. I quote from a report written, painfully, by one of these senior citizens. She is describing a patient in the Euclid Manor Nursing Home in Cleveland, certified for Medicare, which supposedly puts it in the highest category of nursing homes. She writes:
>
>> When I reached the second floor, I had to wait for somebody to unlock the gate for me, then they told me she (the patient) was in the second room to my left. When I opened the door after knocking, to get permission to get in, I found a very frail woman crying very hard, wishing she could die. I got her quieted · down a little bit and then asked her why she was unhappy. She told me how a white nurse and a colored nurse dragged her to the bathroom and threw her in the bathtub.
>>
>> In one other occasion when they were giving her a bath after throwing her in, they broke her tail bone, which hurts her very much, when, sitting her in a hard chair, they tie her in that chair. The meals are very poor, she is parlized

[sic] in the left arm and chronic arthritis in the hands and is unable to walk, she begged me not to tell on her as she does not want to be spit on and beaten anymore. This lady is 81 years of age and has very little company.

The delegation presented me with several similar reports of neglect and cruelty. They pleaded with me for help. They were older citizens and they were frightened. I could offer nothing more than a promise to call the director of the state health department licensure division. I was forced to admit to them that, based on previous experience, I didn't expect much to be done.

I called the director of licensure. I told him only that a delegation of senior citizens had come to my office to deliver some complaints about the Euclid Manor Nursing Home. He did not ask me to enumerate any of their complaints. Unless, he said, there is a witness other then the patient willing to sign his name to a complaint, the health department would not investigate. The health department would not even listen to the senior citizen delegation. Of course, by the very nature of the business, the only witness is the attendant who himself created the agony for the patient. Only in a most unusual situation would anyone else be around to witness a patient being "spit on and beaten" by an aide or nurse. Thus, officialdom has comfortably shielded itself from the necessity of action by requiring nearly impossible documentation of claims of cruelty.[39]

While this account was useless as evidence for an official investigation—the state required that there be another witness other than the patient—it is powerful data for an action research report.

Finally, consumer reports can take any form, be it interview transcripts, case studies, affidavits, or offhand comments. One particularly common and useful form is the letter. Jim Hightower uses this type of consumer evidence in his action research book on the food industry entitled *Eat Your Heart Out*. The report includes economic evidence on how farming has become more and more controlled by a few major corporations. While he finds that many family farms still exist, many family farmers find themselves increasingly at the mercy of monopolistic practices and suffer from the resultant inflation. Hightower illustrates this point through a variety of means, one of which is a letter sent him by a cousin farmer:

June 10, 1974

Dear Jim,

We took a load of steers and heifers to the cattle auction Saturday and came away so sick and disgusted that we went fishing. After catching enough fish for dinner, we came home and I compiled these figures. They are straight from the horse's mouth, and maybe the next time you feel the urge to call Butz a dirty name they will give you a little extra ammunition.

a. After waiting weeks for the ship carrying baler twine to arrive in Baltimore, we paid $31 a bale; last year it was plentiful and we paid $8.50 a bale—265% increase.

b. Barbed wire this year is $30 a roll; last May is was $12.95. The only blessing there is that you can't find any even at $30—132% increase.

c. Oats for seeding last year $5.70 a hundred; this year $10—75% increase.

d. Fertilizer for the grain fields (we don't raise corn, thank goodness) $89 a ton; last year $55.80—60% increase.

e. Of course everybody knows about gas, but farm price is now 52.9¢ compared to 32.9¢ last May—60%.

f. And then there is the friendly Production Credit Association and Federal Land Bank who are charging us 9½% interest on our cattle note this year compared to 7½% last spring—27% increase.
Now comes the good part!
a. Our load of cattle averaged $33 per hundred Saturday. In 1973 the average was $47 per hundred—42% loss over last year. However, we all know that last year beef prices were unusually high. So I went back to 1972: the average that year was $39—still an 18% loss. And then back to 1971 which was our first year of sales: average was $34.30—a modest 4% loss. The clincher is that this is the last year we have in which to show a profit on the farm; otherwise the IRS says our farming operation is just a hobby and we won't be allowed to deduct any of our losses.

Love,
Cousin Velma[40]

With this as evidence, Jim Hightower makes his case: "input corporations (farm supplies) joined the supermarket (a few big chains are their own middlemen buyers) to make a killing off the farmer."[41]

Consumer Involvement

When consumers provide essential data in the form of first hand accounts they are involved in action research. Yet in this role they are subjects as well as participants. That is, they are at once both communicators of data and data themselves. In many action research studies consumers play a more directive role and become the researchers themselves. They participate in designing the study, gather the data, analyze the data, and decide how to use the results (for example, in press conferences, for negotiations, to formulate a legislative agenda).

As the Love Canal case reveals, consumers themselves have performed some of the very best and most influential action research. The advantages of consumer operated action research are obvious. Who but consumers have more interest in seeing that an action research project is carried through to its conclusion? Who but consumers are best able to define issues for action research? Who but consumers will have the greatest incentive to pursue research findings into action? A typical criticism of consumer-led and consumer-staffed action research is that consumers may inadvertently bias the data. Clearly, however, measures can be taken in any research project to double check data, to build in controls, and establish the validity, reliability, and accuracy of findings.

In his article entitled "Citizens as Experts," Nick Kotz tells what can happen when consumers do their own action research.[42] He describes a project, funded by the federal Community Services Administration, to involve community groups in monitoring how cities spend Community Development Block Grant money. The project, called the National Citizens Monitoring Project, trains community groups, poor people, working class people, and concerned citizens in forty-three U.S. cities. The task of figuring out where community development block grants go is not altogether easy. The very nature of federal block grants makes such work difficult. Block grants are intended to redirect federally collected tax money to local communities and, within some general guidelines, allow the local communities, or rather the political leadership in local communities, discretion in how to spend the funds. Because the federal government allows so much local discretion, even large expenditures are hard to track. Thus the citizen has a hard time figuring out just where community development block grants are going. How much community development money goes to improving housing for a city's poorest people? How much of that money goes to subsidize area businesses? If community development funds aid in the rebuilding of poor or deteriorating neighborhoods into middle class and fashionable ones, what benefits are derived by poor people? Are the poor forced to move on in the wake of what is commonly called "gentrification?"

Through the Citizens Monitoring Project, citizens learned how to get answers to these questions. In Birmingham, Alabama, for example, citizens researchers found that the city leaders who controlled community development funds had decided that thirty-one neighborhoods were too poor and far gone to be able to benefit from the block grant money.[43] In New York City, a citizen coalition found that huge amounts of community development funds had been redirected to general purposes use—in other words, to help shore up New York's enormous fiscal problems.[44] In San Francisco, consumers found that the block grant money was "slated for a luxury condominium and for a business and tourist project, both located in affluent neighborhoods."[45] When the citizens brought this San Francisco matter to light, federal officials stopped the projects.

Consumers have tackled research projects in literally every area of living. They have compiled guides to doctors' fees. Banking mortgage policies and tax assessment inequities have also been investigated. Consumers have uncovered job discrimination practices, and have monitored how television portrays older people, women, and people with disabilities. They have issued ratings of politicians on key community issues. And they have documented their own health needs. Consumers have surveyed transporation patterns and matched them with official spending for transportation to uncover bias. In her book entitled *Your Community and Beyond: An Information and Action Guide,*[46] Julia Cheever provides examples of how to engage in simple, inexpensive, but important action research on such broad-ranging topics as criminal justice, economic exploitation, working conditions, education, taxes and welfare, food, housing, and health care. She provides supermarket surveys, housing code checklists, ways to see what it means to live on a welfare budget, how to do research on the rail bond system and legal fees, and methods for surveying occupational health conditions.

As noted above, consumer staffed research into particular issues involves the people who have the greatest interest in defining those issues and in deciding what to study and what to do with the results. In addition to affording opportunities for self-determination, consumer-staffed action research accomplishes several other important goals. For one thing, it promotes greater accountability by public organizations and private corporations. Political scientists generally measure political participation in terms of whether or not citizens belong to a political party, whether they contribute to the party, and whether they vote. Citizens action researchers carry the meaning of political participation much farther by bringing citizens into everyday decision making. They bring accountability to such matters as where to spend block grant money or how much to assess particular parcels of property. They demand accountability from organizations such as corporations which, in many respects, have traditionally operated without political accountability. In other words, action research gives consumers the ability to exercise political force in ways other than through the ballot box. This approach has yielded impressive results in many instances. At Love Canal, for example, citizens were able to force government agencies and a major corporation to deal with hazardous wastes that threatened the health of area residents. In Little Rock, Arkansas, a citizen action group known as ACORN (Arkansas Community Organization for Reform Now) investigated tax assessment practices and found that certain wealthy politicians and leading citizens were receiving extraordinarily favored treatment from the County Board of Equalization. Further investigation by the citizen group revealed such inequities to be statewide. The group ultimately forced the state to seriously address thirty-eight ACORN proposals for reform.[47] In Massachusetts a group called Action for Children's Television has been lobbying for years, with its own action research to back up its demands, for reforms within the television industry. The group has been critical of violence in television, exploitation by advertisers, and television stereotyping of particular segments of the population.

A group in New York State accomplished its action research by interviewing its own members. Syracuse United Neighbors surveyed its membership, mainly citizens from the poorest section of the city, on their experiences in securing homeowners insurance. It found that 26 percent of the 162 members polled felt they had been discriminated against by insurers. Many of those who were able to secure insurance found that the insurance companies charged them as much as 100 percent more for premiums than if they had lived in middle-class neighborhoods. The group cited numerous specific instances of what it called discriminatory practices:

> A Rich Street man said he got a notice from his insurance company stating they were cancelling his insurance because the paint was peeling off his house.
>
> A Midland Avenue woman said she was denied a policy because she had "vicious dogs on the premises." She said, "I bought the dogs for my protection against vandals and robbers. That's the best insurance policy one can have."
>
> One firm refused to renew a Southwest Side family because they had a carport that "made the house look rundown."
>
> A West Ostrander Avenue man said he had done business with an insurance company for 30 years. "I had to file a claim this past winter; when I received my check they notified me that my policy was cancelled," he said.[48]

These results lack the sophistication of many traditional studies. The researchers, for example, did not establish a carefully selected control group for their study. Rather, they followed their hunches and gathered data which seemed compelling. That was really all they needed to do, since their audience was not one of professional researchers, but rather the general public. The group demanded and got negotiation meetings with the major insurance companies. The local newspaper wrote up the study with the following lead: "Syracuse United Neighbors has declared war on insurance companies that allegedly 'red line' local neighborhoods."[49]

The other great asset of consumer-staffed action research is that it is a type of action that involves many people. Action research thus serves not only as consciousness-raising-in-action, but also as a vehicle for involving large numbers of people in meaningful group activity. Action research provides a process for collective development. It fosters group cohesiveness. Participants come to feel a sense of group commitment and group productivity. Individual group members can see their own part in the whole activity. And, finally, because consumer-staffed action research requires attention to detail, a certain amount of detective work, hard work, long hours, perseverance, confrontation with certain prevailing myths, and an ability to weather frequent rebuffs, it serves as an excellent training ground for organizers. For some, action research has been a kind of trial by fire. Note, for example, the transformation of Love Canal's Mrs. Gibbs:

> As the *Times* put it . . . , "Protesting, picketing, being jailed have become a way of life for Lois Gibbs. Two years ago she could barely pronounce the names of the chemicals detected in her basement. Today she tours the country warning of their effects before audiences large and small."[50]

Breaking Conventions

The process by which action researchers challenge discrimination, exploitation, potential dangers and many other things, including common-sense beliefs, is anything but conventional. Action researchers abandon most of traditional research's decorum. Since their audience is the public, they have far more interest than do traditional researchers in making their study exciting, interesting, and compelling. If they present the study in a meticulously, objective way, they do so as a marketing strategy not because they perceive themselves as coldly dispassionate. More often, the action researcher uses subtle and not so subtle strategies to question traditionally revered authority figures and institutions.

Note, for example, how action researchers write about people to whom society usually gives automatic status and respect. The following account appears in Mary Adelaide Mendelson's *Tender Loving Greed:*

The Moneylender: A More Secret Sharer

> He is known, to those few who know both him and the industry, as "King of the Nursing Homes." To the press and the public at large, he is merely a "Boston financier," for his nursing home kingdom does not appear on the public record. Unlike Eugene Woods and Max Strauss, he does not have his name linked directly with the operation of nursing homes, and unlike Bernard Bergman, he does not make his money from owning them. Yet this reputed millionaire has himself declared nursing homes to be his chief source of income.
>
> Joseph Kosow is a moneylender. He belongs to a category of profiteers whose activities in the nursing home industry are still more difficult to trace than the concealed owners. They do not show up in court, for there is nothing necessarily illegal

about high interest rates, no matter what the effect may be on patient care. Only rarely has the baleful influence of the moneylender even been recognized. Once was by Allan Robinson, one-time counsel to a Massachusetts special commission that was studying nursing homes. Testifying in Boston before the Senate Subcommittee on Long-Term Care, Robinson spoke of "the loan sharks who sat, and perhaps still sit astride many of the facilities, like fat spiders and who have waxed rich on their shackled mortgagers."[51]

A "Boston financier" is transformed into a shady, but prosperous "moneylender," a "profiteer," and a "loan shark." Financier and moneylender both describe essentially the same activity, but the former carries with it an image of respect, the other an image of preying on the less fortunate.

Among its other breaks with tradition, action research rarely concerns itself with the strictures of laboratory research. As the Syracuse United Neighbors case demonstrates, the test for action research is not whether it will stand the scrutiny of other researchers—such scholars concern themselves with sample size, the use of double blinds, control groups, data reliability—but whether it will be acceptable to television, radio, and the newspapers, and by extrapolation, to the public. Action research is often quickly done and is openly political in the sense that its stated purpose is to promote change. It must adhere to the test of believability. That is, will people believe the evidence (a term action researchers use more often than "data"), believe that the evidence was fairly collected, and believe that the conclusions based on the evidence are correct?

Action research also parts company with convention in that particular strategies employed are not an extension of traditional research methods. Sometimes these strategies amount to deceit. Indeed, the approach of an action researcher is more like that of the investigative reporter than of the researcher. One researcher, for example, pretended that she was a parent of a multiply disabled child in search of human services, particularly educational programs. She found that if her imaginary child had been real, she would have had no services. All she received from the many public and private agencies in her community was a runaround and, worse, advice to institutionalize her daughter. Another action researcher purposely broke a small part in a television set and then took it to a television repair shop. He did this repeatedly with the same television, but each time went to a different shop. In this manner he collected eivdence of overcharging and dishonesty by the community's television repair shops. He found that some television repair shops told him that many other expensive parts needed replacement as well. In still another study, one sponsored by a Nader organization, college students volunteered at nursing homes in order to secretly gather data on nursing home treatment.

One group of daring researchers went so far as to impersonate mental patients in order to investigate treatment inside mental hospitals. Their work is on the borderline between traditional research and action research; in fact they addressed their findings to the scientific community and to the general public. Their strategy so exemplifies a type of exciting undercover action research that we recount it here in these pages. These undercover "patients" disclosed their findings in the prestigious *Science* magazine.[52] Eight researchers in all took part in the action study. One was a graduate student while the others were "older" and more "established." The three women and five men assumed pseudonyms and, where their own profession was actually mental health, stated another one upon admission. Each researcher gained admission to a different hospital—some were new, some were old, one was private, and the rest were public. Each accomplished admission as a patient by claiming to hospital admission staff that he or she "had been hearing voices. Asked what the voices said, he (or she) replied that they were often unclear, but as far as he could tell they said, 'empty,' 'hollow,' and 'thud.' The voices were unfamiliar and were of the same sex as the pseudopatient."[53] Once inside, the pseudopatients "ceased simulating any symptoms of abnormality."[54] They spoke normally to staff and other residents alike. Visitors from the "outside" could detect no serious symptoms of illness—nor, indeed could other patients. It was quite common for the patients to "detect" the pseudopatient's sanity, but the ward staff and psychiatrists did not. When the pseudopatients asked simple questions of psychiatric staff, they often received disconnected responses:

> The encounter frequently took the following bizarre form: (pseudopatient) "Pardon me, Dr. . . . Could you tell me when I am eligible for grounds privileges?" (physician) "Good morning, Dave. How are you today?" (Moves off without waiting for response.)[55]

The mean daily contact of pseudopatients with psychiatrists, psychologists, (medical) residents, and physicians (combined) was 6.8 minutes, with the greatest average amount for any one of the researchers being 25.1 minutes.[56] All in all, the researchers found their sojourn in total institutions depersonalizing and degrading. They found themselves feeling increasingly more powerless. Depersonalization took many forms. Their experience with medications illustrates the point:

> All told, the pseudopatients were administered nearly 2100 pills, including Elavil, Stelazine, Compazine, and Thorazine, to name but a few. . . . Only two were swallowed. The rest were either pocketed or deposited in the toilet.[57]

The entire experience of hospitalization led the researchers to conclude that mental hospitals impose "a special environment in which the meaning of behavior" are easily misunderstood.[58] Labeled patients find themselves trapped in an impersonal, dehumanizing world. It is, by any standard, an antitherapeutic environment. Thus the researchers suggest alternatives, albeit with some hesitancy, such as community health facilities and therapy without labeling. For the purpose of our discussion it is noteworthy that these findings never would have received the attention they did had the researchers not chosen such a daring and bizarre action strategy.

Because of such controversial strategies, action research often reads like high comedy or drama. How will Mitford uncover the "truth" about embalmers? Will Mendelson discover the hidden owners of the big nursing home chains—one of her strategies was to check license plate numbers on all the expensive luxury cars in a nursing home parking lot during a top level meeting. How will Wooden find out how much money states are willing to expend to ship children out of state?

As the drama unfolds there is usually more than a small amount of macabre humor. Mitford, for example, subscribes to *Mortuary Management,* a funeral industry trade journal. Inside each issue she learns what the funeral directors say to each other. She learns how they plan to profiteer off an unsuspecting and vulnerable public. She finds advertisements telling funeral directors how to make greater profits by selling cutsom caskets, replete with handmade artistic designs, gilt exteriors, and special casket linings. Similarly, Mendelson has us following her through the back halls of nursing homes, watching as the owners pilfer patients' steaks from the home freezer for their own families' use while feeding patients lesser fare.

There are certain kinds of practices and jargon that organization and industry insiders would probably rather keep hidden from the public. Action researchers seem to have a special knack for uncovering them. In so doing, they allow an industry or profession to expose its own myths. One example is a term commonly used to describe an illegal and immoral nursing home practice:

> The gang visit: the physician whips through the nursing home in a couple of hours, glancing at only the most urgent cases, and later the government is billed as if he had given individual attention to each patient, a task requiring days, not hours.[59]

The existence of a slang term for such practice suggests that it is not uncommon. The Government Accounting Office, as we learn from Mendelson, has verified this fact. It has found instances where between eighty and ninety patients were "seen" by a single doctor in one day.[60]

Writing for the Public

We have already noted that action researchers generally regard the public as their primary audience. Hence their interest in using research strategies that will excite their readers and their willingness to inject humor and drama into their research reports. They use a variety of fairly simple strategies to make their points clear to the public: they juxtapose official statements with observations of the day-to-day realities; they use photographs, first-hand consumer accounts, and similarly provocative material; they use the Freedom of Information Act to secure and bring to light public information (see Figure 1); they enlist the news media to disseminate research results; they compose glossaries of technical terms; they translate esoteric, hard-to-understand information into easy-to-understand information; and they welcome rather than avoid controversy.

Figure 1
The Freedom of Information Act
The Federal government and many state governments are required by their respective laws to provide certain kinds of information to the public upon request. For information on state freedom of information or "sunshine" laws, we need to refer to state laws

(see law chapter on how to secure copies of these laws). The basic provisions of the federal Act are as follows:

Each federal agency, federal government controlled corporation, and federally established independent regulatory agency must "state and currently publish in the Federal Register for the guidance of the public" a list of the organization locations, addresses, and employees from whom information can be requested.

Each agency (meaning government agency, government controlled corporation or government sponsored independent regulatory commission) must make available to the public information about how the agency functions, agency interpretations of policy, agency policies, agency decisions in adjudicated cases, policy and implementation manuals, and so forth.

An agency is not required to collect data or other information for the person making the request unless that information is already being collected by the agency.

Agencies may not give out personal information to third parties unless as part of the routine and authorized use of the record.

An agency may deny a request for secret (classified) information or information that includes trade secrets.

Agencies must provide "any reasonably segregable portion" of a record once those sections which are exempt (secret or personal) have been deleted.

Agencies must make information available at reasonable search and reproduction costs and in a timely fashion.

Agencies may waive search and reproduction costs if it is deemed that disclosure of the information is in the public interest.

The law does not require that people seeking information state their purpose.

If any agency refuses to disclose available information, the person making the request may file a complaint (law suit) in Federal District Court.

Since we do not always know the precise title or description of data we want to secure, we need only describe its general nature and purpose. Request all or any portion available. If we suspect an excessive cost of search and reproduction, it may be worth setting a cost limit or asking for a statement of projected cost first.

The best action research studies read like an appeal to the public. Jim Hightower's account of the food industry typifies this approach. He is able to make complex information easily understood and thus take prevailing myths and break them apart. Here is what he has to say about who is to blame for high food prices:

In March of 1974, following a solid year of phenomenal rises in the prices of food, President Nixon pointed to the money that American farmers were making—"the farmers," he asserted in a press conference, "have never had it so good." Farm people did not take at all kindly to that presidential assessment, suggesting that it was the verbal equivalent of stepping in a fresh cow pattie. At the time that Nixon was pronouncing his judgment of the food economy, the *farm* price of food was falling for the sixth straight month. But the *supermarket* price of food still was rising. . . .

If the President had said that oligopolistic middlemen never had it so good, he would have been more on target. The lobbyists for food corporations, as well as Department of Agriculture officials, regularly downplay the profit levels of food corporations, usually by practicing the deception of lumping all food-manufacturing firms together. For example, 1973 was not that great a year for the average of all

32,000 food-manufacturing firms. But the 50 or so oligopolistic firms that dominate the industry and collect about 75% of all the profits had "a year to remember," as *Business Week* put it. The big food makers whined all that year about government price controls squeezing their profits, but (the data) shows a group that whined all the way to the bank.[61]

Later in his report on the food oligopoly he dramatizes his point, saying,

Those who doubt the existence of corporate power in farming might want to RSVP to the menu of conglomerate-produced food, which could be served at their next dinner party:

Appetizers
Sauteed Mushrooms by Clorox wrapped in
Bacon by ITT
Salmon by Unilever

Salads
Tossed Salad of Lettuce by Dow Chemical
and Tomatoes by Gulf & Western
Avocado Salad by Superior Oil

Entrees
Turkey by Ling-Temco-Vought
Ham by Greyhound
Roast Beef by Oppenheimer Industries

Side Dishes
Artichokes by Purex
Carrots by Tenneco
Potatoes by Boeing
Applesauce by American Brands
Deviled Eggs by Cargill
Olives by Zapata Oil

Beverage
Wine by Heublein
Citrus Juice by Pacific Lighting Corp.

After Dinner
Peaches by Westgate-California Corp.
Almonds by Getty Oil[62]

Another way that action researchers attempt to "win the hearts and minds" of the public is by bringing the public along on their confrontations with officials. Dr. Helen Caldicott, medical researcher and antinuclear activist, for example, shared with her readers part of the contents of her letter to then President Jimmy Carter. She briefly listed the dangers of nuclear radiation that attend nuclear reactors, which included genetic damage, cancer, destruction of the natural environment, and military use of certain reactor by-products. She warned him sternly. She then requested an opportunity to meet him face to face, to convince him of the dangers. Carter's aides arranged instead for Dr. Caldicott to meet with a doctor employed by the government's Energy Research and Development Agency (ERDA), but Caldicott turned them down: "ERDA is totally devoted to the expansion and development of nuclear power (it oversees the manufacture of atomic weapons, including the neutron bomb) and any doctor who works for that agency has already sold his soul to the devil.''[63]

Accounts of confrontations and copies of letters portraying them are common in action research reports. Indeed, they are part of the research and the action research. When, for example, Massachusetts Mental Health Commissioner requested a prepublication copy of a report on children in mental health systems, entitled *Suffer the Children,* he got a stern and outraged rebuff from the authors, The Task Force on Children Out of School.[64] The Commissioner claimed that members of his own State agency who had participated in the report had spotted inaccuracies but had been denied an opportunity to correct them. The Commissioner now wanted that right. Writing in response, Task Force chairperson Mr. Hubert E. Jones, then directing the Roxbury Multi-Service Center and later Dean of the School of Social Work at Boston University, informed the Commissioner that those same employees who participated on the Task Force report revealed that the Commissioner himself had asked them not to sign the report and that the Commissioner had threatened to try and cut off the Task Force's funding at its source. Jones then continued to steadfastly refuse the Commissioner's request for a prepublication copy. He did so for three reasons: (1) because all data for the report came directly from the mental health department itself—any errors would have to be in department data, not the Task Force's data; (2) to give the Commissioner an opportunity to edit an investigation of his own department would throw the Task Force's integrity and independence into question; and (3) because the Task Force had knowledge that the Commissioner wanted to try to mitigate the report's impact prior to its release by preparing press releases in advance. Jones contended that no Task Force member had requested not to sign the report, that no inaccuracies had been identified by the Department's participants, and that no Task Force member had, as the Commissioner claimed, requested the right to file a minority report. Larry Brown, the action group's director, responded even more angrily, also in writing. He accused the Commissioner of not only trying to stop publication of the Task Force's action report, but also of trying to threaten the very existence of the Task Force. ''The attempted use of public office,'' he charged, ''to intimidate a private organization can be seen as nothing less than disgraceful.''[65] He accused the Commissioner of exposing his ''attitude toward public service more poignantly than a report could ever do.''[66] As if to settle the debate or perhaps to bring the debate before the public, the Task Force published all three letters, the Commissioner's, Chairperson Hubert Jones's, and Director Larry Brown's.

Blueprints

One reason that researchers have proven so unpopular with policy makers is that they frequently offer no suggestions for policy change. That charge cannot be levelled against action researchers. Every action research study includes extensive recommendations. These take a variety of forms including model legislation, consumer checklists, calls to action for community groups, lists of demands, conversion plans, and so forth. Jessica Mitford suggests we join cooperative memorial societies before we die so that our families will not be exploited by funeral hucksters in a time of grief. Wooden lobbies for government investigations of private institutions for children and an end to the interstate commerce of children. The Massies want a national blood plan and program similar to that which is available in France. They also demand government subsidized AHF for people with hemophilia. The Children's Defense Fund report *Children Out of School in America* recommends due process rights for children with respect to their schooling, review of suspension and exclusion practices by school boards, use of suspension from school only as a last resort and only in instances where a child has been violent, special education programs for those who need it, public education as a right for all children, regardless of their relative wealth or other circumstances, and many more. Many of these recommendations became part of The Education for All Handicapped Children Act passed by Congress one year after the Defense Fund issued its report. These are just a few action researchers' suggestions for change.

One of the most frequently heard criticisms of those who question prevailing social practices and policies centers around their lack of alternatives for existing conditions. "If you think things are so bad, what do you think we can do about them?" "Do you have something better to offer?" "What's your blueprint?" Those questions deserve to be asked. Out of criticism—and action research is, if nothing else, highly critical—must come a vision of change, a blueprint, however rudimentary or incomplete. In the absence of alternatives we can only feel powerless before the urgently stated discoveries of action research. That is, action research usually reveals illegalities, inequities, and suffering. Without an action plan to remedy these findings we might feel overwhelmed by their enormity.

When Geraldo Rivera went to Willowbrook State School and prepared a searing exposé of the degrading conditions there, he also travelled to California and shot television footage of educational and residential programs in communities where retarded people received decent care and treatment. Through this point/ counterpoint strategy he documented that the horrors of Willowbrook—the disease, the denied education, the nudity, the filth, the treatment of people as if they were worse than animals in a zoo—were not inevitable. Rivera's interest in social change is revealed in the subtitle he gave to his book about the Willowbrook exposé: "A Report on How It Is and Why It Doesn't Have to Be That Way." To Rivera, the key question in the end was "Does this documentary make a difference?" He wondered if people would watch it. If they did, he was confident they would see that change was needed and in what direction that change should occur. On the day of the television broadcast, Rivera went home to watch and liked what he saw. Then he thought, what would the ratings be? "Ratings might sound crass and commerical," he later wrote, "but it is a sad fact of life that the impact of a television program is directly related to how many people see it."[67] He wasn't concerned about what the critics would say; he only wanted to know if the people would watch it. "It was supposed to be a catalyst for change. And change is dictated by the masses."[68] The morning after the airing, he called the local ABC studio. "Willowbrook, The Last

Great Disgrace'' had received the highest rating of a local news special in the history of television. Two and a half million people in the New York area had seen it. In Rivera's own words, ''They had seen the horrors of Willowbrook, and they had seen an alternative approach which said that things didn't have to be the way they were.''

Few action research projects can produce the drama and excitement of the Willowbrook exposé. However, that fact in no way lessens action researchers' attention to social change. A study on the barriers to quality health care which confront American children, particularly poor and minority children, point this out. In a report entitled, ''Doctors and Dollars Are Not Enough: How to Improve Health Services for Children and Their Families,'' the Children's Defense Fund documents the financial, cultural, professional, and bureaucratic barriers to quality health care services for children.[69] For instance, some families have no transportation to health care. Some parents have no one to look after their other children when they must take one to health services. A number of health centers do not have staff who speak the language of many of their potential clients. Some health programs do not have service hours on weekends or evenings despite the fact that working parents tend to be able to use health care exclusively at these times. The Children's Defense Fund incorporates recommendations in every section of its report. Moreover, one third of the report is devoted to chapters entitled, ''Improving the Content of Care,'' and ''On Effective Advocacy.'' At the end of the latter chapter on practical change, the Fund provides consumers (and presumably professionals as well) with a conscious-ness-raising checklist by which to evaluate how well a health care delivery system is organized to meet the needs of *all* children. In effect, consumer and citizen groups in any community, urban or rural, wealthy or poor, can use this checklist as a blueprint for change at the local level. That checklist is reproduced here in its entirety as an example of a popular and effective action research strategy of provid-ing concrete alternatives (Figure 2).

Figure 2
MORE EFFECTIVE ENTRY INTO THE SYSTEM

Outreach
1. Is outreach made through personal contact?
2. Is outreach performed by trained workers who share or are sensitive to the background of the people served?
3. Is outreach conducted in a variety of places in the community?
4. Are outreach efforts reinforced and supplemented by trained, nonhealth personnel in the community?
5. Do outreach services link people to a system of care which provides con-tinuing services?

Location of Services and Transportation
1. In medically underserved areas, is there an organized setting which (a) offers combined practice with other professionals and expanded profes-sional contact and activities beyond the immediate area; and (b) makes available support services which one professional on his own could not muster?

2. Are primary care services located in the midst of the target population by (a) taking the needs of the target population into account in the decision about where to build a new facility, or (b) decentralizing the services of an existing program? Might it be appropriate to adopt a regional approach to the allocation of health resources?
3. Where it is impossible to offer comprehensive primary health services in a conveniently located facility, are other approaches being used, such as the placement of health personnel in outlying areas, or the use of mobile clinics?
4. Where health services exist within a reasonable distance, but parents do not have transportation available, are transportation services provided or arranged by (a) modifying existing public transportation systems to arrange schedules and routes that efficiently link users and health care facilities; (b) reimbursing families or patients for transportation they can find themselves but cannot afford; (c) contracting with other agencies to provide transportation to health services; or (d) developing a program-run transportation system?

Telephone Access
1. Is there 24-hour, 7-day-a-week telephone access for emergencies, and day and evening telephone access to medical care for acute health needs?
2. Is there some time during the day when families can consult with health professionals over the telephone concerning more general health questions?
3. Is the person who responds to the telephone call able to communicate effectively with the caller and able to provide the caller with appropriate instructions?

Hours of Service
1. Are hours when care is available designed so that they do not always conflict with school or work?

Appointment Systems
1. Are there appointment systems? Are they designed to accommodate the habits and practical daily problems of consumers?
2. Can parents make appointments in a number of different ways, such as through outreach workers, health aides in the home or hospital, by telephone, through other agencies, etc.?
3. Are appointment systems designed to promote continuous care?
4. Do appointment systems make possible the provision of related health services in an efficient manner?

Care for Other Children
1. Where necessary, are there arrangements for the care of other children when the parent brings a child to the clinic or comes in for care herself?

Reducing Cultural Barriers
1. Are there special provisions to assure that health services do not discriminate among patients by race and that services are responsive to the different cultural and socio-economic backgrounds of the families they serve? Is there staff from or with knowledge about the communities being served? Are there language interpreters when needed? Are there patient advocates from the communities to ease entry to health services and allay children's and parents' fears? Is there a procedure for hearing grievances and allowing consumers to participate in decision making?

Emergency Care
1. Are emergency services designed to introduce patients to a regular source of care when they do not have one?

2. Do parents in every location have a system of emergency care available which includes public information about how to get emergency help, emergency transportation and communication with a health center or hospital, health staff in the ambulance and emergency room who are trained in emergency care, high quality emergency room facilities, and provision for needed follow-up services?

IMPROVING THE CONTENT OF CARE

Unifying Fragmented Services
1. Are most primary care services available in one place and under unified administrative auspices?
2. Does one person have the responsibility of coordinating the diverse services a child or family needs?
3. Are services that are now rendered in fragmented ways being reorganized toward comprehensive primary care?
4. Are services provided separately in those circumstances when providing services separately might be more effective (for example, for adolescents)?

Providing Continuity of Care
1. Is the health program designed to allow each patient to have a continuous relationship with a physician, a nurse-practitioner, or other trained health worker?
2. Are medical record systems designed to promote continuity of care?

Humanizing Care
1. In planning how physicians use their time, is there leeway for the possibility of a leisurely consultation between health professionals and families either when the professional thinks it is crucial or when the child or family indicates a special need? Is the physical setting conducive to easy and private communications?
2. Are there educational efforts aimed at enabling parents and children to become active and knowledgeable partners with health professionals in the process of patient care and health maintenance?

Support and Advocacy from the Health Care System
1. Is a wide range of health support services (such as those listed in Appendix B) available as part of the health program?

The People Who Provide the Health Services
1. Do the criteria for selecting people to provide primary care include a high level of technical competence? Is equal attention given to the capacity to deal with children and parents in a compassionate, supportive, caring and respectful manner, and to work easily with others of different backgrounds and training?
2. Is the program designed in such a way as to provide a setting in which sensitivity, supportiveness, and mutual respect can flourish?
3. Does the design of the health program make it possible for health workers to do those tasks for which they are particularly suited by their training, experience, skills, and personal qualities?[71]

The great difficulty faced by action researchers lies in convincing the public or some segment of it that there are indeed alternatives to existing conditions. Perhaps the problem is that people have been so conditioned to accept "what is as what must be" or that people truly have difficulty conceptualizing alternatives. It may be that those who have an interest in keeping things as they are have access to powerful means of advertising and other forms of public persuasion at their finger-tips. In any case, we as a society do not abandon the status quo easily. It is thus not insignificant that Ralph Nader entitled the last chapter of his action research report on toxic chemicals, "Conclusion: We Are Not Helpless."[70] He begins this last chapter with a call to action. "We are not helpless in the environmental crisis," he tells us. We can stop "the spread of cancer—the plague of the 20th century."[72] We can find alternatives. In fact, the alternatives are here, and available now. We can, he exhorts, recapture our air, land, water and food from pollution. "The proper functioning of our economic system does not require the sacrifice of residents of Love Canal, or the waters of Lake Superior and the James River."[73]

Nader approaches the problem of change or, more accurately, of developing a blueprint for change, pragmatically. He recognized, as the best action research does, that we must address the blueprint issue on a variety of levels. Can we find technical solutions to identified problems? Are the answers largely a matter of organizational changes (as in the case of the health care system)? Do we need to reconceptualize the problem altogether, thus enabling us to think differently about possible solutions? Can we find cost-effective, practical recommendations? In his treatment of the toxic chemicals issue, Nader addresses each of these levels.

In response to the rhetorical question, "Are there technical alternatives?", Nader cites one after another. For example, he demonstrates that American—indeed, world—agriculture uses toxic chemical pesticides far in excess of what it needs. In fact, he argues that we have more or less adopted the false notion that without massive use of pesticides it would be nearly impossible to continue efficient agricultural production. Through traditional methods such as crop rotation, planting of multiple types of crops, and other methods, farmers could reduce their costly dependence on pesticides considerably. This approach has been called Integrated Pest Management (IPM). Nader cites a six-year study by the Environmental Protection Agency, the United States Department of Agriculture, and the National Science Foundation which found that "IPM use on cotton, citrus fruits, deciduous fruits, soybeans and alfalfa (to which are applied 70 percent of the insecticides used on U.S. cropland) could cut pesticide use 70–80 percent in ten years—with no decrease in yield."[74] IPM, then, is one of the *technical* solutions to poisoning by chemicals in the environment. Nader presents it as part of the blueprint for change.

In terms of organizational change, Nader suggests that chemical corporations could be better monitored and would be more morally upstanding if their boards of directors were independent of management. Further, he recommends that Congress establish a superfund to clean up toxic disasters. That fund would be established with money from the chemical industry itself, not from taxpayers. In terms of cost-effective solutions, Nader suggests that the government place stringent regulations on the use of known carcinogenic chemicals and that the industry cut wasteful use of chemical products. "Are we really wed to dangerous chemicals?" he asks. "Some uses are frivolous; more than 10 million tons of plastic are used each year merely for packaging."[75] Companies can easily, and at no great expense, replace the most dangerous chemicals with nontoxic ones.

These recommendations, with the possible exception of the one that would reconstitute boards of directors as citizen boards, probably would encounter resistance only from the industry itself. While such changes might cause industry some minor inconveniences, recent instances of industry reforms confirm their reasonableness. Frequently, however, action research calls for more than simple reforms and technical innovations. In many cases, action researchers ask the public to think differently about an issue. For instance, Rivera asks us to believe that retarded people are full human beings capable of benefiting from quality programs. He asks us to recognize the concentration camp-like conditions in which retarded people have lived for some years. He asks us to take some responsibility for those conditions. Similarly, the Children's Defense Fund asks us to think of health care delivery for poor children, and minority children in much the same way that the health care system has always thought of health care for middle and upper class children, that is, as a service that should be tailored to meet the needs of that group in the best fashion.

In the case of the toxic chemicals crisis, Nader demands no less. He asks us to reconceptualize how we think about industrial waste. Nader suggests that we consider deliberate toxic contamination by a corporation a crime. He names certain companies as "recidivists," and calls for court action. While he notes that a corporation may be unable to visit a probation officer, the probation officer could visit and monitor the corporation. He suggests that the best alternative to continued environmental action and what amounts to industrial lawlessness is a strategy that would take the profit out of such blatant disregard for the public interest:

> If managers considering the marketing of a hazardous product knew that disclosure of the danger would incur not only jail terms and stiff fines . . . , but also the complete return of all revenue derived from the product, the incentive for those actions, too, would be diminished sharply.[76]

By conceptualizing the problem in this way, as a crime, and not just a problem, we can conceptualize a certain set of solutions that might otherwise not come to mind. It is all part of the strategy of developing useful blueprints for change. And change is the ultimate purpose of action research.

NOTES

[1]Kenneth Wooden, *Weeping in the Playtime of Others* (New York: McGraw-Hill, 1976), p. 182.

[2]Peter Schrag and Diane Divoky, *The Myth of the Hyperactive Child* (New York: Dell Pub. Co., Inc., 1976), p. 12.

[3]Robert and Suzanne Massie, *Journey* (New York: Knopf), p. 324.

[4]Mary Adelaid Mendelson, *Tender Loving Greed* (New York: Vintage Books, 1975), p. 42.

[5]Jessica Mitford, *Poison Penmanship* (New York: Knopf, 1979).

[6]Mitford, *Poison,* p. 160.

[7]Charles E. Lindblom and David K. Cohen, *Useable Knowledge: Social Science and Social Problem Solving* (New Haven: Yale University Press, 1979), p. 5.

[8]Lindblom and Cohen, *Useable Knowledge,* pp. 5 and 6.

[9]Lindblom and Cohen, *Useable Knowledge,* pp. 7 and 8.

[10]Lindblom and Cohen, *Useable Knowledge,* p. 7.

[11]Lindblom and Cohen, *Useable Knowledge,* p. 64.

[12]Victor Bach quoted in Nick Kotz, "Citizens as Experts," *Working Papers,* Vol. VIII, No. 2, p. 44.

[13]John Gofman and Arthur Tamplin, *Poisoned Power: The case Against Nuclear Power Plants* (Emmaus, PA: Rodale Press Inc., 1971), p. 133. Also see Anna Gyorgy, *No Nukes* (Boston: South End Press, 1979), p..18.

[14]Gyorgy, *No Nukes,* p. 18.

[15]Ralph Nader, Ronald Brownstein, and John Richard, *Who's Poisoning America* (San Francisco: Sierra Club Books, 1981), p. 349.

[16]Steven Taylor, *A Guide to Monitoring Residential Settings* (*Report*) (Syracuse, NY: Center on Human Policy, 1980), p. 24.

[17]Mitford, *Poison,* p. 24.

[18]Dan Wakefield, "Taking It Big: A Memoir of C. Wright Mills," *The Atlantic Monthly,* September 1971, p. 70.

[19]Russell Mokhiber and Leonard Shen, "Love Canal," in *Who's Poisoning America,* eds., Ralph Nader, Ronald Brownstein, and John Richard (San Francisco: Sierra Club Books, 1981), p. 28.

[20]Mokhiber and Shen, "Love Canal," p. 27.

[21]Mokhiber and Shen, "Love Canal," pp. 281–282.

[22]Murray Levine, "Method or Madness: On the Alienation of the Professional," Invited Address, Division 12, American Psychological Association, Montreal, September 1980, p. 15.

[23]Levine, "Method or Madness," p. 13.

[24]Levine, "Method or Madness," p. 14.

[25]Levine, "Method or Madness," pp. 15 and 16.

[26]Mokhiber and Shen, "Love Canal," p. 287.

[27]Douglas Biklen "Human Report I" in *Souls in Extremis,* ed. Burton Blatt (Boston: Allyn and Bacon, 1973) p. 62.

[28]Biklen "Report", pp. 59–92.

[29]The Center on Human Policy.

[30]*The Community Imperative* (Syracuse, NY: The Center on Human Policy, 1979).

[31]The Children's Defense Fund, *Children Out of School in America* (Washington, DC: The Washington Research Project, Inc., 1974).

[32]The Children's Defense Fund, *Children Out,* p. 31.

[33]The Children's Defense Fund, *Children Out,* pp. 20–21.

[34]The Children's Defense Fund, *Children Out,* p. 22.

[35]Betty Medsger, "The Most Captive Consumers," *The Progressive,* March 1979, pp. 34–39.

[36]Medsger, "Captive Consumers," p. 35.

[37]Medsger, "Captive Consumers," p. 35.

[38]Medsger, "Captive Consumers," p. 36.

[39]Mendelson, *Tender Loving Greed,* pp. 214–215.

[40]Jim Hightower, *Eat Your Heart Out: Food Profiteering in America* (New York: Vintage, 1976), pp. 176–177.

[41]Hightower, *Eat,* p. 176.

[42]Nick Kotz, "Citizens as Experts," *Working Papers,* March/April 1981, Vol. VIII, No. 2, pp. 42–48.

[43]Kotz, "Citizens," p. 45.

[44]Kotz, "Citizens," p. 46.

[45]Kotz, "Citizens," p. 46.

[46]Julia Cheever, *Your Community and Beyond: An Information and Action Guide* (Palo Alto, CA: Page-Ficklin Publications, 1975).

[47]Cheever, *Your Community*, p. 71.

[48]Richard Palmer, "Insurance Firm Still 'Red Lining,'" SUN claims, *Syracuse Herald Journal*, June 25, 1981, p. D1.

[49]Palmer, "Red Lining," p. D1.

[50]Mokhiber and Shen, "Love Canal," p. 289.

[51]Mendelson, *Tender Loving Greed*, p. 123.

[52]D. L. Rosenhan, "On Being Sane in Insane Places," *Science*, Vol. 179, no. 19, January 1973, pp. 250–258.

[53]Rosenhan, "Insane," p. 251.

[54]Rosenhan, "Insane," p. 251.

[55]Rosenhan, "Insane," p. 255.

[56]Rosenhan, "Insane," p. 256.

[57]Rosenhan, "Insane," p. 256.

[58]Rosenhan, "Insane," p. 257.

[59]Mendelson, *Tender Loving Greed*, p. 44.

[60]Mendelson, *Tender Loving Greed*, p. 44.

[61]Hightower, *Eat*, p. 41.

[62]Hightower, *Eat*, pp. 190–191.

[63]Helen Caldicott, *Nuclear Madness: What You Can Do* (Brookline, MA: Autumn Press, 1978), p. 96.

[64]Task Force on Children Out of School, *Suffer the Children: The Politics of Mental Health in Massachusetts* (Boston: Task Force on Children Out of School, Inc., 1972).

[65]Task Force, *Suffer the Children*, p. i.

[66]Task Force, *Suffer the Children*, p. ii.

[67]Geraldo Rivera, *Willowbrook: A Report on How It Is and Why It Doesn't Have to Be That Way* (New York: Vintage Books, 1972), p. 141.

[68]Rivera, *Willowbrook*, p. 141.

[69]Children's Defense Fund, *Doctors and Dollars Are Not Enough: How to Improve Health Services for Children and Their Familes* (Washington, DC: Children's Defense Fund, 1975).

[70]Ralph Nader, Ronald Brownstein, and John Richard (eds.), *Who's Poisoning America: Corporate Polluters and Their Victims in the Chemical Age* (San Francisco: Sierra Club, 1981), p. 311.

[71]Children's Defense Fund, *Doctors and Dollars*, pp. 96–97.

[72]Nader et al., *Poisoning*, p. 311.

[73]Nader et al., *Poisoning*, p. 311.

[74]Nader et al., *Poisoning*, p. 317.

[75]Nader et al., *Poisoning*, p. 349.

[76]Nader et al., *Poisoning*, p. 347.

CHAPTER ELEVEN
WHISTLEBLOWING

INTRODUCTION

On August 24, 1978, Senator Edward M. Kennedy addressed the U.S. Senate on whistleblowing. He spoke of creating an atmosphere in government where government employees could speak out freely on illegalities and immorality in human services, government administration, and every other aspect of governmental action. He spoke optimistically of a day when government workers would courageously embrace whistleblowing. He also spoke of the public interest that would be served. Listen, he said, to

> the message that we have been receiving from an angry public: we have had too much waste in government; we have had too much ineptitude in government; we have had too much inefficiency in government; and we have even had too much corruption in government. And we don't need new ranks of bureaucrats to clean up what others have messed up. We merely need to provide protection and incentives for those presently in public service to bring to light—and to rectify—lawlessness and waste in government.
>
> For whistle-blowing will be amply staffed by our existing army of the conscientious and the dedicated—those who are committed enough, professional enough, and patriotic enough to "blow the whistle" on corruption, waste or illegality that they see around them. That is why I express strong support for S. 2640 (The Civil Service Reform act and Senator Leahy's whistleblower amendment).
>
> But ensuring that the alarm is sounded, and ensuring that the employee is indeed protected, is only the first step in the process. For the true purpose of whistle-blowing is not the public recognition of the dedicated employee, but the correction of government wrongdoing, the saving of tax-payer's money and the prosecution of the corrupt. . . .
>
> I have heard dozens of witnesses recount stories of transfer, demotion, harass-

ment and emasculation in return for telling the public the truth. I am more than happy to see the fruits of these hearings today.

All but the most simplistic of sloganeers know that our federal agencies are not "faceless bureaucracies," but that they are instead made up of individuals who are professional, honest, and hard working. We must maximize the contributions that conscientious public servants can have to good government and increased economy. We must provide our civil servants with an impartial "dissent channel" to which they can direct reports of corruption or waste. We must provide them with the protection that they deserve for speaking out. And we must make the most of their courage and honesty by providing a follow-through mechanism that will correct the wrongs that are disclosed.[1]

Senator Kennedy probably had in mind the Defense Department cost analyst, Ernest Fitzgerald, when he promised savings to the taxpayers from reports of waste. Mr. Fitzgerald was single-handedly responsible for documenting massive cost overruns on the C–5A airplane. In fact, his case became synonymous with whistleblowing in the 1970s because it was so celebrated. Actually, whistleblowing has occurred in a broad range of organizational settings. Employees have blown the whistle on corrupt, dangerous, and otherwise harmful practices in human service organizations, in local as well as national government, and in and out of private and public organizations.

Virtually every instance of whistleblowing confirms the importance of building safeguards for those employees willing to speak out for the public interest. As will become apparent through the examples of whistleblowing presented in this chapter, whistleblowers encounter enormous problems. Some of these "problems" include redbaiting, attacks on the whistleblower's personal motives and morality, threats to themselves and their families, ostracism by coworkers, loss of employment, blacklisting for all other employment in their field, personal doubt, depression and anger, even death. For many, whistleblowing brings a terrible sense of loneliness. For the many who believe in the whistleblower's analysis and actions, giving him or her support proves difficult, even impossible. As baseball star Curt Flood found when he challenged organized baseball's reserve clause which gave baseball owners the right to control where a baseball player would work (Flood's challenge eventually paved the way for the free agent system), challenging the system can prove costly. Once Flood exposed the problem publicly, he never again worked in baseball. Flood was determined to break baseball's system of keeping players in servitude: "I am a man, not a consignment of goods to be bought and sold."[2] But he paid an enormous price for his right to challenge the system:

Do you know what I've been through? Do you know what it means to go against the grain in this country? Your neighbors hate you. Do you know what its like to be called the little black son of a bitch who tried to destroy baseball, the American pastime?[3]

In many ways, Flood's experience should be quite familiar to organizers. Challenging dominant social values and social institutions does not, in the short run at least, win us friends and positive recognition. Yet hundreds of others continue to challenge the system, to blow the whistle on policies and practices they consider wrong and illegal.

In this chapter we will explore the nature of whistleblowing, celebrated and not-so-celebrated examples of whistleblowing, the different forms that whistleblowing can take, the role of whistleblowing as a community organizing strategy, ways in which community organizers can relate to whistleblowers, and strategies for whistleblowing. Hopefully, the chapter will, like the legislation Senator Kennedy praised, encourage organizers who work within social institutions, be they private corporations, public schools, social welfare agencies, other human service settings, or government bureaucracies, to speak out freely. While no one can promise activists that their experience will be significantly different than Curt Flood's, activists can learn from his and other available examples of whistleblowing what to expect and how best to prepare for the act of whistleblowing and its consequences.

THE CASE OF KAREN SILKWOOD

Karen Silkwood was driving a 1973 white Honda Civic when she left the Hub Diner in Crescent, Oklahoma at 7:10 P.M. and headed for a rendezvous with a *New York Times* reporter and a union official at a Holiday Inn 30 miles away. She was reportedly prepared to supply the *Times* with documents which would substantiate union charges (she was a union member) that the Kerr-McGee plutonium plant where she worked was violating Atomic Energy Commission standards for safety, endangering workers, producing faulty nuclear fuel rods, disguising the faulty fuel rods by tampering with photographic negatives, and engaging in other illegal and dangerous practices. At 7:30 P.M. her car was discovered by a passing truck driver. Karen Silkwood was dead. Her car had travelled from the right side of Route 74 to the left side and had gone 240 feet on the left shoulder before careening over a culvert and smashing into a concrete wingwall. The car travelled 24 feet in the air and hit the concrete abutment wall at a speed of 45 miles an hour.[4]

The charges that Silkwood the whistleblower raised would ultimately be aired in court as part of civil suit brought by her estate (her parents and children). But the cause of her death and many events which occurred just prior to and long after her death would remain, at least for the time being, a mystery. Did Karen Silkwood fall asleep at the wheel, as the Oklahoma State Highway Patrol claims, and thus die an unremarkable, accidental death? Or was she murdered? What happened to the packet of documents that was in her car when she crashed? Witnesses report having seen her carry documents when she got into her car and having seen them at the accident scene just after the crash. Who took the documents? The Oklahoma Highway Patrol says there were no documents around when it arrived. Why did the police radio the wrecker which was first dispatched to the accident scene and tell the driver to return to his garage? Why was the Oklahoma Highway Patrol unwilling to admit that certain new dents in the back of Karen Silkwood's car probably were made by another car's bumper and that such marks might suggest that she was driven off the road that night? If the accident was indeed the result of the driver falling asleep, then how could the police explain the fact that the steering wheel was bent in a fashion that was only possible if the driver were fully conscious, clutching the wheel? Why did the police say Karen Silkwood had been drinking before the crash when in fact she had not been drinking? What of the many mysteries that surrounded Karen Silkwood's life just prior to the accident? How did she get contaminated with plutonium radiation at the Kerr-McGee plant? Where did the radiation poisoning come from? Had she contaminated herself as the nuclear health physicist at the plant suggested? Or had she been contamined by accident or by someone else's design? How did her apartment get contaminated? Was someone trying to threaten her, to scare her?

The Kerr-McGee plant where Karen worked produced nuclear fuel rods made out of plutonium. Plutonium is, in the words of one news account, "20,000 times more deadly than the venom from a cobra if ingested, and even minute quantities can cause cancer years later."[5] In her first few years at the Kerr-McGee plant, Karen Silkwood did not know how dangerous plutonium was. The plant's training manual carefully neglected to explain plutonium's carcinogenic properties. When Karen Silkwood first became active in the Oil, Chemical, and Atomic Workers Union, she was still almost completely uninformed about plutonium: "No one had ever taken an anatomical drawing, pointed to lungs or liver or lymph nodes or bones, said that plutonium can cause cancer there in twenty-five or thirty years. It angered her, for she had been in a contaminated room without a respirator."[6] Karen Silkwood would be contaminated much more seriously before her death.

Once aware of the dangers, Silkwood began to investigate more closely the working conditions at the Kerr-McGee plant. She became alarmed when she observed workers in contaminated areas of the building for several hours at a time. Workers were, according to her accounts relayed to union officials, simply not fully aware of the dangers they encountered daily. Karen Silkwood became increasingly concerned as she learned more about plutonium. The union brought in experts to educate the workers. Two nuclear scientists from the University of Minnesota spoke to the workers candidly. They did nothing to allay Silkwood's fears:

> The scientists pounded away at one theme: plutonium causes cancer. No one, they said, knows how much plutonium will cause cancer, or where and when. They said it is difficult to describe just how toxic plutonium really is because it's so different from other poisons. Fiendishly toxic, even in small amounts. Twenty thousand times more deadly than the potassium used in the Auschwitz gas chambers.
> They said the AEC "safe" standards were meaningless, set on faith. The standards for the general population had been tightened by a factor of 100 during the past few years, but those for the men and women who worked with plutonium and who breathed it had not been made more stringent.
> The plutonium at the Cimarron plant, they told their listeners, gets into the air as a nitrate mist or as a fine oxide dust. You breathe it through your mouth or nose. If you breathe it through your nose, they said, the cilia in your nostrils catch the biggest chunks; the rest enters the body. If you breathe it through your mouth, some plutonium

sneaks down the windpipe; some is trapped by mucus and forced into the esophagus. It ends up in your stomach.[7]

Silkwood's major charges against Kerr-McGee were that workers were contaminated, that when they were contaminated they frequently were allowed to track the contamination through the plant where they could contaminate others, that regular production continued in contaminated areas, that nuclear materials were stored improperly, that respirators were inadequately monitored and cleaned, that workers were not given time to shower, that the plant had only two showers for 75 workers per shift, that the company tampered with quality control photographs to cover up flaws in the fuel rods, and that workers were encouraged to disregard certain safety precautions.[8] These were the charges she took to her union and she intended to prove them with evidence she planned to give to New York Times reporter David Burnham.

Just several weeks before her death, Karen Silkwood was contaminated badly. She was contaminated first while working at the plant. No one could figure out where the contamination came from. Her work clothes had forty times the "acceptable" limit of radioactivity. Her skin and hair showed twenty times the limit declared safe by the Atomic Energy Commission. A day later, she still showed signs of being contaminated. Her nostrils—an important place to measure radioactivity because a nose smear indicates possible inhalation of radioactive particles—showed readings higher than the day before. On the third day, tests showed she had been very dangerously exposed. Both nostrils showed 90 times the AEC limit. It was then that the contamination specialist went with Silkwood from the plant to her apartment. Her apartment was so "hot" with radioactivity that the specialist had to go back to the plant to get special clothing before investigating and decontaminating it. A wrapper covering a bologna and cheese sandwich in her refrigerator was contaminated 800 times over the limit. Later tests proved that Silkwood had indeed ingested contaminated matter.[9] But where had the contamination come from? Had someone intentionally poisoned her? The civil suit brought by Karen Silkwood's parents against Kerr-McGee was designed to answer those questions and many more.[10]

In his book, The Killing of Karen Silkwood, investigative reporter Richard Rashke provides an extraordinarily detailed and illuminating account of the Silkwood case. He explains, for example, how the attorneys for Silkwood built their case into something of enormous scope, but then had to narrow it considerably. The attorneys for Karen Silkwood's estate brought in their own investigator, Bill Taylor, to help put together evidence for the trial. Taylor confirmed much of what the union's investigator had discovered. First, Karen Silkwood's car had been pushed from behind. Dents in the back fender would not have been caused during the towing after the accident. Scratch marks on the dents were not made by a cement wall; they were made by rubber such as that found on bumpers. Investigator Taylor then began to probe further into the case. He found that the local police agency which had done the investigation had extensive electronic surveillance gear obtained by a Florida-based spy school. He learned further that the police agency was connected to a private intelligence-gathering federation. He then learned that the FBI had an extensive file on the Silkwood case. But as it turned out, neither Congress nor the Silkwood attorneys were able to secure a copy of the complete FBI file in the case. One of the first judges in the case had been recommended for appointment to the federal bench by Sam Kerr, founder of Kerr-McGee against whom the case was filed. The investigator's life was in danger three times during the probe. The last time was when several White House staff members warned that he could be killed if he pursued certain avenues of investigation. However, despite all of the intrigue in this case, the attorneys for the Silkwood estate kept running up against stone walls. Even though they believed that the FBI and Kerr-McGee had conspired to cover up illegal activities, they could not get enough information to link the Federal Bureau of Investigation with Kerr-McGee. Thus the court put the conspiracy case aside, forcing the attorneys to focus on the civil suit which alleged that Karen Silkwood had been contaminated by Kerr-McGee plutonium, that plutonium is extraordinarily toxic, that Kerr-McGee had been negligent in its handling of plutonium, and that Kerr-McGee thus jeopardized the safety not only of Karen Silkwood, but of all other workers at the plant.

In court testimony, it came out that workers who had complained to the Atomic Energy Commission about safety had been hounded by the company. When these same workers refused Kerr-McGee's polygraph tests which included questions about their thoughts on nuclear power, they were transferred to less preferable jobs. One employee provided a list of design defects in the plant that made it unsafe. Another described a woefully inadequate training program. Still another told of company efforts to literally cover up a nuclear spill in the Cimarron river; workers were brought out at night to bury dead fish. When all the testimony was in, the jury found that Karen Silkwood did not, as Kerr-McGee tried to argue, contaminate herself. Instead, the jury found that "the Kerr-McGee Nuclear Corporation was negligent in its operation of the Cimarron facility" and that this negligence led to escape of plutonium from the plant and contamination of Silkwood. The jury found Kerr-McGee guilty. Indeed, it found Kerr-McGee guilty of willful wrongdoing, for which the jury charged Kerr-McGee punitive damages of $10,000,000, the largest ever in such a case.

Attorneys for Kerr-McGee had attempted during the course of the trial to characterize Karen Silkwood as an antinuclear activist, as an unstable person who was prone to "free" sex and drug use, and as so militantly pro-union that she would contaminate herself in order to embarrass the company and advance the union cause. Much of this line of testimony was simply disallowed by the judge. The rest was successfully refuted by Silkwood estate attorneys. Perhaps because the civil suit was successful, or because so much meticulously gathered evidence came to light in and out of the courtroom, it is now possible to derive many lessons from Karen Silkwood's experiences and legacy as a whistleblower.

As an employee who raised questions about worker safety and environmental safety, Silkwood frequently felt that company officials treated her as naive. She felt as if she were regarded as having stepped out of line, as a troublemaker rather than a serious person with serious and legitimate concerns. She learned early that many people around her were threatened by her outspokenness. Had she not had union support, her tenacious questioning of authority would have been more difficult. Karen Silkwood found that in order to obtain information about the issue that concerned her, worker safety, she literally had to turn into a cloak-and-dagger investigator. Even basic information concerning the carcinogenic properties of plutonium was hidden from the workers, herself included. She found she had to go outside the company gates and official manuals to get straightforward information. Ultimately, Karen Silkwood found not only her livelihood threatened, but her very life. It is entirely possible that her death was caused by her attempt to blow the whistle on unsafe conditions at the plant. Author Richard Rashke believes that the FBI knows who killed Karen Silkwood but is still covering up that information.

Karen Silkwood's case is not typical of most whistleblowers' in that most do not face a threat of death. However, most do experience severe reprisals. Some lose their jobs, some lose their friends, and some lose hoped-for promotions. Many find themselves characterized as troublemakers. Others find themselves becoming the objects of slander. Some find that those they accuse of wrongdoing turn around and charge them with causing the problems they have exposed. Some, like Karen Silkwood, find that whistleblowing provides the impetus for a social change movement to emerge. Many others, though, discover that their actions gather no such broad-based support and sympathy. Despite its obvious potential to foment change, whistleblowing is a strategy fraught with risks. The major question, then, is how to blow the whistle on wrongdoing while at the same time minimizing its personal costs.

THE NATURE OF WHISTLEBLOWING

What is whistleblowing? When is "speaking out" whistleblowing and when is it "sour grapes" or "informing?" Is the whistleblower a protector of morality or a social misfit, an egoist of the first order? If a whistleblower tells the truth and serves the public interest then why do others, even those who are sympathetic, find it so difficult to ally themselves with the whistleblower's cause? These questions surround the topic of whistleblowing partially because it is a relatively new phenomenon. Questions also arise because despite its outward simplicity, whistleblowing is exceedingly complex. It takes a variety of forms and occurs in diverse contexts. Whistleblowing leads to some predictable and some not so predictable outcomes, and inevitably generates controversy.

Whistleblowing means bringing attention to any illegal, immoral, or otherwise wrongful practices in a setting where one works or lives with the intent of stopping or changing them. It usually refers to an action taken by someone who is perceived as a member of the setting that is being questioned. Hence we would not refer to accusations made by a taxpayer against particular governmental actions as whistleblowing. Nor would muckraking journalism qualify as whistleblowing. Similarly, we would not generally regard a consumer's criticisms of a product or service as a kind of whistleblowing. While each of these practices may contribute to social change and improved social conditions, none of them fits the definition of whistleblowing. Whistleblowing is a type of outspokenness and community action that is different from most others in that its initiators are themselves members of a particular social setting being criticized, whether it is a small town, a major corporation, or the U.S. government.

By this definition, was President Nixon's legal adviser, John Dean, a whistleblower? In several respects, he fit the definition. He belonged to the Nixon administration and eventually exposed it. He even participated in many of the illegalities that were brought to light in his Congressional testimony. However, was this an example of whistleblowing or was it merely a case of a man who saw the "writing on the wall" and decided to tell all before he himself became further enmeshed in the administration's problems? The latter seems to be the case. While it is true that John Dean shocked the nation with his candor and excellent recall of events in and around Nixon's Oval Office—he described with script-like accuracy the dramatic sequence of events that occurred as Nixon and his aides attempted to obscure and even deny their part in the burglary of the Democratic headquarters at the Watergate office building and the subsequent cover-up of that involvement—he did so only when subpoenaed to testify before Congress and only when it was obvious that any further complicity in the cover-up would involve perjury on his part. The major difference between his actions and those we commonly refer to as whistleblowing is that he was a collaborator in the illegalities. He spoke out only when his own illegal actions were about to become public information. In fact, it appeared that the Nixon Administration was maneuvering to make it look like the entire Watergate cover-up was created and perpetrated by John Dean, legal counsellor, on an unsuspecting and naive president and his advisors. Dean spoke as much as to save himself as the country.

The case of John Dean raises another question about the nature of the true whistleblower. Dean spoke out willingly, but only after he was faced with possible imprisonment for perjury. Ironically, even though he did not perjure himself before Congress, he did spend four months in prison for his participation in illegal acts associated with the Watergate scandal.[11] This raises the issue of whether whistleblowers act willingly or under coercion from others when they speak out against illegal and dangerous practices. Note the case of one of the most written about whistleblowers, Ernest Fitzgerald. As a Defense Department cost analyst, he was in a position to know about cost overruns on major military projects such as the C–5A transport planes. However, he did not take his knowledge of massive cost overruns to the American people or to Congress. Indeed, he seems to have backed into his celebrated role of whistleblower. Richard Reeves, in an article for *Esquire* magazine entitled "The Last Angry Men," describes how Fitzgerald became a whistleblower:

The troubles—and heroism, if it is that—come gradually, incrementally. Ernest Fitzgerald says that the people who think he is a hero, and the people who hate him, have forgotten that he did not exactly roar into a hearing room in the New Senate Office Building demanding that the government clean up waste in defense spending. He was asked directly, by Senator William Proxmire, about the accuracy of Congressional reports that the C–5A was running $2 billion over Air Force cost estimates. Others lied; Fitzgerald waffled bureaucratically for a few sentences and concluded, "Your figures could be approximately right."[12]

From that moment on, Fitzgerald became a whistleblower, both in his own eyes and in those of the people with whom he worked. He had broken ranks with his colleagues. They had lied. He committed the indiscretion of telling the truth. From that moment on he became a symbol of the conscientious worker who speaks out for what is right. His case is rather typical of many whistleblowers who become activists almost by accident.

In some instances, the substance rather than the form of a person's outspokenness may determine whether or not her or she is a whistleblower. With regard to legal and illegal activities, the whistleblower's role is clear—to expose illegalities by "going public." However, when the substance of the charges involve less easily defined things like immorality, danger, and activities deemed "not in the public's interest," the assessment of whether or not a person is a whistleblower is a bit more difficult. For example, when an employee at General Motors sent information to Ralph Nader about dangerous defects in car trunks (Defects that could asphyxiate passengers), was the worker blowing the whistle or was he simply expressing a disagreement with the company over a merely technical matter? In this case there was a technical controversy but, over time, it became obvious that the employee's charges were accurate. The car design he questioned was potentially dangerous. Eventually the company made a change in the cars. In that case, the employee fit our definition of a whistleblower.

Other examples are more complex. In the early 1950s, Senator Joseph McCarthy engaged in what is now generally regarded as a demogogic witch-hunt of people presumed by McCarthy to be communists in the film industry and in government. McCarthy was eventually discredited because he used tactics that were considered unfair and unconstitutional and because he made accusations that he could not substantiate. But prior to his downfall, McCarthy forced many famous people to come before his committee and tell about their own activities in the Communist party, their own knowledge of the American Communist party, and their knowledge of other people's activities. When people testified, they frequently found themselves implicating their friends. Some people, like Lillian Hellman, refused to do this. She and others were unwilling to testify. However, some people like Elia Kazan, Whittaker Chambers, and James Wechsler, provided the Senator's committee with information on their friends' past involvement with the Communists. At first glance, the testimony of the latter group may appear to be simply "informing." Victor S. Navasky, author of a detailed and thoughtful history of this period entitled *Naming Names,* defines informing as betrayal of a comrade, that is, "a fellow member of a movement, a colleague, or a friend, to the authorities."[13] Interestingly though, several of those who chose to inform on friends saw themselves as blowing the whistle on communism. James Rorty and Moshe Decter summarize this position in their book, *McCarthy and the Communists:*

> A former Communist who testifies frankly about his past associations often thereby helps to expose dangerous current activities of the Party.
>
> Frank testimony of this sort does not make one an "informer," with all the distasteful connotations of that word. On the contrary, if a silent witness must be protected in his right to invoke the Fifth Amendment, a forthright witness must be equally protected from slanderous insinuations against his reputation and idealism. The man who testifies frankly about the past Communist record of former friends and associates performs the same public service as the witness who testifies to his personal knowledge of the past Nazi or Fascist record of former friends and associates.[14]

In reference to one group of informants, those Victor Navasky calls espionage informers, naming names (of people who were communists or thought to be communist sympathizers) was a way of stopping what the informers perceived as communism's threatening advances:

> The collective witness of the self-styled espionage exposers contributed mightily to American's belief that here was an international red menace and that these particular ex-communists deserved our thanks and respect for blowing the whistle on Stalin and his blueprint for world domination.[15]

Here, blowing the whistle meant creating a definition of a problem, perhaps even making up a problem to some extent (that is, the red menace), and rooting it out. In retrospect, creating a near hysterical fear of the presumed menace proved every bit as problematic, perhaps more so, than any actual threat to democracy that may have in fact existed. Indeed, the strategies that McCarthy and others used to gather information are now commonly regarded as profoundly antidemocratic. The term "McCarthyism" is now synonymous with modern day witch-hunting.

To call informers whistleblowers does violence to our sense of what the latter term means. It is true that those who named names may have regarded their actions as patriotic and, thus, in the public interest. However, these informants lacked one quality usually associated with whistleblowers. When whistleblowers stand up for high principles, they do so in opposition to those in power or authority. Karen Silkwood stood up to officials of the Atomic Energy Commission and those at Kerr-McGee. Ernest Fitzgerald stood up, however inadvertently, against "the brass" in the Pentagon. As Curt Flood put it, when you go against the grain, you do not endear yourself to those in power. The people who provided McCarthy with information he requested, even information about their friends, did not challenge authority. However unwillingly, they acquiesced to authority. From this perspective, Lillian Hellman and the others who refused to cooperate, who fought to expose the antidemocratic nature of the hearings themselves, were the ones who laid themselves open to retribution in the form of stunted careers, denied jobs, and clouded reputations. It was the latter group that was willing to risk all, to stand up to the greatest powers in the country, for a principle.

As power becomes more and more concentrated, whistleblowing becomes more and more important as a strategy for maintaining accountability to certain important values. In the world of corporate power, who will ensure that concern for product safety will win out over concern for cutting costs and maximizing profitability? In the back wards of large mental institutions, who can promise that expedience and routinization will not dominate concern for individual, personal care and treatment? As Robert Townsend puts it, we seem to have a double standard about values we expect individuals to adhere to and those demanded of corporations and government:

> Who are we going to look to, to make these giant organizations honest—to make them stop destroying the quality of all our lives (including theirs and their employees') for their own private interests?
>
> The government? Union Carbide has all the know-how in chemistry, the government practically none; General Motors all the know-how in automobiles, the government just what they're allowed to know. And those government officials that can't be snowed can be bought. The military juggernaut owns John Stennis, body and soul.
>
> The law? Union Camp, Inc., dictated the laws which enabled it to turn the Savannah River into an open sewer.
>
> Corporate leaders? No, but why not? In my judgment, there are two reasons. First, we have a double legal standard in this country. If you—Peter Petkas, citizen—walk across the hall and kill your neighbor, you will probably be severely punished under the criminal law. If you—Peter Petkas, a president of the Allison Division of General Motors—release a known defective airplane engine which causes the death of thirty-eight people, you won't be punished at all. Your company may be fined $7500 under the civil code. This they will deduct from taxes as a normal business expense. So corporate murder costs two hundred dollars a head before taxes and a hundred dollars a head after taxes. Standard Oil of California drew a million-dollar fine—the biggest in corporate history. If you earned $168 a week, the equivalent for you would be a two-dollar fine. So there's work to be done to eliminate the double legal standard and let the punishment fit the crime.
>
> The second reason we can't expect leadership from our corporate moguls is that at the moment of assuming command we unfit them for the job. What we should do is tell them to take off their coat, go out among their people and their customers, and find out at first hand what the problems and opportunities are. What we do is give them two more secretaries, a private limousine, a private helicopter, a private elevator, a private dining room, a big increase in pay, and outside directorships. The result is that Lee Iacocca is never heard from again by his own people.[16]

Given that context, where citizens have fewer and fewer ways to check public and private (mainly corporate) power and where power is more concentrated than ever before, the whistleblower's role, while not the only point of accountability, stands out as a crucial one. Whistleblowers have one main advantage and one great disadvantage when compared to other organizers. Their unique advantage lies in their easy access to inside information about a policy, practice, cover-up, or the like. In many situations, insiders are the only ones who have information necessary to verify an illegal or threatening situation. To cite an example with which most people are familiar we might ask, would newspaper reporters Bob Woodward and Carl Bernstein have been able to break the Watergate cover-up had they not had the assistance of an insider whom they referred to as "Deep Throat?" Similarly, would the Kerr-McGee story have ever been told had Karen Silkwood and several coworkers not disclosed information they gathered as insiders. Clearly, the whistleblower needs other qualities as well, like the ability to interpret technical information for the general public, the ability to tell the difference between a big problem and a minor flaw, and the ability to ferret out information without jeopardizing his or her position irreparably. However, the first and most crucial advantage the whistleblower enjoys is the insider's access to information.

The whistleblower's chief problem derives from this first advantage. As a member of the organization or setting, the whistleblower is vulnerable. Government or company leaders can isolate, fire, harass, and otherwise make life miserable for whistleblowers. The numerous cases included in this chapter indicate the kinds of sanctions that whistleblowers encounter when they begin to use their inside information to serve outside interests. In the last section of this chapter, we will examine defensive strategies which whistleblowers can use to safeguard themselves against those sanctions.

The issue that whistleblowers address are usually highly controversial. These issues have involved, for example:

* abuses of patients (for example, overmedication, inadequate staffing, punishment, improper medical treatment) in nursing homes and mental institutions.
* manufacture of automobiles which have known flaws in their design and manufacturing.
* intentional dumping of toxic wastes in violation of state and federal regulations, posing an obvious threat to the public health.
* denial by banks, and other lending institutions, of loans and mortgages to Blacks, Hispanics, and other minority customers who live and work in particular areas of a community (a practice called red-lining).
* overrepresentation of Black, Hispanic, and other minority children in public school special education classes.
* failure on the part of human service agencies and welfare agencies to make appropriated funding available to those people for whom it was intended.
* use of community development funds for politically influential individuals and organizations at the expense of those groups for whom it was intended.
* profiteering by business people from certain municipal projects (for example, the buying of certain parcels of land, owned by politically connected individuals, at exhorbitant prices for use in municipal capital construction projects such as buildings, highways, trash burning plants, and parks).

Unfortunately, such practices have become almost commonplace in most American cities and in most large workplaces. Few people who work in large organizational settings can say that they have not seen illegal or immoral activities occur. Thus, most people face the decision that whistleblowers face. "Should I speak out?"; "If I don't get a satisfactory response from the officials in the setting, should I go public?''; "If I keep quite, am I compromising my principles? Am I becoming part of the problem, a collaborator?''

As with any type of organizing, the individual must answer those questions personally and in the contexts in which they arise. No situation is precisely like another. Many factors (most of which are covered in the final section of this chapter) enter into the consideration of whether or not to speak out.

CASE EXAMPLES:
WHISTLEBLOWERS AT LARGE

Mildred S. Downs

Mildred S. Downs had worked as a public school teacher in Arkansas for 25½ years. Then, the Conway School Board fired her.[17]

Mildred Downs began to have some disagreements with school officials just two years before she was fired. The first encounter over an issue of conditions in the school seemed innocuous enough. Her classroom water fountain broke. Ms. Downs reported the problem to the school principal who in turn reported it to Carl White, the maintenance director. Mr. White discovered that the fountain was under warranty but that the necessary parts would not be available for ten days to two weeks. He so informed Ms. Downs. For the interim, she provided the students with paper cups and a plastic bucket full of water.

One day, while the permanent fountain was still broken and the plastic bucket empty, Ms. Downs was about to start art class. She asked the students to draw pictures of each other. A few of the students drew pictures of each other lying down asking for water, with wilted flowers nearby. The teacher found these cartoons rather humorous. In fact, she showed them to the principal. She then forgot about the whole incident. However, unbeknownst to her, it would surface again later.

On another matter, Mildred Downs had a more serious conflict with school officials. The school operated an open incinerator in the middle of the playground, which posed a hazard to students. Children apparently were attracted to the incinerator and frequently climbed the incinerator walls. Only close supervision by teachers kept them from being injured. When students played basketball or baseball, they were exposed to the incinerator's overflow of burned and rusted tin cans and broken bottles. Also, when the wind blew in the school's direction, smoke from the incinerator entered the classrooms and caused respiratory problems for teachers and students alike.

Mildred Downs complained on numerous occasions to the school principal that smoke was seeping into her classroom. She wanted the incinerator moved or trash removal provided. In fact, she found the problem so offensive that she and her husband offered several times to pay for trash removal. The superintendent made no reply to their offers. He apparently believed that since there were similar incinerator problems at each of the District's five schools, and since the District could not afford to provide trash removal at the other school sites as well, that it would be unfair to allow trash removal only at the Ellen Smith Elementary School where Mildred Downs taught.

As far as Mildred Downs knew, she was the only person who was making serious complaints about the incinerator to the principal. Actually. a group of mothers who had volunteered in the school and who experienced the smoke problem first hand had also complained. Yet despite the fact that the superintendent knew and had been repeatedly warned that the incinerator was a hazard to the health and physical well-being of students and teachers, he did nothing to remedy the situation.

Like so many people who end up being defined as whistleblowers, Mildred Downs did not define her role as such. She was simply trying to do her job, and ensure the optimal health and safety of her students and herself.

Mildred Downs was destined to have more problems. In January of her last year of teaching before she was fired, she presented a lesson, taken from an authorized school text, on nutrition. The lesson included information that raw carrots provide more nutritional value than do cooked ones. Since the students' workbook suggested that they write letters expressing their views on issues, it was natural that one of the students suggested that they write a letter to the food service personnel requesting raw carrots. The letter lacked certain amenities, but since it originated from one of the students and because it emanated naturally from the curriculum, at the students' request, Ms. Downs herself, along with the students, signed the letter. The letter read: ''Dear Mr. Glenn, The people in my room do not like cooked carrots so will you please serve the school raw carrots? Mrs. Downs' Second Grade.'' The second graders sent the letter to Mr. Glenn via the principal.

When the superintendent of schools heard about the letter, he became angry. He charged the teacher with ''going over his head.'' He further expressed, for the first time, his displeasure with the students' water fountain drawings. Ms. Downs was surprised that this issue had resurfaced. In fact, she was unaware until this point that the water fountain drawings were an issue. She told the superintendent that she did not believe she had gone ''over his head'' and that she believed the cartoons were actually quite creative and educational. She told him she felt they were consistent with her duty to awaken students' interest in current events.

About this time, in the spring before her firing, the incinerator problem worsened. Ms. Downs therefore increased her complaints. However, the principal told her that she alone, among the school teachers, was complaining. He did not tell her, and Ms. Downs did not know, that several parents had also complained. Mildred Downs then asked the other teachers to express their concerns in writing. One teacher did not respond, but instead complained about Ms. Downs' request to the superintendent.

On April 27, the Ellen Smith School Parent-Teachers Association requested that the School Board remove the incinerators. On May 25, the superintendent notified Ms. Downs that her contract would not be renewed. The reasons were as follows: (1) insubordination; (2) lack of cooperation with the administration; and (3) teaching second graders to protest.

The central question raised by Ms. Downs' case is ''What protection do whistleblowers have when speaking out for such reasonable concerns as health and safety?'' Or, put another way, can an employer require, as a condition of employment, that employees agree to keep their concerns to themselves? Mildred Downs took her case to Federal Court for an answer to this and several related questions. On the basic question of employee rights to speak out, the U.S. District Court, Eastern District Arkansas, cited a Court of Appeals decision, *Lucas v. Chapman*, 430 F.2d 945 (5th C.A. 1970):

> While the school boards in Arkansas have the right to decide whom they are going to employ or re-employ, the basis for failing to re-employ must not be on impermissible constitutional grounds.[18]

And, citing another case, *Norton v. Blaylock*, 285 F.Supp, 659 (E.D. Ark., 1968) aff'd 409 F.2d 772 (8th C.A. 1969), the court found

> that a State may not constitutionally impose arbitrary or discriminatory employment criteria and may not in general condition public employment upon the willingness of an employee or would-be employee to forego the exercise of rights protected by some of the first ten amendments to the Constitution as brought forward into the 14th Amendment.[19]

In other words, the State may not demand that employees choose between being employed and exercising their rights under the Bill of Rights of the U.S. Constitution.

The School District tried to justify its firing of Ms. Downs on the grounds that she violated a school district policy, namely that: ''No petition for any purpose may be circulated in any building without the approval of the Superintendent of Schools.'' Not surprisingly, the court found the School District's policy unnecessarily broad and therefore, unconstitutional. It might be permissible for the district to disallow petitions that would interfere with operation of the school, but to outlaw all petitions was, as the court put it, ''total censorship.'' Further, after reviewing the evidence in the Downs case, the court found no evidence, nor was any presented by the school district, that Mildred Downs' activities interfered ''with discipline in the operation of the school.''[20] Indeed, the Court seemed amused that the superintendent simultaneously expressed his belief in freedom to discuss controversial issues and his own intolerance of such behaviors.

Another issue that arose in the Downs case was whether she had been insubordinate. On the contrary, Mildred Downs had always gone through appropriate channels. The Court confirmed this when it found:

> In the incident concerning the carrots, Mrs. Downs discussed the matter only with the cafeteria supervisor as he was the party most immediately concerned. With respect to the water fountain, again only the maintenance supervisor and later the principal were involved as it was unnecessary to enlist the aid of a successively higher authority re: the superintendent. Lastly regarding the incinerator, Mrs. Downs again only went through the hierarchy as the need became evident.[21]

Had Mildred Downs not pursued standard hierarchical channels she might have been open to the charge of breaching school policy and therefore, of insubordination. Therefore, the manner in which she presented her own and her students' concerns ultimately shaped the final determination of her case.

Finally, the court took an aggressive stand in protecting the right of Ms. Downs to speak out on issues, even controversial ones:

> When a School Board acts, as it did here, to punish a teacher who seeks to protect the health and safety of herself and her pupils, the resulting intimidation can only cause a severe chilling, it not freezing, effect on the free discussion of more controversial subjects.[22]

To some extent, the court seemed to be saying that schools have a special obligation to protect the free flow of discussion. This special obligation is derived from the historical role of schools as instruments of education for citizenship. The Court cited the district's own policy in this regard:

> In conclusion this Court hopes that the defendents (the District) . . . will adopt a reasonable attitude which will allow its teachers to comply with Policy III F 4e which provides, as to teachers that: "He shall demonstrate that principals of democracy at all times in the operation of his classroom thereby providing each child with the opportunity to develop from actual experience a real understanding of the democratic way of life." The Board shall not allow naive and chimerical fears to disrupt the above objective as was done in this case.[23]

One year later, on the 23rd day of June, Ms. Downs won her job back. The court ordered her reinstated, with full back pay, and full compensation for attorney's fees which she had incurred while defending her rights.

Haverford State

When the *Philadelphia Daily News* published an article entitled, "Drug, Sex Charges Leveled at Hospital,"[24] Linda Rafferty had no idea she would lose her job as a result of remarks she made that were quoted in the article.

Linda Rafferty was a former president of the State Psychiatric Nurses Association and a former employee (for five years) at Haverford State Hospital. She was employed as a psychiatric nurse at the Philadelphia Psychiatric Center when she went public with her charges against Haverford State. She spoke out because she wanted "to help the patients." She has previously taken her complaints to her supervisors and to the Haverford Director but with, in her view, little effect.

The condition and incidents she exposed were serious:

1. signed drug prescription forms left in unlocked drawers where anyone could come in and write down a drug and any name.
2. "forced homosexuality among patients and seduction of mentally disturbed youngsters by outsiders."
3. gross misdiagnoses of medical conditions.

4. inaccessible fire extinguishers.
5. institutional peonage; residents forced to clean buildings.

Ms. Rafferty produced a copy of a signed prescription order as well as detailed accounts of incidents involving exploitation of residents to document her charges.

The State of Pennsylvania fired Ms. Rafferty from her job at the Philadelphia Psychiatric Center, which she had held for one week. The State admitted the firing was related to her remarks in the *Daily News* article, but claimed a legitimate interest. Namely, the State argued that she was incompetent and that her remarks would be anxiety-producing for the staff with whom she worked in the new Center. The Court found the incompetence charge totally without merit: "We find the allegations of inadequate performance afterthoughts to justify the firing rather than reasons for it."[26] In regard to the second charge, that her remarks were anxiety-producing, the court showed equally little patience with the State:

> It can hardly be doubted that conditions at a state mental hospital are matters of considerable public concern on which citizens, including former employees of the hospital, would ordinarily have the right to comment freely. And it is equally clear that defendents' interest in allaying the anxieties of some of their employees is . . . totally insufficient to outweigh Mrs. Rafferty's interest in speaking freely about Haverford State Hospital. . . .
> The First Amendment does not stop at the hospital door. A hospital should be given every possible latitude in maintaining a proper environment for the treatment of its patients. It may not, however, be permitted to mask its arbitrary suppression of protected speech behind claims that such speech creates an "antitherapeutic situation" when no ill effect on patient care has been shown. It may not stifle one employee's freedom of expression by professing a duty to create a sterilized, anxiety-free vacuum for its other employees, all of whom should by training be able to weather minor upsets without totally disintegrating. Free speech may create tumult; it may offend some of its hearers. *Cohen* v. *California*, 403 U.S., 15, 91 S.Ct. 1780, 29 L. Ed.2d 284 (1971); *Organization for a Better Austin* v. *Keefe*, 402 U.S. 415. 91 S. Ct. 1575, 29 L.Ed.2d 1 (1971). It may also create "staff anxiety." However, staff anxiety over working with someone who is critical and outspoken, who adds to the dialogue that the First Amendment was designed to foster and protect, is no reason for firing a public employee for exercising her First Amendment rights.[27]

Finally, the court ordered the Commonwealth of Pennsylvania to reinstate Linda Rafferty to her job, with full back pay. She won. And, in the process of winning through litigation she helped clarify and establish the rights of whistleblowers to expose conditions which they find harmful to the public.

Drug Testing

Karen E. Test and Stephen Blythe are former research assistants who worked for a Boston-based doctor engaged in drug research. The doctor had a contract with a drug company to experiment with a "branched-chain amino acid" drug.[28]

According to their testimony before the Health Subcommittee of the Labor and Human Resource Committee, Test and Blythe observed other lab technicians removing labels marked "not for human use" from drug bottles. When Blythe questioned the doctor about the practice, the doctor assured him that all was legal. The doctor claimed he had the pharmaceutical company's approval. In fact, it appears he did not. Test and Blythe called the drug company to check. The company said the drug was not for human use yet and that it was "shocked" to learn of its application to human patients.[29]

At the same hearings, a Food and Drug Administration official reported on other instances where experimenters falsified data on research performed for drug companies. Senator Edward Kennedy, chairperson of the Health Subcommittee charged that such violations had persisted for a long period of time.[30]

The purpose of whistleblowing in this case was to expose the problem of fraud in drug testing and to provide support for legislation that would improve monitoring of such experimentation and better protect human subjects.

Jean Reilly, Hooker Chemicals and Plastics Employee

The Love Canal community near Buffalo, New York became infamous in America, a household word, when it was disclosed that Hooker Chemicals had used the site to dump toxic wastes. Since it had been turned into residential property, families who lived at the site were reporting abnormally high incidences of respiratory problems, birth defects, and cancer. Eventually, New York State saved many families from bankruptcy by buying the homes located closest to the site. In so doing, the government acknowledged that the chemical company had contaminated the area and that citizens were suffering from the corporation's actions. Thus it came as no particular surprise when lab technician Jean Reilly revealed other unsafe practices by the corporation.

Jean Reilly worked for 13 years at Hooker Chemicals and Plastics before she was fired. She believed that she was fired because "we (the union) have complained about working conditions in the lab."[31] Two weeks earlier, Jean Reilly testified before a state legislative committee in favor of proposed legislation that would "require companies to tell employees when they may be working near dangerous substances."[32] In her testimony she complained that while Hooker Chemicals did perform health monitoring of employees, she, for one, had never received the results of such tests. Only after the legislative hearing did she receive test results done on workers' exposure to asbestos in 1978. Results of the 1977 tests were not forthcoming.

The company fined Jean Reilly for failing to wear a gas mask. She claimed that the company policy required that an employee wear such a mask *or* have it readily accessible. She kept hers on a nearby bench. Jean Reilly and her union believed that the gas mask incident was a smokescreen for company anger at her legislative testimony. At the time she was fired, the union intended to fight on Reilly's behalf. A 65,000-strong union coalition announced: "We'll do everything we can do to support her in getting her job back."[33]

Dr. Capurro: An Informed and
Concerned Citizen Whistleblower

Whistleblowing is usually thought of as an inside-the-organization strategy. Karen Silkwood was an insider, a prototype whistleblower. So was Ernest Fitzgerald. Actually, the context for whistleblowing is sometimes larger than a single organization. In the case of Dr. Peter Capurro, the context was the small, seemingly innocent community of Little Elk Valley. As it turned out, the community was a site ripe for classic whistleblowing.[34] Author Larry Agran recounts Dr. Capurro's experience in an article which appeared in *New Times*.

Dr. Capurro and his family moved to Little Elk Valley to get away from chemical hazards. But when they arrived at their new home, Dr. Capurro immediately noticed chemical smells. When he inquired of a neighbor, he was told that the only chemical plant in the area was engaged in dumping. When Capurro called the plant, a worker confirmed the dumping. Capurro inquired further. He suspected the plant was processing certain toxic chemicals, among them toluene, carbon tetrachloride, and benzine, an assertion the company president denied.

The more Capurro investigated, the more certain he became that the Galaxy Chemical Company was dumping toxic chemicals in Little Elk Creek and contaminating Little Elk Creek air. The evidence was all too clear. Capurro used a gas chromatograph to examine air and water samples which contained, as he discovered, benzene, carbon tetrachloride, and methyl ethyl ketone. When he tested the blood of Little Elk Valley residents, they showed unusually high levels of these same chemicals. Finally, as a pathologist at the nearby hospital, he began noticing an abnormal number of cancer deaths among Little Elk Creek residents. Further tests of people's homes in the area revealed that the sickest people, as well as those who were presently dying, lived in the path of air and water flows that led away from the plant.

Despite all his evidence, Dr. Capurro found that officials in the community, at the company, and in State government ignored, trivialized, or were angered by his investigation and concerns. Finally, the State Health Department hired a specialist to investigate Dr. Capurro's concerns. However, when that specialist, Dr. Karlin, came up with concerns of her own, she too, according to Capurro, became a "nut," "no good" in the eyes of state officials. Dr. Karlin, like Dr. Capurro, would not drop the issue. She gave her story to a local paper. It did not take long for national media, namely the *Washington Post* and *CBS Evening News* to pick up on the story. Dr. Capurro's account for the media was simple, measured, and compelling:

> I can't say that the deaths in the valley from cancer were the result of specific exposure to chemical fumes. But there have been a lot of chemicals in that valley's air and water and the blood of those people we tested, and some of these chemicals cause cancer. And we know there are a lot more malignancies there than you would expect . . . if you're in a room where everyone is scratched and there's a lion in there, too, then you've got to suspect a lion.[33]

The Elk Valley incident stirred public interest partly because it fit the David and Goliath model that so typifies most whistleblowing cases and partly because the chemical company sued Dr. Capurro, charging him with an anti-Galaxy attitude and bad scientific technique. But it also stirred interest because Elk Valley was isolated. As Larry Agran suggests in his account of the Galaxy case, Elk Valley was a kind of environmental test tube, an isolated geographic area with one chemical plant and, therefore, a sole source of toxic chemicals. If people were dying in this test tube or, as Dr. Capurro put it, in the vicinity of a lion, then some kind of relationship could safely be assumed. Ultimately, the State of Maryland did study cancer deaths in the area and found that among other causes of death, "valley residents were dying of lymphatic cancer at a rate thirty times greater than normal" (that is greater than would be expected).[34]

Capurro's immediate public gave him mixed reviews. For many in the community, Capurro was a villain. They blamed him for threatening the community's livelihood by exposing the plant's illegal practices. His home and car were the objects of vandalism. Some treated him as an obsessed "nut." Others welcomed his determination. Some joined his campaign to protect the town by uncovering the coverup. Dr. Capurro and his family moved out of the area to protect their own health.

Willowbrook

Whistleblowers prove controversial because they pose an enormous dilemma for nearly everyone around them. They bring to the fore the issue of "whose interests does the worker, whether corporate executive, government bureaucrat, or line level staff, represent." They pose moral questions, forcing people to take sides. What makes matters worse, at least from the perspective of powerful people who occupy positions of authority and who are not accustomed to having their authority challenged, whistleblowers tend to point out potential conflicts of interest between those in authority and those less powerful. To the extent that superiors do not respond honestly and effectively to the whistleblower's concerns, the superiors find themselves embarrassed, threatened, and exposed by the whistleblower.

Human service workers are a case in point. Who are their clients? The agency directors for whom they work, the government officials who distribute funding for their programs, themselves, or the consumers to whom they provide services? In part at least, the manner in which we answer that question will determine whether or not we have the potential to engage in whistleblowing. Unless we see our own and the consumer's interests as the ones which need and deserve protection, we will probably not adopt the whistleblower role. In other words, as long as the employee sees the organization's self-interest (that is, maximizing profit, perpetuating age-old, but long since bankrupt policies and practices, permitting corruption which benefits certain members of the organization) as the interests to defend, then whistleblowing will have no place. Whistleblowing occurs where values and interests conflict.

The Willowbrook State School is an excellent example. Willowbrook is an institution for mentally retarded people located on Staten Island, a short ferry ride away from New York City. While the institution was called a school, it was, in the words of *Time* magazine, "a school in name only."[35] *Time* preferred to call it a "human warehouse."[36] In December of 1971, a few staff members at the institution began meeting with several parents who had sons and daughters in the institution. They discussed conditions at the facility. At the time, Willowbrook was the largest institution for the retarded in America. It housed over 5,000 inmates. At one time, in the 1960s, it housed over 6,000 residents, twice the number the institution had been built for in 1941.

For the majority of residents, the institution provided no programming, education, or developmental programming. On any given day, a visitor could walk through the institution and observe building after building, ward after ward, filled with thirty and fifty people, many of them severely and profoundly retarded locked in large, barren "day rooms." Many residents had no clothes on. Many had bruises and scars from the rigors of ward life. As one doctor testified in court, after the whistle had been blown on Willowbrook, one staff member had cut a resident by hitting him with a fist full of keys. Residents' teeth were in near total disrepair. Some had had their teeth removed to prevent them from biting themselves or other residents. Some rooms housed residents who could not walk. These residents lay in carts against the wall. Others had been drugged with tranquilizers so that they spent most of the day sleeping or in a drugged stupor.

The staff who met with the parents included two doctors and a social worker, among others. They described conditions at Willowbrook, conditions some of the parents had not seen because they had not been allowed on the wards. They brought the parents into the facility to see the actual conditions, which were so bad that they could not be easily or quickly cleaned up. Months after Willowbrook became a cause celebre, the conditions were still outrageous. Some buildings were seriously overcrowded, to the point where staff and residents occasionally had to climb over one bed in order to reach another. In such environments training was simply absent. *Time* described one part of the institution: "the girls spend their days sitting, standing or lying in a large, marble-floored room that resembles Sartre's vision of hell."[37] Rooms smelled of urine, feces, and disinfectant. Hepatitis raged through Willowbrook. Actually, 100 percent of the residents contracted hepatitis within six months of entering the institution. In fact, the hepatitis problem was used by one scientific experimenter as justification for injecting some of the Willowbrook residents with hepatitis—he reasoned that if all residents contract the dread disease anyway, why not use them for experimental purposes—as part of an effort to develop an effective vaccine against hepatitis. Ten years later when the same scientist suggested testing a vaccine on retarded persons in institutions, leading members of the medical profession expressed their outrage at the thought. But in 1971, Willowbrook permitted such practices. It was all part of an incredibly grim picture that the world would come to know as the Willowbrook exposé.

The parents of those institutionalized became more and more politicized. They and the handful of professionals from the inside met with a reporter from ABC television by the name of Geraldo Rivera. Rivera was a young attorney turned television newsperson. He had a knack for going after stories with social meaning. Willowbrook was just such a story. The whistleblowers, Drs. Bronston and Wilkins and social worker Elizabeth Lee, talked with the media. They invited Gerald Rivera to bring his cameras into the wards, and to hear the whistleblowers' complaints. Wilkins told Rivera that because of overcrowding and short staffing, staff were forced to feed residents at breakneck speed, the end result of which was that residents would develop pneumonia, a condition that could prove deadly for severely retarded people who have other respiratory complications. Rivera took pictures of residents languishing on the wards. He spoke with residents who had received only limited or no educational services. He asked, rhetorically, why these conditions had to continue.

The Willowbrook media coverage made institutional abuse a national issue. Institutional conditions had been exposed five years earlier in a *Look* magazine article by special educator Dr. Burton Blatt, but even though that issue of *Look* outsold all others, it could not match the coverage achieved by Willowbrook. After the ABC news accounts, the media flocked to the institution. *Time, The New York Times, The Village Voice, The Staten Island Advance,* and the *Dick Cavett Show* all reported the Willowbrook scandal.

Willowbrook's administration blamed institutional problems on overcrowding, lack of money, and on "militants and radicals" among staff personnel. In other words, they attributed the problems either to forces beyond the administration's control or to the people who reported the problems. The administration moved quickly to fire two of the whistleblowers, Dr. Wilkins and Ms. Lee. Both were "provisional employees" meaning that they had worked at the institution for less than three years and thus had no right under department policy to appeal the firings. Wilkins, Lee, and Bronston were accused of trying to take over the parent organization. The administration could not summarily fire Bronston in the same fashion because he had worked at the institution for more than three years and was a permanent employee. Despite reports from coworkers and parents that Bronston's work habits and medical abilities were outstanding, he became the first doctor in the history of the institution to receive a negative peer review, this after receiving only positive reviews prior to the exposé. As for Wilkins and Lee, the institution director took the position that he need not inform them about why they were fired. He sent them each a letter at 1 P.M. on Janurary 6th, 1972, informing them that they were fired as of the end of that work day. When asked by a local newspaper to comment on the firings, the institutional director, Dr. Jack Hammond, reportedly said, "No comment, I don't have to tell you anything."[38] Lee's immediate supervisor expressed shock at the firing: "Mrs. Lee is an excellent worker. She is a concerned caseworker who has tried to plan for her families and children as effectively as possible. She was one of the best things that's happened to Willowbrook. She was able to effect change when necessary."[39] Similarly, Wilkins' prior work evaluations had included only positive comments. Both were model employees, at least until they spoke out.

Parents of Willowbrook residents demanded reinstatement for Wilkins and Lee. They called for the director's ouster unless Lee and Wilkins were reinstated. For a brief moment, it appeared that there might be a reconciliation. In the face of

mounting pressure, the director agreed to reinstate the two. However, that settlement was short lived. The State Mental Health Commissioner vetoed the reinstatement. In the middle of all this, the parent-run Benevolent Association announced
that it was appointing Dr. Wilkins and social worker Lee as ombudsmen for the
association. The Willowbrook Benevolent Association charged Wilkins and Lee
with representing the rights of parents and the rights of children.[40]

Like so many whistleblowers, the Willowbrook group demonstrated extraordinary tenacity. Wilkins and Lee stayed around for months, helping the parents and
the community to organize for change. One group of parents filed suit against the
State, charging it with neglect under the child abuse and neglect statutes of New
York State. A family court judge dismissed the case on the grounds that the statute
was meant to monitor families, not State agencies. But the parents returned to
litigation. They enlisted the help of the New York State Association for Retarded
Citizens and the American Civil Liberties Union to bring a class action lawsuit
against the Governor and the institution. In a preliminary court order, a federal court
judge ruled that residents had a right to protection from harm. Eventually, the case
was settled in the form of a "consent decree" whereby the State admitted to the
alleged conditions and agreed to find quality, small, homelike community placements for all but 250 Willowbrook residents. It was an historic decision.

The State continued to question Dr. Bronston's competence. To protect himself, Dr. Bronston secured the services of leading labor attorneys. He eventually
agreed to leave state employment, but only after winning agreement that the state
would give him a year's paid leave from Willowbrook during which time he could
develop training programs for community living alternatives and continue to organize for change. As of this writing, Dr. Bronston works as a special consultant to
the Commissioner of Rehabilitation in the State of California. He spends most of his
waking hours as an organizer for change in the field of disability rights.

Actually, Bronston never saw himself as a whistleblower. Rather, he defined
his role as that of an organizer. Blowing the whistle on Willowbrook was one of
many strategies to bring about social change. From the beginning, he conceptualized the Willowbrook struggle as a struggle of ideologies. It was, to him a
national and not a local struggle. Willowbrook simply afforded one of the many
possible sites where the battle could be waged. It was an excellent site, the largest
institution for the retarded in America, as bad as any, located near a major media
center. Dr. Bronston helped mobilize physically disabled activists from New York
City, parents of handicapped children living in the community, parent organizations
attached to area institutions, leading national civil rights attorneys, special education leaders and scholars, and people who had spent years in Willowbrook to plan a
major assault on the institution. As it turned out, many of these people with whom
Bronston allied himself in 1972 would become leaders in a national disability rights
movement in the decade to come. They included many of the people who would
push for deinstitutionalization as national policy, leaders of the independent living
movement, leaders in the battle to secure the right to education for students with
disabilities, leaders in the self-advocacy movement, and the people who coined the

term handicapism, which would become shorthand for prejudice, stereotyping and discrimination toward people with disabilities.

The foundation of the social movement that Dr. Bronston predicted and helped to foment was a vision which challenged prevailing beliefs in custodialism, which dominated institutions for the retarded at the time. It was this value conflict that motivated Bronston, Wilkins, Lee, and others to blow the whistle at Willowbrook and to organize for change there and nationally. Bronston stated the conflicting views this way:

> The parochialism of (the) Willowbrook director and the Department of Mental Hygiene in trying to convince anyone that Willowbrook alone is under attack, or that the issue has arisen from mass media exposure and parent outrage, denies historical reality.
>
> In the United States there has been a steady drive from the community of families of the handicapped and progressive professionals to foreclose on the legacy of charity for the handicapped and the second class, hat in hand citizenship which befalls these families.
>
> At issue are two fundamentally antagonistic outlooks: on the one hand, a philosophy which accepts the brutalization and reduction of human beings to a subhuman condition, as has been amply documented in the state institutions.
>
> Opposing this, our position, that people with special needs, the handicapped, the retarded and others, must be accorded the full spectrum of human and constitutional rights with regard to care, treatment and education.[41]

WHISTLEBLOWING STRATEGIES

Why do whistleblowers have so few friends and supporters? That is a question whistleblowers frequently ask themselves and it is asked with bitterness. Actually, the whistleblower's coworkers often ask a similar question, "Why is it so hard to lend support to whistleblowers?" Clearly, there are a number of plausible answers to both questions. In "committing truth," as Ernest Fitzgerald puts it, whistleblowers may implicitly say, "Other people lie and cover up or ignore what we uncover and disclose." The whistleblower thus lives up to a standard that may embarass others. Whistleblowers take risks with their jobs, their futures, and their families. Others, particularly coworkers, may fear the fallout that could result from being associated too closely with whistleblowing. Thus when whistleblowers speak out they run the risk of being characterized by those they criticize as troublesome, unbalanced, and individually problematic. In other words, attention becomes focused on them as individuals. People around the whistleblower, coworkers for example, may simply come to believe the organization's allegations.

Available examples of whistleblowing suggest that whistleblowing, almost no matter how it is done, involves great risk to one's career, livelihood, and friendships, and inevitably leads to some measure of alienation for the whistleblower. However, the evidence also suggests that whistleblowers are not entirely the pawns of circumstance. They may be able to control some of the things that happen to them. In other words, whistleblowing can be more than "committing truth." It can be an organizing skill.

Learning whistleblowing as a skill means knowing how to define issues and solutions to issues. It means knowing how to document concerns and how to communicate them through a chain of command in the organizational setting before ever "going public." It means knowing what to expect when we blow the whistle. It means knowing our rights and the limitations on these rights to speak out with impunity. Finally, it means having an action plan.

Define the Issues

Some whistleblowers find that the issues have been defined for them. This was the case for Ernest Fitzgerald, who literally backed into the whistleblower role when subpoenaed before a Senate subcommittee that was investigating cost over-runs on military projects. In most situations, though, it is the whistleblower who must identify an issue, formulate it clearly, and communicate it first to superiors and then, if no action has been taken, to the public. Thus the whistleblower needs to consider how to make an issue compelling. At first, the issue may arise as a personal concern. In order to translate that concern into an issue, and one that organization or public will act on, we need to present it effectively. Again, whistleblowers' experiences offer some guidance. First, we must ask, what is the nature of the objectionable activity, policy, or practice? Is it illegal? If so, what specific laws have been broken? Is it immoral? If so, what common social, religious, or moral standards can we cite in reference to the activity or policy? Does the policy or practice violate some organizational, professional, or social standards? If so, which ones? Is the policy or practice dangerous? If so, in what way? With respect to each of these questions, we might ask, "Who will be harmed, and to what extent, if the policy or practice continues?"

Good problem identification requires good evidence and clear thinking. Before we decide to blow the whistle on a policy or practice we need to gather evidence. We may find it through first hand observations, through collection of affidavits from consumers of services, through official reports, memoranda and other organizational documents, through available statistical data, through photographs, through personal testimony, through carefully administered surveys, and through other forms of investigation. Once the evidence is collected, we must then formulate the problem succinctly, including a definition of the problem, how it was identified, its extent, the harm that will come from its not being corrected, the cost for correcting it (optional), and how it could be corrected. This last point deserves special attention. People who speak out often find that their audience wants to know if and how the organization should deal with the problem. People expect critics to offer a blueprint, a solution.

Of course, no amount of good documentation and problem definition will have any effect if the whistleblower cannot communicate the evidence and recommendations in plain, everyday English. As with nearly every organization strategy, whistleblowing requires good communication skills. In most cases, such as Edward Gregory's criticism of the 1965 Chevrolet, explaining the issues raises no real difficulties.[42] After a rock hunting expedition, Gregory noticed that his friends' 1965 Chevrolet had accumulated road dust in its trunk. Gregory, an inspector for General Motors, noticed that the trunk was inadequately sealed. He thought about the problem and became worried that if dust could seep into the car trunk, so could carbon monoxide. Once in the trunk, carbon monoxide could then threaten the welfare of a car's passengers. Because of this, he spoke up about the problem. He explained the problem by showing his supervisors defective car panels in the production line. He found cars that had been produced and sold with the defect. He explained how the problem could be overcome, at relatively little expense. He also warned about the threat of carbon monoxide if a consumer had a leaky exhaust system, something that occurs quite frequently when an exhaust system rusts away before the owner has it replaced. General Motors transferred Gregory "far from where he could act as a daily watchdog over the suspect quarter panels."[43] Two years later, several Chevrolet owners died from carbon monoxide fumes which escaped from rusted exhaust systems into their cars. General Motors reportedly never admitted a relationship between the faulty panel problem and the deaths, but three years after Gregory's suggestion, General Motors recalled 2.4 million Chevrolets made between 1965 and 1969.[44] Gregory's case serves as a good example for effective whistleblowing because it includes so many of the essential elements for identifying and communicating issues—definition of the problem, identification of who would be harmed by inaction, a proposed solution, warning the company of possible negligence charges (legal issue) if the problem went uncorrected and if consumers were harmed by the fault, and showing the cost of repairing the problem during production as compared to the cost of recalling thousands of autos or of paying off on negligance suits. In his case, defining the issue was straightforward and simple.

In many other situations, whistleblowers have a more difficult time explaining their problems. Many health-related issues impose just this burden on whistleblowers, that of "how to explain what is not easily understood." The experience of Drs. Tamplin and Gofman provide a good example. The Atomic Energy Commission asked Dr. Tamplin to prepare a scientific paper that would dispute claims by University of Pittsburgh professor Ernest Sternglass that increased cancer incidences and deaths could be projected from AEC estimates of how much radiation exposure should be allowable for people.[46] Unfortunately, the AEC did not like Dr. Tamplin's findings that, indeed, one could project significantly increased rates of cancer and deaths if current standards for radiation exposure were not drastically lowered. Tamplin predicted 16,000 extra cases of cancer and leukemia per year.[47] A year later, as the AEC insisted on trying to defend its "allowable dose" standards, Tamplin teamed up with Dr. Gofman to produce more reports. Instead of backing off from the 16,000 projection, they doubled their estimate to 32,000 new cases of cancer and leukemia.[48] The problem with such claims, of course, is that neither Sternglass nor Tamplin and Gofman could point to actual cancers or actual deaths and say for certain, "Here is the evidence; this is the causal relationship between radiation exposure of certain levels and disease or death." Cancer usually takes years to develop. Thus the danger of certain doses cannot be easily demonstrated. Moreover, scientific data on the effects of low level radiation are still relatively sparse. Even though few scientists would say Tamplin and Gofman were wrong, neither could they absolutely say that they had more than a solid hypothesis. The two scientists found themselves battling the AEC, a government-created body that had the dual and seemingly contradictory roles of regulating and promoting the nuclear industry. Unlike other whistleblowers who could point to solid and incontrovertible evidence (for example, a leaky trunk compartment on a car, a massive cost overrun on a military contract), Drs. Tamplin and Gofman had only their ideas and their warnings, albeit based on available evidence and careful scientific thinking, all of which were, in the end, debatable. Perhaps that was sufficient in this case—to keep the debate before the profession and the public.

Follow the Chain of Command

When the Conway School District tried to fire Mildred Downs, it accused her of failing to observe school policy and of going over the heads of her immediate supervisors. However, the court found that she had actually taken her concerns to the responsible individuals and in the correct sequence. Thus the court found no support for the District's contention. Since government agencies and private organizations alike may fire employees for insubordination, so long as they do not define all free speech as insubordination, it behooves whistleblowers to pay attention to lines of command.

As a general rule, whistleblowers would do well to separate the matter of style from substance. That is, whistleblowers can predict that expressing their concerns over a substantive issue will probably offend their superiors. Yet they have decided to take that risk. On the other hand, whistleblowers can probably minimize their own risks and difficulties by observing all of the correct etiquette (style) of the setting. In so doing, they can protect themselves against diversionary issues which, if valid, can undermine their effectiveness.

Be Prepared

Whistleblowing is not for the faint hearted. If we learn anything from the many reported cases of whistleblowing it is that whistleblowers invariably encounter hard times once they have spoken out publicly. A look at the evidence shows this to be true. When Ronald H. Secrist first blew the whistle on Equity Funding, some thought he would escape unscathed. By the time he blew the whistle on "one of the biggest bamboozlements in American business history"—Equity officials were making up fake insurance clients, fake records, and fake accidents, all in an effort to fool auditors and to make the company appear like an exceptionally good stock for prospective investors—he had secured an executive job with another insurance agency. However, the minute he began questioning illegal practices, albeit of a much less serious nature, in his new firm, he ran into trouble. Secrist now works for himself. He operates a small store. He says he quit the insurance business because he believed that it was a "rat race" that led inevitably to practices on the edge of the law.[49] Others have had even tougher struggles. Ernest Fitzgerald was fired from his job. It cost him $400,000 in court fees to get it back. Dr. J. Anthony Morris, the virologist who questioned the Ford Administration's claim that a 1976 swine flu would be as virulent as the infamous 1918 swine flu and who warned that the government-sponsored swine flu inoculations could produce dangerous side effects, was fired for "insubordination and inefficiency."[50] Henry Durham, a whistleblower who provided evidence of Lockheed's mismanagement, "false documentation, and waste in . . . production of the C–5A military transport aircraft,"[51] encountered great hostility even though he resigned his job voluntarily before going public:

> "Turncoat is what Henry Durham was called around here," says William Kinney, associate editor of the Marietta Daily Journal.
> "Kill Durham" signs appeared on bulletin boards at the Lockheed plant. Life-long friends refused to speak to the Durhams or allow their children to play together. Automobiles drove slowly past the family's split-level home at night, prompting Mr. Durham to sleep with a 22-caliber magnum pistol by his side. His wife Nan now doubts that her husband's action was worth it. A thin woman, she lost 15 pounds during the ordeal.
> The harassment abated after two armed U.S. marshals moved in with the Durhams for two months.[52]

Henry Durham, like so many whistleblowers, wonders why people do not want to hear the truth. In his own words, "There's certainly a defect in our society when people who call attention to wrongdoing are ostracized, fired, criticized, and virtually abandoned."[53]

While it is probably impossible for anyone to truly be prepared for losing close friends, job, and security, it might be easier were it more understandable. However, few of us learn or are ever taught why many people regard whistleblowing and other forms of speaking out and social change activism so negatively. Is it that people learn to respect authority, whatever that authority espouses? Is it that people believe their grasp on a livelihood is so tenuous that they can ill afford any stepping out of line, even by others around them? Is it that people are willing to go along with the system, however corrupt or dangerous, in order to achieve personal rewards? Is it that people believe loyalty, almost at any price, to be more sacred than other social values such as public safety, honesty, and free expression? Or is it a combination of these things? Frank Serpico, the New York City Police Officer who, at the risk of his own life, blew the whistle on police corruption, points to poor leadership and peer pressure to "look the other way" as the culprits:

> I saw that happening to men all around me, men who could have been good officers, men of decent impulse, men of ideals, but men who were without decent leadership, men who were told in a hundred ways every day go along, forget the law, don't make waves, and shut up.

So they did shut up. They did go along. They did learn the unwritten code of the department. They went along and they lost something very precious: they weren't cops anymore. They were a long way towards not being men any more.[54]

An analyst of whistleblowing inside private corporations suggests several explanations for employee silence and acquiescence.[55] One notion held by at least some employers and employees is that the worker, like a feudal vassal, owes everything to the employer. In this view, the employer has all power over the employee. Another argument holds that industry's architects know what is best and it is the employee's role to keep quiet and follow orders. A third explanation likens the employee to a consumer. The employee who does not like the wages and working conditions can pick up his belongings and move on to another place of employment. In short, "love it or leave it."

As long as Americans place the ideal of "committing truth" below certain other beliefs (for example, "getting along," "looking out for self before others," "trusting blindly in experts"), whistleblowers can expect to encounter enormous personal difficulties with each act of outspokenness. Thus aside from warning family and friends about possible fallout from our actions, we must seriously consider whether or not to blow the whistle. Is the issue worth the personal costs involved? Have we built up a strong enough record as employees that our credibility cannot be easily undermined? As whistleblowers are we prepared for and able to accept or at least endure the predictable suffering? Are we prepared for the fact that even in speaking out we may not succeed in our cause? We may not win. How will we handle rejection by friends and associates? Do we have the physical and psychological stamina to see the whistleblowing through to completion? It may take years.

Know Your Rights

Jack Muller was a detective on the Chicago City police force. In October, 1967, he was assigned to an auto theft unit. During the course of his work he discovered that certain of his fellow officers were taking some of the stolen property which they had recovered for their own use. Muller reported this fact to the city-wide commander for auto theft units. But when Muller saw no action taken, he reported his charges directly to the Superintendent of Police. When interviewed several weeks later by a television newsperson about the charges, Muller was asked why he had not taken his complaints to the police Internal Inspection Division. Muller was not circumspect in his response. He said, "The IID is like a great big washing machine. Everything they put into it comes out clean."[56] That comment apparently angered some officials in the department. The Deputy Chief of Detectives summoned Muller twice to give him an oral reprimand. Each time, detective Muller refused the reprimand. Instead, he demanded a hearing before the department's Disciplinary Board. The Disciplinary Board did hear the case, but decided against detective Muller. The Board found that he had violated department rule 31, which prohibits all officers from "engaging in any activity, conversation, deliberation, or discussion which is derogatory to the Department or any member or policy of the Department.''[57] The Board then ordered that the department place a written reprimand in Officer Muller's record, the same record that the department uses when considering employees for advancement. Eventually, Muller won his case in court. A federal appeals court found the police department rule against any critical comments overly broad, vague, and inclusive. It is not fair, the court found, to completely deny a public employee his or her right to free speech as a prerequisite for employment.

Muller's victory was actually based on a similar appeal by a school teacher, Marvin L. Pickering, also of Illinois. Pickering had written a letter to a local newspaper in which he criticized the School Board for spending money on athletic rather than academic programs and of hiding information on the issue from the public. The court found that while some of Mr. Pickering's comments were unfounded, he believed them to be true. The School Board argued that Pickering's charges were ''detrimental to the efficient operation and administration of the schools of the district'' and that the interests of the school district required Pickering's firing. As it turned out, Pickering's case raised the central legal question that is present in most whistleblowing cases. Did Pickering merely exercise his First Amendment right to free speech when he sent his letter to the editor or did he also disrupt the efficient operation of the organization for which he worked? By the same token, the court in Muller's case had asked if he simply spoke out about a topic of concern to him or if he jeopardized the integrity of the department as well. The court set a general, if somewhat nonspecific, test for such cases when it decided in *Pickering* that the teacher could speak out as long as his comments did not interfere with his ''proper performance of his daily duties in the classroom or to have interfered with the regular operation of the schools generally.'' Even though his public statements were erroneous, as long as there was no evidence that he made them recklessly or knowingly, the court would defend his right to make them.

Unfortunately for whistleblowers, the Pickering rule only applies to public employees. People who work in places of private employment do not have the same guarantees against being fired for speaking out. The law is not altogether clear about an employee's rights. As it currently stands, ''employees of a company selling 80 percent of its products to the government have a right to free speech, but not the employees of companies doing little business with the government.''[58] Similarly, employees who cite violations of certain federal acts such as the Coal Mine Safety Act, the Water Pollution Control Act, and the Occupational Safety and Health Acts are protected in their right to be outspoken.[59] Others may find protection under provisions of the National Labor Relations Board. Still others may argue successfully that they have been prohibited from speaking out because they are members of a minority or women, thus opening up protection under civil rights and affirmative action statutes. The point here is that, in the final analysis, whistleblowers are far from having achieved blanket protection from recrimination by employers. The basic rule of thumb is that employees are most often protected when their issues concern illegalities or public interest and when their actions do not interfere with their work or with efficient operation of the work setting.

Action Plan

It takes a bit of luck and a lot of strategy to achieve more as a whistleblower than isolation and exile. An action plan is a necessity. Since most people come to whistleblowing accidentally, even innocently, they have no plan of action. This means that they have no ready store of ways to effectively recruit and involve allies within and outside the organization. They may have no good way to keep the issue alive once they have raised it. They may have no means of projecting their analysis of the issues to their fellow workers and to the public once the organization has begun to present its perspective. An action plan would include strategies for dealing with each of these potential problems.

One of the reasons Karen Silkwood posed such a threat to Kerr-McGee was that the company could not easily isolate her. She had allies. She shared her commitment to safety with several coworkers who, like her, were willing to make their charges openly to the Atomic Energy Commission and to their union. Through her union she had access to nuclear contamination experts who spoke to other workers and explained the highly technical issues of radiation exposure to the workers. She also had access to news reporters who, even after she had been killed, were able to carry on the battle she began. Also, because she belonged to a union and was a health advocate for the union, she had an official justification—it was part of the union contract—for assisting workers in their health related concerns. Moreover, while her outspokenness could win her disfavor with Kerr-McGee officials, those same officials would find it difficult to fire or transfer her. Her union position gave her at least limited protection under National Labor Relation Board guidelines.

The lesson of Silkwood's whistleblowing is clear. It helps to have an organization behind the whistleblower such as a union, a group of friends who can act as an informal sounding board against which to test ideas and findings, and allies on the outside, whether they be experts, mass media contacts, important citizens, or professional associations. Some whistleblowers have informants at the very top levels of the organization so that they know about recriminations and official responses even before they are officially revealed. Thus they can plan for and defend against them. Others simply have established enough outside support that insiders are fearful of the storm of protest and bad press that may result if they do fire or exile the whistleblower. One such well known whistleblower is Al Louis Ripskis, a program analyst at the Department of Housing and Urban Development (HUD). He has been exposing waste and corruption at HUD for years. This role, as well as outside contacts, has won him protection. He publishes a newsletter, a kind of whistleblower's journal, called *Impact,* in which he regularly exposes abuses, incompetence, and illegalities. He considers himself relatively secure in his troublemaking role: "I have managed to survive with a minimum of harassment, and it was not by accident. The critical choices came in the beginning. If they decide to fire you at the start, it's hard to reverse the bureaucracy once it gets rolling. But I started muckraking and kicking up a lot of publicity, and I became well known so the department knew it would be bloody if they canned me.''[60] Ripskis had allies and, equally important, a means (his newsletter and media exposure) of reaching those allies.[61]

Aside from careful attention to locating and nurturing allies, a whistleblowing plan should include multiple actions. We tend to think of whistleblowing as a single moment of exposure such as Ernest Fitzgerald exposing government cost overruns and a conspiracy to cover up the overruns, Henry Durham's testimony on the reasons for cost overruns, or Ronald Secrist's phone calls which blew the whistle on Equity Funding. However, the most effective whistleblowers have been dogged in their pursuit of change. A few stand out because they knew how to keep an issue alive over a long period of time. The Willowbrook whistleblowers, for example, formed an organization to push for change and started a newspaper to communicate their perspective. They held press conferences in which they made demands of the institution administration. These people wrote guest editorials, started a lawsuit against the institution and the state, and held training sessions for workers, parents and interested citizens on alternatives to the institution. They revealed additional evidence on every few weeks of continued abuses in the institution and gathered first-hand accounts of this abuse and made them public. Additionally, they appealed to major professional associations and parent organizations for support. Such a barrage of strategies, spread over a period of year guaranteed that the issue would remain alive and potent. These strategies put enormous pressure on the system to change. With these multiple approaches to change, the administration could not isolate the whistleblower.

Finally, the action plan must have both creative and practical elements. On the one hand whistleblowers need, like all organizers, to consider such things as timing, pressure points, and symbolism. When is the best time to blow the whistle? This may depend on upcoming elections, availability of media coverage or other factors. At what point in the system should whistleblowers direct their attention? Is there a particularly vulnerable spot such as stockholders, congressional watchdog committees, public opinion (media) exposure, the executive branch of government, the corporate board? Are there particular symbols which the whistleblower can exploit in order to better impress upon the public the urgency of the issue? If, for example, the organization prides itself on safety, as did the Kerr-McGee plant which Karen Silkwood found so unsafe, can that fact be exploited in press releases, posters, newsletters, and others of the whistleblower's communication outlets? On the less creative and more practical side, whistleblowers find it useful, particularly if their case ever reaches litigation, or even formal negotiation, to keep detailed, meticulous notes and files on every bit of evidence, every action, and every accomplishment. Most practical of all, the whistleblower's action plan is not complete without a clear sense of the goals to be achieved and the degree of compromise permissible.

NOTES

[1]Senator Edward M. Kennedy (D., Massachusetts). "Statement on Leahy Whistleblower Amendment to S. 2640, the Civil Service Reform Act." August 24, 1978, U.S. Senate.

[2]Curt Flood quoted in Richard Reeves, "The Last Angry Men," *Esquire*, March 1, 1978, p. 42.

[3]Reeves, "Angry Men," p. 42.

[4]Richard Rashke, *The Killing of Karen Silkwood* (Boston: Houghton-Mifflin Company, 1981).

[5]"Poisoned by Plutonium," *Time*, March 19, 1979, p. 35.

[6]Rashke, *Silkwood*, p. 20.

[7]Rashke, *Silkwood*, p. 29.

[8]Rashke, *Silkwood*, pp. 22–23.

[9]Rashke, *Silkwood*, pp. 58–59.

[10]The account of the Karen Silkwood trial and investigation are drawn from Rashke, *Silkwood*, 1981.

[11]John Dean, *Blind Ambition* (New York: Pocket Book, 1977).

[12]Reeves, "The Last Angry Men," p. 44.

[13]Victor Navasky, *Naming Names* (New York: Viking, 1980), p. xviii.

[14]Navasky, *Names*, p. 57.

[15]Navasky, *Names* p. 19.

[16]Robert Townsend, "The Whistle Blower as Entrepeneur," in *Whistle Blowing*, eds. Ralph Nader, Peter Petkas and Kate Blackwell (New York: Grossman Publishers, 1972), pp. 20–21.

[17]*Downs* v. *Conway School District*, 328 F. Supp 338 (1971). This case study is drawn entirely from the U.S. District Court decision, Eastern District Arkansas.

[18]*Downs* v. *Conway*, p. 344.

[19]*Downs* v. *Conway*, p. 344.

[20]*Downs* v. *Conway*, p. 347.

[21]*Downs* v. *Conway*, p. 348.

[22]*Downs* v. *Conway*, p. 349.

[23]*Downs* v. *Conway*, p. 350.

[24]"Drugs, Sex Charges Leveled at Hospital," *Philadelphia Daily News*, Tuesday, September 5, 1972, p. 4.

[25]"Drugs, Sex," p. 4.

[26]*Rafferty* v. *Philadelphia Psychiatric Center*, 356, F. Supp. 500 (1973), p. 507.

[27]*Rafferty* v. *Philadelphia*, pp. 507–508.

[28]Associated Press, "Senate Panel Told of Falsified Data in Drug Studies," *New York Times* October 12, 1979, p. 14.

[29]"Falsified Data," p. 14.

[30]"Falsified Data," p. 14.

[31]Associated Press, "Hooker Employees Protest Dismissal," *Syracuse Herald-Journal*, February 28, 1980, p. 2.

[32]"Hooker Employees," p. 2.

[33]"Hooker Employees," p. 2.

[34]Larry Agran, "Death Valley Days," *New Times*, December 9, 1977, pp. 57–67. Information for this case study is drawn exclusively from Mr. Agran's account.

[35]"Human Warehouse," *Time*, February 14, 1972, p. 68.

[36]"Warehouse," *Time*, p. 68.

[37]"Warehouse," *Time*, pp. 68 and 99.

[38]Jane Kurtin, "Willowbrook Head Fires 2 Who Spoke Out," *Staten Island Advance*, January 7, 1972, p. 1.

[39]Kurtin, "Willowbrook," p. 2.

[40]"Union Urges Action for Willowbrook," *New York Times*, January 28, 1972, p. 20, col. 2.

[41]William G. Bronston, "Willowbrook Continued," *New York Times*, 1972.

[42]Ralph Nader, Peter Petkas, and Kate Blackwell (eds.), *Whistleblowing* (New York: Grossman Publishers, 1972).

[43]Nader et al., *Whistleblowing*, p. 79.

[44]Nader et al., *Whistleblowing*, p. 82.

[45]Nader et al., *Whistleblowing*, p. 83.

[46]Nader et al., *Whistleblowing*, p. 62.

[47]Nader et al., *Whistleblowing*, p. 63.

[48]Nader et al., *Whistleblowing*, p. 63.

[49]Joann S. Lublin, "Spilling the Beans," *Wall Street Journal*, 1976, pp 1 and 19.

[50]Helen Dudar, "The Price of Blowing the Whistle," *New York Times Magazine*, October 30, 1979, pp. 41–54.

[51]Lublin, "Spilling," p. 19.

[52]Lublin, "Spilling," p. 19.

[53]Lublin, "Spilling," p. 19.

[54]Nader et al., *Whistleblowing*, 1972, p. 166.

[55]David E. Ewing, *Freedom Inside the Organization* (New York: Dalton, 1977), pp. 34–35.

[56]*Muller* v. *Conlisk*, 429 F.2d 901 (1970), p. 902.

[57]*Muller* v. *Conlisk*, 902.

[58]Ewing, *Freedom*, p. 112.

[59]Ewing, *Freedom*, p. 112.

[60]Helen Dudar, "The Price of Blowing the Whistle," *New York Times Magazine*, October 30, 1977.

[61]On June 8, 1981, Al Ripskis, a Housing and Urban Development Program Analyst charged that up to 1 billion dollars may have been "thrown down the rat hole" (wasted) between 1975 and 1981. See "Hud Accused of Wasting Millions," The *Syracuse Post Standard, Monday, June 8, 1981, p. 1.*

INDEX